W9-BSC-979

This book presents a side of Russian life largely unknown in the West – the world of popular culture. By surveying detective and science fiction, popular songs, jokes, box office movie hits, the stage, radio, and television, Professor Richard Stites introduces the people and cultural products that are household names to ordinary Russian people.

Spanning the entire twentieth century, Professor Stites examines the sub-cultures that draw upon and enrich Russian popular culture. He explores the relationship between popular culture and the national and social values of the masses, including their heroes and myths, and assesses the phenomenon of the celebrity from the silent screen star to the latest rock music idol. He pays particular attention to the dramatic battle between elite and popular culture and to the intervention of revolutions, wars, and the state in the production and control of this culture.

Russian popular culture demonstrates how popular culture has had more impact upon and reveals more about the lives of Russian people than the giants of high culture. It will be widely read by students and specialists of Russian studies, history, literature, and popular culture as well as by anyone interested in the cultural world of the ordinary Russian citizen.

RICHARD STITES is Professor of History at Georgetown University. He has published extensively on Russian and Soviet society including *The women's liberation movement in Russia: Feminism, nihilism, and Bolshevism, 1860–1930* and the highly acclaimed *Revolutionary dreams: Utopian vision and experimental life in the Russian Revolution*.

Russian popular culture

Cambridge Soviet Paperbacks: 7

Cambridge Soviet Paperbacks is a completely new initiative in publishing on the Soviet Union. The series will focus on the economics, international relations, politics, sociology and history of the Soviet and Revolutionary periods.

The idea behind the series is the identification of gaps for upper-level surveys or studies falling between the traditional university press monograph and most student textbooks. The main readership will be students and specialists, but some 'overview' studies in the series will have broader appeal.

Publication will in every case be simultaneously in hardcover and paperback.

Russian popular culture

Entertainment and society since 1900

RICHARD STITES

Professor of History,
Georgetown University

CAMBRIDGE
UNIVERSITY PRESS

Published by the Press Syndicate of the University of Cambridge
The Pitt Building, Trumpington Street, Cambridge CB2 1RP
40 West 20th Street, New York, NY 10011-4211, USA
10 Stamford Road, Oakleigh, Melbourne 3166, Australia

First published 1992
Reprinted 1994, 1995

*A catalogue record for this book
is available from the British Library*

Library of Congress cataloguing in publication data

Stites, Richard.
Russian popular culture: entertainment and society since
1900/Richard Stites.
      p.   cm. – (Cambridge Soviet paperbacks: 7)
Includes bibliographical references and index.
1. Soviet Union – Popular culture. 2. Soviet Union –
Civilization – 1917   I. Title.   II. Series.
DK266.4.S76 1992
947.084 – dc20   91-33592 CIP

ISBN 0 521 36214 8 hardback
ISBN 0 521 36986 X paperback

Transferred to digital printing 2000

To my beloved son, Andryusha

Contents

Illustrations

Preface and acknowledgements

This introductory survey of Russian popular culture and entertainment in our century is designed to fill a gap in our knowledge of the Soviet Union. The subject has interested me from the time of my first visit to the USSR in the early Brezhnev period (1967) – from the first glimpse of Soviet reality, the first party, the first pop concert, the first dinner at a Soviet restaurant. I have been in the USSR over thirty times since – the most recent of the longer sojourns being six months in 1989–1990 – in homes, dorms, hotels of every sort in a dozen cities. I have studied, socialized, attended performances of all kinds, and observed how popular entertainment has changed over the years. This book attempts to make sense of that experience by putting it into a historical framework. It is meant to be serious but not solemn. I have spent hundreds of hours in places where historians are usually found – libraries, reading rooms, documentary collections – as well as in places that are off the beaten path: nightclubs, restaurants, variety theaters, pop concerts, film archives, workers' clubs, and movie houses. Much of the coverage for the years 1967–1990 is based on personal viewing or listening.

I have kept documentation to a minimum, citing in short form in the notes only the most important of the sources used or those quoted. Full references along with other basic works are in the bibliography which contains many English language titles for the guidance of the general reader. This is followed by a discography, a filmography, and a videography, particularly meant for those interested in teaching the subject, since Soviet phonograph records, films, and video cassettes are now widely available. For Russian words in the text, I have anglicized many names and used a modified Library of Congress system of transliteration for ease of reading; in the notes and bibliography, I have adhered more strictly to that system but without diacritical marks.

My greatest thanks go to Professor Dorothy Brown of Georgetown University, a precious colleague and partner in our course on Soviet and American popular culture, who has enriched my understanding of both; to Professor Mary McAuley of Oxford University who invited me to write the book; and to IREX and the Soviet Academy of Sciences for financial and logistical support in Moscow and Leningrad. For my stay in Helsinki, I thank the Fulbright-Hays Fellowship Committee, the staffs of the Finnish Film Archive, the Finnish Literature Society, and most of all of the Slavonic Library of the University of Helsinki. In Moscow, I am indebted to Elena Kartseva, Lyudmila Budyak, Tatyana Eliseeva, and Anatoly Shumlyansky of the All-Union Research Institute of Cinema (VNIIK) for arranging film showings; to Anya Salnykova and Lydia Zaitseva of the All-Union Institute of Cinematography (VGIK) for granting me access to lectures and films; to Maya Turovskaya for showing me her archive on Soviet film attendance; to Viktor Vladimirov, director of the Circus Academy for conversations and access to repertoire manuscripts. Alexander Sherel of the Institute for the History of Art has my eternal gratitude for allowing me to listen to old radio programs and to view old television shows, for providing me with archival documents, tapes, and clips, and for taking me to Gosteleradio studios at Ostankino to see how Soviet TV works.

In Leningrad, I thank Grigory Tishkin and the faculty of the Institute of Culture for inviting me to give a lecture course there on Soviet and American Popular Culture in 1990; Irina Balod at the library of Kinotsentr; Tatyana Demidova and Lev Shvarts of the Institute of Theater, Music, and Cinematography; Roman Kopp of the Jazz Club; Nikolai Mikhailov of the Rock Club; Tatyana Fomkina, German Korotkov, and Mikhail Zeger for their kind hospitality at Leningrad Radio Center; and my longtime friend, Valery Shinder, for tracking down song lyrics and comedy recordings for me. I wish I could enumerate all the nightclub artists, musicians, film people, entertainers, staffs of workers' clubs and Houses of Culture, and ordinary Soviet citizens I have talked to over the years. I thank them all collectively here. Hubertus Jahn kindly shared his knowledge and research on World War I and guided me to new information storehouses.

Tanya Stites deserves a special thank you for first taking me to Leningrad movies, restaurants, and *estrada* concerts in the old days. My warm gratitude goes to Deans Richard Schwartz and Gerald Mara of the Graduate School of Georgetown University for generous research support over the years; and to my research assistants, Michael Skidan, Dawn Hanahan, Seth Lerman, Margo Mallar, and Charlene

Bell. I also owe a debt to the many students at Georgetown and elsewhere who have shared their research, insights, and knowledge with me; and to colleagues in various fields who have given me generous assistance and advice: Vasily Aksenov, Harley and Marjorie Balzer, John Bowlt, Jeff Burds, John Bushnell, Katerina Clark, Maurice Friedberg, Peter Kenez, Walter Laqueur, Ellen Mickiewicz, Anthony Olcott, Samuel Rachlin, Robert Rothstein, Gerald Stanton Smith, S. Frederick Starr, Richard Taylor, Mark von Hagen, James Von Geldern, and Denise Youngblood. David Goldfrank and Howard Spendelow, as colleagues, friends, and computer mentors, have helped me more than they can ever know. Anna Lawton has a special place in this book as friend, advisor, moral supporter, and devotee of Soviet movies. Most of all I dedicate this book to one of my best teachers: my son, Andryusha Stites.

Research for this book was supported in part by a grant from the International Research and Exchanges Board (IREX), with funds provided by the National Endowment for the Humanities and the United States Information Agency. None of these organizations is responsible for the views expressed.

Glossary

Not all of these terms are used in the present text but they may help researchers who know Russian but are unfamiliar with the terminology of popular culture.

artist, artistka: performing artist
boevik: box-office movie hit
detektiv: detective, crime, or mystery story, including thriller and spy novel (see *sledopyt*)
dosug: leisure time
estrada: the popular stage and arena
estradnaya muzyka: popular music
goluboi ekran: (blue screen) television
kafe-shantan: *café chantant*
kassovyi: popular, i.e. successful at the box office (*kassa*)
konferanse: conferencier or master of ceremonies
korol: king or male superstar
koroleva: queen or female superstar
kuplet: ditty
legkii zhanr: entertainment art
lubok: illustrated popular literature
massovaya pesnya: mass song
myuzik-kholl: (English style) Music Hall
myuzikl: (American style) musical
narodnaya pesnya: folksong
narodnyi: folk
nauchnaya fantastika: science fiction
nomer: circus act or variety number
pinkerton: see *detektiv*
priklyuchenie: adventure
shansonetka: *chansonette*
shlyager: popular song hit

sistema: the hippie counter culture

sledopyt: sleuth or detective

stilyaga: style hunter or zoot-suiter

tsyganshchina: music in the gypsy manner

tusovka: hangout, crash pad, or "happening" among hippies and rock fans

VIA (*Vokalno-instrumentalnyi ansambl*): vocal and instrumental ensemble, i.e. guitars, keyboard, percussion, and singer

zhestokii romans: urban or cruel song

zvezda: entertainment star

Introduction

What is popular culture? This discipline is still in its infancy and clear definitions have not yet been canonized. In a pioneering work about early modern Europe, Peter Burke defined popular culture as that of peasants and artisans. This does not work for modern urban societies in Europe, the United States, or the Soviet Union. Industrialization, social mobility, mass communications, politicization, commercialism, musical, theatrical, artistic, and literary professionalism, and a dozen other forces have changed the whole notion of popular culture. Popular culture, as presently understood, is distinctly urban and markedly different from folk culture. The term "mass culture," which in the West often denotes the content of the mass communications media, is sometimes used as an alternative and pejorative term for the modern variety.

Popular culture, whether urban or folk, is a ceaseless bubbling up of stories and tales – told or sung or acted – with twists and tricks and plots that give shape and shock to our emotions. It is thus not only contemporary but very often temporary. The spatial metaphor of high and low commonly used to distinguish the two levels of culture is apt. High culture – lofty, elevated, exalted, and ethereal – is constructed as "thin" like the air it grows in, delicate like the flower that pokes up out of the ground, brainy like the topmost organ of the human body. All this is in contrast to the earth that is moist and fertile, dirty by definition, and rich in odors. The stern critic will complain here that this metaphorical lexicon applies only to the natural juxtaposition of real art and authentic folk culture which is indeed rooted in the earth of forest and plowland; and that modern "popular culture" is urban, alienated, artificial, inorganic. Such arguments miss the point that all culture is organic, that the "folk" of teeming streets who consume a culture participate in its creation as much as do the media manipulators.

Why study popular culture? High culture and the classics address

1

the eternal truths, the deepest values, and the big questions. But people often operate on the basis of "superficial" values and the ephemeral trends of their own time that are reflected in the popular culture which rarely concerns itself with the great enigmas of human experience. The study of popular culture, like any other intellectual enterprise, can descend into trivial antiquarianism. But recent scholarship has shown that light can emanate from below as well as from above. Patterns of popular taste reflect, among other things, attitudes to the city, the state, the nation, the family, money, foreigners, minorities, the arts, and the "system." The consumption of culture is part of a people's biography and popular culture can be a means of bonding for most people in a way that high culture cannot. It is hardly antiquarian for a historian to inquire what large bodies of people did in their spare time (about one-third of their lives) if this part of life was important to them.

Urban popular culture has been interpreted both as a foe and a friend of the status quo. When it began to be seen in the nineteenth century as a "problem" in the West, advocates of social control saw in it a potentially dangerous force that fostered prurience and violence and weakened good work habits among the lower classes. But in our century, one of the most influential theories about it claims that, like religion, popular or mass culture is an opiate concocted by the ruling classes to maintain the masses in a supine posture of apoliticism and undeveloped class consciousness. The theory was elaborated by Marxists of the Frankfurt school and has a wide following among Western intellectuals. A variant argues that popular culture does function as a narcotic, but independent of anyone's intention. Cultural elitists fear that mass culture diminishes the impact of "real" art. These fears are sometimes joined by anger at the creators of popular culture who allegedly impose base values on consumers or at the very least cater to their lowest instincts – all in the name of profit. Herbert Gans has persuasively argued that the theory has no empirical basis and is itself partly motivated by aesthetic elitism and sometimes professional self-interest. He concludes that "popular culture reflects and expresses aesthetic and other wants of many people, thus making it culture and not just commercial menace."[1] I believe that Gans' position holds not only for market societies but for societies, like that of the USSR, where political control of culture has been a hallmark in this century.

Culture is not exactly a neglected field in Soviet studies: we have many works on high culture as well as political culture. They tell us much about the ruling and educated elites; but most people in this and any society do not belong to the elites. There is also a large body of cultural anthropology dealing with peasants and ethnic or "tribal" groups in the USSR. But this country is now an urbanized society and has been for many years; and even in the early part of the century when the rural element was still large, urban life, values, and culture – high and low – set patterns for mass taste and cultural consumption and interacted with village culture. Urban songs and dances, light reading, the entertainment stage, and cinema are the basic ingredients of popular culture, though by no means exhausting it. Sports and leisure activities loom very large in the lives of Soviet people and I shall touch on them briefly. Audience reception is a crucial element in this history. Cultural consumption must be observed not only as particular ways to deploy leisure time, money, and energy but also for the subcultural affects adopted by consumers – songs they sing together for certain functions, clothes they wear, styles of behavior, gestures, emulative postures (e.g. of cinema stars), dances, and even speech patterns, jokes, and narrative styles.

Most works on Russian culture deal exclusively with high culture, particularly literature, including dissident or underground masterpieces that had little or no popular resonance. Such studies are morally and aesthetically necessary because they keep alive the genius, the spirit, and the conscience of Russia's great seekers after truth. But they offer an incomplete and one-sided understanding of ordinary Russian people living in the USSR. The present work deals with the culture and entertainment of the people, the masses, a word I use neither in a demeaning nor exalting sense. Therefore it is not about *belles lettres*, *beaux arts*, legitimate theater, classical music, ballet, or art cinema; it is rather about pulp fiction, mass graphics, the variety stage, radio, television, popular songs, dances, and the movies. The last is the only Soviet popular art that has been extensively studied in the West, but that study has until recently focused on works of high aesthetic value and thus ignored popular movies. I will try to show the historical relation between art cinema and popular movie and relate them to other realms of popular culture.

Culture created by elites and for elites – in or outside the market – can also be presented as popular. High culture has been made accessible to mass audiences in our age by schooling, mass media, highbrow stars, and cultural establishments. Mass audiences may differ in tastes and sensibilities from those of people who mainly frequent the temples of exalted art, but the interaction of high and "low" culture is dense and continuous, especially in countries like Russia with very old and highly revered cultural traditions. The use of folktunes by nine-teenth-century Russian composers (universally welcomed by concert audiences) and the jazzing up of classics by Soviet bands of the 1920s and 1930s (often condemned by purists) are two familiar examples. Similar combinations can be found in all the other arts. Therefore, although historians of high culture generally neglect popular culture, it is impossible for the historian of popular culture to neglect its relation to high culture.

The focus of this study is the entertainment arts and their con-sumers. Soviet entertainment possesses certain universal features and mechanisms dictated by the desire of producers to have their products consumed in some kind of market, however controlled: adaptation of one medium to another; the periodic revival of works or genres; spinoff (the movie hit song being one of the best-known examples); and the movement of stars from one medium to another by the sheer force of their celebrity. It has also been shaped by social forces. The migration of ethnic minorities – especially Jews – to the Russian capitals under the impulse of economic pressure or political cataclysms brought about the spread and adaptation of local musical and per-formance styles into mainstream metropolitan culture – in the same way that the egress of Black musicians from the Mississippi Delta reshaped jazz music or the movement of Jews from Europe to New York and Hollywood gave a special form to American popular culture. The most striking instance of this in Russia was the transfer of Odessa comedy and song patterns to Moscow and Leningrad stages.

But Russian popular culture also has its peculiarities. Most of the thematic ones will be readily apparent. But the most important by far was the impact of political forces. Much of the prerevolutionary popular culture described in chapter 1 was destroyed or periodically prohibited after the revolution. Nostalgia for it, long nourished in the underground, is now in full ascendance in the age of openness. This prerevolutionary culture took shape as an amalgam of folk, high, and light urban entertainment genres of old Russia in a context of commer-cialism, the quickening of technology, relative openness after the revolution of 1905, and increased contact with foreign culture. World War I curtailed some of this natural growth through isolation, censor-ship, xenophobia, and official solemnity; on the other hand, the iso-lation gave Russian native forms – for example in cinema – a chance to flourish.

In the West, some aspects of popular culture – such as vaudeville and its variants – were eliminated by the rise of new media technologies. This happened in Russia too, but the main agent of destruction was the 1917 tidal wave of revolution after which political and aesthetic revolutionaries tried to suppress the allegedly dangerous old world of commercial popular culture. In the 1930s, Stalinism completed this suppression and created a fusion of the old and new to produce "mass culture," utilizing the modern media but closely controlling the content for State purposes. *Massovaya kultura*, as it was called, was a culture constructed, promoted, and even financed by the state. But it was designed with the people in mind and was, as I shall demonstrate, popular none the less. In the decades since Stalin's death, the system of mass culture has been eroding in the face of continuing urbanization, education, exposure to the West, the rhythms of political reform and popular expectation, and the birth of new media – especially television.

The other peculiarity of Russian popular culture is related to cultural politics but also has its own native roots. This is its relative conservatism and homogeneity until very recently; and the presence in it of themes, conventions, and commonplaces – many of them traceable to folklore and high culture – that are repeated again and again in every popular genre. Separate studies of the popular arts – song, fiction, stage, and cinema – have not always demonstrated the rich and powerful interconnection that allows culturally conditioned Soviet audiences to decode effortlessly the various quotations, allusions, and symbols that recur so frequently in popular entertainment. This cultural code is the secondary language that connects the artists and entertainers with their audiences and reveals certain values, characteristics, and aspirations of Russian people not easily discernible in ideology or constitutions. The astonishing durability of these themes has been a mighty wall defending Russian cultural forms against the trendiness, rapid-fire obsolescence, and kaleidoscopic changes of style so characteristic of the dominant Americanized world culture. Russian cultural stability – its establishment, its social base, and the prospect of its diminution in our time – is an underlying theme of the book.

Two complementary and conflicting aspects of self-attributed Russian "national character" can be found in permanent interlock throughout the history of popular culture. One is openness or simplicity, without pretense or pretensions. It implies not so much formal honesty, but "bigness," generosity, lavish hospitality, and a sense of adventure – a sense admired by a people generally known for its own tendency to avoid risk. All of it is seen as a pendant to cunning and calculation. This is related to another self-proclaimed cliché about national character: spontaneity and impulsiveness, the kind of behavior that skirts danger, indulges in excess, acts without rational calculation. Many of the heros of Russian popular culture in fiction and in life – Stenka Razin, Varya Panina, Sergei Esenin, Chapaev, Vysotsky, Alla Pugacheva – possessed precisely the rash temperament that leads to impossible romance, hopeless battle, imprudent spending, or oceans of vodka.

The other aspect is moralism – officially sponsored and rooted in traditions of intelligentsia preaching and village life – which saturates the educational system, the media, the arts, and popular culture. Appeals for kindness and human decency and exalted expressions of love, patriotism, self-sacrifice, and friendship are constantly voiced. Ethical injunction, sometimes descending into pious moralizing, has been an enduring element in Russian popular culture long before its politicization by the Bolsheviks. This has always been accompanied by an antiphonal chorus of impious jokes, underground satire, and mockery of existing platitudes, including moral ones. Anecdotes, parodies, and songs about Soviet leaders and heroes – particularly sanctified ones like Lenin, Chapaev, and Zoya Kosmodemyanskaya – have been in continuous official circulation for decades. They are as much a part of the popular culture as are their targets. But no more so. There is no cause to believe that only underground culture is "authentic" and that all the rest is merely state-imposed mystification. The sentimental reverence toward certain Soviet traditions, heroic episodes, and sainted figures is as genuine as the carnivalic mockery that emerges to puncture pretensions. The striking thing about the present era is that almost the entire range of old counterculture has emerged into public view alongside the official conventions.

The collective impulse or social bonding, so often noted among Russians and attributed wrongly to Marxism or totalitarianism, is a powerful and enduring element in Soviet life. It predates the revolution by many eons and is rooted in village structures. One may observe it nightly in Soviet restaurants as tables full of men and women from the workplace gather to celebrate an occasion. The women, finely dressed, are especially prone to recreate the village milieu with folksongs and rural steps on the dance floor to whatever music is being played. Communal practices that are found widely in everyday life are reproduced, reinforced, and even exalted in the productions of popular culture in forms as varied as collective singing in war films, dramatic wedding scenes, non-erotic tenderness within genders, and the constant invocation of the language of social emotional solidarity.

In providing a context for things known and in introducing things not so well known, I have mentioned many people – lyricists, singers, musicians, filmmakers, movie actors, impresarios, comedians, writers of pulp fiction – and their works. The reader will hopefully forgive the multitude of names that appear in this book. Only with a sense of the concrete can one begin to appreciate the enormous scope and influence that mass culture has had in the Soviet Union in our century. Furthermore, many of these names, though virtually unknown to outsiders, are household terms for the average Russian. A Western historian of Russia, for example, will likely know more about Grigory Orlov than about the actress Lyubov Orlova; more about Count Panin than about the gypsy singer Varya Panina; more about Emelyan Pugachev than about the pop star Alla Pugacheva. For most Soviet people, the reverse would be true.

In choosing a particular story, song, comedy routine, movie, or entertainment figure from the immense body of popular culture, I have had to be severely selective and have sought those most firmly lodged in the memory of Russians and that seem to have been the symbols of their times. When possible, I have documented this with numerical evidence of popularity. For movies, preference was given to those I have seen, ranging from 1908 to the present. Fiction presents a dilemma because Russian classics, Soviet mainstream literature, and foreign translations have been very popular at various junctures in Soviet history. A discussion of everything that was actually "popular" in reading tastes, would have burst the limits of this survey. Since those works and their readerships have been thoroughly treated in easily available books,[2] I have focused on the less-studied forms – detective, adventure, science fiction and other "light" genres, particularly those that treated a theme that was visible in the other popular arts at the time.

Thirty years ago, a keen firsthand Western observer of Soviet life had this to say: "To the foreigner in Russia, a far clearer picture of Russian life, ways of thinking, and inner problems emerges from a study of entertainments than from enquiry into politics – by meeting artists and talking about theater rather than by interviewing officials."[3] The range of inquiry has changed drastically since then, to be sure, but the rewards of cultural study still remain. Part of comprehending a people's culture is knowing what they know. Soviet people have much greater information about Western popular culture than we do about theirs, and this is not necessarily because ours is "better." Although outsiders like myself and most of my readers cannot aspire to a full understanding of Russian popular culture, we can at least try for some balance in mutual knowledge and understanding.

1   In old Russia 1900–1917

Those were the days

The Russian Empire in the years 1900–1917 entered the throes of industrialization, urbanization, parliamentary life, agrarian change, ethnic and class tensions, two revolutions, and two wars. Beneath the clamor of these events and processes could be heard the marching feet of peasants into the factories and of ethnic minorities rattling their way to Moscow by train. Before it was dramatically destroyed in 1917, Russia's urban morphology had begun to resemble that of many earlier industrializing societies. A growing class of affluent businessmen and their wives consumed high-toned and middle class commodities – including culture. Modern merchandizing and architecture were wedded in new structures: the Shopping Arcade (now GUM) in Moscow, the Singer Building (now Dom Knigi) in St. Petersburg, and the ornamental Eliseevsky Delicatessens. Rapid advances and transfers of technology brought an expanded railroad net, trams, automobiles, telephones, phonographs, cameras, new kinds of printing, electric illumination, and the cinema. A massive intake of foreign styles and artifacts helped shape the Silver Age of the arts. On its fringes flourished an appetite for exotic cultural forms – Caucasian, Jewish, Gypsy – and the elite's discovery of Russian folk culture. Below it all rumbled the momentous sound of revolutionary subcultures.

Behind the rising façades of modernity lurked human and material poverty. Possessed of ancient Slavic cities and spectacular capitals such as Kiev, Moscow, and St. Petersburg, Russia was also the scene of slum-infested "migrant towns," socially unstable and lacking in amenities. The technical wizardry of modern engineering that built street lights and iron bridges also brought the bombs fashioned by insurgents and the field pieces deployed by pacifying troops in the vicious conflicts that beset the country between 1900 and 1914. The delights of parliamentary elections and debates, an emergent civil society, and the diminution of censorship were accompanied by a quickening of social animosity, strikes, and pogroms. The immense gulf between the propertied, the landed, and the empowered on the one hand and the lower classes on the other was crosscut by a chasm between educated society and the masses.

In culture this was reflected in the tendency of Silver Age artists to avert their eyes from social problems; and in the obsessive hostility of a moralistic elite toward the burgeoning popular culture. The growth of street hooliganism with its theatricality and socially iconoclastic energies was matched by avant-garde provocations in cafe performances; all of popular culture seemed to take on a sharper edge and a coarser tone as if in visceral revolt against the "culture" of the respectable. It also revealed a discernible shift in mass taste, especially in the bigger cities, whose population's growing urban consciousness was reflected in newspaper readers' thirst for sensation, crime, scandals, disasters, vice, social tension, and muckraking, as well as news in general – in other words the real world of the throbbing metropolis as chronicled in the big, colorful popular dailies of Moscow and St. Petersburg.[1] Although returning workers brought urban fiction, phonograph records, stories of things seen and heard, new dances, and pictures from the towns, villages were remote from the high culture of the urban intelligentsia. Traveling theater companies, Sergei Kusevitsky's Volga River concert boat tours of classical music in 1910–1914, and upper class artists who went into the villages all barely touched the surface of the agrarian realm of folktales, sayings, songs, dances, and woodcraft.

Russians then – and to a great extent now – spent most of their leisure time simply in self-entertainment: visiting friends, having company, or going out together – on village street, urban park, or sylvan wood for a picnic or excursion. For the peasantry, the main diversions were the tavern, religious rituals, family events, and the frequent and colorful calendar and church holiday feasting – which sometimes lasted for days. On the estates and in the towns the variety of self-generated entertainment was as varied as the classes themselves: for the highly placed there were seasonal balls, salons, sleighing parties, yacht receptions, midnight suppers, and the races. Modest versions of these entertainments prevailed among the middle range of urban classes and merchants. All of it was dictated by inherited values, sizes of income and leisure time, and even quality of wardrobe.

Although much interplay between habits of town and country persisted, urban forms were taking shape. In the city, workers tended toward bonding in factory groups, hometown affiliations (*zemlya-chestva*), residential communes, or neighborhoods – thus creating urban subcultures, in-groups, or even gangs. These found expression in both harmless and harmful activities. In the tavern they produced the warm glow of conviviality – an exceptionally important feature of lower class male lives – and sometimes belligerent drunkenness. A contemporary foe of Russian urban popular culture freely admitted that the tavern was far more popular than reading, shows, or other entertainment. Another side of working class leisure was courtship and dating. *Progulki*, in village terminology, meant strolling up and down the street in gender groups to flirt, to show off, to make friends, to sing and joke. This reappeared in the city's industrial zones as simply promenading, or "going out" (its present meaning) to streets and gardens or to a tavern or dance hall.[2]

Gang mentalities throve on institutionalized working-class violence – directed at each other and not at police or employers. A dramatic example of this was the "wall-to-wall" fistfight match between associated groups of male workers on a combat ground for the sheer purpose of beating each other up with bare hands and sometimes with knives or clubs. The custom has survived in variant forms down to the present and was recently depicted in the film *Little Vera*. In fact almost all of these activities, however modified in style by the changing shape of town and country in the past hundred years, have proved astonishingly tenacious. From the public holiday which throws thousands of promenaders, shoppers, and singers onto the streets to the vicious gang fights, Russian urban leisure forms contain much that is traditional, even in the age of perestroika.

Radical or "politically conscious" workers were pulled into a counterculture that differed sharply from everyday working class subcultures. First of all, it was much smaller. Its main venues were circle and study group where political texts and revolutionary fairytales were read, underground holiday picnics with songs of protest, and street demonstrations with red flags and slogans. But this did not constitute an all-embracing cultural movement for the masses of the kind envisioned by the Left Bolshevik intellectuals Gorky, Lunacharsky, and Bogdanov, who were trying to forge a proletarian culture movement in this period and who would try again after 1917. Radical workers, although part of a counterculture, continued to consume the works of other cultures. An old Bolshevik recalled that at gatherings, his circle of radical friends sang "prison, Volga, student, folk, and revolutionary songs." Politicized workers also mingled with other workers and with other classes in their consumption of popular culture – the movies, the fairs, People's Houses. Popular tastes and class feelings – both of them authentic – may have seemed incompatible to radical intellectuals; but they coexisted very well among the common people, and indeed still do.[3]

A major theme in the history of popular culture is the hostility of educated elites to it – a hostility that cut across political lines and endures right up to today. Vladimir Mikhnevich, writing in 1886 of the hopelessly "dark world" of the lower classes, explained it partly by the "false" culture that was fed to them: "fairbooth theater, the tavern, dancing classes in the *cafes chantants*, and the poisonous output of book-stall literature – *The Bandit Churkin* and pornographic novels."[4] This ill-tempered but accurate digest of the main forms of urban popular culture at that moment would be greatly amplified in the next three decades by electrical and mechanical inventions. The intelligentsia assaulted all the varieties of popular culture in the last decades of the Old Regime partly because of greater awareness of it and partly because of its wider dissemination. Intellectuals, censors, priests, physicians, and revolutionaries – however sharply they differed among themselves – were often united in their animosity to the new culture which they linked directly to vice. And yet that culture was, after all, a folklore of the city: the product of the urban masses' desire to read, hear, watch, and sing about their own city life – even if and especially if much of it was a lament about its cruelty.

Song and dance in the city

In the nineteenth century, Russian village songs were part of folk art: solo, chant, responsive dialogue, humorous couplets, laments, bandit epics, soldier and boatman songs, and ritual pieces. They varied in time and place because of the oral tradition that housed them. Instruments were scarce – a balalaika or a modest concertina. The urban song – including composed "folk songs" – that emerged in full force around 1900 – written by people of various social classes and often published anonymously in penny song-books – differed from the art song and the folk song in content, melody, style of performance, and scope of its social appeal. It was broader, more "vulgar," accessible, and sensual; its words, melodies, and rhythms possessed a sharpness rare in earlier song genres. The style of delivery, a combination of facial expressions, gestures, and postures, differed strikingly from the body language of salon and village street and suited well the broadness and even banality of the words and music; it also frequently suggested individualism or a mild posture of lawlessness and contempt for respectability – which of course explains its appeal to "the better sort" who were out on the town.

The dominant style of the new urban song was *tsyganshchina* – "gypsy" song. Upper-class fascination with Gypsies is well attested in literature. The Gypsy was an emblem of freedom and looseness in Russia even more than elsewhere in Europe. In Russia, the freedom evoked by the Gypsy had nothing to do with political liberty. It was the peasant and cossack *volya*, signifying the open steppe, rolling wagons, savage dignity, and wanton abandon. Gypsies were not only homeless but did not even know where their homeland was; they thus excelled in evoking a favorite Russian mood, *toska* – ineffable longing for something lost or far away. Officers and nobles, rich merchants, and socially catapulted persons (such as Rasputin) found utter release from "civilization" in the great Gypsy choirs of taverns and restaurants. But turn-of-the-century "gypsy" singing stars were no more Gypsy than their songs. The new singers shaped wild sensibilities into a manageable performance art suitable for stage and the intimate cabinet of a restaurant. The gypsy idiom contained violent and rhythmically exotic flourishes of uncontrolled passion – intimations of sex, hysteria, flights of fancy, and floods of champagne. Particularly effective was the shock of sudden changes in tempo and the accelerando–crescendo phrasing that became its hallmark – brilliantly displayed in staples of the genre, "Endless Road," "Dark Eyes," and "Two Guitars." Such songs offered socially unifying entertainment perfectly suited to the mixed milieu of the urban restaurant and tavern.[5]

The repertoire of Anastasia Vyaltseva (1871–1913), one of several stars of the era, combined the sweep and rebelliousness of the older gypsy song with the bitter-sweet nostalgia of urban life. She elicited unabashed tears and sighs of upper and middle class patrons who were, through her art, enabled to make contact with the "primitive" without ever being engulfed by it. Her big hit, "I Fall in and out of Love at Will," celebrated the capricious and seductive woman. Vyaltseva made annual tours all over the empire and became a national figure. Like many celebrities of that and other times, she recapitulated the style of her art in a private life of extravagant love affairs, conspicuous consumption, lavish spending, and the heavy drinking that shortened her life. Plevitskaya (1884–1941), another gypsy star, toured Europe and was even able to melt the "starched audiences" of

London. Varya Panina (1872–1911; see fig. 1), a true Gypsy by birth, dominated the famous Yar Restaurant in Moscow with her ensemble until lured into the concert circuit. Although Panina acquired huge wealth, she died penniless. All three were the subject of rumors and legends – the kind that tracked later Soviet stars such as Vysotsky and Pugacheva. People who adored gypsy music – including Tolstoy, Blok, the actor Mozzhukhin, and many others – sometimes articulated their worship; those appalled by it voiced their hostility in racist references to "hot blood" or tropical passion in almost the same way Americans of the time did about urban "Negro" music.[6]

The cruel song or romance (*zhestokii romans*), sometimes called "urban romance," was more elegiac and more Russian than gypsy in its makeup, but differing from the salon romance which had featured exalted worship of the beloved, sad disillusionment, and nostalgic recollection. The cruel song added a coarsening element in the music and a verbal formula of blatant self-pity. It contained some of the social lament found in folk song (coachman, recruit, and prisoner genres) but not the political bite of the radical song. It spoke to the individual and served the needs of a growing city clientele which flocked to restaurants and cafes. These songs did not emanate collectively or spontaneously from the masses but were designed for them by professional songwriters and were ubiquitous in the towns and ready made for migration to sheet music, film, recordings, and live entertainment.[7]

Alexander Vertinsky (1889–1957) drew a somewhat different clientele, though there was much overlapping of audiences in this era: artists, intelligentsia, students, and a wide assortment of high-society people who liked their sadness and *toska* adorned with a touch of cosmopolitan chic. Vertinsky was an immensely talented and cultivated figure who began his career as a poet and stage actor. A tall, slender man and a master of expressive, nuanced gestures, he performed in the costume of Pierrot with powdered face and closed eyes his own bittersweet songs of broken love, elegant variants of gypsy and cruel song. His rendition of "Endless Road" ("Dorogoi dlinnoyu," known in English as "Those Were the Days") is one of the classics of his repertoire. Vertinsky bathed his verses in images of palm trees, tropical birds, foreign ports, plush lobbies, ceiling fans, and "daybreak on the pink-tinted sea," treating his patrons to such songs as "Jamais," "Little Creole Girl," "Cocaine Lady," "Lily White Negro," and "Your Fingers Smell of Incense." The blending of refined irony, decadent wit, and elegiac sorrow made Vertinsky a star of the intimate stage from 1913–1914 onward. His fame was broadcast throughout the country through concert tours, movies, sheet music, and phonograph records that were played in Russia long after he emigrated.[8]

The Russian dance revolution of the early twentieth century was European and American in both form and social function. The tango, the cakewalk, the one-step, and the foxtrot were brought into Russia by foreign visitors and Russian travelers abroad and by choreographic spies sent out to record the new steps. The new dance was originally an upper class affair, part of its revolt – as in New York cafe society of the same period – against the stiffness and formality of traditional balls and suppers. In America, the popular dance filtered up from Blacks, immigrants, and workers; in Europe and Russia, it came in at the top and then filtered down to a larger public. The charm of ragtime and jazzy dancing lay in its exotic chic and its suggestion of rebelliousness, sensuality, and bodily freedom.[9]

Gypsy music, cruel song, the rarefied effervescence of Vertinsky and other cafe singers, ragtime, and the new dance emerged at a moment when technical possibilities allowed them to be dispersed far and wide via traveling companies on railroad tours, shipboard concerts, recordings, and large-scale printing of sheet music and colored photos of stars. Celebrity, previously the monopoly of high-culture figures in opera, theater, and ballet, along with dynastic, military, and government personages was now shared by entertainment stars through records and sell-out concerts. Migration from genre to genre and medium to medium accelerated: opera stars appeared in restaurants, novelists turned to screen writing, popular singers, dancers, and legitimate actors stood in front of the movie camera. Vertinsky enjoyed the first of his two film careers during World War I.

Not only singers, but songs themselves became celebrated as "hits" (*shlagery*). In the years 1900–1907, a half million gramophones were sold in Russia. Movie producers capitalized on the immense popularity of song hits and simply adapted their simple narratives and titles to films of the same name. The songs "Postal Sleigh" (Vot, mchitsya troika pochtovaya) – still well known today among Soviet listeners – "Dashing Merchant" (Ukhar-kupets), and "Coachman, Don't Race the Horses" – all familiar as songs of the road in folk and popular culture – were scripted into films. The title of a major song hit written by the classical composer Yuly Bleikhman, "Do You Remember?," was given to a tear-jerking movie melodrama (see p. 32). Scenarists would scratch out movie treatments as they listened to restaurant singers. Dance routines were also screened. In fact, every form of popular musical entertainment was coopted for the movies in the 1910s. Silent films were always accompanied by music played by an orchestra, a small band, or a piano. Thus sound – much of it popular music – occupied half of the audience's attention, however badly it was coordinated with the flickering images on the screen.[10]

The world of radical music was remote in spirit and purpose from mainstream popular culture. Revolutionary subculture flourished in a tiny segment of the radical intelligentsia, and a small but growing layer of industrial workers, among whom singing was almost the only form of performance possible in an underground milieu. Some indigenous songs dated back to the revolutionary movement of the 1860s and 1870s, but many were European in origin, such as "Workers' Marseill- aise," "Internationale," and "Varshavianka." The last was a French tune with Polish words translated into Russian. Its ominous opening verse about "the hostile winds raging about us" and the oppressive forces of darkness and evil moved the hearts of revolutionaries in and out of power for decades. The melody, dressed in a driving staccato march beat, was incorporated by Dmitry Shostakovich into his Eleventh Symphony (1957), a celebration of the 1905 revolution. Russian radical song writers – like those elsewhere – discovered that almost any kind of music could be radicalized by adding the right words. The melody of the rousing, "For Soviet Power" was a cafe song of the period, "White Acacia" (still sung under that title in Finland, then part of the Russian Empire). Revolutionary lyrics were funereal, visionary, accusatory, or menacing, but the tunes were overwhelm- ingly mournful. As illegal sounds of protest, they had small audiences but they unquestionably deepened and defined radical sentiments of those who sang them. After 1917, as hymns of a Bolshevik religiosity, they nearly drowned out all other forms of public celebratory music.[11]

The world of *estrada*

Beyond the proscenia of the great theaters of St. Petersburg and Moscow, performance art of all kinds flourished in the last decade of the monarchy and formed the bases for modern Soviet *estrada*. The Russian term *estrada* (from Spanish through French: small stage) indi- cates a very broad range of live entertainment from rural and tradi- tional outdoor shows to modern nightclub revues. *Narodnoe gulyane*, meaning carnival, folk fair, or folk festival was a traditional seasonal event with deep roots in pagan and Christian rites, minstrel com- panies, and folk games. It offered fairbooth satire, sleigh rides, dancing bears, carrousels and swings, ice hill sledding, food stalls, and general drinking and merrymaking. In the last years of the old regime, folk fairs were organized on designated grounds or indoors by private enterprise, government, and civic societies who hoped to woo people away from politics or the tavern. Their ban on drinking and stringent rules marked a shift from spontaneous popular festival to greater social control.[12]

Live entertainment in folk festival included the peep show (*raëk*) and the fairbooth (*balagan*), both eagerly adapted by high culture before the revolution and for revolutionary satire in the Soviet period. *Raek* combined a panoramic scene inside a curtained booth and lively routines by the carnival barker (*raeshnik* or *raeshnyi ded*) who regaled customers with topical wit and good humored insults – occasionally sliding into social or political satire. The *raeshnik* personified the humor of the market place – both as meeting place and a mart of which he was an agent. The need to induce passersby into a sideshow or a carnival ride developed in him resourcefulness, social alertness and topicality, the power to read an audience, and a sharp tongue ever poised to improvise. The style of the barker has been traced by folklorists to the toastmaster or best man at village weddings who regaled the company with witty and off-color jokes. He was also an ancestor of the urban variety show entertainer and of Soviet standup comedians – and, like them, subject to censorship. The *balagan* stage was dominated by folk drama, melodrama, knights' tales, harlequinades, and reenactments of Russian battles and sieges, all filled with action and visual excitement.[13]

Folk drama, dating from the early modern period, was performed by itinerant companies in villages, fairs, and military units. The plays were lengthy outdoor productions or smaller pieces full of social lampoon and stuffed with fragments and remnants of pagan motifs, rituals, songs, and puppet shows. They were all structurally "unstable," that is without script and open to change and improvisation. The absence of a stage or "fourth wall" allowed intermixing of audience and public. Folk drama's consciousness of itself as theater is what made avant-garde experimentalists so fond of it and related entertainments. Of the two most popular longer plays, *Tsar Maximilian* dealt with Christian martyrdom through the disturbing theme of a father, the pagan emperor Maximilian, ordering the torture and execution of his Christian son. *The Boat*, derived from folk songs and poems about the seventeenth-century cossack bandit and rebel Stenka Razin, was performed to their accompaniment.[14] Thus, the image of cossack-bandits floating on the Volga with no apparent destination was firmly fixed in the popular memory when in 1908 it became the subject of Russia's first successful feature film, *Stenka Razin.*

Popular theater, in contrast to folk drama, was an elite enterprise designed to bring literary drama and moral uplift to the masses. Launched by the intelligentsia in the 1860s, popular theater troupes eventually included amateurs from various social classes. By 1914 their number stood at 300. The founders of one of the Mobile People's Theaters (1903), Pavel Gaideburov and Nadezhda Skarskaya, typified the mentality of most organizers. They disliked traditional lower class leisure pursuits, especially the folk fair, and offered spiritual and cultural uplift through the classics of Russian drama. Audiences at the free or inexpensive popular theaters were startled by the "realism" of the performances in contrast to the stylized character of folk drama. The public tended to reify abstract ideas, identify with characters, and applaud righteousness and the punishment of sinners. Like the producers, they saw theater as a moral instrument. But they also ignored the niceties of audience-theater relations and felt free to *kibitz* and shout at actors who "misbehaved" or admiringly throw vodka bottles on stage. They sometimes laughed or reacted in the "wrong" way: during the chopping scene of Chekhov's *Cherry Orchard*, the public cheered. Some things were beyond their grasp; lawyers, for example, were to them a puzzling and alien species.[15]

In the early twentieth century, the *locus* for most urban popular theater was the People's House (*Narodnyi dom*). Dating from the 1880s, it was one of many attempts to offer culture as social prophylaxis by the intelligentsia, factory owners, government agencies, and charities. People's Houses usually contained a reading room, a tea room, and a theater where melodramas, patriotic plays, and "extravaganzas" were staged. The most famous was the Ligovsky People's House, south of the Moscow railway station in a very poor section of St. Petersburg, founded in 1902 by the wealthy member of the Liberal Kadet party, Countess Sofia Panina, and partly designed to win young girls away from the enormous red light district nearby. Its permanent theater and school for amateur working class actors were accessible to the poor. In 1903, Gorky founded a People's House in Nizhny-Novgorod. By 1913 there were 147 of them in the empire. People's Houses were the models of the later Soviet houses and palaces of culture. They were augmented by a large network of rural cooperative cultural affiliates – ancestors of the Bolshevik reading cabins and agit-points of the 1920s.[16]

Circus, one of the most enduring forms of mass entertainment in

Russia, was established on a permanent basis in 1853, and was largely dominated by foreigners: the Salomanskys of Berlin in Moscow and the Cinizelli family of Italy in St. Petersburg whose houses are now the Moscow and Leningrad circuses, respectively. Russian entrepreneurs, such as the Nikitin Brothers, entered the scene later. Circus, dating from Roman times, is deeply conservative; it has long been enmeshed by family acts and dynasties stemming from the itinerant character of early circus life and the need for trust and teamwork. The colorful and kinetic qualities of the arena and a distinct aura of sexuality made the circus a natural theme in show business and fiction. Alexander Kuprin wrote stories about circus life; theatrical innovators such as Meyerhold were attracted to it; its acts were pulled out into the variety stage, and several popular movie melodramas of the time revolved around circus life.[17]

The clown was the key figure in circus entertainment who linked the acts, broke the tension through slapstick humor, and ridiculed a wide range of behavior by exaggeration and deflation. One of the most renowned teams in pre-revolutionary Russian circus was Bim-Bom, formed by I.S. Radunsky and successive partners who specialized in parodying operatic music – a recurrent theme in modern popular culture. Bim-Bom became celebrities through films and recordings. The Durov brothers, Anatoly and Vladimir, founded the best-known clown dynasty in Russian history. They developed the so-called Durov method of humane animal care and training, based upon scientific theories, a method still used today in Soviet circuses. In a famous act called "The Durov Railroad," all the passengers and personnel were played by animals. The Durovs sometimes ridiculed bureaucratic arrogance. In 1905, Anatoly Durov insulted the notorious anti-Semitic governor of Odessa, Admiral Zeleny (which means green), by leading a pig painted green into the arena to the general amusement of the public. The capacity of circus to accommodate satire in a setting of mass entertainment[18] would make it a perfect instrument of Soviet mass culture.[18]

Urbanized folk entertainment, an activity that some call folklorism or even fakelore emerged at the end of the nineteenth century. The conception and adoption of folk culture was variously motivated by dedication to the people, nostalgia, nationalism, anthropological sentimentalism, profit, and combinations of these. The intelligentsia endeavored to rescue "authentic" folk culture from looming oblivion, package it, and present it to urban audiences, mostly of the middle and upper classes. Song, dance, and instrumental folk ensembles became a major segment of *estrada* entertainment before 1917.[19]

Its pioneer, Vasily Andreev (1861–1918), a member of the lesser provincial gentry, mastered the peasant balalaika and then founded the first major ensemble of folk instruments. He "rescued" folk music but drastically transformed it by creating a giant balalaika orchestra, with instruments of seven different registers from soprano down to the bulky octobass (later amplified by domras, gusli, svirels, and zhalei-kas) which played lushly harmonized folk tunes and classics in lavish settings (see fig. 2). All of this was alien to village musical culture, where the three-stringed balalaika was known, if at all, in one size and usually played only to accompanying dancing. Andreev – like most impresarios of invented culture – enjoyed his greatest success with middlebrow audiences but reached a far wider market through record-ings and outdoor performances. The band included trained pro-fessionals and ordinary peasants and it toured Russia and Europe in the years 1908–1912, bringing "folk" music to urban audiences. Although assaulted by cultural elitists who detested the rendering of classics on "primitive village instruments" and by the political right wing who despised the cultural exaltation of the peasant ethos, the concerts of the Andreev ensemble won great popularity.[20]

Mitrofan Pyatnitsky (1864–1927), another folk revivalist, was the son of a village deacon, who in 1905 assembled a song and dance ensemble composed of real peasant singers and dancers from the provinces decked out in folk costume and employing the pristine forms and styles of byliny, folk songs, and lamentations from their villages. Pyatnitsky's company performed at outdoor fairs and folk festivals around the country. But its 1912 theatrical debut was played to a stylish audience in the Moscow Club of the Nobility, where Pyatnitsky tried to reduce the jarring spectacle of peasants performing on an indoor stage by what he called the scenic method – replicating a village street and erecting cabins right on the stage. It was the familiar attempt to de-theatricalize by means of realistic sets. This realism of the unreal resembled the cultural construction of village life by painters and photographers of postcards who framed rural landscapes, romanti-cized them, and sold their representations in large numbers. Both Andreev and Pyatnitsky dreamed of making folk music a national pastime and cultural industry and this dream was realized on a massive scale in the Stalin period.[21]

Like its counterparts in London and Paris, the Russian variety stage – estrada in the narrower sense – combined and popularized all kinds of novelties: hit songs, vocal stars, visiting companies, short operettas, new dances, imported numbers, satirical comedy, circus acts, even films – all in one performance with an emphasis on action, surprise, and fun. Invading parks, People's Houses, and cinemas, variety attracted huge audiences with its deployment of the crude, the flashy, the energetic, and the exotic. By 1907 fifty were in operation. Offshoots of *estrada* could be viewed also in the larger restaurants and *cafés chantants*. Nightclubs in the capital took such names as Hermitage, Orpheus, Folies Bergère, and Alcazar. A 1908 program of the Restaurant Yar, with its luxurious two-story hall of malachite columns, balconies, and palms (a favorite haunt of Rasputin) included comedy and clown acts such as Bim-Bom; Gypsy, Russian, and Ukrainian singers; and acts billed as Hungarian, Viennese, Spanish, and French. In the Hotel Metropole, one could have 5 o'clock tea, drink at the American Bar, and listen to Viennese and Romanian salon orchestras. Indeed "foreignism" was a hallmark of urban popular culture. So was sex: a Moscow Farce Theater presented "Sarah Wants a Negro," "Don't Walk about in the Nude," and a drag show with female impersonators dressed as Vyaltseva, Panina, and Plevitskaya. Both the foreignism and the "pornography" were purged from *estrada* culture after the revolution.[22]

Estrada and the movies fed on each other: gypsy themes, operettas, and variety acts were made into films; cinema helped spread *estrada* by opening houses all over the country where stage shows shared billing with popular films. When the tango, imported from South America through Europe, captured Russian nightclub audiences after 1910, studios released a rash of tango films including, at the peak of the craze, *Everyone Tangos in Russia*. At the very end of commercial movie history appeared *The Last Tango* (1918), taken from the repertoire of the salon singer Iza Kremer and ending with the murder of the Argentine heroine (Vera Kholodnaya) by her jealous lover on a Paris dance floor.[23]

The main vehicle for the delivery of satire was the couplet (*kuplet*), a rhymed verse or ditty, spoken or sung, with an urban theme that differentiated it from the village *chastushka*. At the turn of the century it was popularized in the circus by Bim-Bom and was even used for beer advertisement jingles. During the revolution of 1905 it was given a political edge as comedy shows echoed the bitter cartoons of the satirical journals. But although some performers were arrested, the political dimension of stage satire was quite small. Odessa – a multiethnic and international harbor city – became renowned as a breeding ground for satirists, among whom Jews were especially prominent. But they dealt far more often with infidelity, high fashion, and in-laws than they did with tsarist repression. After the revolution, stage comedians would have to learn the proper formula for the use of satire.[24]

Cabaret, a high counterculture, did not enjoy wide patronage, but it adopted some of the attributes of the lower arts in its habitats, its bohemian façade, and its slumming clientele. Cabaret held up a "crooked mirror" to high society and its art, encouraged the mixing of ethnic, class, and gender orientation (including homosexuals), and possessed a fringe of the disrespectable. Affluent businessmen and professional patrons – contemptuously called "druggists" – were kept on the fringe of the fringe. As a social margin, cabaret offered escape from the rigors of upper class life, a passage to adventure, an arena of controlled chaos, and a nearby exit back to normality. It combined the contrived menace of the circus with the trendy sheen of in-group company and high-toned entertainment. The Bat (Moscow), the Stray Dog, and the Crooked Mirror (St. Petersburg) were the chief cabarets in the years 1908–1917. The Bat punctured the portentous Moscow Art Theater and its famous Stanislavsky pauses; its bat logo was a jibe at that theater's revered production of Chekhov's *The Sea Gull*. Crooked Mirror parodied urban popular entertainment – gypsy singers, music hall performers, and film comedy. It gave a start to the famous Soviet comic, Vladimir Khenkin. Banished after the revolution, cabaret has been revived in the years of glasnost.[25]

Especially suggestive for the coming revolution was the growing diversification of tastes among working class and upper class audiences in the capitals. Many workers – while still frequenting popular movies – showed by their attendance at People's Houses aspirations to understand the classics of drama, music, and poetry in places set up for them by the intelligentsia. This quest for upward mobility and respectability would clash with Proletcult and avant-garde designs for workers after the Bolshevik Revolution and would thus enrich and confuse fixed notions of popular taste and culture. Equally interesting was the Russian version of slumming. It came in two styles: the straightforward rush by members of the elite into dens awash with gypsy music or into vulgar vaudeville and burlesque houses catering to a wide urban stratum; and the more ambiguous habituation of the avant-garde bohemian milieux where generals, ballerinas, sailors, bums, foreign celebrities, besotted poets, and starving artists congregated in order to shock the bourgeoisie. At the core of all this was commingling of classes, a jumble of tastes, and the proliferation of genres.

From page to screen

Russian fiction, oral and written, has long been a part of popular culture in its own right and as raw material for other arts and media. Folk literature was largely oral, a performance art in which tellers told; its most popular genre was the fairy tale. Literate peasants – a rapidly growing community – had access to the chap book or illustrated broadside (*lubok*), religious texts, and secular handbooks. Peasants tended to approach a text as something sacred and true, designed to excite the emotions and teach moral lessons. The folk-tale cycle, *Ivan the Little Fool*, with its elements of reversal, illustrates in most readings the moral superiority and even resourcefulness of the poor, the weak, and the low born. Other tales reflected peasant notions of *pravda* (truth, right, justice, fairness) and popular monarchism (belief in a benevolent but isolated tsar). Folk heroes – thieves, bandits, and rebels – abounded in this corpus, especially Stenka Razin and Emelyan Pugachev.[26]

Folkloric themes and styles were adapted to urban popular media just as they had been used by high culture in the nineteenth century. Figures, conventions, and commonplaces of folk culture appeared in popular writings and then made their way to stage and cinema: repetition, contraction of visual images, and stock descriptive phrases such as "furrowed brow," "swift boats," "fiery steeds," "menacing eyes," and "white hands." After 1917, they were coopted into revolutionary culture and into official Stalinist mythology. Razin and Pugachev were worked into Bolshevik rhetoric and art in the early years. Anti-clerical images of greed and lust were magnified and distorted in anti-religious campaigns. Popular monarchism was incorporated into the "invented folklore" of the Lenin and Stalin cults. The moral superiority of the poor – very strong in folklore – became the central myth of the revolution.

Popular fiction written and published in the cities for peasants and urban lower classes came in two varieties. That sponsored by the state, the church, and the intelligentsia was designed to elevate the tastes and morals of the masses by means of "good" literature. Much greater in volume was that written mostly by lower class authors and sold in cheap commercial mass editions. Jeffrey Brooks' masterful study of an immense body of materials from *lubok* literature to detective and adventure stories in the penny press points to shifting attitudes of writers (and, by implication, readers) from rural contentment to an urban ethic of ambition, an expanded perspective about Russia, and a rational view of the world; although some of it suggests a primitive, racist, and anti-modern sensibility as well. Pulp fiction created a large unified reading culture and thus a natural audience for adaptations into other popular arts such as movies.[27]

Readership included lower middle class clerks, artisans, and small merchants, some peasants, urban workers, servants, and non-proletarian laborers, with an admixture of other classes. This corresponded roughly to the mass movie public. Many works of popular fiction were made into films: the bandit stories *Anton Krechet* (serialized 1909–1916) and *The Bandit Vaska Churkin* (also made into a popular song); detective stories and the crime epic, *Light-fingered Sonka* (one of the greatest hits of early cinema), based on the real criminal exploits of Sonya Blyuvshtein; and the romantic melodrama, Verbitskaya's *Keys to Happiness* (two films, 1913, 1917). Melodrama, high adventure, action, suspense, and satisfying resolutions were the stuff of popular fiction and films – then and now; facile writers like Alexander Amfiteatrov, Lydia Charskaya, and Count Amori (Ippolit Rapgof) became successful scenarists. The detective genre was largely derived from American, English, and French mass market pulp stories. *Nat Pinkerton, Nick Carter*, and *Sherlock Holmes* were the kings of Russian crime fiction featuring in such titles as *Boston Flesh Merchants, Oka Yuma, Japanese Spy*, and *Thames Pirates*. Young boys adored them and waited frantically for each succeeding episode. The Soviet writer Valentin Kataev recalled his childhood infatuation with detective tales.[28]

Highbrow critics hated the "vulgar" and "frivolous" stories and were especially scandalized by the popularity of "boulevard" literature or pornography – as the word was then understood – which began to flood the book-stalls after the easing of the censorship in 1905. Mikhail Artsybashev and Anastasia Verbitskaya were the most popular and best-remembered writers of that genre. Artsybashev (1878–1927) became a negative cultural icon in twentieth-century Russian literary and social discourse, endowing it with two terms of anguish and anger among the intelligentsia: *artsybashevshchina* and *saninshchina*. His 1908 novel *Sanin* is a tale of post-revolutionary social withdrawal, incest, suicide, and hedonism, with a touch of cheapened Nietzscheanism. Its author was skilled in the use of formulaic language to indicate physical traits of female characters – sensual mouth, broad shoulders, and ample breasts – and in delivering the expected clichés of love, passion, and betrayal.

Verbitskaya (1861–1928) used the same devices, but treated female ambition and sexuality through such themes as the talented woman

breaking with social convention on the road to success in the entertainment world. The emergence of that world as a topos of popular
fiction indicates its growing importance on the social landscape after
1905. Verbitskaya also employed the realia of luxury, refinement,
travel, and exotica – the 1910 equivalents of technologies, procedures,
foreign locales, and brand names that fascinate present-day readers of
bestsellers. In Verbitskaya and Artsybashev, contemporary political
events or social processes are no more than a backdrop – as in a movie
poster – to the main heroes and the flow of action. But although critics
rightly contrast the tinsel pretense of these works with the straightforward and primitive action tales of the serial genre, boulevard fiction
possessed and created its own public and was eminently suitable for
screen treatment in its time. Charskaya, another practitioner, wrote
movie scenarios such as that for *Mirages* (1916), a melodrama about an
actress, seduced from an idyllic family life by success and wealth,
abandoned by her lover, and then led to commit suicide.[29]

The fiction of muckraking contributed much to the new "openness"
in this era. Its most artistic practitioner, Alexander Kuprin – trained as a
newspaperman – produced fine novels and stories about prostitution,
regimental life, corruption, urban crime, and the underside of the
entertainment world. His *Yama*, a fictionalized report on life inside a
brothel caused a scandal and brought the author much publicity. The
exposé was made into a hot commodity in the daily press by muck-
rakers such as V. M. Doroshevich of *The Russian Word* who explored
exile and prison life and many other social evils. The literate urban
population was surrounded by "stories" – of crime and disaster,
perfidy and war, seduction and violence, heroism and triumph. The
new journalism was sharp, topical, and accessible. Ads and stories
about the entertainment world and illustrated popular science journals fed the fascination with celebrities, foreign places, discovery, and
invention and helped create consumers of the new popular culture;
and journalists of the mass circulation press and the craftsmen of
popular fiction imitated each other's racy styles.[30] This crucial nexus
between a free mass press and the popular arts was destroyed by the
revolution and reborn again only in the recent years of glasnost.

One genre that remained largely in the shadows until 1917 was
radical popular fiction. A crucial stratum of the laboring classes, the
so-called worker–intelligentsia, came to admire propaganda tales, anti-
religious fables, and revolutionary fairy tales such as *Four Brothers*, a
parable about oppression the world over that was often adapted in
Russian popular culture. Maxim Gorky was one of the few leftist writers

who successfully combined literature and radical politics with a broad readership – primarily through his autobiography, sketches of lower class life, and the revolutionary novel *Mother* (1906) which became one of the models for Soviet socialist realism. It was based on the Somov strike of 1902, in which a mother and son figured. Gorky molded it into an enduring tale about the burgeoning political consciousness and martyrdom of a proletarian mother from which three Soviet films have been made, one of them Pudovkin's masterpiece. Science fiction and urban Utopias also caught on when the works of H. G. Wells and Jules Verne flooded Russia in these years and helped inspire a Bolshevik science fiction Utopia: Alexander Bogdanov's *Red Star* (1908), a stirring tale of the 1905 revolution combined with a journey to Mars where high technology, social justice, and communism reigned. But the Utopia of hope was more than matched by Utopias of fear beginning in the 1890s. Some of these were war-scare novels, filled with xenophobia, anti-modernism, and anti-Semitism. Others warned of the dangerous allure of socialism which could grow into hideous regimentation.[31]

Picturing Russia

Pictorial material has always been a key element in mass culture. At the moment of the movie industry's birth, popular graphics had long been undergoing change. *Lubok*, the illustrated popular chapbook for the peasantry, often satirized various aspects of Russian life. Through the efforts of an artistic intelligentsia and the financing of industrial patrons, *lubok* art was reworked into book illustrations, postcards, and stage sets for ballet and opera. Later, foreign advertising began to move on to Russian pages to join the cartoon and the political caricature of various *fin-de-siècle* art styles. Pictures, posters, and *affiches* played an important role in changing tastes since they were used to illustrate texts, frame nature, evoke nostalgia, arouse political anger, and promote recordings, movies, plays, and shows of every kind.

Postcards were instrumental in teaching a mass audience – including peasant buyers – what peasants and the countryside were supposed to look like, thus spreading a romanticized image that many educated people already possessed from cheap engravings and pastels. A postcard series called "Russian Types" offered images (often distorted) that helped people "envision" social categories. Popular entertainment of the time was partly shaped by the kind of representation it received at the hands of graphic artists. Pictorial art was both a means of spreading popular culture and a segment of that culture. The movie poster and the illustrated film journal prepared viewers for what they were going to see and fixed in their minds a summary of what they had seen. The covers and illustrations of pulp fiction were visual mediators between story and film. A 1915 story by Count Amori, *Secrets of Nevsky Prospect* has a picture captioned "Disaster at the Hotel Fontanka" showing an officer holding a discharged pistol, the woman he has just shot askew on a divan, and an intimate dinner table between them with the remnants of supper and a champagne bucket. Almost literal copies of this scene were common in film melodramas of the era.[32]

Graphic satirists turned political during the Revolution of 1905 when a new array of artists arose – Brodsky, Kustodiev, and others – who would play a big role in 1917. Over 400 satirical journals came and went in the years 1905–1907, replete with anti-government cartoons. In them artists produced extraordinarily violent and morbid depictions of government repression, filled with religious and satanic images. The cover of the journal *The Jester* (*Payats*) showed a hand holding a severed Christ-like head of the martyred people against a blood red Kremlin and a raven-filled sky. Another presented Mother Russia as a young girl being devoured by the serpent of reaction. In the 1910s, cinema employed the satanic and serpentine images for the content of films and the imagery of their posters (see fig. 3). Both the pictures and the films were inspired by the dark occultist and mystical aura that enwrapped Russian society in these years.[33]

Electrotheater: moloch of culture

The movies embraced all of popular culture: folkloric themes and narrative styles, popular music and dance, *estrada*, fiction, and pictorial representation. Movie moguls in Russia, as elsewhere, were omnivorous; they would devour anything with a story line that promised to pull the film through the camera, unroll on the screen, and draw people into the dark houses. The greed of the studios for profit was no greater than the insatiability of the public for more movies. There were never enough scenarios; a screen veteran recalls that producers "would take any foreign adventure tale, change Pierre to Vladimir and Henrietta to Larisa and the script would be ready."[34] When these ran out, studios hired hacks to create scripts right on the set – exactly as was done on the meadows of Astoria and the backlots of Hollywood. The facile Count Amori, instant contriver of such lurid tales as *Secrets of the Japanese Court*, *Slave of Passion*, *Gold and Blood*, would stand on the set in his famous red necktie and crank out lines for each scene as the cameras were shooting. He is universally scorned in the film literature; but he reached mass audiences both in print and on screen.

The coming of the movies to Russia – first film showings in 1896, first native features in 1908 – brought the partial smudging of the boundaries of class, taste, and nationality among audiences. Cinema made foreign culture and Russian classics in vulgarized form directly available to the mass public for the first time in Russian history. The film industry also created a vast archipelago of democratized space and an unprecedented revelation of the power of the cultural marketplace. It spurred arts and artists into new directions (as the camera had previously done to painting), generated wholesale defections from high art into money art, and – being new and relatively uncontrolled – opened yet another door for ethnically non-Russian entrepreneurial energies. The power of movies both shocked and seduced people like Tsar Nicholas II, Chaliapin, and Tolstoy and deepened the line between moral elites of government, church, and intelligentsia on the one hand and producers and consumers of popular culture on the other. Most of all, film art provided sheer entertainment, fascination, and fun for a huge number of people of all classes.

Foreigners commanded about 80 percent of the domestic market until after the war began; then Russian producers largely took over. Of the half-dozen big native studios, those of two giant rivals, Alexander Drankov (1880–?) and Alexander Khanzhonkov (1887–1945), embodied the adventurous and vulgarian side of the new art. Drankov, a former parliamentary photographer and an energetic, enterprising, and charming man, was willing to take big risks – a distinctly modern trait. Besides bandit and detective tales, he filmed hunting and wrestling, a railroad crash, Tolstoy at Yasnaya Polyana, and the under-life of Moscow's Khitrova slum. To later Soviet filmmakers, the term *drankovshchina* indicated cinematic hackwork, a not entirely fair judgment. Khanzhonkov, an ex-cossack officer, built the best studio in Moscow and, like other major producers, launched prestige films with sumptuous decor as well as popular trivia such as *Lunar Beauties, Magic Tango*, and *Aza the Gypsy*. Lesser producers (called "little beetles") came and went in quick succession – like the humble cook who became a major distributor or the businessman who went bankrupt due to an error in camera loading. They were profiteers who turned out interchangeable junk films, shooting two or three on the same set in one day. The small producers were often swallowed by the "whales" in the vicious studio wars.[35]

When top directors and movie stars emerged, studios took on greater identity. Evgeny Bauer, Yakov Protazanov, Viktor Gardin, and Peter Chardynin were directors of great talent who made some of the best films in this era. The first screen celebrities achieved fame as imitators of the foreign stars Asta Nielsen and Max Linder. In 1914, with Russian films now dominating the screens, star billing began to replace other credits; and writers created vehicles especially for the "kings, queens, and stars of the linen sky." Russian movie stars were heroes of urban folklore, embodying both the ordinary people who viewed their films and the fantasy they came to see. They earned fabulous sums and were well publicized on placards, photos, screen magazines, postcards, and recordings. Most films were oriented toward male matinee idols: Ivan Mozzhukhin, Vitold Polonsky, Vladimir Maximov, Amo Bek-Nazarov, and others. Urbane, slightly cruel, and impeccably dressed, they broke the hearts and shattered the lives of beautiful women on screen.

The most famous of them, Mozzhukhin (1889–1939), abandoned a mediocre theater career and became king at the Khanzhonkov and Ermolev studios. The expressiveness of his eyes and his ability to cry on camera gave to cinema history the term "Mozzhukhin's tears." Tens of thousands of postcards bearing his image were treasured by their owners. In the last major film made before the Bolshevik revolution, he joined Protazanov in the unforgettable *Father Sergius*, based on a story by Tolstoy. His portrayal of Kazatsky, the youthful cadet who flees the torment of carnal temptation by joining the church is a masterful exercise in facial evolution and psychological transformation, all acted out in front of the static cameras of the age. The female superstar, Vera Kholodnaya, reigned from 1914 to a premature death in 1919, and made scores of movies. The former dancer with the sad eyes got into films without previous acting experience, a fact that unleashed a stampede of young girls aspiring to a movie career. Kholodnaya's magic brought to life the celluloid world she dwelled in, a world of tainted money, opulent restaurants, lavish champagne picnics, luxurious autos careening through the night, and illicit love ending in tragedy.[36]

The earliest films were shown in the Aquarium music hall of St. Petersburg, the Hermitage Garden of Moscow, *cafés chantants*, and shop premises. When permanent houses were built, cinema shared billing with variety acts of every kind. Music was provided by pianists, string ensembles, and even military bands (for war movies). Gramophones and electric pianos in the lobby, the wires and sparks of the whirring projector, and the bright lights outside justified the widely used term "electrotheater." In 1912, there were 134 permanent houses in the capital, sixty-seven in Moscow (New York at the time had 600 nickelodeons), and 1,412 in the empire. As elsewhere, they bore evocative names such as Mirage, Fantasy, Wonder World, Illusion, Globe, and Ambrosia (in a few years, they would give way to the revolutionary names Barricade, Shockworker, and Spartacus). Distributors journeyed from town to village with projector and a few cans of film. Even movie barges were tried in the early 1900s. By 1914, movie audiences exceeded those of all other popular entertainments and included students of both sexes, policemen, writers, prostitutes, officers, the intelligentsia "with spectacles and goatees," workers, clerks, businessmen, "women of the world," milliners, officials – in other words, almost everybody. In 1916 movie tickets outsold theater tickets by twelve times.[37]

Distributors used catchy ads ("Women's Day – Maximov is Playing!"), promised to show a woman clawed to death by a panther on screen, or presented live lions on stage before the showing of a jungle movie.[38] When short of new films, they would rename the current showing and exhibit it as a new feature. Successful expansion and entrepreneurial adventure were not matched by much cinematic experimentation. There were a few efforts to try out sound: at the Edison Cinetophone studio in St. Petersburg, singers tried to mouth the words to an operetta while a phonograph was playing and the camera rolled. Another failed innovation was to stage half a play and film the other half. On the screen, "theateritis" prevailed. In cinematography, that meant "Khanzhonkovism" as it was called by later filmmakers: long takes, intermediate shots, and a stationary camera standing as an imagined theater audience. In acting it meant "Delsartism," a repertory of exaggerated poses and gestures coded to emotions, developed on the stage by the Frenchman Francois Delsarte, and taken into popular melodrama and then films. It was against this art that most of the great film masters of the 1920s rebelled.

What kind of films were made? The market, perceptions of the market, artistic inclinations, logistical factors, and the personality of the producer combined to generate a rich array of genres. The tsarist censorship, though forbidding pornography, the depiction of royalty, the church, or labor unrest, interfered rarely, although it did kill an attempt to film Kuprin's popular novel *Yama*. Local authorities could sometimes intervene: a Don Cossack chieftain forbade movies dealing with theft and murder and another prohibited films where the hero dies at the end.

One of the first fiction films shot by Russians was *Stenka Razin* (1908), made by Drankov and lasting eight minutes. Its story line is as sketchy as the folk drama and song which inspired it: Razin's men, resentful of the attention he bestows upon his captive Persian mistress (who dances on an oriental rug!), forge a letter that suggests her infidelity and in a rage, Razin casts her from the boat into the Volga waves. Drankov's "broad Volga River" was a small inlet near the capital where it was filmed in a single day amidst great chaos with a cast from a People's House. The action is interspersed with drinking and singing the familiar folk song, "Stenka Razin." It was a commercial success because of the familiarity of the material to virtually all Russians and the *lubok* character of its *tableaux vivants*. The robber band motif probably helped the popularity of the cossack, bandit, and detective serials that soon emerged on screen.[39]

What later were called "prestige" films – costume dramas and spectacles – appealed to filmmakers everywhere from the very birth of the industry. In Russia, many were taken from novels on the widely held but erroneous belief that good literature guaranteed a good film. In most adaptations, narratalogical and psychological complexity were simplified by dropping subplots and by flattening the characters, especially bad ones. This often meant personalizing evil instead of making philosophical or social commentaries. The classics were often disguised by retitling or serializing them: Pushkin's *Mozart and Salieri* became *Symphony of Love and Death*. Screen versions of literary classics were touted as quality products, but were usually cheap and flashy. A major exception was Gardin's *Kreutzer Sonata* (1914), a work of great psychological sensitivity and masterful construction. Big historical pageants were modeled after the Italian prototypes, *Spartacus* and *Julius Caesar*. At least two films were based on the romantic Caucasian resistance leader, Shamil, a perennial favorite in Russian popular entertainment. For a 1911 spectacle, *The Defence of Sevastopol*, Vereshchagin's Crimean battle canvases were carefully studied in the Khanzhonkov studios (a device used by Eisenstein for *Alexander Nevsky* in 1938).

The films that packed in mass audiences were comedy, adventure, and melodrama. The major comic attraction was the suave Frenchman Max Linder who inspired a number of Russian imitators and who partly immunized viewers in Russia to the cruder art of Charlie Chaplin who in 1914–1917 was at the zenith of world success. One of the best native contributions to film comedy was the farcical *Little*

House in Kolomna (1913), which displayed the versatility of Mozzhuk-hin playing both a hussar officer and a female servant. Primitive and cheaply made adventure, bandit, and detective movies based on Russian boulevard pulp fiction flooded the market. *Light-fingered Sonka* brought that popular criminal and adventuress from the pulp original to the screen.

The dominant genre after 1913, was the domestic or "bourgeois" melodrama – often called "psychological salon melodrama" – which accounted for half of the 2,000 or so Russian made films of the era. Neya Zorkaya has analyzed a few hundred of these using a method inspired by the classic work of the folklorist Vladimir Propp whose "morphology of the folk tale" proclaimed the structural unity of all folk tale plots.[40] Most silent film melodramas bear the marks of standardized production – formulas and repetition of stories, themes, situations, and endings; cardboard characters, psychological shallowness, and lack of historical-sociological content. Almost all are variants on a masterplot: the idyllic life of a young girl, marred only by a vague malaise, is disrupted by the appearance of a seducer; her passion for him gives way to disenchantment and, at the end, to suicide, ruin, or vengeful murder. The stuff of these drawing room thrillers – with titles such as *Satan Exultant, Slave of Passion – Slave of Vice* – was temptation, seduction, adultery, betrayal, false accusation, fraud, and tawdry relations of every kind, all set in an affluent milieu.

Verbitskaya's bestselling novel, *The Keys to Happiness*, was made into the number one box office success in Russian pre-revolutionary cinema. It broke all records in advanced sales, standing room in mammoth theaters, and jacked up prices. *Keys* traced the stormy career of an aspiring actress caught in the crosscurrents of ambition, romance, ethnic ambivalence (one of her lovers was a wealthy Jew), and politics (always marginal). The life style of the principles is baroque in its extravagance, thus made to order for the dreamers in the dark theater who viewed it. Bauer's *For Happiness* (1917), related the painful story of a mother vs. daughter love triangle. Chardynin's *Do You Remember* (1914) brought together three great talents of the period in a typically bathetic story that epitomized the cinematic sensibility of the day. A young wife (Vera Koralli), adored by a doting older husband (Chardynin), is lured by a romantic young violinist (Mozzhukhin) away from husband and daughter to a rendezvous on a Christmas eve. Delayed by a blizzard and touched by the spectacle of a warm and happy family that she meets along the way, she returns only to find her husband killed by his own hand.[41]

Vera Kholodnaya was the queen of melodrama. In *Children of the Age* (1915), she played the loving wife and mother who succumbs to the temptations of high society when her husband is forced out of work by the wealthy playboy who lusts after her. In *Life for a Life* (1916; see fig. 4), she is again victimized by a rich good-for-nothing (played by the handsome Polonsky) but is avenged by her foster mother who kills him. Bauer's direction lent distinction to this conventional plot. Chardynin's *Be Still, My Grief* (1918) – the last of the salon-psychological melodramas – again juxtaposed the vulnerable world of the poor (an unemployed circus couple) to the cruelty and sexual depredations of the upper classes. It was the ultimate example of the genre, replete with Gypsies, circus people, street begging with guitar and violin, and billows of pathos. The gradual emergence of contempt for her weak husband in the wife was vividly rendered by Kholodnaya.[42]

It is more than probable that films like these which enjoyed a wide showing influenced the feelings of the lower classes in the revolution. Hatred and collective indignation can be engendered by the popular media – war films alone are proof of this. If hostility is already festering, it can be reinforced by a cultural product that tells viewers that the makers of the movie and the public share their feelings about social morality and its outward affects – scenery, raiment, and manners. It is no wonder that slicked hair and bowler hats, prime emblems of the slimy seducers, were angrily rejected, satirized, and even assaulted under the new Soviet regime. The privileging of classical motifs in architecture and furnishing in the *mise-en-scène* of the Chardynin and Bauer films – classical busts, statuettes, columns, cornices, Grecian urns – was meant to signify perfection, beauty, and aesthetic honesty and provide ironic contrast to the degraded values of their owners. But to the masses, they must have been simply emblems of the excessive luxury of the owning classes. This may have deepened the "vandalistic" behavior of the riotous urban lower classes in 1917–1918.

Russian melodrama had its own code. Its heroine was rarely as lucky as the American "damsel in distress": she was almost always seduced and forced to undergo suffering and either death or repentance; the villain was punished but not until he had wrought his evil work. This reflected one aspect of the Russian sensibility: the fatalistic attitude about the inevitability of tragedy, loss, and deep suffering. Some melodramas verged on pornography. *Praise of Madness* from the novel *Venus in Furs* by Sacher-Masoch, featured nude bathing and sado-masochistic relationships; and the sexy heroine of Count Amori's *Amorous Adventures of Mme. V.* tempted high school boys by undressing in front of open drapes. The Moscow cinema Magic Dreams showed off-color films after midnight. Decadence was the mood of the years after 1908, partly a European import, partly a result of the aftermath of a failed revolution. Since the Russian cinema was born in that year, it could hardly escape its influence. For those who came to power in 1917, decadence – including mysticism and the occult as well as eroticism – was a major cultural malady.

Russian jingo

The popular arts turned easily to patriotic themes during World War I. One facile producer of racy stories offered a salacious treatment of the German Kaiser in *Wilhelm in the Sultan's Harem* (1914). Philanthropic societies flooded Russia with patriotic graphics – executed mostly by realistic artists of the Itinerant Movement – which promoted war bonds, hatred of a barbarous foe, and sympathy for the suffering victims at home, on the front, and in allied countries. The most famous was Leonid Pasternak's 1914 "Aid for the Victims of War," adapted by the Bolsheviks after the revolution for their own program. Artists employed antique Slavonic lettering, Christian motifs, and *lubok* styles on war posters depicting German and Turkish atrocities and Russian war heroes. The most famous of these was the cossack Kuzma Kryuchkov who killed eleven German soldiers in 1915. His face appeared everywhere – in the papers, on posters, and on postcards – and a rash of verse was poured out in his honor. *Carnival Sideshow: the German War* invoked the folk festival in a malicious rhymed satire on the Kaiser embellished with a crude cartoon of him with insane eyes and twisted moustaches. *Scourge*, a journal of satire, flogged the draft dodger in foppish monocle and morning coat.[43]

Supporters of the war took to the stage in large numbers. M.I. Dolina, a monarchist and reactionary propagandist, gave hundreds of benefit concerts that offered folk songs, balalaika bands, martial ensembles, regimental choirs, songs set to the words of the famous anti-Semitic publicist Pavel Krushevan, and readings of official edicts and texts provided by the Russian Right. Dolina presented *tableaux vivants* – actors dressed as Suvorov, Kutuzov, and other national-military heroes, frozen alongside common people for the visual contemplation of the audiences. The mixture of social orders was designed to promote a picture of all-Russian solidarity and loyalty. Folk art was enlisted in the war effort in 1915 when the seventy-two year old folk song teller, Maria Krivopolenova, was discovered in the Archangel region and brought to Petrograd. Reciting on stage for the first time in her life, she captured the hearts of a nation at war – as many saw it – in the cause of culture. Much of this was anticipated in the rituals and performances of the prewar Russian Right which had employed religious, nationalist, and dynastic iconography and music to frame speeches resounding with aggressive chauvinism and ethnic intolerance. They always ended their meetings with the thrice sung tsarist national anthem, "God Save the Tsar" – a habit which Bolsheviks (singing another tune) found hard to break with.[44]

Artists took their talents to military hospitals and their organizations gave concerts that avoided the chauvinism of Dolina but also combined the high culture of the intelligentsia with military bands and folk songs – thus portraying the social–cultural unity of the Russian people in the face of a dangerous enemy – a unity that turned out to be fictitious in 1917. The Soviets would mount similar cultural operations in the civil war and World War II. Circus performers expressed patriotic feelings by means of allegorical processions celebrating Tsar and country. Drawing on old circus enactments of Russian battle scenes, they performed The Inundation of Belgium and Russian Heroes in the Carpathians. On December 16, 1914, the great clown Vitaly Lazarenko (1890–1939) – who would soon be a hero of Bolshevik circus – presented The Triumph of the Powers, honoring his country's allies. In 1915, the Nikitin Circus staged as an aquatic pantomime The Capture of Przemysl, a major Russian victory that also inspired a motion picture.[45]

Movie producers rushed to inscribe every new headline from the front onto the screen. Bauer's crude and hastily made but exciting Glory to Us, Death to the Foe (1914) was one of the first. Like a hundred other war films around the world, it shatters the idyll of a manor house party and an officer's proposal with news of war. When her fiance (Mozzhukhin) goes off to war, the heroine joins up as nurse only to find him dying in the lazaret. She then crosses the lines disguised as an Austrian nurse and serves in the enemy field hospital in order to spy on them. When a young Austrian officer who has been paying attention to her is given a secret message to deliver, she lures him to a rendezvous, stabs him, and flees with the document back toward her own lines and is rescued by Russian men. In the finale, she is decorated with military honors.

In Tears of a Ravished Poland (with the Chopin funeral march played on the piano), patriotic producers tried to project an image of German barbarism, Polish suffering, and Slavic solidarity. (A half-truth at best, in view of the historic relations of Poles and Russians; the image was repeated as a full lie in Soviet documentaries of occupied Eastern Poland in 1939–1941.) The exploits of the first heroes – Kryuchkov, the pilot Nesterov, and Vasily Ryabov – were put on film. Studios raced to film Tolstoy's *War and Peace* – indeed two of them were made in 1915. A whole sub-genre was devoted to the Turkish atrocities at the front and in Armenia. The detective thriller was easily adapted to spy stories such as *The Secret of the Krupp Works* which combined adventure with patriotism, a politicized precursor of the Bolshevik "red detective" movie. All the devices of early film were present in *Amid the Thunder of Cannon* which treated the war as merely a backdrop. In it, Fritz Muller, the son of a German factory owner in Russia lusts after the young Vera (Faith) who is loyal to the Russian Sorokin. When war comes, he and Sorokin are drafted into the Russian army and Vera becomes a nurse. Fritz deserts to the Germans and captures Vera and Sorokin whom he threatens to dispatch unless she gives herself to him. But Sorokin, tied to a tree, is released by a shepherd boy and kills Fritz. When the German troops are about to execute the Russian hero, a squadron of cossacks appears on the scene to save all – a standard ploy of adventure cinema even then.[46]

But any focus on the wartime use of cinema – or any of the arts – as propaganda or simply war-related morale building is misleading because both the producers and the public continued to rivet their attention on purely entertainment genres. Indeed the movie melodrama's popularity increased enormously during the war years. Russian jingoism took tsarist popular culture down the road to state service, but not very far. In all the belligerent countries, culture – high, low, and middle – was enlisted for patriotic purposes. Though hardly novel in 1914, it was intensified by the technical means of communication. One can find in the techniques of patriotic popular culture a preview of some of those used by the Provisional government and the Bolshevik regime to legitimize their revolutions: the *tableau vivant*, the historical spectacle, the imaging of enemies in circus, graphics, and movies (which used not only plot, but casting, lighting, and costuming to satanize political and social foes). But nothing like mass mobilization or nationalization of the arts took place. Private enterprise continued to churn out lurid graphics, mystical and satanic movies, detective tales, vulgar songs, straight comedy and dance routines with no political or national content. This went on unhindered and indeed amplified after the fall of the monarchy in March 1917. It was only when the Bolsheviks came to power that state authorities took upon themselves the onerous and arrogant task of regulating the people's taste in a serious way.

2 Revolutionary reassortment 1917–1927

To the people and for the people

As a turning point in the history of Russian popular culture, 1917 was, like 1985, a harbinger of drastic change but in the direction of state control. The onset of Stalinism and the death of Stalin also brought momentous changes in degree. 1917, the year that brought revolutionary Marxists to power, marked a great change in behavior and thought. For those who made it, it was a revolution of salvation, for Russians and for mankind. No later distortions made in its name and no new revelations about its inhumanities can ever change the undeniable fact that hundreds of thousands of people saw it as a new dawn of human freedom and justice. But in their attempt to deliver that human liberation, they committed monstrous atrocities.

After the Bolshevik Revolution of 1917, the new Soviet regime moved the capital to Moscow and unveiled a program of startling social radicalism. The new hammer and sickle flag of angry red emblematized the revolutionary government's social bases among the poorest classes – peasants and workers. To their enemies, it symbolized the triumph of satanism. For almost three years of bitter warfare, the Bolsheviks defended the heartland of Soviet Russia against the White armies who occupied the fringes of the immense land and were assisted by troops and supplies from America, England, France, and a dozen other nations desirous of bringing down the red regime. The Russian Civil War was a brutal experience that implanted bitter remembrance on both sides. The red army prevailed and its victory achieved the mythic proportions of a religious crusade of good against evil, a heroic struggle against the forces of capitalist hell, a euphoric moment of history filled with martyrs, saints, and legends. The defeated Whites and hundreds of thousands of Russians cast anchor and made their way to other shores – to Paris and London, to China and California.

One of the effects on Russian popular culture of the upheaval was the dramatic emigration of cultural figures later destined to achieve fame in another country. Artists, musicians, and filmmakers carved out brilliant careers in the West. Vladimir Dukelsky became Vernon Duke, composer of the American hit songs, "Autumn in New York" and "April in Paris." Dmitry Tiomkin won acclaim writing Hollywood film scores. Maria Uspenskaya (Ouspenskaya), Akim Tamiroff, Reuben Mamoulian made screen careers in the United States, as did Ivan Mozzhukhin (Mosjoukine) in France. Cameraman Boris Kaufman left behind his two brothers Mikhail and Denis (Dziga Vertov) to help revolutionize Soviet cinema in the 1920s while he himself helped revolutionize cinematography in such American films as *The Pawnbroker*, *On the Waterfront*, and *Twelve Angry Men*.

Inside Soviet territory, events and policies conspired to bring about the near demise of old time popular culture. War redirected energies and caused an exodus from big cities, massive dislocation, generalized poverty, social disorder, and material shortages – for example of newsprint, film stock, fuel, and electric power – shortages sometimes invoked by the Soviet regime as it shut down newspapers or closed theaters. The Bolsheviks associated commercial popular culture with the old regime. The spectacle of private profit in the midst of suffering and deprivation, the continuing celebration of "bourgeois" values in song, story, and film, the perceived immorality and triviality of their themes, and the fear of the cultural power of their styles – all coalesced in the decision, taken after about two years of haggling, to shut down private entertainment, kill the market mechanism, and nationalize film companies, publishers, sheet music houses, recording studios, music halls, theaters, and dance-halls. Makers of commercial cultural commodities fled southward behind the lines and continued to produce until the defeat of their White protectors forced them into expatriation.

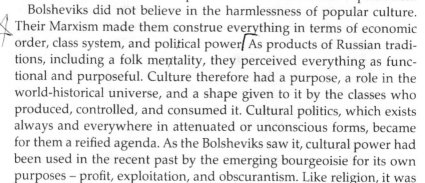

Bolsheviks did not believe in the harmlessness of popular culture. Their Marxism made them construe everything in terms of economic order, class system, and political power. As products of Russian traditions, including a folk mentality, they perceived everything as functional and purposeful. Culture therefore had a purpose, a role in the world-historical universe, and a shape given to it by the classes who produced, controlled, and consumed it. Cultural politics, which exists always and everywhere in attenuated or unconscious forms, became for them a reified agenda. As the Bolsheviks saw it, cultural power had been used in the recent past by the emerging bourgeoisie for its own purposes – profit, exploitation, and obscurantism. Like religion, it was a drug for the masses. But culture also possessed the power to enlighten and ennoble the masses. This was essentially an ecclesiastical view of culture's place in society. For the state, ideological correctness was paramount, mass appeal was important, and artistic excellence was desirable to the extent that it fit the other two.[1]

The Bolshevik propaganda style illustrated these views. All kinds of people were enlisted in brigades touring the front and the remote regions on agitation trains and boats; and in the cities huge parades and spectacles were mounted on every possible occasion. A whole array of new symbols and rituals were introduced and infused with anti-capitalism, the collective spirit, atheism, and machine worship. Bolshevik artists and propagandists went to the people with a culture for the people and in doing so they tried to combine the new with the old, self-consciously infusing circus, fairbooth, *lubok*, folk ditties, songs, and dances with revolutionary content. The agit-train was a traveling political carnival with live entertainers, phonograph recitals of Lenin's voice, and motion picture projectors. Folk language, repetition, and encores fit right into the popular notions of what a performance should be. But this was neither folk nor popular culture; it was elitist revolutionary enlightenment and pseudo-religious missionary work for moral uplift and political persuasion. Aside from the educational establishment, the main forces in this cultural crusade were the avant-garde and the Proletarian Culture movement (Proletcult).[2]

Many of the artistic avant-garde were dedicated revolutionaries who genuinely wanted to reach the masses with their new art. But they also fiercely desired aesthetic self-expression in a revolutionary idiom. Avant-garde experiment released a free flight of magnificent fantasy which delighted the creators and the cognoscenti, but only occasionally the mass public. Futurist and transrational poetry, constructivist theater and art, machinery orchestras, innovative cinematography, and geometric forms of the dance – all predating the revolution – rose up to challenge the older styles in high culture in a vigorous aesthetic and generational revolt. And since this revolt was embedded in a social revolution, many experimental artists saw it also as *the* revolutionary culture for the masses: something exalted, modernist, futuristic, and mechanical in celebration of the industrial technology that imbued this revolution more than any previous one. Such artists held commercial popular culture in contempt; and they were puzzled and offended when workers did not respond well to factory concerts with machine sonatas or "ballets" whose dancers were dressed as flying lizards.[3] Ordinary people displayed indifference or hostility to experimental art or political propaganda that obstructed the flow of entertainment. This became clear from the very outset of the revolution, though few would admit it.

Proletcult was also visionary, but it was a mass organization reaching a membership of almost a half million during the civil war. Founded in 1917, it combined notions of the prewar elitists who preached high culture, the Left Bolsheviks who dreamed of a new (though vaguely defined) revolutionary proletarian culture, and the workers themselves who wanted these and other things as well. The uneasy alliance generated continuous tensions. Essentially a plebeian organization, Proletcult was wracked by disputes among the leaders – many of them intellectuals – and between workers and intellectuals. It heralded "the new" but found that masses of workers also wanted to enter the cathedrals of traditional high culture. In practice, depending on local conditions and the preferences of assertive leaders, Proletcult promoted not only a culture of the factory floor and industrial motifs, but also folk singing, avant-garde experimentation, and the treasures of old high culture. Although the spokesmen of Proletcult contested the avant-garde on many issues, they shared its hostility to commercial popular culture. As a mass organized movement, Proletcult collapsed at the end of the civil war for internal and external reasons and lingered on in vestigial form in the 1920s as self-styled proletarian cultural formations devoted to art, architecture, theater, music, cinema, radio, and literature. These were smaller, less proletarian in social makeup, and lacking in the universal visionary qualities of the Proletcult.[4]

During the era of the New Economic Policy (NEP, 1921–1928) which followed the civil war, private business was partially restored. Old forms of popular culture reappeared with the resurgence of private trade. Russian cities were once again the *locus* of well-dressed merchants and profiteers and their berouged and silk-stockinged ladies in fancy restaurants who devoured caviar, drank champagne, and listened to sobbing violins playing gypsy tunes. The Bolshevik or Communist Party controlled the mainsprings of the economy and kept a tight rein on political life. Its cultural code proscribed eroticism, mysticism, religion, or upper-class fluff (except as objects of derision). As a counterweight it promoted a new proletarian morality based upon mutual respect and equality of the sexes; atheism rooted in science; a spirit of collective comradeship; and a veritable cult of technology and the machine. The 1920s was an era of uneasy coexistence and constant struggle among the ruling communists, the avant-garde, and "the people" over what constituted culture and popular culture.

Revolutionary adventure

The Russian Revolution almost wholly destroyed the popular literature of the past. The early communists, like much of the intelligentsia, had a low opinion of the oral traditions and native culture of the peasantry and were simply blind and deaf to its richness and immensity. Artists adopted elements of folk culture into their own productions, but dismissed the main body of folklore. *Lubok* literature, saints' lives, knightly and religious tales, songbooks, lore, and the serial adventures and bandit stories so popular before the revolution were discontinued and existing stocks were pulped. The communists held a monopoly of information in the print media and used it to advance their own programs and interdict the kind of material made available through the market before the revolution in the penny press. The lower classes were deprived of "popular" themes of olden times because of the authorities' censorship and monopoly, arbitrary choice of content, and failure to find out exactly what the people wanted – or, if informed, ignoring what they found. Thus, the common people probably read less in the 1920s than in the years before 1917.[5]

The communists did by fiat what the old intelligentsia had wanted to do: give the people what they thought was good for them and not what they wanted. Officially sponsored popular writing took many forms – few suitable for mass consumption by the population at large. One was self-produced workers' journalism, wall-newspapers, short plays, songs, and rhymes, some rooted in older forms but dealing with agronomy, the factory, and the new politics. A whole body of invented folklore arose about the revolution and civil war and the political and cultic heroes of the state. Proletcult and futurist writers attempted to reach the workers by exalting machinery, dynamism, and the factory – with limited success. The most popular of the official writers was Demyan Bedny (a pseudonym) who styled himself *muzhik vrednyi*, "dangerous peasant." He wrote witty fables about old regime landowners who tried to win peasant votes to the Duma and about saplings, once used to flog peasants, that were maturing into the oaken cudgels that would destroy the regime.[6]

Soviet authorities pumped their publications into the villages in the name of "good reading." But a 1922 inquiry in a region of central Russia revealed that Soviet newspapers were used as cigarette paper by peasants who could not comprehend their politicized language. A 24-year-old Red Army veteran in 1923 was found to be unable to understand the terms "USSR," "Soviet," and "socialism"! Foreign and abstract words, complex syntax, and arcane references all defeated the common reader. Communist journalists and publishers did try to incorporate popular values into the mass press: *The Poor* (1918–1931), *The Worker's Newspaper* (1922–1939), *Workers' Moscow* (1922–   ), and *The Peasants' Newspaper (1923–1939)*. Interaction with readers was provided by letters to the editor and worker correspondents. *The Peasants' Newspaper* far excelled the others in circulation with a million readers at the end of the decade. But the weight of circulation fell heavily on Moscow and Leningrad with a total of 4.6 million copies in 1925 compared with 3.4 million for all the rest of the country.[7]

Surveys of mass readership in the 1920s showed clearly that the people wanted to read books for relaxation with adventure and action or vivid descriptions of everyday life and without political rhetoric, ornamental prose, bad language, or elitist attempts to reproduce lower class jargon and slang. They wanted either to see themselves or to escape into entertainment. Ready to accept the new plots about revolutionary struggles, they scorned stylistic novelty or experimentation in favor of linear narrative, positive heroes, and realism. Happy with a moral message as well as a story, readers also wanted unadulterated adventure. Yury Tynyanov lamented the fact that "the unknown reader" thirsted for novelty; and thus publishers went from Tarzan to Tarzan's son, his wife, his ox, and his donkey. Another critic announced that "the Russian reader is in the grip of the apes." He was right. The combination of familiar characters and settings generating new adventures was and is still irresistible to mass readers. NEP partly revived the private book trade, whose 223 firms provided one-quarter of all books printed in 1922, although the number of books published had fallen drastically from 34,000 titles in 133 million copies in 1913 to 4,000 titles in 28 million copies in 1921. Native, imported, and prerevolutionary popular fiction was on the market and people were buying and reading Tarzan stories and – *horribile dictu* – the works of Artsybashev and Verbitskaya.[8]

Writers sympathetic to the regime responded to the problem with "revolutionary adventures" that were politically correct but written in a popular style. Members of a small literary coterie, the Serapion Brothers, called for Soviet versions of Wells, Verne, Kipling, Stevenson, and Dumas; a major communist leader of the time Nikolai Bukharin suggested the term "red detective story" (*krasnyi detektiv*) or "red

Pinkerton story" (*krasnyi pinkerton*). Writers of them tried to serve the interests of the state, of the masses, and of their own art by blending propaganda, adventure, and parody. In an obviously self-conscious and good-natured way, they adopted the tricks of popular culture and especially the conventions of silent cinema. Their output was in fact cinematized fiction, another striking example of the mutual fertilization of the popular arts.[9]

The first and most famous "red detective story" was not a conventional one, though it possessed features of the prerevolutionary pulp and serial genre that went by that name: Marietta Shaginyan's (1888–1982) *Mess-Mend: or a Yankee in Petrograd* (1923–1925), written under the pseudonym "Jim Dollar" as a serialized yarn issued with lively photomontage covers by Alexei Rodchenko (see fig. 5). It employed folkloric figures – "fairhaired Laurie Lane," "taciturn Ned," and characters allegorizing good and evil – and added the cliff-hanger episode endings of old popular fiction and film. The plot was delightfully unbelievable – even ludicrous – and included a Utopian Soviet society, a workers' revolution in America, an evil capitalist plot, and a virtuous Russian man who rescues an innocent proletarian girl from a satanic villain, all punctuated by generous doses of pursuit, escape, murder, and espionage. The novel celebrated not only revolutionary elan, but also two important political doctrines of the time. One was the cult of science, as represented by a secondary hero, Mick Thingmaster, who uses the magic of technology to defeat the Black Magic of the villains. The other was the inevitable degeneration of capitalism into fascism (just being articulated at the time in Comintern theory), as symbolized by a biological disease in the spines of capitalists that transforms them into four-footed beasts.[10]

Intellectuals, when invited to recreate the popular forms of the past with a new revolutionary idiom, could not resist the lure of parody. Faced with the stereotypes and clichés of the detective story, they played with them. Parody became an in-game for informed readers and an occasion for one to parody the other (as with Valentin Kataev's sendup of Ehrenburg in his *Ehrendorf's Island*). Later, musical artists such as Leonid Utësov and Igor Moiseev would try to parody Western jazz and rock in public performances. But audiences did not always catch the jokes; they were perfectly willing to "read" all these texts as straight. Audiences and readers again and again displayed their liking for whatever had become familiar and internalized.

A closely related genre was revolutionary science fiction (*nauchnaya fantastika*). Some of it was purely Utopian projection of communism into the future. Some was a variant of the "red detective story": intrigues by capitalist villains resulting in war or the threat of war employing infernal engines of mass destruction and ending in a communist victory. The most famous of these were written by mainstream writers. Alexei Tolstoy's *Engineer Garin's Death Ray* (1925) featured the ubiquitous madman. In Ilya Ehrenburg's *The D.E. Trust* (1923) a villainous figure plots to take over Europe. More accessible versions of these were written in a simple style and sometimes issued in mass circulation serials. But the most popular and least political of the science fiction writers, Alexander Belyaev (1884–1942), who is still read today, specialized in technological innovations, biological novelties (flying and shrinking men), and exotic settings. His *Amphibian*, a perennial bestseller, contained pearl diving in tropical waters, seaplanes, and a plot full of maritime action. The hero, Icthyander, the son of a doctor, has been turned by his father into an amphibian by implanting shark gills in order to save his life. Like his prototype Tarzan, he dwells in a Utopian realm – in this case under water – which contrasts with the dirty world of business and imperialism on shore.[11]

The historical novel – with some exceptions a popular rather than an artistic genre in the Russian literary tradition – also achieved a high level of consumption in the 1920s. Alexei Chapygin's *Razin Stepan* (1925–1926, in serial format), Georgy Shtorm's *Tale about Ivan Bolotnikov* (1929), and Artëm Vesëly's novella about Ermak, *Gulyai-Volga* (1930), were typical of those dealing with historical peasant rebels and cossacks. Readers liked them because of their mass style, knightly heroes, elaborate descriptions of cossack costumes, and scenes of drinking and revelry. The anachronistic atheism and Utopianism inserted into the novels made them politically respectable but did not enhance their popularity. Like the detective story of the period, these "revolutionary" historical tales were influenced by cinema – especially prerevolutionary or "bourgeois" cinema – in the costumes and the accessories of the characters.[12]

The "light genres" did not crowd out the Soviet political novel of revolution. A survey of 360 young peasants in the Leningrad region produced the following list of nine favorite books: Ivan Neverov, *City of Bread*; Dmitry Furmanov, *Chapaev* and *Red Landing*; Lydia Seifullina, *Virineya*; Pavel Dorokhov, *The Irtysh River*; Alexander Serafimovich, *The Iron Flood*; Sikhachev, *The Kulak*; Upton Sinclair, *King Coal*; and Jack London, *The Sea Wolf*. Neither the proletarian novel nor the avant-garde made this list which included six revolutionary adventures and two foreign books about workers fighting capitalist exploitation. But most of them, including the foreign ones, were too difficult for those with only two years of schooling. Other favorites were Russian classics by Chekhov, Tolstoy, and Pushkin, Gorky's *Mother*, Fadeev's *The Rout*, Gladkov's *Cement*, Sholokhov's first "Don" volume, Alexei Tolstoy's *Road to Calvary*, and foreign works by Hugo, Zola, and Erkman-Chatrian.[13]

The civil war provided ample adventure material. Furmanov's *Chapaev* (1923) begot an entire cultural industry: the novel reprinted dozens of times up to the present; the sensational movie of 1934; the songs (and parodies); the children's cults and games; and the (unofficial) jokes. The immense popularity of this novel can be understood at once merely by perusing the chapter (five) introducing the hero, Vasily Chapaev, and his men. Fresh from a battle on the steppe, they are like cowboys back from the range: tough, dirty, rude, even menacing, but also humorous, brave, loyal, and egalitarian except in their universal deference to the leader. Before the revolution, the cossack was the analogue of the American cowboy; in Soviet times it was the civil war partisan, the last hero to ride horseback into battle. Chapaev himself is folkloric; he is part of the male bonding but wiser and more cunning than his men. Contemptuous of brass and bureaucrats, he embodies a style – common in this war – of independent command based on close knowledge of the topography and the local people and on the personal bond of trust with his own men. Chapaev is a universal type in popular military, frontier, and colonial literature. In terms of communist discourse, he is the irrepressible spontaneity that must be tempered by party consciousness. His commissar (Klychkov in the book) is the instrument of the party and of central power, the mentor who harnesses the energy of the steppe warrior to the cause of Bolshevism. The complex Chapaev–Furmanov relationship became a model in socialist realist fiction of the 1930s.[14]

Discordant melodies

Music presented another dichotomy between the values of the regime and the tastes of the people. The music that accompanied the early years of the Russian Revolution reflected the official cultural configuration: reverence for the high art of the past heard in classical music; and pious celebration of the revolution heard in proletarian songs – a potent marriage of the mind and the heart. The writer Serafimovich recalls a "concert meeting" in Moscow on New Year's

Eve, 1917 which was in every way typical of the time: Wieniawski's *Legend* for violin followed by a choir singing the revolutionary favorite, "Blacksmiths" and then the audience spontaneously singing the "Internationale." The pattern was repeated over and over: Glinka, Chaikovsky, and Beethoven establishing cultural solemnity and legitimacy; the proletarian songs providing the emotional release. The canon did not go unchallenged; throughout the decade avant-gardists experimented with machine music, factory whistle concerts, and electronic sonorities. But these found little favor either with the regime or with the people.[15]

The revolutionary songs that rent the air in the early Soviet years filled hundreds of thousands with euphoria and were cherished by them to the end of their days. The authorities were immensely happy about this. "Begin and complete your work," urged Trotsky, "to the sound of socialist songs and anthems." Thousands of choruses were established in workers' clubs throughout the land. On every possible public occasion the old radical songs were intoned. Although audiences never seemed to tire of singing or hearing them, there was a drive for new ones. One of the most enduring was "Chapaev the Hero" by Marusya Popova, a machine-gunner from his unit. Old popular tunes and folk songs were set to political words; even the notorious "Two Guitars" was reworked for Komsomol events. Martial and folk styles were enlisted in 1920 to create stirring war songs. A 20-year-old pianist at the Crooked Jimmy in Rostov Dmitry Pokrass and the poet A. A. D'Aktil (Frenkel) wrote the "Budenny March" after the general liberated the city from the Whites. Another Pokrass brother wrote the equally famous "White Army, Black Baron." Yuly Khait and Pavel German created the future hit song "Avia-March." Most of these men became famous later as mass song composers. During the civil war, fighters were content to sing all kinds of songs – folk, radical, and soldier songs, as well as love ballads.[16]

But the more "leftist" song writers first in Proletcult and then in the Russian Association of Proletarian Musicians (RAPM; earlier called APM, later VAPM) tried to write "pure" political or factory songs cleansed of all folk elements and with lyrics about foreign enemies and lazy workers. A modern critic has called them "freak songs, so bombastic, complicated, and cold that nobody would sing them."[17] The fetish over "proletarian music" led to one of many cultural wars of the twenties and early thirties against all forms that were considered alien to working class sensibilities by those – mostly intellectuals – who waged it. RAPM, with increasing vigor and shrillness, came to oppose all other music except its own: classical for its association with the past; jazz for its links with the West; gypsy and related genres for its roots in the bourgeoisie; folk for its "backwardness."

Not all musicians associated with "proletarian" organizations opposed folk music. A vigorous promoter of it and a power inside the Moscow Proletcult was Alexander Kastalsky, the famous folklorist, choral director, and arranger of the "Internationale." His pupil, a major composer of new working class and revolutionary songs was Dmitry Vasilev-Buglai (1888–1956), a professional choral director who after the revolution became a leading force in the musical life of the Proletcult movement. He took his choir of 150 voices to the civil war front to sing revolutionary, anti-religious, and satirical agit-songs, as well as folk songs. The Pyatnitsky and other folk ensembles played regularly at state affairs during the civil war. Andreev, who had performed for the wounded during World War I, appeared again at the head of his ensemble and toured the civil war fronts on behalf of the Bolsheviks. He died in December 1918 from illness contracted during these tours. In 1919, his band was reorganized as the State Russian Folk Orchestra. But musical folklorism in general went into the doldrums in the 1920s; most performances of it were done by proletarian choirs. At the end of the decade, folk culture came under assault.[18]

The people – proletarians included – continued to like light melodies, popular songs, dance music, and words that were fun to sing.[19] Even in official parades, the masses sometimes broke into such favorites as "Gypsy Girl," or "O Why Did You Kiss Me?" Private sheet music firms had been nationalized during the revolution. NEP allowed their return along with private restaurants and cafes with their familiar strains of prewar dances, sentimental gypsy ballads, and foreign hits. An Association of Moscow Songwriters – a near equivalent of Tin Pan Alley – was established and urban popular music began pouring off the presses, reaching a peak in the last years of NEP. Censors decided which gypsy songs were suitable for proletarian ears and which ones promoted "decadence and unhealthy exoticism, so-called free love, and drunken tavern debauchery." Singers from the Caucasus, such as Keto Dzhaparidze and Tamara Tsereteli (1900–1968) made their careers with these songs. The foreign-inspired dance tunes included foxtrot, Boston waltz, tango, and telephone step; works by Viennese operetta composers and the Americans, Irving Berlin and Vincent Youmans; and exotica such as "Rickshaw from Nagasaki," "Creolita," and "Thief of Baghdad" (the film was showing in Moscow at the time).

Songwriters who tried to have it both ways produced songs about the "new socialist life" (*novyi byt*) with catchy but very unsocialist melodies. Valentin Kruchinin's "The Brick Factory" (or "Little Bricks" – Kirpichiki) inspired hundreds of versions as well as a comedy film. Proletarian composers sniffed at such songs, calling them "music hall *chansonettes*." But those who were able to graft the new onto the old became major song writers of the Stalin period: Khait, Kruchinin, Matvei Blanter, and the Pokrass brothers, Dmitry (b. 1899) and Daniil (1905–1954); the third, Samuil, emigrated to America and died in New York in 1939. These men, along with Dunaevsky and a half-dozen others, most of them Jews, succeeded, by collaborating with facile lyricists, in creating Stalin era popular music known as "mass song." Their versatility should come as no surprise: Irving Berlin wrote the hymn-like "God Bless America" as well as "Alexander's Ragtime Band."

Urban folklore, or songs popular among workers and taken out to the peasants in the countryside were usually unpublished. Cruel song predominated: a simple, doleful narrative of unrequited love, a touch of violence, and a sentimental plea for pity. These were popular in the 1920s among workers in small towns. Closely related in theme but harsher were the underground songs (*blatnye pesni*) of unfortunates, criminals, convicts, homeless children (*besprizornye*), and ordinary youth gangs. One of them, "Forgotten and Forsaken," though banned during the cultural revolution, was sung in a hit movie of the 1930s, *Start in Life*. The most popular unofficial song of the twenties, "Bublichki" (Pretzels or Bagels), was written by Yakov Yadov for an Odessa cabaret. Its lyrics about a drunken father and a whoring mother were later adapted to an indecent underground parody song on Chapaev. All through the 1920s, musicians such as Leonid Utesov who were later canonized as Soviet culture heroes cranked out songs about Odessa thieves and jailbirds.

Jazz returned to Russia after the hiatus of war and revolution for the same reason other popular forms returned: the political climate allowed it and the social climate sustained it. As in the previous epoch, jazz was initially an elitist trend. The first jazz concert (1922) shared billing with poetry reading; Meyerhold on the stage and Vertov on the screen used jazz to symbolize capitalist decay. By the late twenties, new Soviet bands had replaced the visiting Negro ensembles and formed the base of the jazz era of the 1930s. The original Soviet jazzmen came mostly from educated ethnic minorities – A. K. Lvov-Velyaminov, Sigizmund Kort, Georgy Landsberg, and the better-known Utesov and Tsfasman – just as the pioneers of rock music decades later were usually the sons of the intelligentsia. This followed a pattern in many societies where marginals, intellectuals, and elites spearheaded the innovation (and often importation) of popular culture. Early Soviet jazz, highly derivative, had by 1928 conquered large segments of the urban middle classes, NEP businessmen, some workers, and a few powerful official sponsors. Some government officials even considered it suitable to play at congresses. Both the foreign and the domestic bands ranged from hot and swingy to smoother salon styles.[20]

With jazz came the dance craze again. On stage and in the higher-toned dining rooms, the salon dance reigned – imported and erotically suggestive acrobatic steps such as "Tango of Death" that were some-times performed by celebrity dance couples. The new and revived dance styles won over young and old. But some prudish party and Komsomol moralizers saw *fokstrotizm* and *tangoizm* as harmful mala-dies. A Leningrad club official urged a struggle "against the proclivity of some members who, waiting for the end of a lecture impatiently, run off to the dance." Though many a party member "trotted" through the 1920s, some thought dancing was counter-revolutionary or morally indecent. The Russian official revulsion for the swaying of female bottoms that so outraged Khrushchev in his day predated the revolution, but its self-assertiveness began right here. The remedy? One leader promoted evenings of revolutionary marching for young people. Another suggested creating a Soviet "mass dance" – the first of many unsuccessful attempts to head off the spontaneous and near universal Russian passion for shaking the body to the sound of music which prevails to this day. Opposition to jazz and the dances it spawned sprang, as elsewhere, from a fear of the body and of mass corruption. These dance-and-music battles were sporadic in the first decade of the revolution; they would escalate into a long war begin-ning in 1928.[21]

October in the showplace

The whole concept of *estrada* as popular stage entertainment was twisted into a new shape by the October Revolution. Every possible kind of theater, stage, and arena was pressed into its service – from the *agitki* or propaganda skits performed on flatcars of agit-trains to the large theatrical institutions – all of them more amenable to control than song and dance. Officials wanted shows appropriate to the spirit of the

revolution and they insisted on injecting political purpose into entertainment. Knowing the importance of the "intermediary" in popular
performance – the ringmaster, the emcee, and the conferencier – they
used it to build bridges in all the arts between "correct" culture and the
still unprepared masses. The so-called monographic concert taught the
"meaning" of classical music: a lecture would precede the concert and
interpret the historical-class significance of the composer and the
piece. At the unveiling of revolutionary statues, speakers orated about
the life of each hero. When a foreign film was shown, officials sometimes rewrote the intertitles and warned the audience against harmful
messages. In staged events, the emcee could explain the inner significance of the acts to come, starting with a political speech to a
captive audience which was then treated to live entertainment. This
compulsion to gloss art for its social meaning was part of an old
intelligentsia critical tradition of the nineteenth century and also a
continuation of elite distrust of unmonitored popular entertainment.[22]

The diversity of revolutionary entertainment conducted in those
years was endless. At literary concerts for workers, Mayakovsky and
the young proletarian and Komsomol poets bellowed out verses. Foes
of Bolshevism were mocked in giant spectacles, tramcar shows, parade
floats, anti-religious carnivals, factory theaters, and workers' clubs.
Proletcult theater cloaked older works in revolutionary garments.
Krylov's "Quartet," a fable about a monkey, a goat, a bear, and an ass
was redone as a meeting of the Entente powers. Glinka's patriotic
anti-Polish opera, *A Life for the Tsar* was set in the Russo-Polish war of
1920. *The Voyage of Old Eremei*, a civil war *raek* about a journey to distant
worlds where the traveler finds exploitation was inspired by *Four
Brothers* (see ch. 1) and it anticipated one of Arkady Raikin's comedy
acts (see ch. 5). Even popular melodrama was enlisted: Lunacharsky
and Gorky believed that its optimism could be harnessed to political
purposes – as long as the element of action was retained. Gorky
sponsored a melodrama competition in 1919 and it rapidly evolved
into a special form of short, pungent, political playlet that was baptized
the *agitka*. The prefix *agit* (from agitation) came to denote almost
anything that could combine political message with rudimentary art
forms: thus the agit-train freighted with revolutionary minstrels and
embellished with poster art, the agit-song, and the agit-film.[23]

One of the most curious of the popular political melodramas of the
era was the *agit-sud* or mock trial, staged by amateur and professional
actors and aimed at various targets: political enemies; harmful behavior such as child abandonment, drunkenness, and prostitution; and

dangerous beliefs, such as religion. In all but the last, "courtroom" audiences were often successfully led to believe in the literal truth of the trial and took the judges, witnesses, and defendants as genuine. The playwright Vsevolod Vishnevsky recalled an outdoor "trial of Wrangel" held in the Kuban district in 1919. The actor assigned to play the White general, notorious for his cruelty, tried to decline this role out of fear that he would be lynched by the attending audience of thousands. The same thing happened in the 1930s when casting began for the villains in the notorious Stalinist purge film, *Great Citizen*.[24]

The Blue Blouse workers' theater movement was the melodramatic equivalent of red detective story and film. Operating as a collective and as a "living newspaper," the company put on one-hour shows in cafeterias and workplaces, acting out the day's news, commenting sharply on current events, and delivering satirical songs, couplets, and anti-capitalist skits. In 1924, fourteen such collectives were giving thousands of performances. Some of them toured abroad and were widely imitated in the West. But Blue Blouse was ultimately a semi-intellectual cabaret and its rapid rise to fame was followed by a rapid fall. The same fate befell the parallel movement in the countryside, the Red Shirt. During the staging of the great spectacles of the revolution, artists dipped into the rich fund of popular performance culture, particularly circus and folk drama. In the earliest revolutionary specta-cles, soldiers, armed with a loose plot idea, would improvise about the overthrow of the autocracy just the way it was done in old folk drama.[25]

Circus, as a branch of the popular arts, held immense fascination for revolutionary artists like Eisenstein, Meyerhold, Bedny, Kataev, the Erdman brothers, and Nikolai Ekk who used it in their work. Maya-kovsky wrote a skit for the clown Lazarenko called *World Wrestling Match*, featuring the great wrestlers Lloyd-George, Wilson, Pilsudski, and Baron Wrangel facing off against "Revolution." But this was avant-gardist cooptation and had little to do with traditional circus which many intellectuals attacked in 1917–1918. They saw magic acts as superstition, animal acts as cruelty, clowning as vulgarity, and sensa-tional stunts as inhumane and demeaning. Lunacharsky, ever the mediator, argued that circus exalted the human body and offered novel modes of presenting historical and political themes through pantomime and satirical clowning. In 1919, circus was nationalized and a new department created for it in the theater section of the Commiss-ariat of Enlightenment. Circus took to the streets and the front in the civil war. Acrobats, tightrope walkers, and cruder acts were muted in favor of verbal clowning and pantomime. Pro-Bolshevik clowns Durov and Lazarenko revived the political couplets and the patriotic circus shows of the wartime period and turned them to revolutionary uses. But the stress on ideological abstraction weakened the dynamic of true circus and turned these shows into panegyric theater. Ridicule could be directed only against the enemy. Thus, when the clown team Bim-Bom turned its satirical arrows at the Bolsheviks an angry soldier threatened to shoot up the act.[26]

One ought not to think that the revolutionary-political idiom was wholly uninteresting to the masses. Workers participated eagerly all through the twenties in festivals, amateur productions in clubs, and in skits taken from the papers or from their own lives. But, workers wanted other things as well, and not everybody was a worker. As with revolutionary music, the political stage simply did not offer enough to fill a hunger for general entertainment. People still wanted variety shows with light music, comedy, and novelty acts. When the elan of the early years wore off and NEP restored part of the market, people began rushing back to private places of diversion. Soviet scholars admit that they were more popular than performances of political satire because audiences preferred to be entertained. The occupation of the stage by Spanish clowns, German hypnotists, Czech ice skaters, Negro operettas (see fig. 6), sea lions, dogs, and crocodiles perturbed the critics. Many entertainers were criticized at the time for engaging in "beerhall" *estrada*, i.e. unlicenced restaurant and cafe stages; and faulted by later Soviet scholars for succumbing to the lure of NEP audiences and placing vulgarity over art and politics.

Comedians always face a dilemma in an authoritarian state: whom can they ridicule? When political themes prevailed, audiences lost interest; and when prerevolutionary acts were parodied, the old material was so good that the parody went unnoticed – a perennial problem for those who tried to mix art, politics, and entertainment. Comics had to walk this rope and find new targets. Boris Borisov (1873–1939) once reduced Lenin to spasmodic laughter with his gesticulations. A veteran of The Bat, Borisov applied its parodic traditions to NEP and added a word to the Soviet language: in one of his routines, he played "the Nepman," the first use of this term which was immediately and universally adopted as the designation of a trader or capitalist of the era. Nikolai Smirnov-Sokolsky (1889–1962) an ex-reporter with a wicked tongue and an acerbic personality began his stage career in vaudeville, toured the front for the Reds in the civil war, and then worked the provincial towns in the 1920s. His art was a composite of village judgmentalism, Marxist politics, and eighteenth century satire of manners. One of his political parodies was Vertinsky's "My Pierrot" which he performed by dressing shabbily like a hungry worker. Vladimir Khenkin (1883–1953; see fig. 7) had been a borscht-belt comic in the southern port towns before the revolution, specializing in mimicry, impersonations, and satirical couplets. In the 1920s and 1930s, he was considered the unequaled virtuoso of comic *estrada*. It is now all but forgotten that Khenkin introduced into Soviet usage the ancient Roman gesture of the closed fist and the upright thumb as a sign of approval.[27]

Operetta had the hardest time adjusting to the new order. Up to 1905, it had been largely satirical buffoonery and drawing room comedy. When Strauss, Lehar, Kalman, and other masters of the Viennese school conquered Russian operetta houses, scripts were modified to reflect Russian conditions. Operetta had been a great feeder of popular culture, endowing it with songs, singers, mannerisms, gypsy motifs, and the chorus line. But the Bolsheviks called it the purest of bourgeois art and its Parisian and Viennese fluff unsuited to the revolution. In 1919, feeling some pressure, the managers of one theater put on a "revolutionary operetta" – practically an oxymoron. They renamed Imre Kalman's *The Little King*, inspired by the abdication of King Manuel of Portugal in 1910, as *The Revolutionary Woman*, an idea sillier than the original plot itself. For this and other sins, operetta theaters were closed and reopened several times in the first years. Attempts to politicize old forms had no success until 1927 when Soviet operetta was finally born with *The Suitors* (Zhenikhi). Set in a provincial town, it spoofed NEP philistinism and its social types by surrounding a supposed rich widow with greedy suitors. A classic *comedia* variant of the Ulysses–Penelope story, it was filled in by the catchy songs of Dunaevsky. After this, the first state theater of operetta was established and it became an acceptable Soviet popular art form.[28] But like all other stage arts, it was in for an even bigger assault.

Red *lubok*

The graphic revolution recapitulated the experience of other popular arts: assault on traditional forms of representation – especially vulgar book covers, religious iconography, and *lubok*; the intersection of political revolution and avant-garde revolt; the partial cooptation by the avant garde of popular forms; the limited success of this and the resultant tension. Lenin wanted to replace *lubok* with inexpensive reproductions of classical paintings. But popular and folk idioms were alluring to revolutionary artists and they adapted them to various uses. Since peasants were indifferent to iconography lacking in verisimilitude, Futurist and other avant-garde styles of art had to be abandoned or modified. Artists working for the various organs of government, party, army, and educational establishments – Moor, Deni, Mayakovsky, Apsit, Simakov – drew from a wealth of prerevolutionary forms: theater and film *affiches*, advertisements, political satire of the 1905 revolution, and patriotic art of World War I.

The deep traditions of icon and *lubok* served the needs of some artists. They used religious motifs in two ways: to mock religion directly with images of fat and greedy priests; and to suggest quasi-religious feelings through allegory – the proletarian as knight slaying the dragon of reaction, the pagan moloch redone as capital, Satan in the dress of a White officer, and Old Slavonic script for the captions. *Chastushki*, children's ditties, and familiar passages from popular lore were used as texts. Deni was especially effective in making the fat, top-hatted, cigar smoking, and vile looking capitalist – a European import – a durable Soviet cliché that gravitated to the stage and screen (for example, the gargantuan factory owner in Eisenstein's *Strike*). Posters produced by the thousands in Proletcult studios were put up everywhere on walls, trains, public buildings. Agit-trains took revolutionary art out to the front and to the countryside; at first their sides were painted up in avant-garde designs which the peasants could not comprehend; later a more folkish style was employed. ROSTA, a network of rail and telegraph stations became the focus of a huge national art distribution system for political cartoons and posters whose windows bore about 1,600 pictures by February 1922 in Moscow alone.[29]

Great silent

In spite of the monumental political and military crises facing the young Soviet regime, it took vigorous measures to overhaul the Russian cinematic world: to "liquidate" what it saw as the trashy, decadent, and obscene movies of the prerevolutionary studios, with their motifs of light comedy, melodrama, affluent society life, and sordid crime and sex; and to make politically correct films of high quality that would attract the masses. Like other elitist moralizers of the time, the Bolsheviks feared that the "dark forces" dormant among the lower classes could be evoked by sitting in the darkened chamber of the commercial cinema. After a complicated and turbulent coexistence with the private studios – who were churning out films on Rasputin, erotic and satanic mysticism, nineteenth-century revolutionaries, and anti-Bolshevism along with some fine melodramas – the regime nationalized the industry. Some private filmmakers fled to the south behind the lines of the White armies and continued to turn out potboilers in the sunny seaports of the Black Sea, a moment in history captured brilliantly in the later Soviet film *Slave of Love* (1976).[30]

But eliminating private cinema was much easier than building up new industry that could produce the kind of films the Bolsheviks wanted. Hardly one important feature film was made during the civil war due to emergency conditions and shortage of both skilled personnel and film stock. The authorities settled for short propaganda pieces (*agitki*) that were made quickly and cheaply and bore simple posterlike political messages. Like the ROSTA windows and the agit-plays, they drew on *lubok* and folk idioms. Some of the great documentary film figures got their start in this way. And indeed the earliest Soviet features were hardly more than extended *agitki*. During the 1920s – the golden age of Soviet cinema – the rulers of the country whose primary desire was for "films of persuasion" faced two major obstacles: avant-garde filmmakers who wanted to create a new cinematic art; and popular audiences who wanted entertainment.

The films of the avant-garde – Eisenstein, Pudovkin, Kuleshov, Vertov, and Dovzhenko – are known the world over and have been studied as pioneering masterpieces of the directorial art: shooting, *mise-en-scène*, and especially the cutting and assembly of the film, known as montage or editing. Nothing like their best films was produced in Russia before the revolution. But these masters were possessed not only by self-expression and aesthetic innovation; they clearly wanted to reach the masses in their revolutionary spectacles, documentary "truths," and cinematic poems. No thinking filmgoer can remain unmoved by Eisenstein's *Battleship Potemkin* (more popular abroad than in Russia), Pudovkin's *End of St. Petersburg*, or Dovzhenko's *Earth* – to name only three. But the masses did not respond with enthusiasm to the language of montage because of its conceptual and stylistic difficulties. This was a problem even for those directors, such as Trauberg and Kozintsev, who were deeply inspired by popular culture: street language, circus posters, pulp magazine covers, jazz, and cafe entertainment. In their films, *Oktyabrina*, *The Devil's Wheel*, and *The New Babylon*, these things were intellectualized.

Eventually, the political leaders began to berate filmmakers because of this for their lack of success with the mass public.[31]

That public was impatient with too much moralizing politics or experimental techniques. They preferred to be entertained as in the old days. The movie world was never the same as in its early, dreamy years under the tsar. But some things made a comeback – for awhile. Just as melons appeared on Moscow street stalls a few days after the inauguration of the New Economic Policy, in 1921 the red necktied Count Amori showed up at a newly reopened private film studio auguring a return to the fast-breaking movie schlock of which he had been a king. The old-style yarns of romance and adventure, cleansed only of counter-revolution and blatant sex, became again the mainstay of movie audiences through the 1920s. The most popular movie genres of the revolutionary period were the same as the foreign and prerevolutionary Russian ones: costume drama, action and adventure, literary works adapted for the screen, melodramas, and comedy. Those who patronized them were not merely the *nepmanskaya auditoriya*, that is the bourgeoisie, alleged to be addicted to lurid sex films. Working class clubs sponsored by the Communist Party also had to show some entertainment films or risk losing their audience.[32]

Most people preferred European and American films precisely because they contained the familiar formulas of popularity: zany comedy, melodramatic catharsis, high life, adventure narratives, crime stories, action, surprise, romance, intrigue, and exotic settings. *Tarzan*, *The Mark of Zorro*, and the Pearl White series were hits. The most popular film stars by far in Soviet Russia of those years were not Nikolai Batalov, Vera Baranovskaya, or Alexandra Khokhlova but Charlie Chaplin, Mary Pickford, Douglas Fairbanks, and Conrad Veidt. Soviet actress Nina Lee adopted an American sounding name and was known as "the Russian Mary Pickford." Audiences adored the comic insanity of Chaplin and his clownish reading of the little man's lot in life, the perky personality of Pickford, and the athletic prowess of Fairbanks as he bounced from jar to jar in *The Thief of Baghdad*. Years later, the popularity of the last was sarcastically attested by the makers of the Stalinist film, *Great Citizen* (1937). The authorities could not drive the public away from Fairbanks and into the arms of Eisenstein. His *Potemkin*, for example, was dislodged from one of Moscow's movie houses by Fairbanks' version of *Robin Hood*. Another Eisenstein classic, *October*, was called "unintelligible to the millions"; and it was concern for the millions that led film authorities in the 1930s to a search for a new kind of Soviet popular movie.[33]

But the 1920s also yielded popular Russian films, some of them made by prerevolutionary directors such as Protazanov. They were supported by the film trust, Sovkino, because they generated big revenues for the industry – which the masterpieces of experimentation did not. Protazanov has been called the "king of the popular film." *Aelita* (1924) based loosely on Alexei Tolstoy's fantasy about a voyage to Mars was as distinctly old fashioned as the novel itself. Its main charm is the acting of Nikolai Batalov and the comic Igor Ilinsky and the futuristic sets on Mars. But it also contained sharp visual comments on the past and present as when nobles arrive at an illegal ball with high heels and gowns hidden beneath shapeless peasant boots and coats. Protazanov's *The Case of the Three Million* was a hilarious comedy about thieves, capitalists, and bourgeois infidelity. His *Forty-First* was adapted from a popular civil war story by Boris Lavrenev about a Bolshevik woman sniper who has forty notches on her rifle – her kill count of White soldiers. When she becomes the guard of a young aristocratic White officer they fall in love. But when he tries to escape, she kills her "41st." The book and the film put a woman into an active role as a warrior in her own right and – like the "admirable Crichton" whom she resembles – as a tougher survivor than her thin, delicate, and beautiful captive. This alluring theme was taken up again in the Khrushchev era with great success.

The first major "Soviet" hit was *Little Red Imps* (1923; see fig. 8), about three youngsters, one of them a black, who fight on the side of the Bolshevik commander Budenny to defeat the peasant anarchist army of Nestor Makhno. The film contains a barroom fight right out of an American western. Its heroes are delightfully clever and resourceful; their enemies are the cruel Makhno who scowls throughout the film and his mercenary German body guard – a perfect cinematization of the anti-Kaiser cartoons of World War I. The director Ivan Perestiani (a veteran of tsarist era cinema) introduced here many a future theme of popular culture: the use of circus performers for his actors; the armored train – a particularly cinematic object deployed later with great effect in many films, notably *Man With a Gun* (1938); the bared chest of a Bolshevik about to be executed (made famous in Dovzhenko's *Arsenal*); a black youth (played by a Senegalese deserter from the French interventionist forces in Odessa) as the emblem of racial equality (used in *Circus*, 1936); and the satanization of Makhno, employed in circus spectacle, operetta, and the marvelous film comedy *Wedding at Malinovka* (1967). The cultural fate of Makhno was ironic, since if any epic ever deserved romanticized and sympathetic treatment in fiction and cinema, it was that of his Ukrainian Insurgent Horse Army that outwitted both Reds and Whites for years before being subdued. Their story is closer to the legends of Stenka Razin and other folk rebels than anything in the Bolshevik hagiography, including Chapaev. But since the Bolsheviks feared having the Makhnoists treated as underdogs, they enshrined them for decades as sadistic and degenerate bandits.[34]

One of the biggest box-office draws of the decade was the imaginative *Bear's Wedding* (1926) directed by Konstantin Eggert with a script by Lunacharsky and a huge cast – including Eggert himself and Lunacharsky's wife – who swarm through the movie's unstoppable action. The title is that of a famous *lubok* but the story was taken from Prosper Mérimée. The film version is a romantic costume gothic with the deep forests and medieval castles of Lithuania as exotic backdrop for a nineteenth-century vampire tale of a jealous count, a beautiful countess who is impregnated by a bear, and their accursed offspring who periodically turns into a were-bear. The plot drives relentlessly through the torments of the crazed old countess and the love-sick young bear count who murders his new bride in their nuptial bed and is slain by enraged retainers and villagers – exactly in the manner of the Frankenstein movies. To a modern viewer the film suffers from bad continuity and superfluous characters. But these did not perturb the mass audiences who packed the theaters to see it.

The Extraordinary Adventures of Mr. West in the Land of the Bolsheviks (1924) by Lev Kuleshov offered an affectionate parody of the American western and the cops-and-robbers chase, with a large dose of broad humor. It is a delightful miniature picaresque that pretends to mock the bigoted American view of the USSR at the time. A Texan (Mr. West) visits Moscow and brings along a wild-west cowboy (played by Boris Barnet) as his body guard. When the two become enmeshed with a local criminal gang, the movie comes alive with autos and sleigh chases and cowboy acrobatics. The gang moll was played by the witty and versatile Alexandra Khokhlova (1897–1985) who later starred in Kuleshov's dark and moving – but never popular – *By the Law* (1926). she was the Soviet tribute to the Western vamp. *Mr. West* competed successfully with Chaplin and other favorites. Cinematically, it is infinitely superior to *Bear's Wedding* because a master filmmaker and teacher combines visual dynamism and energy with the largely unnoticed "economy and efficiency of shots" that he so admired in the classical Hollywood cinema – legibility, continuity, framing, narrative clarity.[35] Komarov's *The Kiss of Mary Pickford* (1926) was also a montage of international styles (American and Russian) as well as a blend of studio film and newsreel footage of the visit of Pickford and Fairbanks to the Soviet Union in which the comic star, Ilinsky, delivers a virtuoso performance, replete with the gestures and sight gags that established his career.

Melodramas set in the NEP, unable to replicate the class content of prerevolutionary ones, dealt with the ambiguous realities of a mixed economy, social reversal, and underground life. One of the best was *Katka the Reinette Apple Seller* (1926) directed by Fridrikh Ermler (1898–1967), a former Chekist of working class background, who aimed his camera at the contradictions of NEP society. The topography of Leningrad is a major star of *Katka*: the Klodt Horses, Mars Field, the monuments and squares function differently both from the antique props of the old melodramas and the heroic *mise-en-scène* of an Eisenstein canvas. They are the backdrop to the pressing business of survival in a tough world of illegal commerce, street bums, fat merchants, the spicily pretentious flapper girls in lipstick and sailor blouses, cheap hoods with guitars and dangling cigarettes, and smoky casinos alive with jazz and the foxtrot. This retelling of an old story of a village girl arriving in the capital to be seduced and abandoned by a handsome but brutish villain touches almost every social type of the era. Especially well treated are Verka, the vulgar, sexy, but desperate *nepka* (NEP woman), whose dead end is cinematically depicted in a dawn scene as the converging skyline of geometric edifices of the slum-like Ligovsky Prospect seem to close her in; and Vadim, the former *intelligent* reduced to pathetic impotence and penury by the revolution and played with marvelous sensitivity by a great actor of the era, Fedor Nikitin.[36]

As elsewhere, Soviet movie life in the 1920s was characterized by continuous fighting among studios and personnel over prerogatives, scripts, production values, money, equipment, and virtually everything else. But here, government played an important role. Contrary to the accepted image of this era as one of total dedication to innovative cinematography, the public and many party leaders, cultural figures, and movie-makers shared a vigorous desire for realism in the movies. Sovkino favored the production of "popular" domestic and imported films – *kassovye* or box-office grossers – over either political films (*klassovye*) or the experimental masterpieces. This engendered a fierce debate about the utility of foreign films and the "Hollywood invasion" *per se*, a debate echoed in many countries during the silent era – and echoed today in Moscow. Although some actors made their mark in the silent era, it produced no stars comparable to those of the West or of the past. Fan magazines, fan mail, and screen bios flourished, but these revolved around Western stars. The actress Olga Zhizneva related that, though a member of her union's executive and married to director Avram Room, she lived with him in two sparsely furnished rooms. When an adolescent wrote in the Young Pioneer paper that she wanted to be in the movies, she was criticized by other youngsters for aspiring to a "millionaire" and a "Mary Pickford" instead of an agronomist![37]

The Soviet Union was not yet a mass "movie society." The number of films was always much lower than in the West. In 1928 – the end of the period and its peak – 123 films were released and 300 million tickets were sold. All told in the 1920s, the Soviets produced 1,172 feature films. In the United States, by comparison, there were 100 million viewers a week and a vaulting system of studios, agents, publicity organs, stars, and scandals. As for exhibiting, Moscow had 143 houses in 1914, but none until late 1921 when the first opened its doors on Tverskaya and showed *Be Still My Grief* from morning to night to full houses; and less than 1,500 in 1927. In 1922 the Malaya Dmitrovka showed new American movies every week. In the countryside, old silents were almost the only viewing available through the 1920s. A campaign of "cinefication" (*kinofikatsiya*) to provide movies for peasant audiences met the same kind of problems encountered in fiction and the press: the wrong themes, alien stories, puzzling characters, and inappropriate cinematic language. One major exception was Olga Preobrazhenskaya's beautifully wrought *Peasant Women of Ryazan* (1927) dealing with a painful women's theme: male peasant sexual abuse of daughters-in-law. Peasants seem to have reacted to movies the way they did to popular theater before the revolution. In one case, a girl was terrified by closeups on screen which she saw as people "cut into pieces." Much audience research was conducted but little came of it. The problem was exacerbated by the technical shortages. In remote areas, movies had practically no impact on village life.[38]

Semicapitalism and demimonde

Readers and scholars would love to know which kinds of people – by age, gender, ethnicity, and class – enjoyed which kinds of culture. What were the "taste cultures" and "taste publics" in the early Soviet period? This is not easy to determine, because often the choices were restricted. The masses clearly preferred popular to high culture or political propaganda. When they did consume high culture they liked the traditional better than avant-garde. Many people also "straddled" up to high or revolutionary art and down to entertainment genres – just as they had before 1917. Women, particularly of the working classes, had less leisure time than men; when they had time for a movie, they certainly enjoyed a romantic angle more than a military adventure. Workers by no means displayed uniformity of cultural tastes. Again as in the old days, they diverged according to craft, skill, age, education, and other things. Peasants had less access than urbanites to mass culture but were by no means immune to it or indifferent to it.[39]

What about the despised nepmen? In retrospect, the demimonde of NEP was a culture of desperation acted out under an overhanging sword. But it did not always seem so at the time. Created largely by nepmen and their satellites but joined by all kinds of people, it revived the urban popular culture of the prerevolutionary era: restaurants, gypsy music, the old movies, and a host of other cultural artifacts seen as precious reminders of a better day by their consumers and as lurid vestiges of a decadent past by the revolutionaries. Just as NEP was an economic hybrid, so the popular cultural scene was one of uncertainty, unclarity, and ambivalence. Nevsky Prospect was a vivid insult to socialism: it sheltered not only the petty private stalls soon to be liquidated, but also casinos, clubs, and hotel bars, favorite haunts of foreigners and nepmen who could escape for a time into a nostalgic past at tables with soiled linen set amid dusty palms and the whining of a jazz clarinet. When Soviet writers such as Kataev, Ilf, and Petrov or filmmakers such as Barnet set out to satirize these remnants, the results were hilarious; but many readers and viewers must have enjoyed the refreshing descriptions of drunks, gamblers, and swindlers for their own sake.[40]

Another subculture of the era was that of the "homeless children" (besprizornye), orphaned or abandoned waifs whose normal numbers were swollen immensely by the disasters of 1914–1922; estimates run as high as 7 million at peak. These children, 75–80 percent of them boys, inhabited a realm of human misery marked by begging, petty crime, prostitution, hunger, and homelessness. Fiction and film often depicted the pathos of their lives spent in railroad stations, cellars, caves, dumps, and heating vats. As social outcasts or self-made marginals, homeless children created their own subculture – nicknames, jargon (part of the larger and older blatnaya muzyka – rough music – the language of the urban underground), a repertoire of underworld song, a code of honor about group loyalty, debts, and desertion that was harshly enforced, and a cult of the leader (*vozhak*). All this resembled the subcultures of criminals, convicts, even robber bands of yore and street gangs of the present day. Gambling and movies were the favorite leisure pursuits of the *besprizorniki* – sources say that they liked both the American film *The Mark of Zorro* and *Battleship Potemkin*. In a tiny survey, thirty out of thirty-three homeless boys took American actors as their idols, well over half naming Douglas Fairbanks as number one.[41]

This twilight world was not wholly novel: gambling, drugs, cheap vice, petty crime, shady dealing, prostitution, abandoned children, and street gangs were all known to imperial Russia. What made the dens and denizens of NEP so striking compared to tsarist times was the political and moralizing forces that surrounded them on almost every side. Militants who had fought in the civil war and aspired to liquidate capitalism and build a moral communist society associated popular culture with the "decadence" of the old regime and with the sleazy, if not criminal, side of NEP civilization. Jazz, gypsy songs, and tangos got victimized by their association with sordid haunts and patrons, even though they had a far wider following than NEP types. Just as jazz was linked to the bootleg liquor and speakeasies of prohibition America, and to offensive cabaret in Weimar Germany, so in Russia it was identified with a world alien to Marxists and revolutionaries.

But that alien world had some appeal even to the stalwarts of the new society: working class youth and students. Sex, alcohol, smoking, and hooliganism were regular features of dorm and street life for many of them. Furthermore a whole cult arose around the poet Sergei Esenin after his suicide in 1925; a cult which included individualism, soulful verse, sexual machismo, heavy drinking, and even suicide. Like the gypsy song artists of bygone days and like the modern figures of Pugacheva and Vysotsky, Esenin as a rebel cult hero symbolized youthful longing for nonconformist behavior and became a link between alienation and counterculture.

Party and komsomol authorities fought "bourgeois" popular culture sporadically in the 1920s with carrot and stick. Komsomol activists, fearing that working class youth would succumb to its charms, infiltrated their parties to find out what kind of music and dancing was going on, a device used periodically up to the late 1980s whenever a new dance seemed to pose a decadent threat to decency; and they mounted "red parties" with revolutionary songs and marches and readings aloud from journals! Workers' clubs and parks of culture and rest were built to introduce workers to a "rational" style of recreation and to supplement holiday spectacles, healthy sports, and pedagogical excursions. All of this was part of a naive but genuinely idealistic effort to promote an official moral culture through educational reform, anti-religious campaigns, new rituals, a proletarian morality, children's books and theater, and the overall remolding of the leisure habits of the working class – and thus eventually of all. The attacks on popular commercial culture that were merely bothersome in the NEP era took on menacing force in the years of the first five year plan.[42]

3   Stalin by starlight 1928–1941

Mass culture

In the 1930s – a decade that rocked many a nation's values – Russian popular culture got the shape it would have for the next fifty years. The "great change" launched by Stalin in 1928 transformed the economy of the USSR. The NEP, with its capitalism, private trading, landowning, and private demimondes, was brutally abolished. The new Soviet bosses outdid themselves and each other in the dramatic surge for building. Youth, propelled by exuberant idealism, rushed to the great construction sites in order to forge a new world. Shock workers and later Stakhanovites led drives for productivity that were replete with military and religious imagery.

In the accompanying cultural revolution, critics claiming to speak on behalf of the proletariat in art, architecture, music, literature, radio, and film demanded a parallel liquidation of the NEP cultural system. They wanted to upturn the world once again and for the last time, to silence the noisy purloiners of vulgarity, to drown out the sickly whimpers of gypsy violins with the shrill of the factory whistle. But the main figures in the "proletarian" camps of the cultural revolution were intellectuals not workers; and they scorned the eclecticism and pluralism of the original Proletcult movement. Indeed, their program ought to be called – in an analogy with folklorism – "proletarianism": the adaptation of certain features of working class life and culture to their own aesthetic and political demands. The proletarianists assaulted science fiction, detective stories, fairy tales, folk music, jazz, urban song, and escape movies as the effusion of decadent intellectuals produced for the unhealthy appetites of degenerate businessmen and allowed to flourish in dark and noisome corners of the NEP. The self-proclaimed guardians of proletarian sensibilities almost succeeded in destroying what was left of popular culture in the years 1928–1932.[1]

The cultural revolution as such ended as suddenly as it had begun.

By 1933–1934, a turnabout had begun, iconoclasm and anti-intellectual-
ism was curbed, and a partial restoration of older values enunciated.
Party leaders angrily denounced the arrogant reductionism of the
proletarianist movements, their vulgar sociologism, their hostility to
everything old and foreign. The reaction to the excesses of the cultural
revolution coincided with a huge blast of triumphant euphoria that
came with the end of the five year plan and with the mood of many
people who were happy for the chance to celebrate. The result was an
outpouring of spontaneous fun and joy for three or four years.
Popular culture reemerged with great vigor – as it had done after the
storms of the civil war. But in 1936, another reversal took place:
"excesses" were checked in jazz music, *estrada*, and the movies and
solemn joy in a dignified setting replaced the zany fun. The popular
culture of the 1930s, even after the restraining orders of 1936, was more
pluralistic than that favored by the fanatics of the cultural revolution.
But it also promoted optimism over self-pity, exuberance over intro-
spection, comradely devotion over sex, directed satire over open-
ended comedy, and systematic formula over experiment.

The constant gyrations in popular culture reflected the leadership's
desire to capture mass audiences and to respond to the new taste
culture generated by the Stalinist social revolution. When the political
intelligentsia was purged and replaced by people of a lower middle or
working class background with a technical schooling, the newcomers
were invested with privilege and expected to develop respectable
habits and tastes. The new elite had their own tailors and haberdashers
and displayed status symbols (such as Parker pens and Troika cigarettes) to illustrate and embellish their power. Promotees from the
working class were instructed by their bosses to wear business suits
and carry briefcases. Having risen from proletarian origins, they had
little taste for narrowly construed "proletarian" culture. They thirsted
for old high culture as a badge of distinction; for entertainment they
enjoyed sentimentalism, fun, uplift, and an affirmation of their values.
Late love is a powerful force, and when leaders and managers who
had spent their youth in a village or a factory dorm discovered
traditional high culture they canonized classical music, ballet, and
architecture, realistic theater, and didactic painting. At the same time
they helped fashion a "mass culture" of socialist realist fiction, state-
sponsored folklore, mass song, military bands, parades, movies, and
radio – accessible to all, politically impeccable, and bearing some of the
solemn hallmarks of high culture.[2]

The thematics of mass culture in this era mythically fused national accomplishment, social mobility, and personal success. Construction, mechanization, and the promethean battle against nature through exploration, aviation exploits, and production heroism were made palpable and attractive in the same way that military valor and colonial conquest were romanticized in earlier eras. The immense canvas of achievement – displayed to the Soviet public through all the arts and media – sanctified the leaders but also depicted common workers loyal to the principles of Soviet socialism climbing the triumphal stairway to the top of an edifice through hard work. One stairway provided the familiar ascent from the menial world of physical labor to white collar management or professionalism; the more novel one rose from the lower reaches of manual work to the extraordinary heights of superlabor. This only partly resembled the American myth of success whose main ingredient was the rise of a poor and humble male to high places and private fortunes. In Russia it meant rank, decorations, titles, better pay and privileges bestowed by the state; and for the very best men and women, a journey to the enchanted castle of the prince.

The cult of Stalin was a key ingredient in the myth. It portrayed him as a poor man from a backwater of the Russian empire, a friend of Lenin, a dashing hero of revolution and civil war, a father to his people – a prince, hero, wise elder, and godlike figure to be worshipped and obeyed. The industrialization of the country was heralded as Stalin's public achievement. His systematic invitation of working class and peasant achievers to the theaters and palaces of the Kremlin not only honored the guests but "plebeianized" the host. Stakhanovites and aviators marveled at the simplicity of the great leader and were impressed by his small gestures of politeness to "ordinary" people. All of this was wreathed in sunny optimism and jubilation and celebrated in story, song, and movie, integrated and carefully monitored by censorship, prescriptive orders from above, and the corporate responsibility of producers. It was also regulated by a highly centralized bureaucracy which required planning, fulfillment, and ideological correctness from all its branches.[3]

Fairy tales can come true

During the literary battles of the early 1930s that strewed the field with many a corpse, the proletarianists assaulted "our Mayne Reids and Jules Vernes" – light entertainment fiction in general. But influential figures such as Maxim Gorky and others wanted a fiction that would reach the masses. After much fierce debate, a "solution" was reached. Commercial popular writing and avant-garde literature as well as the mysticism and eroticism of the old regime were rejected in favor of a single literary art that would teach the people and serve the state. After such terms as "proletarian realism" and "revolutionary romanticism" were rejected, it came to be called "socialist realism," a syncretic blend of theories inspired by Gorky's *Mother*, Furmanov's *Chapaev*, Gladkov's *Cement* (1925), and Fadeev's *The Rout* (1927). Popular tastes rooted in tradition were to be recognized, though purged of religious or other harmful elements. As one scholar has put it so vividly, "it projected Tarzan as well as adventure stories and Pugachev and his rebellions onto the positive hero constructing dams, and St. George overcoming the dragon as well as Ivan the simple-minded or the *bogatyri* of the *chansons de geste* and traditional *byliny*."[4] The official status of the new art meant that writers were provided with standardized character types, resolutions, and even settings.

Socialist realism gave the public part of what it wanted: "realism," adventure, and moral guidance. Realism meant simple and readable prose and the here and now or a heroic past for the plot and setting – enterprise, factory, collective farm, research institute, and revolutionary or national battlefield. Socialism meant fantasized political personalities and a masterplot about a young person, under the tutelage of a mentor, achieving consciousness by doing battle with obstructionist forces. The masses consumed the new literature partly because no competition was permitted, but also because its characters were largely folkloric: firm and self-controlled, but loving and good and brave – people that the common reader could recognize from popular notions of how characters should act and speak. As in most popular fiction, the plots were formulaic and the writing contained the familiar complement of "furrowed brows" and "shining eyes." The descriptive lexicon was coded to exalt reason, technology, and the city and to enwrap such impulses as sex in the dark shades of chaos. The result was a peculiar variety of didactic middlebrow literature whose rules and codes quickly migrated to statuary, film, radio drama, and song. Socialist realist culture as a whole was a tortuous compromise between the art of old masters, folk culture, ideology, and some elements of popular commercial art. Its output was enormous and it embraced not only fiction, but fictionalized history, communist hagiography, travel prose, and folk materials, as the following few examples will show.

Nikolai Ostrovsky's *How the Steel Was Tempered* (1932–1934) became the classic novel of socialist realism and its hero Pavel Korchagin the quintessential positive hero. It is a crude semi-autobiographical chain of episodes that begins with the portrait of a lowborn, uneducated, and undisciplined boy resembling in some ways the orphaned and homeless children of the time. During his civil war adventures, Korchagin is gradually shaped into consciousness by a series of mentors. The theme of the foolish but brave and decent hothead who grows into a hero had and still has enormous power. It enlivens not only many Soviet boyhood and military adventures – on page, stage, and screen – but also American cowboy, orphan, street gang, and aviation tales. The success of Korchagin's saga was also due partly to its heavy promotion by the Komsomol. The only historical novel that gained wide popularity in the 1930s was Alexei Tolstoy's epic *Peter the First* (1929–1945). Tolstoy erected a mighty symbolic ancestor of Stalin in the energetic Peter, surrounded, as in Stalin's mythic hierarchy, by enterprising engineers and proto-proletarians who ascend the ladder of mobility provided by his revolution from above. Its screen version of 1936 was a huge hit with Soviet audiences. Illusion and allusion are used with great effect at the novel's end: a dreamy vista of a bright future suspended over a concrete reality. It would be the trademark of many a novel and film of that age.[5]

Utopian science fiction was suppressed in the early 1930s because of its dangerous comparisons to the present and its revolutionary idealism. So was the "red detective story" which was blasted during the cultural revolution for its alleged vulgar qualities. In the 1930s, the manichean struggle of socialist heaven and capitalist hell that had infused both genres was reduced to crude plots about espionage and military vigilance. The crime motif was preserved by Yury German who used the ordinary militia as his force of heroes but broke sharply with the style and content of the old Pinkerton stories, red or otherwise. His best-known work, *Ivan Lapshin* (1937), was a police novel in a provincial setting whose main theme was the integration of criminals into society through order and labor. In this sense it resembles old bandit tales in which outlaws are reintegrated into society by colluding with the authorities. The novel incorporates a vision of collectivity (the policemen live in a commune), rationalism, culture, and social tranquility unperturbed by the black discord of crime. For good measure, Lapshin acts as mentor to his junior colleague. All of this is captured, with a twist, in the brilliant film version, *My Friend, Ivan Lapshin* made by the author's son, Alexei German in the 1980s.[6]

In the Stalinist fairy tale, figures from real life were transformed into living legends or martyred saints. The most famous martyr was Pavlik

Morozov. According to the mythical official account, in 1932 during the collectivization wars, the 13-year-old country lad appeared in his Pioneer uniform at the local courthouse and, standing beneath Lenin's portrait, denounced his own father as a friend of *kulaks*. Shortly after, he and his younger brother were brutally murdered by their grandfather and an accomplice. At the urging of Gorky, Morozov became a legend. His village in the Urals was made into a Young Pioneer shrine, streets and youth groups were named after him, and mythologized stories flooded the schoolroom. The Komsomol commissioned Alexander Rzheshevsky to fictionalize the episode. His story, which combined Turgenev's "Bezhin Meadow" with the Morozov case, became the basis of Eisenstein's ill-fated film of the same name. Morozov's early childhood was romanticized and he entered the Bolshevik martyrology alongside the victims of tsarist police and counter-revolution.[7]

A literary and journalistic theme that had much resonance in the popular arts was the romance of exploration, settlement, and production. During the twilight period of European overseas imperialism, from about 1900 to 1940, arctic and antarctic exploration captured the fancy of the reading and filmgoing world, a fancy later caught by World War II and then by space travel. The new Kiplings and Haggards of the newsreel cameras thrilled world audiences with adventure on the ice. One of the first Soviet writings to bring to life the hardships and heroism of polar exploration was Alexei Garri's *Ice and People* (1928), a self-consciously cinematic travel adventure based upon the author's harrowing experience in the rescue of the Nobile expedition. For Soviet readers, Garri's vivid reportage fed the fascination and also delivered heavy doses of machinolotry in its prose closeups of engines, ski-planes, and icebreakers. Movie screens, radio waves, and even the variety stage were filled with their images and sounds throughout the decade.[8]

Pilots and aviators played a special role in the mythology of the 1930s – and not only in the USSR. They embodied the leading edge of applied science and technology, the frontier spirit, bravery and adventure in distant and forbidding locales, and spirited youth tempered by fatherly mentors. Record flyers and the heroes who soared over arctic wastelands became overnight media personalities. Stalin adopted them as his "falcons"; and writers, actors, singers, and comedians feted them at their clubs and made radio shows and films about them. The hit song "Aviamarsh" or "Ever Higher" (see ch. 2) blended aviation and optimism. Valery Chkalov (1904–1938), the ultimate romantic aviator, was the star of stars whose audacious stunts such as flying against orders beneath a Neva River bridge in Leningrad were as endearing as his spectacular transpolar flights. He became an idol among the actors of the Moscow Art Theater. The fame of the female flyers, Osipenko, Raskova, and Grizodubova, was employed to recruit women aviators in World War II. The fact that the geophysicist and arctic explorer Otto Schmidt held high-ranking scientific and government posts helped make aviation and exploration media fetishes.[9]

The pioneering urge to break new ground and create cities and factories in the wilderness led tens of thousands of young people out to construction sites in the mountains, steppes, and riverbanks of the Soviet land. Youngsters and seasoned workers pitched their tents on the emptiness of the Urals and erected Magnetic Mountain (Magnitogorsk); and they created gigantic complexes on the Dnieper, the Don, and the Volga. These exploits unleashed a deluge of folklore. The most distant of the projects of those days was Komsomol City-on-the-Amur, begun in 1932 deep in the primeval taiga of the Soviet Far East. It was a construction epic adorned with a promotion campaign extravagant even for those days of state-sponsored hoopla. Like the Virgin Lands and the Baikal-Amur campaigns of later years, it helped to slake youth's thirst for the euphoria of trailblazing in exotic places. One of the most popular children's stories of industrial romanticism was written by a trained engineer from a famous family of children's writers, M. Ilin (Ilya Marshak): *Story of the Great Plan* (1930), widely translated and once a bestseller in the West. Its descriptions of the hydroelectric dam at Dneprostroi, the Donbass mining community, and a tractor assembly plant were couched in a simple and sometimes poetic language that also throbbed with the dynamism of the age – omitting of course all the hardships, mismanagement, and suffering that accompanied Stalin's industrial revolution.[10]

Alexei Stakhanov (1906–1977) and his numerous imitators on the front of industrial superheroism were mythologized in the romance of production. Stakhanov was endowed in the popular literature and media with an idealized childhood, an older mentor, a heroic deed, and an immortal persona. Less famous now, but universally known at the time was the tractor driver, Praskovya (Pasha) Angelina (1913–1959), the most famous young woman in Russia of the early 1930s, whose minidrama was captured by the playwright Sergei Tretyakov, in "Nine Girls" (1935). Her family was presented as a model of upward mobility and technical, military, and agricultural attainment. Her achievement and style provided the lexicon of the Stalinist success story: peasant simplicity, toughness, a struggle against all odds (including sabotage), a production promise to Stalin, triumph on the furrow front, and the climactic journey to the Kremlin (in an olive-colored Lincoln!) to be received by the Great Leader. When Angelina decided to marry, the anxiety on her tractor team about the loss of a champion gave birth to a fertile plot idea that seeded innumerable tractor novels, *kolkhoz* operettas, and rustic film comedies. Pasha Angelina was the socialist Cinderella supreme. She and other worker prodigies were turned into postcard heroes and cultic idols of kitsch, models for youth and paragons of virtue.[11]

Industrial folklore invaded the printed page on a grand scale in such works as *People of the Stalin Tractor Works* (thirty-two autobiographies) and *White Sea Canal*, written by a collective of thirty-seven writers, one of the most extraordinary apologias for slave labor camps ever written, complete with eulogies to Yagoda, head of the security police, and Berman, director of its camp complex. A huge corpus of factory histories, workers' memoirs, and the reports of factory, village, and barracks correspondents flooded the press in these years and a synthetic folklore was woven around heroic workers in proletarian periodicals such as *The Stakhanovite*, *Club*, and *The Worker of Magnitogorsk*. These were bourgeoisified proletarian success stories containing idealized biographies, pious homilies on sobriety and the work ethic, a cult of victory in life (by "conquest" of a mountain or winning at sport), and earnestly minute descriptions of the trophies that victory could bring: a good apartment with fine furniture, a bicycle, a phonograph, a free vacation, or a bottle of Crimea Rose perfume.[12]

Peasant or folk culture, after years of neglect or abuse, finally became legitimized – though in adapted and coopted form (and minus one of its key ingredients, religious rituals and festivals). At the 1934 congress of writers, Gorky urged the use of folklore in the new Soviet literature because it was earthy, optimistic, and artistically precious and because its heroic types were dear to the people. In 1934–1935, ethnographic teams were sent into the countryside to gather remnants of authentic folk culture. But at the same time a whole new industry of folklorism or pseudofolklore was created as an instrument of propaganda. Workers were given folk tales to read as models for their own autobiographies. By the mid 1930s a whole array of tellers and bards had surfaced, including the Russian Marfa Kryukova (1846–1954) and the Kazakh Dzhambul Dzhabaev (1846–1945). Using traditional forms they fashioned *novinki* or new folk tales such as Kryukova's improvised narrative on Lenin's death, "All Stone-Built Moscow Went a-Weepin'" or on the exploits of Stalin (Joseph Bright), Voroshilov (a wondrous knight), Chapaev (an eagle), and the aviation heroes of the day. The writers and singers were guided by political tutors to insure correct ideological content and their works were read on the radio, recorded on the phonograph, printed in huge runs, and adapted to stage and screen in various forms.[13]

It is hardly an exaggeration to say that after 1936 virtually all of Soviet mass culture became "folklorized" under the impact of literary models. It differed substantially from that of the 1920s, in that it was nearly monopolistic, suffering little competition from spontaneous forms (except for the highly constricted underground subcultures of the streets, schoolrooms, barracks, and prison camps). Its themes of optimism, affirmation of life, healthy work and construction, collective ambition and success, hot-blooded heroism yoked to cool-headed wisdom made their way into song lyrics, circus acts, and movies.

Sing a song of joyous life

The first five year plan stirred the Russian Association of Proletarian Musicians to feverish militancy. Quasi-religious preachers against sinful music called Western popular music "the song and dance of the period of the catastrophe of capitalism," foxtrot a "dance of slaves," and tango "the music of impotents." The Association of Workers on the Revolutionary Radio Front assaulted *tsyganshchina, fokstrotshchina*, and Viennese waltzes as "counter-revolutionary." "We send [composers] to the factories," complained a musician, "to learn the new rhythms of trip hammer and blast furnace, and they compose their works, and then [the radio programers] play Chopin and Schubert and Bach." When RAPM forces captured the conservatory in 1929, they abolished solo singing, grades, and examinations, taught primitive music history, and excoriated all forms of music – gypsy, jazz, folk, operetta, and classical – except that propagating industrial construction. The Moscow composers group and the "light music" department in the Commissariat of Enlightenment were dissolved. Popular singers such as Tsereteli were tested and graded by high culture commissions and their old repertoires branded by RAPM as not only "sickness" but "sabotage," a dangerous charge in an era when "wreckers" in industry were tried and jailed. Private sheet music publishing ended in 1929 and gypsy music was banned on radio. Proletarianist composers formed themselves into shock brigades to churn out songs for workers and collectivized farmers.[14]

The bitter campaign against jazz codified a decade of invective; all subsequent onslaughts on popular music have been ritualistic reissues of this one. In 1928 the recently returned Gorky identified jazz with homosexuality, drugs, and bourgeois eroticism – charges that were later recycled to fit the rock culture of our time. Even a ban on saxophones was suggested in 1929 (and would be carried out twenty years later). Komsomols patrolled public dance places and anti-jazz lecturers marched into schoolrooms. On the folk front, the Pyatnitsky choir was given a mock trial on the radio and then banned from the airwaves because it allegedly encouraged a cult of the old village and was thus harmful to socialism. But the proletarian musicians still failed to produce popular substitutes. They were generally poor composers who could create only simple songs with primitive harmonies, march-like rhythms, and some folk elements.[15]

The iron musical dictatorship of proletarian musicians was broken in the same reversal that recast the canons of fiction. The success enjoyed by songs from the first sound film hits revealed that the masses wanted more than proletarian hymns to sing. In 1932 RAPM was abolished and in 1933 the end of the first five year plan was heralded as a major national victory worthy of jubilation. The leaders now promoted a lightening up of feelings. Popular music of every kind reemerged. The old gypsy favorite "Dark Eyes," the orphan song "Forgotten and Forsaken," and the foreign hits "Ramona" and "How Do You Do, Do, Do, Mr Brown" were heard all over Moscow. With Ziegler's Czech Jazz playing the Hotel Metropole and the Tsfasman and Utesov bands the National, tea dances on Sunday afternoon, and the novelty song "Little Lemons" blasting out at the cellar cafe Kanatik, it seemed like a return if not to 1916 then at least to 1921. At the Praga Restaurant on the Arbat, the same Moscow gypsy band that used to accompany Varvara Panina and serenade Rasputin in the Yar Restaurant before the war was rending the air with passionate music. But the revival of competition also induced envy: gypsy performers began to hate jazz for its popularity, just as jazzmen would one day resent the success of rock.[16]

The 1930s brought the restoration of the "star system" in popular entertainment. Celebrity, as a socio-cultural phenomenon, returned along with officers' ranks and other signs of privilege. In popular music, Tsereteli and Izabella Yureva (1902–?) revived the gypsy tradition. Klavdiya Shulzhenko (1906–1984), began her long career as a big band singer. The queen of popular song, the peasant-born Lydia Ruslanova (1901–1973), made "Over Hill and Dale" and "Katyusha" into huge hits on radio and records. The major male non-jazz vocalist of the 1930s was Vadim Kozin (1903–   ), the son of a singer of gypsy songs. Possessed of a marvelous lyric tenor voice and a gift for song writing, Kozin had begun as a movie house singer in the 1920s and in the 1930s performed and recorded urban songs and tangos – personal, introspective, and nonpolitical, like those of his emigre contemporary Vertinsky. In Kozin's rendition of "Lyuba" one can hear woodwind arabesques that combine Yiddish and gypsy acceleration with Dixie-land syncopation. His "Farewell My Tabor" is a parting lament to the Gypsy world with sudden modulations into a dark minor key. And in the haunting "Autumn," all the sentimental stops are pulled out in a gloriously nostalgic evocation of lost love. By 1938–1939, Kozin had become a national star. These singers represented 1930s Russian popular song at its best.[17]

In the years of the "red jazz age" (1932–1936) European and Soviet bands were heard in dozens of cities. The kings were Alexander Tsfasman and Leonid Utesov. Tsfasman, the son of a Jewish barber in the Ukraine, rose to become one of the richest men in the USSR, leading a half dozen bands, and a star of radio, concert hall, and film. Tsfasman cultivated an American style, called himself "Bob," married an American, and saturated the Soviet musical scene in the 1930s and 1940s with songs like "The Man I Love," "Shanty Town," and the Glenn Miller classic, "Chattanooga Choo-choo" from the movie, *Sun Valley Serenade*. Utesov – musically far less gifted – was actually more popular than Tsfasman, partly because of the spectacular success of his comedy film *Happy-Go-Lucky Guys*, but mostly because his Odessa background and his circus and carnival road experience on the southern borscht belt gave him a clowning manner. He resembled his idol, the personable Ted ("Is everybody happy?") Lewis more than he did any of the great jazz figures of the time. In fact Utesov was the typical *estrada* entertainer – quick witted, versatile, and funny. He was not only one of the stars of the 1930s but also a personal favorite of Stalin.[18]

Utesov's mature jazz style was more European than American. When jazz migrated from the river ports of the Mississippi, it adapted local strains and styles – some of them quite alien to its original spirit. There is nothing impure about this process; it is endemic to all popular culture. The glossy syncretism of Paul Whiteman or Guy Lombardo was a natural product of adaptation. In European jazz, the same thing occurred, but with different local ingredients: English music hall styles, German oompah, central European folk and gypsy genres. Utesov certainly had, as a historian has noted, one ear cocked to his masters in the Kremlin; but he had the other ear wide open to the tastes of his audience and to the styles around them. His band music was made for the dance of his time. Like jazz, it employed bouncy and slightly syncopated sounds of saxophones, muted trumpets, and drum traps. But the melodies were mostly Slavic, gypsy, and Jewish, the rhythms often tangoesque rather than swinging, and the jazz horns backed by strings and accordions. The strains of an Odessa Jewish wedding were never far away. Jazzy solos were passed around, but nothing like the great riffs of Western 1930s jazzmen were heard. If urban jazzmen in the States adapted black music motifs to their art, their Soviet counterparts did the same thing with the materials at hand – gypsy, Jewish, and folk.[19]

With the triumph of jazz, a new dance craze set in. A blonde Swede and an American black taught steps to the actors of the Vakhtangov Theater. Dance classes were made mandatory for officers in the Red Army by its commander, Kliment Voroshilov; he and Vyacheslav Molotov studied the tango. Dance halls sprung up even in small towns. As in many hierarchical societies, elites began dancing with one another as witness this news item on a New Year's Eve party, a stunning summary of the new cultural values:

The *brigadir*-welder V. I. Baranov (28, the best Stakhanovite at Elektrozavod) glided across the floor in a slow tango with Shura Ovchinnikova (20, the best Stakhanovite at TsAGI). He was dressed in a black Boston [wool gabardine] suit that fully accentuated his solidly built figure; she was in a crêpe de Chine dress and black shoes with white trimming.

The tango revival was partly an import from neighboring countries. Kozin and others rode upon the wave. Ballroom dancing to Soviet jazz bands became the thing at diplomatic affairs and Kremlin functions. But the dance also captured ordinary people. A visitor in 1936 recalled the popular rage for American dances and recordings; nighttime dancing in the parks of culture included foxtrot, rhumba, and the Boston waltz.[20]

The jazz age corresponded with the breathing spell that gave way in 1936 to a new wave of violence unleashed in the form of bloody purges. At the moment of its peak, jazz fell victim to a new assault by envious musicians from other genres and nationalists and conservatives resentful of imported culture. Division and ambivalence reigned for a while, even among the leaders. But when the purge came, it hit hard. One bandleader was arrested on the podium. Others were sent to camps. Tsfasman, Utesov, and a few others remained untouched, but only at the price of converting their jazz into a Soviet product, cleansed of "decadence." State Jazz (later *Estrada*) Orchestras were formed, large well-dressed ensembles that played an assortment of ballroom music, classics, and smoothed out "jazz" in carefully written arrangements with an emphasis on orchestral color and texture rather than on swinging spontaneity. A famous example of this was Utesov's rendition of "Suliko" a favorite song of Stalin. American tunes were often dished up with Russian words as in Utesov's "Smugglers" sung to the tune of "My Blue Heaven." As a whole, Stalin's cleanup of jazz resembled that in Hitler's Germany where dance music had to be slow and smooth, with strings and some "folk" instruments added to the "jazz" complement.[21]

Folk music (see next section) and a genre that came to be known as "mass song" (a term from the 1920s) filled the gap left by the purge of jazzy dance music. The new mass song was infused with a pathos of affirmation rather than revolt and negation. Its motifs were optimistic, humanitarian, and positive; the tunes were accessible and the lyrics uplifting. Jazz figures clung to their melodies for a while but were gradually replaced by folkish ones. In the 1930s mass songs were given a tremendous boost by their association with Soviet musical films, which in turn were made popular by the songs performed in them by stars like Lyubov Orlova and by recordings and radio. A song contest 1935–1936 yielded 6,575 entries. Mass song swelled to a crescendo in the years 1936–1941 when jazz was being Sovietized.[22] Most of the song writers were Jews from the Pale – Blanter from near Mogilev, Khait and the Pokrass brothers from Kiev, Feltsman from Odessa – who had received classical training and then had turned to light music. This was also true of the main figures of the operetta and jazz worlds. There was thus a musical connection between mass song, jazz, and Jewish motifs and rhythms.[23] Matvei Isaakovich Blanter (1903–) turned from classical music to the variety shows of Leningrad in the 1920s and then became one of the half-dozen masters of mass song – brisk, popular, and politically impeccable. In their promotion of national values, Jewish origin was no more an obstacle to this than it was for the American Irving Berlin or patriotic Jews of other lands.

Isaac Osipovich Dunaevsky (1900–1955; see fig. 9) was the acknowledged master of the genre, producing hundreds of marches and songs, twenty film scores, two ballets, music for thirty dramas, and a dozen operettas in collaboration with librettists Lebedev-Kumach, Matusovsky, and d'Aktil. He was born near Kharkov of a Jewish family, studied classical music, flirted with avant-garde trends, and then moved into jazz and variety in the 1920s. In the 1930s he was decorated, highly paid, and honored throughout the country. Dunaevsky intersected professionally with virtually every major figure in music, theater, and film of his era. Facility and a melodic gift brought him success. He has been accused of plagiarizing Russian, Mexican, American, and Neapolitan songs. But his compositions, especially the film tunes, were and are undeniably enchanting and they became enormous national hits precisely because he fused different styles: revolutionary hymn, light romance, operetta, and jazz. In his relationship to Stalin, power and culture met in the way it often does in lands of princes and their courts. Dunaevsky might have been sincere in his privately voiced admiration for Stalin, although the song he wrote for him disappointed the leader. Stalin for his part enjoyed Dunaevsky's music but disliked the man.[24]

The 1932 "Song of the Counterplan" (Shostakovich/Kornilov) for the sound film *Counterplan* became the model for movie hits of the decade. A rousing, optimistic march, its catchy melody was adopted as hymn of the United Nations during the war (and then dropped at the onset of the Cold War). The movie *Happy-Go-Lucky Guys* (1934) launched Dunaevsky's famous "Heart" into the hearts of millions, many of whom recognize at once a half century later its opening words:

> How many lovely girls there are!
> How many tender girlish names!

The biggest non-movie hit was Blanter's "Katyusha" (1938) destined to achieve world renown during the war. The rocket mortar invented by A. G. Kostikov and first used in the Russo-Finnish War of 1939 was named after it. The lyrics of Mikhail Isakovsky (1900–1973) are strictly folkloric in their use of repetitive figures:

> Little apples, little pears were blooming,
> Soft did mist upon the river lie.
> To its bank wandered peasant lass Katyusha
> To its steep bank, to its bank so high.

Military, sports, and youth organizations provided occasions and patronage for mass songs, performed by dance bands, huge orchestras, and choirs, which saturated air waves, soundtracks, stages, and public parks. A major vehicle for them was the brass band. Semen Chernetsky, Inspector General of Red Army Bands, organized elaborate contests for composers of marches attended by the cream of Soviet song writers – Khait, Dunaevsky, and others – as well as Voroshilov and the top brass. Bands were mandatory on holidays; in the big November 7 celebrations of Red Square, the United NKVD Band of

400–500 players would blare out music all through the day as the parades passed by. The most famous military ensemble was that of General Alexander Alexandrov (1883–1946) who had studied before the revolution in the St. Petersburg conservatory and then rose from a provincial music teacher to a professorship at the Moscow conservatory. His Red Army Band, formed in the 1920s with a dozen members, gained a huge following during the five year plan, and reached 200 players and singers in the 1930s. The military band was a metaphor for official culture – just as it often was of the patriotic culture of other lands.[25] An honest film about the early 1930s, *My Friend Ivan Lapshin*, employs the metaphor throughout as a counterpoint to the otherwise grim surroundings; one of its characters comments that "there is a band for every soul in this town." In the finale – following the violent climax – a tramcar adorned with the face of Stalin carries a brass band into the town square to play a bright military march.

Return of the folk

Folklorism – politicized folk adaptation – became a major industry in the Stalin era. After undergoing assault during the cultural revolution, folk performance rode back into favor on the wave of the literary folk revival. In 1936 a Theater of Folk Art was established in Moscow with Igor Moiseev (1906–) as its choreographer and dancing coach. A former ballet dancer and – along with George Balanchine – a disciple of the great innovator Kasyan Goleizovsky, Moiseev wanted to extend the plasticity of the body in dance. After a 1936 youth festival, he founded his folk dance ensemble which brilliantly combined the rigor of classical ballet with folkloric steps and village scenes. The State Russian Folk Orchestra, still bearing Andreev's name, was reorganized several times under various leaders and made part of the Leningrad Philharmonic organization in 1936. In the next four years its sixty players gave 571 concerts in fifty-three towns in eight republics at clubs, barracks, factories, and concert halls. Solemn cantatas, revolutionary hymns, and mass songs were added to its repertoire, thus blurring its folkish character. In 1940 the balalaika player Nikolai Osipov became the orchestra's director and it later took his name, while a Leningrad branch of it took the name of Andreev. The Pyatnitsky folksong ensemble (whose founder had died in 1927) was upgraded and legitimized, spawning a dozen imitators.[26]

The names Moiseev, Osipov, Virsky, and Pyatnitsky are known the world over due to this revival of the original Andreev and Pyatnitsky cultural forms. The pioneers of folklorism had wanted to democratize the art, to give it back to the people and not just play it to the cities. This now happened: a nationwide network of amateur folk choirs and ensembles was sponsored by the state, thus making folk a participatory as well as a spectator art. Amateur choirs, bands, singers, reciters, solo instrumentalists, and dance companies from all over the country made pilgrimages to Moiseev's theater in Moscow to perform folk and popular music, a social episode that inspired one of the great musical comedy films of the era (*Volga, Volga*; see below). An elaborate system of vocal, instrumental, and dance companies was established with state support, training schools, and guaranteed bookings. By the late 1930s, Soviet factories were producing a million and half balalaikas and domras a year. By the eve of war, folklorism had become a thoroughly Soviet national art and remains so until this day.[27]

But the victory of folk music in Stalin's Russia also meant the strengthening of conservatism and nationalism in music. Competition for state resources led to animosity reinforced by personal tastes and ideological-cultural perspectives. Jazzmen were notorious in their contempt for the balalaika and accordion even though those instruments were sometimes forced on their big bands to add "national" flavor. The animosity was deepened in wartime when both these forms of music were set loose in frontline entertainment. After the war, one of the harshest voices against deviation in music was the co-leader and composer for the Pyatnitsky ensemble, Vladimir Zakharov (see fig. 10). The composition and deployment of the sexes in the folk ensembles also reinforced the gender and authority images of the Stalinist era. Building on prerevolutionary precedents and their lingering remnants, the prettified and theatricalized Stalinist ensembles – like those in Eastern Europe – served to symbolize collective values (as in the ring-dance) and promote images of national solidarity, reverence for the past, and happy peasants. As with literary folklore, the ensembles were used to endow collective farm and factory life with cultural legitimation.[28]

Although circus was battered like everything else during the cultural revolution and almost drowned in the alphabet soup of TsUGTs, GOMETs, and GUTs – acronyms of the successive bodies controlling it and *estrada* – it survived very well. Once circus managers learned that it was wise to do so, they had no trouble adapting political texts to its entertainments because circus had done this long before the revolution. The first fully Soviet circus extravaganza was *Makhno's Escapades* (1929). In it the clown Lazarenko, interpreting Makhno as a crude and volatile bandit in the manner of *Little Red Imps*, was assisted by Dunaevsky's musical score played by two orchestras, a libretto by V. Z. Mass – scenarist of the Blue Blouse – and direction by Vilyams Trutstsi (Williams Truzzi) in a staging that included newsreel film, a watery arena, an armored train, a detonated bridge, a *corps de ballet*, and an assortment of social caricatures. Makhno's drunken banquet and the attempted forced wedding of a Bolshevik woman were later used in the *Wedding in Malinovka* (operetta, 1937; film, 1967). The "apotheosis" features a hydroelectric power and radio station with female gymnasts radiating from it. Of the new clowns, influenced by cinema stars Chaplin and Harold Lloyd, the most famous was Karandash ("pencil"; real name Mikhail Rumyantsev) who mastered the art of targeting things like gypsy songs, religion, alcohol, and fascism and exalting female flyers and metro workers. Circus continued to inspire other popular arts: a review at the Music Hall, *Under the Big Top* by Ilf, Petrov, and Kataev contained the original story line for the movie *Circus*.[29]

After multiple crises, the Moscow Music Hall finally mounted a show that was both successful and satisfactory to critics: Demyan Bedny's *How the XIV Division Got to Heaven* (1932). But in 1936 the music halls of Moscow and Leningrad were closed down. Modern Soviet historians of *estrada* claim that they had reached a dead end. What really happened is that the authorities could not abide a popular art that was thematically so distant from the image of society it was trying to project – one of solemn joy in the midst of heroic construction and not one of simple tomfoolery and light-hearted fun. The same kind of anger that was vainly hurled against the film *Happy-Go-Lucky Guys* (see p. 88) was successful in ending free-form comedy on the variety stage. But "revolutionary comedy" did not work either; in 1938 the Moscow Theater of Miniatures presented a one-act play about Spain which bored audiences. Revolutionary themes were then abandoned for motifs from everyday life – in-laws, shoddy work, stodgy bureaucrats – which, along with lambasting current foreign foes, became the staple of Soviet comedy for decades.

Although Vladimir Khenkin remained the big name on the popular stage of the period, a younger figure, Arkady Isaakovich Raikin (1911–1988), emerged in the late thirties. He was born in Riga, grew up in provincial Russia and Leningrad, and switched from a chemical vocation to serious theater and then to *estrada* satire. He scored his first successes right before the war and emerged after it as the major comedy star of the Soviet stage, a position he held until his death. By the outbreak of war, *estrada* had been reduced and narrowed to verbal comedy routines, usually revolving around a central figure, and embellished with music and dance. The creators of this synthesis, Raikin, Menaker, Garkavy, Rina Zelenaya, and others (almost all Jewish) were the equivalents of the stars of American radio comedy shows of the thirties (Jack Benny, Eddie Cantor, Fred Allen) which replaced (and sanitized) the vaudeville of earlier days.[30]

Operetta tried again to politicize itself in an anti-capitalist piece called *The Black Amulet* (1928) about a plutocrat in a donkey mask who hands out wads of money to half-naked women. But it was another example of parodic backfire. The audience apparently enjoyed the flesh more than the sarcasm – and the critics panned it. After more groping, operetta turned to folk musical with Gogol's *Sorochinsky Fair* (1937), performed with 300 artists at a huge outdoor theater in Moscow, and *Wedding at Malinovka* (1937) – another bash at Makhno – both set in the countryside. The Vienna style (*venskii* in Russian) adapted to the Russian village (*derevnya*) was dubbed *derevenskaya operetta* or "rustic Viennese." The role of the choir was greatly amplified and it became the model of one of the greatest popular genres of the Stalin period: the *kolkhoz* film comedies of the 1930s and 1940s. The versatile Dunaevsky was the premier composer in both media, making operetta a crossroads of the popular arts. The Vienna style (which was really Hungarian) and Soviet creations have shared the operetta stage up until today. The all-time favorite through the decades has been Imre Kalman's *Silva* (*Csardaskiralyno*, 1915). When managers have tried to parody the West with bolder works – as in the notorious *Ball at the Savoy* in the 1950s – their theaters filled up until indignant critics forced these pieces off the stage.[31]

Estrada continued on as a vague term for the entertainment stage, particularly where comedy met popular music. It lost the brilliant vitality and variety of the prerevolutionary days, became more purposeful, and occasionally solemn. Its music followed the tastes of the day; its comedians walked the line and targeted only established enemies of their state or obvious and eternal shortcomings of daily life. Nevertheless, that music continued to entertain and quicken the heart; and that comedy managed to open the laughter valves of the audiences who kept this lively art alive and on stage decade after decade.

Radio Moscow

Radio became a mass medium in the Soviet Union only in the 1930s. Although developed independently of Marconi in 1895 by Popov, it had been limited largely to use by the Imperial Navy; the first public broadcast came in 1919 and regular airing began in 1924. Lenin called radio "a newspaper without paper or wires" and officials spoke of the "radiofication" of the country in the twenties, but this had about as much practical impact as cinefication. The Russian-born David Sarnoff was speaking at the same moment of putting "the radio music box" in every American home, but with much greater results. In the late twenties there were sixty Soviet stations and a radio "university" was beaming to 80,000 pupils. During the first five year plan, transmission power was augmented eight times. By 1937 there were 3.5 million receivers, almost all of them speakers wired to one station. Music took up about 96 percent of air time in 1928, with speeches and news accounting for the rest. Like everything else in the cultural realm, radio fell under the blows of yet another proletarianist assault team – AWRRF, the Association of Workers on the Revolutionary Radio Front, who wanted to capture the airwaves for their own uses.[32]

The success of radio drama in England led to emulation, but also to misunderstanding of the medium: actors sometimes arrived at the studio in costume and gesticulated wildly for a public who could not see them. Radio had to face the same problems that early movies had: the tyranny of theatrical traditions. Some critics opposed the whole idea of disembodied voices performing plays. In 1930 therefore, a national conference introduced the term "radio art" as a mode of cultural expression peculiar to itself. In 1931 the All Union Committee of Radio augmented the programming to include reports of achievements on the industrial front, drama, and literature. Radio drama got its start in the early 1930s with comedy skits written by Ilf and Petrov. In the mid thirties radio drama and "theater at the microphone" (plays recorded at performance in the theater and then broadcast) blossomed along with serialized and condensed novels recited by "readers' brigades." O. N. Abdulov (1900–1953), a professional stage actor, employed "voice makeup," and taught his actors to tell instead of reading their parts. With the help of great artists of the Moscow Art Theater such as Ivan Moskvin and V. I. Kachalov, Abdulov wove story, music, and voice into a genuine radio art in more than 200 plays and shows. As happened in Europe and America, radio introduced high culture – particularly epics that lent themselves to non-visual reading – to more Soviet people than any other medium in the era.[33]

Programming throughout the 1930s was dominated by music (78 percent of the cultural sector), often introduced by "explanations." The Moscow central station possessed its own symphony orchestra, two choruses, and a folk orchestra. A January 1934 program included exercise, music "from the era of imperialism," the life and work of a young Stalinist shockworker, news, readings from Heine and Turgenev, a children's amateur hour, technical information, a literary-art segment on defence, reports from village and factory correspondents, party school hour, a Red Army Show, and foreign languages. By 1937, radio was offering Kornei Chukovsky reading his classic children's tale, *Telephone*; Hawaiian guitar music – a big rage at the time; news from the arctic explorers and fliers; and a segment on political vigilance. At every step, radio offered live broadcasts of Soviet achievers: icebreaker skippers, mountain climbers, airmen, and the production stars, Stakhanov and Angelina. In 1931 emerged the remarkable voice of young Yury Levitan (1914–1983). After exchanging his Vladimir accent for a Moscow dialect (many radio voices including that of Goebbels had to retune) he became Stalin's favorite announcer, the man who introduced the Stakhanovs, the Angelinas, the Chkalovs to the listening world of the 1930s. In 1941, he would become a national icon.[34]

Iconology and ideology

In Erwin Panofsky's terms, iconology studies the values and attitudes beneath images. Graphic representation during the 1930s underwent a number of iconological changes. To serve the leader cult, a virtual industry arose for the mass production of Stalin portraits and busts to hang or stand alongside those of Lenin. The allegorical element in political posters gave way to more "realistic" and "thingish" art, particularly the photomontage combining photography, airbrush technique, and poster paints. Depiction of certain key social icons underwent a shift: the proletarian, formerly a mature skilled craftsman, was now more often just a youthful worker. In the representation of females, stout matrons with many children began outnumbering the thin, no-nonsense heroic proletarian women of revolutionary imagery. Conversely, the robust peasant woman of the civil war was replaced by a younger activist – part of the campaign to construct the collectivization process in a female idiom. One facet of gender construction, born with the revolution, remained unaltered and was even deepened: the identification of women with the countryside, and thus subliminally with backwardness, passivity, and nurturing; and the man with city, industry, and power. It was emblazoned on many medallions and posters of the early years – man with hammer, woman with sickle – and it found codification in Vera Mukhina's renowned statue, The Worker and the Collective Farmer (1935–1937) – a syntactically symmetrical pair but with the man wielding the mace of modernity: the industrial hammer.[35]

Industrial dynamism and kinetic youth enlivened the graphic arts. But the counterweight was heaviness and control to reflect the tightening and hardening of society. In the early 1930s, the borders were sealed even tighter than before and the sealing was reinforced in the popular mind through song and picture, film and statue depicting the stern frontier guard with rifle in hand and dog at his side – protector of the workers' state. Migration into cities was closely controlled and elaborate rituals were required to enter buildings. Moscow sprouted massive buildings whose façade ornament inspired by folk and classical art was standardized and mass produced in the way "model façades" had been in the eighteenth and nineteenth centuries. The ornament – vertical piers, columns, entablatures, recessed windows, porticos, statues, prominent cornices, large square entrances, and small windows – emitted an aura of monumentality and bureaucratic power. The mosaics, sculptures, and friezes of the new Moscow Metro carried this symbolism beneath the streets. Ornamental reliefs were even applied to the floodgates of the Volga-Don canal.[36]

But should we assume that architecture's celebration of state grandeur was only meant to underline the insignificance of the citizen on the street? The bright new harbor building (or River Station) in Moscow was designed to extend a dignified but warm welcome to newly arriving passengers from the hinterland. Daily contact with the massive ornament of the metro may have swelled some citizens with pride. Commenting on the newly finished Hotel Moskva which was then used for worker and peasant delegations, a Soviet citizen told a foreign visitor that staying in this hotel "increases their self-respect and strengthens their allegiance to a regime which affords them such princely hospitality." When a provincial woman in Moscow first gazed upon it she exclaimed: "I do not know if this a hotel or a fairy tale palace." In August 1939 the massive Agricultural Exhibition opened in Moscow and was visited by as many as 20–30,000 people a day. It was a fairyland – in many ways resembling its contemporary, the New York World's Fair in opulence and monumentality – of domes, gothic buildings, fountains, broad walkways, a giant statue of Stalin, and the huge Mukhina ensemble. These and other examples of Soviet construction and decor were deployed in the movies of the 1930s not to depress and not only to impress – but to enliven and animate the viewer with self-esteem and communal pride.[37]

Movies for the millions

The cinema industry was also slammed by the proletarianists during the cultural revolution. One critic wanted the "iron script" to reduce the power of the director – the cinematic equivalent of written scores for the State Jazz Orchestras; another wanted films abolished altogether, a reversion to the more extreme currents of prewar thinking. In 1930 Sovkino was transformed into Soyuzkino and placed under the direction of Boris Shumyatsky (1886–1938). As a result of tension and distraction and the emergence of talkies, film production fell from 148 in 1928 to 35 in 1933. The masses were not patronizing films of genius: for example in the very year that Shumyatsky took over in the name of popular audiences, Dovzhenko released his immortal filmic poem, *Earth*, whose famous finale shocked and puzzled ordinary viewers by its nude scenes and its striking montage; Dziga Vertov's *Enthusiasm* with Shostakovich's machinery-like music and the brilliant camera work of Mikhail Kaufman suffered the same fate. Though greatly reducing the number of films made, Shumyatsky managed to fill movie houses whose number grew dramatically; the number of copies of each film produced increased from the tens to about 1,500. Shumyatsky believed that films should not be the personal expression of a tyrannical director but should be endowed with strong plots and clearly defined heroes, be accessible, and avoid cinematic experimentation. Though lambasted by art film devotees ever since, Shumyatsky helped create a new kind of Soviet movie.[38]

A few examples can give a sense of what the masses saw on the screen in those turbulent years. The first real sound film was *Start in Life* (released in the USA as *Road to Life*, 1931), directed by Nikolai Ekk. Inspired by a children's colony outside Moscow made famous by the pedagogue Anton Makarenko, it presented an unusual kind of mentor: a sympathetic but tough savior of abandoned, unloved boys, a sensitive theme in an era of massive homelessness in the USSR. It resembled the equally popular American movie of the same decade, *Boys Town* (1939): both pitted a grown man (Batalov and Spencer Tracy) against a difficult but basically good adolescent (Tsyvan Kyrla and Mickey Rooney). *Start in Life* was immensely popular then and is still considered a classic. The story, set in 1923, is a moving fictional document that contrasts the life of the *besprizorniki* amid the criminal world of NEP (scored to urban "decadent" songs "Bublichki" and "Forgotten and Forsaken") with the purifying nature of communal life (set against work songs and band marches). Labor was sanctified in the construction of a railway which, at the end, bears the body of the reformed but murdered little hero back for burial in his new Soviet home. Though *Start in Life* spawned no immediate copies, its theme of homeless children has recurred regularly down through the decades.

Chapaev (1934; see fig. 11), directed by the Vasiliev "brothers" is one of the most popular Soviet films of all time. Youngsters kept going back to see it, played Chapaev games, and aspired to "be" Chapaev. Some even ran around to other movie-houses, hoping to find a happy ending. Its colossal success lay in the tale on which it was based (see ch. 2); the charismatic performance of the ex-stage actor, Boris Babochkin (1904–1975); its fast-paced action; and the revolutionary pathos that is underlined by the folksong "Black Raven" (still heard today in restaurants) and by the score's doleful ascending and descending chromatic theme. *Chapaev* also offered comic relief in the person of young Petka, who is fond of both "his best friend," the machine-gun and of the bosomy Anka the machine-gunner. Their trench romance (absent from the novel) has inspired hundreds of indecent underground jokes. Scenes from the movie are etched in the memory of millions: long shots of horse soldiers, Chapaev teaching tactics by moving potatoes around a table, the "psychic attack" of the White forces displayed brilliantly as an evil machine, peasant carts assaulting the enemy, a beastly armored car with gun turrets, and closeups of the White Russian colonel fully encoded with a Germanic pince-nez and haircut playing Beethoven's "Moonlight Sonata." Chapaev-Babochkin – cunning, alert, and kinetic – was beloved as no intellectual or political hero ever could be; he was the man of the people, unlettered but thirsting for knowledge – like many of the film's viewers – as well as witty and brave. Shumyatsky, who generated the production of *Chapaev*, proclaimed it best of all Soviet films. Many Russians still share that opinion.[39]

The Chapaev tradition of civil war adventure survived in popular films such as the famous *We Are from Kronstadt* written by Vsevolod Vishnevsky. Like the contemporary American cowboy–Indian or colonial epics, it underlined the evil of the enemy by means of a savage execution scene. Historical hero-worship dominated most films about the revolution. *Man with a Gun* (1938), to take one example, offered a variant of the story of the peasant *khodok* setting out with a message for the tsar (Lenin, played effectively by Maxim Shtraukh). The talented director, Sergei Yutkevich, stuffed this film with political and cinematic clichés: Lenin is witty and democratic but harshly intolerant of liberalism; and the Whites are fat and angry with clipped voices and bejeweled fingers. But there are also powerful visual moments, as when Lenin "reads" the revolution on film footage through a hole in his newspaper, or when a snarling and vicious armored train assaults the idyllic palace park of Tsarskoe Selo near Petrograd. The film is also a landmark in popular culture because it was the on-screen singing debut of a handsome fairhaired boy with a wide grin, the future movie, radio, and television star, Mark Bernes (1911–1969).

Much less famous and hardly mentioned in the chronicles of the 1930s was *Karo* (1937), a favorite among youngsters who went to see it again and again. The viewing records of film scholar Maya Turovskaya show that this film outstripped many of the well-known movie classics of the time in terms of multiple viewing. Based on a tale by Arkady Gaidar, *Karo* was a simple but very busy civil war adventure set in the wilds of Armenia during the strife between nationalists and Bolsheviks. Like *Chapaev* and *Little Red Imps*, it demonized the enemy (in this case the Dashnak movement); and like them it was packed with action. With its child hero, clever tricks and narrow escapes, exotic scenery, and beautiful songs with words by Lebedev-Kumach, *Karo* was the Soviet equivalent of Tom Sawyer, The Thief of Baghdad, and Gunga Din; and it answered the tastes of Soviet youngsters as well as offering the "right" politics and history.[40]

Contemporary adventure was offered in films about flying, building, and exploring. At least a dozen Soviet aviation films were made in the 1930s, a time of tremendous fascination with aircraft which, until the brutal bombing of Guernica by German Stukas during the Spanish Civil War, seemed romantic and harmless even in war. Some are strikingly similar to American pilot movies of the time: flight training enlivened by a love triangle, a hotheaded young stunt man vs. a seasoned instructor – as in *Flyers* (1935) – dangerous rescue missions, and foreign spies.[41] The culmination of the genre was Mikhail Kalatozov's *Valery Chkalov* (1941), a fictionalized film biography released in the States as *Wings of Victory*. This ultimate flight epos was encased in socialist realism and the mythology of the 1930s. The headstrong fighter pilot, grounded by his beloved mentor after the bridge stunt, is sent to the Volga where he marries. Brought back as a test pilot, he proves out a new monoplane for aircraft boss, Grigory Ordzhonikidze, and then goes on to captain transpolar flights. The tale is enhanced by shots of leather-clad airmen and the visual exploitation of the aeronautical designs of the age. Kalatozov's mastery (later revealed in *The Cranes are Flying*) is on display in the low-angle shots and heroic composition of frames. Chkalov's vaunted love of high culture is captured in a stroll with his fiance through Leningrad's Summer Garden of classical sculpture; his national character underlined as he nets fish on the Volga; his socialism unveiled when he answers an American reporter's question, "Are you rich? How much are you worth?" with the words "Yes, I have 180,000,000 – Soviet people."

Sergei Gerasimov's very popular Komsomol pictures of the 1930s mixed good politics with exotic adventure. *The Valiant Seven* (1936) provided arctic blizzards, prop-sleds, ski-planes, rescue, and romance. A fine cast of seven, portraying young communists locked in battle against the elements, is brought to life in a deft story which also depicts human heroism and ethnic solidarity (one hero is a Jew; another risks his life to save a dying Chukchi). *Komsomolsk* (1938), portrayed a town rising in the taiga amidst broken and mended love, sabotage, and euphoric youth. The director is at his best shooting scenes of trains, river boats on the Amur, lumber technology, ski matches, and festive balls. But characterization is weak and the element of villainy in the plot is crudely grafted onto the main story of adventurous construction, an obvious nod to the hysterical atmosphere of the purge going on at the time. Films of adventure and action along the Soviet frontier, one featuring a Rin-Tin-Tin-like border dog, were similar to the Canadian Mounted Police sagas made in Hollywood. *On the Frontier* (1938) combined a struggle against infiltrators with singing heroes.[42]

A truly remarkable phenomenon of Stalinist cinema were musical comedies, particularly the four musicals produced at two-year intervals by the major entertainment figures of the 1930s: Shumyatsky the executive, Lyubov Orlova the singing star, Grigory Alexandrov (her husband) the director, and Dunaevsky the composer. These films perfectly embodied the official theme of joyful life and sunny optimism. The first of them was *Happy-Go-Lucky Guys* (1934), a loose chain of *estrada* numbers performed by Leonid Utesov and his band in zany situations; it was – as critics lamented – Soviet Hollywood with white pianos and pearl-studded cellos. The original script by Erdman and Mass was "depoliticized" by Alexandrov who just wanted fun on screen. Its charm lies in the easy, smiling manner of blond and bland Utesov, the energy of Orlova as a house maid, and the sprightly tunes of Dunaevsky, especially "Heart" and the march which 2,000 Stakhanovites sang out spontaneously at the conclusion of their congress in 1935. The only Marxism in the movie was that of Groucho and his brothers at the moment when the jazzmen created havoc in the Bolshoi theater. Some politicians were hostile to its frolic, but Gorky – the arch-enemy of commercial culture – liked it for some reason and persuaded Stalin to see it. His approval assured its release; audience attendance did the rest. In his book, *Movies for the Millions*, Shumyatsky ridiculed critics for "pathetically beating their breast" over the success of this picture and identified them with the elitists and bourgeois snobs depicted in the movie itself.[43] The film fit the mood of 1934 perfectly and coincided with the onset of the short-lived jazz age.

By the time Orlova, Alexandrov, and Dunaevsky teamed up again to make *Circus* (1936), the reversal had begun and now fun had to be solemnized. Alert to this, the director toned down the slapstick of his previous film and politicized the comedy that Kataev, Ilf, and Petrov had written as *Under the Big Top*. *Circus*, in many ways the ultimate Stalinist film, blended satire and comedy, the popular arts of the era – cartoon, song, stage, arena, architecture – with the political ideas and cultic motifs of the Stalin state: antifascism, ethnic equality, the democratic constitution, the cult of aviation, the new Moscow construction, and the joy of life under Stalin. *Circus* was the culmination of a rash of earlier "American" theme films about Indians, Jews, and Blacks who find a safe, nonracist haven in the USSR (the best of them before *Circus* was *The Return of Nathan Becker*, 1932). Orlova starred again and Vladimir Volodin, as the Soviet ringmaster, established himself in a career of corny overacting. The Black baby, Jim Patterson, child of a Negro (who had come to Russia in 1932 to make a movie about Blacks) and his Russian wife, later became a Soviet naval officer and a well-known poet.[44]

In this exciting musical melodrama, an American circus star, Marion Dixon (the name itself is an arctic reference) played by Orlova, bears a Black child and is driven out of a Kansas town by White racists. Her protector and tormentor is the German ringmaster Franz von Kneischutz, a caricature of the popular movie star Conrad Veidt and a perfect cinematic Nazi – lustful, vindictive, anti-Russian, and inflated (literally by means of rubber tubing beneath his vestments). When the circus performs in Moscow, Marion falls in love with a handsome Russian acrobat – square-jawed and clean cut, in fact a Kirov look-alike – who, garbed in a white peasant tunic, sings "Song of the Motherland" to her at a white piano in the recently completed Hotel Moskva overlooking the Kremlin. Kneischutz in a jealous rage reveals Marion's secret by showing the Black child to the circus audience at the peak of her triumph. But the multi-ethnic Soviet public lullabies the baby in a half-dozen languages. The Yiddish words were sung by the famous actor Shlomo Mikhoels. The movie includes a lavish Hollywood dance number, a "flight" around the tent by Marion's aerial boyfriend, and an irrelevant Red Square parade with the principals marching into the camera, smiling at each other the way Mickey Rooney and Judy Garland used to do in the finales of their musicals, and singing about the land of the free in the year of the "most democratic of democratic constitutions."

Dunaevsky's songs from *Circus* were given massive distribution. Long before the movie reached the provinces, radio listeners were singing them as if they were folk songs. The melody of the theme "Song of the Motherland" (with an opening phrase that resembles both that of "Internationale" and "Stenka Razin") attained such stupendous popularity that it became in May 1939 the station signal of Radio Moscow and was played on the Kremlin chimes for many years. It sold in editions of 20 million and was heard among leftists in France, Britain, Italy, Spain, and the United States. Alexandrov heard 9,000 Londoners sing it in English in 1953! Opening with the words "Shiroka strana moya rodnaya" – O, Vast Country of Mine – the lyrics by Lebedev-Kumach (1898–1949) embodied some major myths about the early Stalin era. In the great purge trial of 1938, a prominent Old Bolshevik defendant, Aron Rozengolts, uttered these final words (he was shot the next day):

For the first time now we have a life, a full-blooded life, scintillating with joy and colour. Millions, tens of millions of people, children and citizens of the Soviet Union, including my own children, sing the song: "Native land of mine, so beautiful [O Vast Country of Mine] .../ There is no other land the whole world over/ Where man walks the earth so proud and free."

In the words of a former Soviet citizen, *Circus* "helped stifle the shots that killed several generations of revolutionaries, it masked Stalin's ruthlessness and Great Russian chauvinism, and it presented to the world the benign face of an idealistic socialist state on the march." At the same time, it publicly endorsed racial tolerance and entertained millions of ordinary people.[45]

Volga, Volga (1938) – a reference to the Stenka Razin song which is quoted in the film – was the third great musical comedy triumph for Alexandrov, Orlova, and Dunaevsky, this time with the brilliant performance of Igor Ilinsky as a bureaucrat who scorns folk music. Over against him were set the deeply Russian Volga River itself, birch trees, balalaikas, folk costumes, rich language, and simple peasant souls and hearts who yearn to sing their songs in Moscow. The idea sprang directly from the recently launched amateur folk music movement (see above). Orlova resembled the peasant messenger of olden times sent to Moscow to talk to the tsar: she races the bureaucrat up the Volga to Moscow to tell the prince the true story of the people and their musical culture. The river is the path between people and tsar; the bureaucrat is the eternal obstacle. In 1938 as the purges still raged, this was a warning to enemies of the people. Dunaevsky's patriotism is once more on display with songs about the length and breadth of the Russian land. The final scene shows the beautiful steamer "Joseph Stalin" docked alongside the gleaming new white columned River Station on the Moscow River, built to punctuate the completion of the Volga–Moscow canal. Its staircase leads up to the capital where the heroes find success and instant popularity for their music.

The Radiant Road (1940; released in a cut version in the USA as *Tanya*) is the pinnacle of social and political fantasy in prewar Stalinist cinema. Orlova, Volodin, Alexandrov, and Dunaevsky served up once more their winning recipe of patriotism, cornball sentiment, spectacular cinematic effects, and celebration of the new Moscow. Tanya (Orlova), a classical Cinderella with a smudged nose, rises through the textile industry to become a Stakhanovite superworker who can run hundreds of looms simultaneously and beat world records. (Orlova studied intensively on the mill floor to prepare herself for the exploits she performed on screen.) Along the way, Tanya learns her letters and wins the love of a clean-cut engineer – a Soviet prince charming with a pipe and a briefcase. She makes the dreamed-of pilgrimage to Moscow, and is decorated by the "peasant" President Kalinin in the opulent Kremlin Palace. The finale contains a splendid visual treatment of the just completed Agricultural Exhibit in Moscow, whose Central Pavilion resembled a palace. In one of the final shots, the living couple is foregrounded in front of Mukhina's statue of the male industrial worker, hammer in hand and the female agricultural worker, sickle in hand – thus suggesting equality of the sexes and simultaneously assuring the male engineer the dominant role in this "equal" partnership.

The movie asserts constantly that this is real life and not a fairy tale. In the finale, a chorus sings the aviation song, "Ever Higher" which opens with the words: "We are born to make fairy tales come true." Indeed the film is roughly modeled on the rise of the then famous Stakhanovite textile workers, the Vinogradovas. Orlova is the victorious plebeian, as she was in *Happy-Go-Lucky Guys* and in *Volga, Volga*. Social mobility through the Soviet system, a breakthrough to "consciousness" with the help of a mentor (in this case, a female schoolteacher), and triumph over a languid bureaucrat and a wrecker – all the ingredients of socialist realism are present. But Alexandrov and his associates rise above the usual drabness of the masterplot by use of the fantastic *mise-en-scène* at the conclusion where monumental structure is framed by dream-filled billows in the sky. The uncut original (which I have not seen) has an automobile flying over the rooftops of Moscow![46] The fusion of the traditional fairy tale with the metallic and mechanical furniture of modernity and with the official scenario for success accounts for the immense popular triumph of this movie – designed for and consumed by "the millions."

These films established Alexandrov and Orlova as the royal couple of popular movies in the 1930s. Born in Kharkov, Alexandrov (real name, Mormonenko, 1903–1984) began in theater, then became an active collaborator of Eisenstein in the 1920s and played Chief Officer Gilyarovsky in *Potemkin*. Alexandrov accompanied Eisenstein to Hollywood where his ideas for mass film germinated. Back in Russia, their ways parted, Alexandrov turning to popular marketable films, his mentor trying to keep alive the aesthetic traditions of the 1920s. Under the sponsorship of Shumyatsky and Stalin, Alexandrov became the main cinematic impresario for fun movies in the thirties and forties and was even brought in to coach the State Jazz Orchestra on matters of dress and style. Orlova (1901–1975), who appeared on screen as an ideal rustic and Slavic blonde beauty with ample hips and bright eyes, was actually the product of a Moscow intelligentsia family who claimed Tolstoy and Chaliapin as acquaintances. She began as a conservatory piano student then went into operetta and silent films and reached maturity in her thirties in the prewar films. Orlova was perfect as the open and honest foil to snobbish ladies, cruel racists, and flabby bureaucrats. She was the most popular movie star of the era – and the light of her star was reflected onto the lofty dictator, rumored to be her admirer.[47]

The musical comedy films of Ivan Pyrev were the rustic equivalents of those of Alexandrov. Pyrev was a genre director who used carnival and fair not as an intellectual metaphor (as in *Dr. Mabuse* or *The Third Man*) but as a "realistic" setting for his depictions of a Soviet rural arcadia. His three prewar examples of this genre were *The Rich Bride* (1938), *The Tractor Drivers* (1939), and *The Swineherd and the Shepherd* (1941). All their plots revolve around socialist competition on the *kolkhoz*, mutual misunderstanding between heroine and hero, and the satisfying closure of a joyful wedding. The films are adorned with engaging music by Dunaevsky, peasant choruses, vigorous scenes of friendly agrarian contests, and folkloric settings and costumes. They were in fact fairy tales designed to entertain and to demonstrate the happy life and superior life-style of the Soviet collective farm.[48]

Of the many films that mythologized revolutionary history, two deserve brief mention. *The Maxim Trilogy* (1935–1938) joined the talents of Trauberg and Kozintsev – who had learned to produce for mass audiences – Maxim Shtraukh, and Boris Chirikov in an epic stretching from 1910 to 1918, full of revolutionary songs, police repression, Duma politics, Menshevik and Anarchist "treachery," executions, and assassinations. But the movie that fueled the fear and hate of the purge years was Ermler's *Great Citizen* (1937–1939), a partial portrait of Sergei Kirov (Peter Shakhov in the movie) who was assassinated in 1934. It has recently been paired by Soviet film scholars with Leni Riefenstahl's *Triumph of the Will* as a representative "film of the era of totalitarianism."[49] Through *mise-en-scène*, lighting, and photography, the villains are rendered as devils, gangsters, and vermin, exactly as in the trial transcripts published in the press and in the graphic art of the time. So loathsome is the arch-villain of this movie, Kartashev, that the actor Ivan Bersenev was reluctant to take it on for fear of being lynched on the street after release of the film. Kirov-Shakhov was presented as a handsome populist and a hero-martyr (played by Nikolai Bogolyubov, the handsome hero of *Valiant Seven*); two of his friends were partly encoded as Lenin and Stalin. For good measure, Chirikov made an appearance as the mature "Maxim." Movies like *Great Citizen* were key ingredients in the cultural system that, among other things, explained and justified the terror.

The much vaunted *Alexander Nevsky* (1938) by Eisenstein was *lubok* entertainment executed by a genius. The hand of the master is discernible in the ice battle formations inspired by Uccello's fifteenth-century battle painting. But the popular and the political clearly dominate this film. The Teutonic enemy is totally demonized (with the help of Sergei Prokofiev's brilliant music): the atrocity scenes are pictorially reminiscent of Russian World War I postcards and posters. The Russian people are enveloped in folk fantasy and myth. *Nevsky* was an early effort to glorify ancient Russian national leaders and it was widely emulated during and after the war. The leading actor Nikolai Cherkasov whose radiant good looks were sanctified by Eisenstein's lighting and camera work was clearly a composite portrait of the Stalinist folk hero of the 1930s: stern, brave, fair, and at one with the people. With the signing of the Nazi–Soviet pact in 1939 this and all other anti-

German films were withdrawn from circulation, only to be reissued in 1941 after the German attack.

The filmmakers of the 1930s combined politics and entertainment to produce popular art of a special kind. As in tsarist times, cinema reflected what was happening in the other genres of popular culture and in society. Folklorism, adventure, optimism, and labor hagiography were blended into scripts, acting styles, scenery, casting, and music. Although the battles that wracked the twenties were largely over, Soviet cinema was scarred in a number of ways. There were shortfalls in the production quotas (one of which led to the arrest of Shumyatsky in 1938; he was later shot). Wholly eliminated from the Soviet screen were the innovative experiments of the great masters: the magnificent art deco film, *Stern Youth*, by Avram Room was one of many consigned to the shelf for decades. Largely excluded also were foreign films that would certainly have rivaled the Stalinist ones in mass appeal. Monopolization, though not unique to the Soviet movie industry, was nevertheless a major feature in producing "movies for the millions" in this era.

Many cultural differences divided Nazi cinema from Soviet Russia, including the total exclusion of Jews from the industry in the former and their active participation in the latter; the open teaching of racism in the former – *The Eternal Jew* and *Jew-Suss* being the most notorious examples – and its repudiation in the latter. Both regimes used the medium consciously for political–ideological purposes to a much greater degree than did the studios of Western Europe and America in that epoch. Both held sway over the industry, controlled the import of foreign films, imposed heavy censorship (in Germany Goebbels was the highest court; in the USSR it was Stalin himself), commissioned certain directly political themes, and used the escapist adventure and musical indirectly for state and national purposes. But the Soviets were far more active, intensive, and successful in harnessing the cinematic screen to these purposes, a fact even admitted and lamented by Nazi leaders. Stalinist cinema was a key element of his spectacle state.

The greatest show on earth

The popular culture of the Stalinist period was a conservative one rooted in the dogmatism of a church-like Communist party, the authoritarian traditions of the state, the tastes of the lower classes, the moralizing elitism of the intelligentsia, and the cultural aspirations of the new Soviet middle class. As in Nazi Germany and Fascist Italy, it was a culture of comfort and tradition amid the imagery of power, modernization, and technology. The folk revival was equally striking in all three of these and served not only the obvious nationalist aims, but as a reassuring social compact wherein the hearts of the leaders and the people beat as one to the national rhythms of *Volk, popolo,* and *narod.*[50] The Soviet case, however, differed dramatically from the others in that it promoted folklorism in all the national republics and regions as a binding force to the center, a signifier of loyalty, and a commitment to ethnic equality. In the USSR, Stalin set the tone and the bureaucrats helped to shape the popular culture that dominated public places and events for decades; under different conditions artistically untrained movie, radio, and music executives did the same thing in the American entertainment world at about the same time. In both cases decision makers of rather humble background relied on their own instincts and the able assistance of talented and facile composers and directors as to what the masses would respond to; and they were usually right.

The horrors of collectivization, the great famine, the recurring waves of purge and killings, the vast network of slave and death camps were not only totally absent from popular culture; their possibility was culturally denied by visions of rural prosperity, urban harmony and success, and a new dawn of freedom. A web of fantasy and a giant political coverup deflected dissatisfaction of the masses against alleged enemies of the people. Fantasists ascribed all achievements to the great leader and all failings to saboteurs, traitors, and spies. Agricultural shortfalls were hidden behind paintings, operettas, and movies about *kolkhoz* feasts with tables groaning under food and wine (see fig. 12). Industrial misery and brutalization in the workplace were not permitted to blemish the lives of fictional or idealized super-workers. Ethnic tensions were belied in cinema and fiction. And the sound of execution trenches being dug and bullets crashing into skulls of NKVD victims were inaudible beneath the soaring and joyful songs of enthusiasm and accomplishment. Millions sang these bright and cheerful mass songs and saw the ebullient musical comedy films that begot them. The Russian intelligentsia is still debating the legitimacy and the morality of those who produced this culture.

How could political and expressive worlds diverge so widely? If one views the popular culture of the 1930s only as an immense mask or an engine of fraud, then no further analysis is needed. Those who interpret the function of mass culture in purely ideological terms are inclined to read it as simply an imposed system of mystification.

Common sense and evidence belie such a reading. The Gramscian concept of hegemony is certainly more useful because it describes culture as not only an implement of the ruling class, "but also its acceptance as 'normal reality' or 'common sense' by those in practice subordinated to it."[51] In many realms of culture – high and low, democratic, market driven, or otherwise – there is no necessary contradiction between fraud, deceit, and manipulation on the one hand and authentic popular enjoyment on the other. The violation of reality, the call for suspension of disbelief, the assault on plausibility are central to popular genres, even "realistic" ones. When people read or watch something that is palpably untrue (as in opera, science fiction, or most movies), they do not "believe" it: they do or do not enjoy it. But they do not "disbelieve" it either: they look for a core of truth inside the art they consume, whether or not it is objectively true. And a core of truth indubitably existed for millions of people in the popular culture of the Stalinist 1930s. To call such culture "escapist" is a truism.

But this culture was not a unified or homogeneous culture. It served many functions, in the words of film historian Maya Turovskaya – "escapist, socializing, compensatory, informational, recreational, prestige-giving, aesthetic, and emotional," among others – and not only mobilizational and mystifying. The late Lydia Ginsburg, an eminent semiotician and literary scholar, put it another way: "People are wrong to imagine the calamitous epochs of the past as totally taken up by calamity. They also consist of a great deal else – the sort of things which life in general consists of, although against a particular background. The thirties is not just hard work and fear, it's also a mass of talented people with a will to carry things out."[52] Neither of these women have or ever had any sympathy with Stalinism whatsoever.

The officially sponsored cultural system encouraged people to have "fun" within a context of order, morality, and labor, without succumbing to frivolity and vice. Popular culture functioned at two levels: direct political communication and controlled spontaneity – the vaunted safety valve. The former was served by mass song and the more politically charged of the novels, films, and stage shows; the latter by smoothed-out jazz, fairy tales and adventures, message musicals, and the light variety stage. Banished altogether were hot swing music, open satire, and slapstick. Rosalinda Sartorti provides a brilliant analysis of how this worked in organized leisure. The great holiday parades in the 1930s were solemn rituals separated from fun and relaxation. But a major drive was launched to organize leisure fun as well in Moscow's Gorky Park of Culture, the largest in the country with its huge swimming pool, an *estrada* theater, a "dance island," a theater seating 25,000, and scores of radio speakers. This park hosted tens of thousands of visitors on workdays, hundreds of thousands on days off and admission was free. From 1935 until the war, great "carnivals" were mounted in the park, partly modeled on the traditional folk festival (*narodnoe gulyane*) with carnival figures, masks, torch-light parades, fireworks, amusements, music, and dance – "a true fairy-tale world" but one that was highly planned and controlled and, as Sartorti notes, "another form of Socialist Realism."[53]

One must not exaggerate the scope of Soviet organized leisure in the 1930s. John Scott, living at the great construction site of Magnitogorsk, saw parks, singing clubs, gramophones, radios, guitars, and balalaikas. But the countryside obviously contained little of it. Leisure time surveys, prominent in the 1920s, ceased being made from 1936 until after Stalin's death. But one of the last of them claimed that residents of selected cities spent only about an hour a week each on books and radio listening, less than that on theater and film, much less (0.3 hrs.) on sports, but over seven hours in traditional pursuits – visiting or going out. Research on workers' culture reveals that they spent less time on reading than in the 1920s and on other cultural pursuits as well, that libraries had been severely censored and curtailed, and that the lower classes continued to prefer Russian and foreign classics to Soviet works.[54]

The prohibition of genuine public satire created a void for some people who filled it by means of illicit jokes whose currency was very limited; people were thrown in jail for much less than reciting one of them. No counterculture could be built around them and they could never reach the media. But in outcast and underground collectives, such as gangs, orphan homes, and prison camps, countercultures flourished, complete with argot, customs, jokes, songs, violent cult figures, martyrologies, and hagiographies. When NEP and its demi-monde were eliminated and a large segment of criminals, homeless children, and prostitutes were swept off the streets in the great round-ups of the early thirties, the *blatnaya kultura* of the Russian urban underground was relocated en masse into the jails and camps, joining that of the older inmates to create an extraordinarily huge and rich cultural system that lasted for thirty years.

4   Holy war and cold war
1941–1953

Narod and Rodina

Understanding a nation's experience of war is often difficult for outsiders. War creates myth and memory, sometimes embodied in great
art but more often in popular culture. The latter helped to shape the
mood of the Russian people during those dreadful years and the
persistent recollection of that mood in the minds of millions has
continued to configure popular culture in the decades since 1945. The
wartime feeling was, in the words of a literary scholar, "the blending of
unspeakable grief, love of country, and fear." The human losses in this
war were forty times greater than those of Britain and seventy times
those of the United States – greater indeed than those of all the
belligerents combined. Soviet people may not know these comparative
figures, but they know through family memory as much as through
public reminders that their collective suffering was colossal. In the
Soviet memorialization of the war, "memory enshrined" by the
government has often converged with the actual recollection of it by
the people. To this process popular culture has contributed a major
share.[1]

When the German legions tore into Soviet territory on June 22, 1941,
a huge nation was thrown into agonizing panic and confusion. Stalin
withdrew to his dacha for two weeks. Whole armies were swallowed
up in the cauldron. Towns, villages, airfields, and industries were
systematically destroyed by Wehrmacht troops, Panzer divisions, and
Luftwaffe pilots. The ears of citizens were assaulted by the terror raids
of Stuka dive bombers with their inhuman siren wail. Leningrad was
encircled, Moscow was approached, and the Ukraine was overrun.
Within weeks, news began to trickle down about the massive losses at
the front. In later months the picture of the horrors of occupation took
on an even more vivid and hideous shape: executions, massacres of
hostages, POWs systematically starved, peasants dragged off as slave

laborers to German factories, beleaguered Leningrad slowly perishing. On the home-front, vast undulations rocked society: mobilization, the evacuation of industries and populations, and the relocation of government offices and cultural establishments – including film studios and theaters. Over a million women were pulled into the war to serve as flyers, soldiers, tankers, and partisans as well as in traditional wartime roles of nurses, doctors, and anti-aircraft gunners. The cultural community was enlisted to popularize the major wartime themes: heroism and love of country; hate and ridicule of the invader.

Military valor was the first theme to occupy the media. Cities were heroized for their endurance or resistance; Leningrad, Brest, Kiev, Odessa, Sevastopol, and Stalingrad were eventually named Hero Cities. Mythic cults of human heroes and martyrs arose around the partisans, the twenty-eight Panfilov men, the five sailors of Sevastopol, Dovator's cavalry, the Young Guard of Krasnodon, and Captain Gastello who plunged his burning plane into an enemy armored column. After the fabled Alexander Matrosov in February 1942 threw his body across a German machine-gun nest to block its fire, an entire movement arose around this remarkable combat suicide, including 332 recorded cases of direct emulation. Film and song exalted his valor. Matrosov's image was magnetic: a tough orphan boy and convict released from incarceration to fight for the nation. The whole episode is now subject to a searching revision by historians. The legend of the partisan high-school girl, Zoya Kosmodemyanskaya who was tortured and hanged by the Germans early in the war was stamped into the memories and devotional life of wartime Russia in poetry, drama, radio, movie, photo, statue, and children's tale (see fig. 13). Few Soviet citizens today do not know her exploit; in the 1950s her bobbed partisan hairdo was adopted by thousands of young women in the People's Republic of China. In the mythic version of her life, Zoya was not only courageous, but also a model pupil and an admirer of Lenin, Stalin, and the heroes of the 1812 war against Napoleon. Furthermore, she never lied or smoked.[2] In all Soviet cultural icons, personal habits were linked to ideological soundness.

The broadcasting about German atrocities soon evoked the theme of hatred in Soviet public life. Implacable loathing pulsed through both high and popular culture. The verses of Alexei Surkov recorded indescribable bestialities committed by the invaders. In the poem 'I Hate" he declared:

> My house has been defiled by the Prussians,
> Their drunken laughter dims my reason.
> And with these hands of mine
> I want to strangle every one of them.

Konstantin Simonov's "Kill Him" was the culmination of a frenzied rage:

> If you do not want to have
> The girl you courted
> But never dared to kiss
> Because your love was pure –
> If you don't want fascists to bruise and beat
> And stretch her naked on the floor
> In hatred, tears, and blood,
> And see three human dogs despoil
> All that you hold dear
> In the manliness of your love ...
> Then kill a German, kill him soon
> And every time you see one – kill him.

Hate alternated with ridicule. Germans, especially Hitler and his minions, were variously portrayed in the media as doomed descendants of Napoleon, physical degenerates – brutish, sly and stupid, gross, fat or bony, effeminate, and evil. After Stalingrad, the theme of imminent victory began to emerge and it fused with a refashioned optimism of the 1930s.[3]

The deepest and most comprehensive theme of wartime sensibilities was home and country. Visions of simplicity, family joys, a rustic cabin, or a broken fence were framed again and again in the popular culture. The motherland (*rodina*) – often represented as a maternal figure – became an object of unabashed idolatry, along with a cult of Russian history, traditions, cultural treasures, and the Russian terrain itself. The political and high cultural establishments revived great heroes of the tsarist past, reached an accord with the Orthodox church, and linked the Russian classics with the national liberation. The land – its rivers, steppes, meadows, birch trees, and endless forests – was woven into wartime culture by means of nature symbolism. To it was added the special thematics of such sacred and endangered places as Moscow and Leningrad. This allowed the reemergence in Russian public culture of personal life, intimate feelings, a deep emotional authenticity, and even quasi-religiosity that had been absent from it during the "optimistic" thirties. Although partly offset after Stalingrad by bombastic motifs of victory and military might, they suffused and characterized the entire wartime experience.

Arsenal of words

Soviet printing presses vied with machine-guns and artillery as weapons of war: they cranked out a hail of periodicals and a barrage of books. Poetry, a national preoccupation, became more than ever an art of popular culture. Russians adore the music of their language, the expressiveness of verse and rhyme; they listen with rapture to public readings live or on the radio. During the war, the regime published hundreds of thousands of pocket editions of verse; and thousands of amateur poets wrote down or recited their works. Poetry and song were ubiquitous. "When war flared up," wrote Boris Pasternak, "its real horrors and real dangers, the threat of a real death, were a blessing compared to the inhuman reign of fantasy, and they brought relief by limiting the magic force of the dead letter." The most popular epic poem of the period was Alexander Tvardovsky's *Vasily Terkin*, a semi-picaresque tale of a simple soldier, a Russian Schweik, wise and witty and humane – the universal "little man" in the ranks who personified for the multitudes the notion that this was a war of the simple people who sometimes forgot the rules and who liked to speak in a salty and folksy idiom. The absence of piety and pomposity and the honest touches of folk culture made *Terkin* a major signpost of the emotional shift in wartime culture. The remarkable flood of versed "replies to Terkin" written by warriors of all ranks demonstrates how deeply Tvardovsky penetrated the feelings of the ordinary Russian at war.[4]

But it was Simonov's "Wait for Me," an elegiac if inelegant love poem, that millions recited as if it were a prayer; that women repeated as tears streamed down their faces; that men adopted as their own expression of the mystical power of a woman's love; that can still moisten the eyes of elderly Soviet citizens.[5]

> Wait for me and I'll come back,
> Wait with might and main.
> Wait when you are drowned by grief
> In floods of yellow rain.
> Wait amid the driving snow,
> Wait in torrid heat.
> Wait when others cease to wait
> Forgetting yesterday.

It was made into a mediocre play by the author and into a now forgotten movie. Seventeen song versions of it appeared, some of them still enduring. The focus was on personal life, the agony of separation and loneliness, the towering belief in fidelity and endurance. The same poet's "Remember, Alesha, the Roads Round Smolensk?" (addressed to Surkov) was bathed in another image, deeply national and suffused with religious emotion.

> I guess you know what the homeland really is –
> It's not the house in the city of my happy days.
> It's the backwoods of our long-gone ancestors
> And the simple crosses on Russian graves.

Novels and stories flooded the reading market. Tolstoy's *War and Peace* – now read for its parallels and promises – was issued in a print run of 500,000 copies in Leningrad alone. Journalists wrote fiction and novelists turned to reportage; of the thousands of writers who went to the front, 275 were killed including the beloved Arkady Gaidar. Simonov's *Days and Nights* (1944), a reportorial saga of the battle of Stalingrad, attained wide popularity by its minute detail, its folkloric ornament, its evocation of mother Russia and mother Volga (into which a character dips his helmet as in ancient Russian epics) and its frank depiction of suffering, courage, compassion, and faith. Fadeev's *Young Guard* (1945), employed a classic device for many a war novel and film: a rustic idyll disrupted by the terrors of invasion. The story concerns a band of youthful resisters in a Donbass city, but it is framed by nature, the steppe, the forest, and the Don; its characters are medieval princes and warriors, this time in a holy quest for consciousness.[6]

Journalism, a major vehicle of popular communication in the war years, was not only an informational lifeline but, like the radio, an emotional instrument of morale and a fund of stories used in other branches of popular culture. So close did reportage relate to fiction that sometimes they were almost inseparable – as in Simonov's *Days and Nights*. The master of journalistic morale-building was Ilya Ehrenburg (1891–1967). As a onetime modernist writer, a longtime resident abroad, a Jew, a participant in the Spanish Civil War, and a close friend of many purge victims of the 1930s, Ehrenburg seemed an unlikely bearer of the torch of national resistance to the enemy. Yet "marginal" figures have often been spokesmen of the mainstream – in Russia and elsewhere. His non-Russianness may have added poignancy to the vitriolic – even racist – hatred and contempt for the Germans (called "fish-eyed oafs" and "green-eyed slugs") that he poured into the pages of *Red Star*, the military paper that was devoured by the soldiers. He was wise enough to catch the Russian spirit and the right note of harshness and bitter irony. Simonov wrote in the pages of *Red Star* at an earthier level. Like his American counterpart, Ernie Pyle, he aimed at the "little guy," the dog soldier of the infantry who slogged through mud and fear, year after year. Simonov's evocation of the siege of Stalingrad is among the best writing of the war and achieves pictorial and even cinematic magnificence as he describes droning bombers soaring over the wide steppe and gushers erupting in the Volga. And in a different voice, he etches the human marginalia of war in his vignette of a petite army nurse singing cossack songs from the fender of a truck on its way to the front.[7]

Song of Russia

The warring nations of 1939–1945 showed an extraordinary tendency to exalt and revere classical music and, through media promotion, turn it into something like a popular art. The occupied nations treasured their own musical heritage, particularly the romantic productions of the previous century. The music of Dvorak, Chopin, Rachmaninov, and Grieg in American radio and movies was associated with the heroic struggles of beleaguered peoples. In war-wracked Russia the most mournful strains of Chopin, Beethoven, and Chaikovsky filled the concert halls and airwaves. On the radio, Russian classics lorded it over folk music, lyrical songs, and military band music.[8] Soviet composers turned their talents to war-related subjects – Shostakovich's "Leningrad" Symphony being the most famous of these.

But it was popular song that really took possession of the masses. As the author of an otherwise bad book put it, "when great events are unfolding, art does not always keep pace with life. But the people do not wait. They want to sing songs that reflect reality."[9] Thousands were written by professional and amateur composers – 200 on Stalingrad alone. Over 100 songs were composed in Moscow in the first four days of the war. Contests and festivals abounded. A virtual song frenzy was released by the invasion, indicating a deeply held belief in the magic power of word and melody. Soldiers, sailors, nurses, and officers wrote their feelings into songs, set to old Russian pieces such as "Volga Boatmen" (Ei, ukhnem) or "Atop the Volga Stands a Rock" (Est na Volge utes) and to prewar mass songs. Variants sprung up for every branch of service. A female sergeant, Tatyana Ivanchuk wrote a song about how her friend, the fighter pilot Lieutenant Valeriya Khomya-kova shot down a German Stuka. Since formula and cliché were so much a part of prewar song, it was not difficult for amateurs to grind out lyrics about the Volga, the Don, the steppe, the white birch, and the vast space of the Russian land. Prewar songs evoked associations from school and teenage years, the golden days of youth, courtship and romance, home town and loved ones – or older genres that sang of the Russian folk and land.[10] As in all the fighting armies, song was closely linked to nostalgic recall.

The prewar "Katyusha" was a universal soldiers' refrain which generated dozens of new versions, making Katyusha now a soldier, a nurse, a partisan, or – in the most famous one – the rocket which "embraced Fritz" and "kissed [the fascists] on the forehead." It achieved international fame and was a marching song of leftist Italian partisans fighting against the German occupiers. Movie hit songs, especially those from Orlova's films, were sung by the troops. Although Dunaevsky's optimistic and joyous songs suffered a decline during the war, in September 1942, during the defence of Stalingrad, someone began singing his "Song of the Motherland" and it was taken up by thousands of troops across the front. Pessimism was taboo: soldiers and commanders criticized the line in Konstantin Listov's song "Zemlyanka": "I am far away from you, but only four steps to death."[11]

Big band jazz was freed up in the looser cultural milieu of the war. In 1941, at the Hermitage Garden in Moscow, Utesov put on a jazz program called Beat the Enemy. He successfully blended sweet jazz elements into the wartime mood: his "Bombardiers" (sung in English and Russian by his wife Edit Utesova) is a straight adaptation of the American hit, "Comin' in on a Wing and a Prayer"; and "Golden Lights" sounds like a Russian theme being played by the Glenn Miller band. When Utesov sang "Danube Waves" (Anniversary Waltz), he employed the kind of topical pathos that the American Al Jolson did at about the same time. Even the anti-Nazi novelty tune, "Baron von der Pshik" (Baron Zilch) is reminiscent of Spike Jones' once famous "Right in der Fuhrer's Face." American tunes such as "All of Me" and "Sunny Side of the Street," were played by Soviet frontline bands. Rail-waymen, aviators, cooks, and the NKVD had their own jazz bands and publishing houses produced "anti-fascist" songs and marches for them.

The ensembles of Boris Rensky, Skomorovsky, Tsfasman, Utesov (who now led the USSR State Band), and others were warmly received at the front and in the fleet. There was never enough jazz music for the troops. When *Sun Valley Serenade* appeared on Soviet screens in 1944, the popularity of Glenn Miller's style rose even further. The wartime jazz star was "Eddie" (Adolph, but called Adi or Edi) Rosner (1910–   ), born in Berlin, the son of a Polish-Jewish shoemaker. Rosner fled into Soviet territory at the beginning of the war. Along the way from Berlin to Russia, he made the transition from violin to trumpet and from conservatory music to big band. As head of the Belorussian jazz ensemble before the invasion of 1941, he was an affluent Soviet prince under the protection of the local satrap, an avid jazz fan. In 1941 he moved to Moscow and then toured the front. An admirer of the American trumpeter and band leader, Harry James, Rosner banished the balalaika and concertina from his orchestra and played straight American jazz.[12]

Among the big wartime hit songs were "Little Blue Scarf" (the theme song of Klavdiya Shulzhenko who sang it at the front and in blockaded cities; see fig. 14), Blanter's "My Beloved" (1941), and "Dark is the Night" (Bogoslovsky/Agatov) – the last made famous in the film *Two Warriors* which starred Mark Bernes (see below). It sings of bullets whistling across the steppe in fierce battle while far away the soldier's wife wipes away a tear beside the cradle of their child. Ambiguity about impending death intrudes in this and many other songs: the singer believes that his wife's fidelity and love will protect him from the bullets of the dark night; but death which stalks him daily is not to be feared. "Wait for Me" (1941) set to music soared to success on the wings of Simonov's lyrics (this and "Blue Scarf" remained popular even in German-occupied Latvia where anti-Russian feeling ran to murderous proportions). "Ah, the Roads" (Novikov/Oshanin) sang of everyday frontline life. Purely political songs, such as the Kompaneets-Oshanin "Into Combat for the Motherland – and for Stalin," were exceptional. Most evoked the countryside – Vladimir Lugovskoy's "Russian Land" – or the home town. The oft-cited "Beloved Town" (Bogoslovsky/Dolmatovsky), though written in 1939, was popularized in the movie *Destroyers* (and here the "town" is wreathed in pastorale: "familiar home, green garden, tender glance").[13] There were also a few semi-scatological anti-German satirical songs, one of them set to "Bei mir bist du shein," a Jewish song popular in the States in the 1930s and 1940s.

The song that generated the greatest emotional reaction was "Holy War" (or Sacred War – Svyashchennaya voina) with music by General Alexandrov of the Red Army Ensemble and words by Lebedev-Kumach:

> Rise up, rise up o mighty land
> And in mortal battle join
> To smite the evil fascist spirit
> That wretched and accursed horde.
>
> Let our righteous fury
> Boil up into a raging wave
> This is a people's war
> This is our holy war.

Even in Russian, these words, though moving, are restrained and declamatory. But the immense cumulative effect of all the verses – Russians tend to sing songs entire – is augmented by the melody, ascending and descending majestically in a minor key in a marching rhythm written in waltz time! Stories abound in soldiers' memoirs about its impact. Heard on the radio after a long isolation, it could bring tears or bursts of martial valor to hardened partisans. Some older songs had the same power: when a unit of sailors in Kharkov was ordered by Hitler to be executed by drowning, they sang an old Russian song, adopted for the Black Sea Fleet, and revived in the 1930s: "The Ocean Covered Vast Expanses" (Raskinulos more shiroko). Some soldiers' songs from 1904–1905 and a few from the civil war period were revived.[14]

In June 1943 as part of the renationalization campaign, Stalin decided to replace the "Internationale" as the Soviet anthem. There were 172 poets and 76 composers competing and the winning entry, again with the music of General Alexandrov (actually the former Party hymn) and words by the writer Sergei Mikhalkov (1913–) and the Uzbek poet Garold El-Registan, was announced on the radio in December 1943 with the explanation that the old anthem did not reflect the social changes undergone by the USSR in recent years. It was first heard on the air New Year's Day 1944. "Internationale" now became the party anthem. The lyrics of the new national anthem were as pompous as the music is solemn and pretentious.

> Our union by great Mother Russia was welded,
> A country of mighty republics are we.
> Long life to the land that the people created,
> The great Soviet Union, united and free.[15]

Soldiers and ordinary citizens of course continued to sing their own songs, including folk, prerevolutionary popular, and even underground songs. When the mood of war lightened somewhat in 1944, "the year of ten victories," the journalist Alexander Werth heard these often; one was an indecent version of one of Mark Bernes' hits, "Kostya." Jokes were heard about "Roosevelt's eggs," a pun ("eggs" in Russian also means testicles) on Lend Lease food; and a charwoman, hearing talk about a second front, was heard to say that one front was enough. The general mood was also less somber in the deep evacuation centers beyond the Volga. In Saratov – called Professaratov by wits in reference to the density of evacuated educators – theaters, the opera, and the movies were going strong in 1943.[16]

In the rear, at the front, and on the air

The production of popular culture during the war was a result of both voluntarism and mobilization, but the latter occurred to a degree undreamed of in other belligerent states, even Nazi Germany. This was especially true of live performance. Plays in the unoccupied towns were of course both censored and commissioned by the regime. The earliest were short one-act plays, manufactured at top speed like the *agitki* of the civil war. Relevant classics were brushed off and updated; more than fifty new productions were on the boards by August 1941. Dramas about the military leaders Alexander Nevsky, Suvorov, and Kutuzov dominated the historical genre – with the parallels heavily underlined. The most famous of those set in the war itself was *The Front* (1942) by Alexander Korneichuk – well-known in his own right and also as the husband of the ardent Polish pro-Soviet publicist, Wanda Wasilewska. This play was designed to discredit the old civil war style of cavalry charge, individual heroism, and lax discipline – known as *partizanshchina* – and endorse the innovative use of planes, tanks, and mechanized units. The conflict was dramaturgically embodied in a generational struggle between young and old. *Front* was staged simultaneously at several theaters and serialized in *Pravda* in August 1942. Soviet wartime theater contrasted starkly to that on Broadway where comedies and musicals reigned unchallenged.[17]

Light entertainment on stage receded in the rear area for a while due to the harsh psychology of the moment and the need for blackouts. But it too was soon enlisted for the war. In June 1942 – a low ebb in Soviet military fortunes – a variety show at the Moscow Hermitage theater featured the singing of "Tipperary" and a Soviet–American dance with allied flags as decor. Circus clowns had only to re-costume the old targets Kerensky, Lord Curzon, and Makhno into Nazi villains. The Durovs put on The Three Gs: Gitler (Hitler), Gimmler (Himmler), and Goebbels, all played by dogs. The Moscow Operetta Theater shared the stage with the army's Red Banner Song and Dance Ensemble and a few operettas adopted a wartime theme: *Forest Tale,* which dealt with the partisans; and *The Ocean Covered Vast Expanses,* taken from the song mentioned above. But the undying *Silva* continued to amuse audiences.[18]

A great flurry of performance art took place in mobile "frontline brigades," show-business troupes of actors, singers, ballet dancers, folk musicians, circus acts, and other kinds of entertainers who regaled the troops in mixed genre shows right behind the fighting lines. One participant claims that some 45,000 artists serving in 3,720 brigades performed over 400,000 concerts at the front. The cultural offering was eclectic: at one end were all the light genres; at the other, poetry readings and scenes from Chaikovsky's *Swan Lake* and Shakespearean plays. The Obraztsov Central Puppet Theater alone put on more than 400 shows in towns and villages, army camps and hospitals, frontline dugouts, and partisan forest encampments. Elena Gogoleva, a dramatic actress at the Moscow Maly Theater, traveled to the front early in 1942 and gave forty concerts a month. After performances, she recalled, pilots would take off on bombing missions "to give our own concerts" for the Germans. Her frontline brigade staged excerpts from classical drama, poems and fables, folk songs and dances. Other frontline audiences heard Chaikovsky played on the violin followed by a singing of "Dark is the Night" and a spontaneous outbreak of folk dancing. The dancer Tamara Tkachenko – later famous as a folk choreographer – recalls giving fifty-one performances in seventeen days in the region of the old Napoleonic invasion route. Her company included *estrada* and radio stars, and the extremely popular folk singer Lydia Ruslanova. Movie actress Lyubov Orlova visited almost every sector of the front.[19] Comic satire and *estrada* of every sort flourished at the front. In 1943, a comedian acted out a Kukryniksy poster of Hitler in a wedding dress, crying because he lost his "ring," i.e. the twenty-two German divisions encircling Stalingrad.[20]

Folk culture rose to full magnitude in the patriotic war. A dozen ensembles were added to the old and sent to the front. In the summer of 1944 the folk revival erupted into a major cultural wave of festivals in Moscow, recently liberated Leningrad, Rostov, Gorky, Sverdlovsk, and Srartov; at the last concert 900 singers from thirteen choirs joined forces. The giant Red Army Ensemble split itself into four detachments and went off to different sectors. Half of their 1,500 wartime concerts were made at the front. The Osipov balalaika ensemble added a whole new range of ancient folk instruments and went on tour. Military units with no access to the mobile brigades put on their own entertainments. In the forests of Belorussia partisan detachments staged amateur folk productions. Folk music swelled majestically in this war and in the years to come, reflecting the depth of national feelings evoked by the struggle for existence.[21]

Radio became a powerful cultural medium during the war, and not only in the Soviet Union. In his radio address on July 3, 1941 after a two-week absence, Stalin addressed the nation as "brothers and sisters," a rhetorical modification of the father–children metaphor in the Stalin cult of the 1930s. It also linked people, state, and leader in a posture of adversity and common danger. The great voice of radio Moscow in those years was that of Yury Levitan, the first man Hitler promised to hang after the capture of Moscow. The resonant voice of the boyish-looking announcer, a ten-year veteran of broadcasting, possessed all the qualities needed for wartime radio: a deep, rich timbre, an overtone of gentle reassurance, an undertone of male, paternal authority, and a pure Russian intonation (Levitan happened to be Jewish). Leningrad radio played a special role under the awful blockade. Poets and dramatists filled the airwaves with radiant words of hope and optimism as well as wrenching sorrow.[22]

Radio served as a lifeline for the troops, the partisans, and civilians under occupation. Luftwaffe bomber pilots marked the radio stations in Moscow and Leningrad as their prime targets. The possession of a receiver was punishable by death in the German occupied areas. Receivers – wired loudspeakers – were the only radios permitted for civilians in Soviet controlled areas. All others were designated for the armed forces and war-related institutions. Broadcasting tied the population to radio central. Listeners lived for the news that was fed into the station by some 7,000 correspondents and conveyed over the radio by the familiar voice of Levitan and dozens of other announcers. The airwaves linked front and rear, occupied and freed zones, besieged cities and Moscow. Waves of hope and pride were fused with radio frequencies when receivers intoned the solemn words: "*Slushai, front, govorit Moskva*" (Attention, frontline people, Moscow Speaking); or "*Slushai Moskva, govorit Leningrad*" – a notice to the nation that Leningraders were holding out against the brutal blockade. When Orel was liberated on August 5, 1943, armored cars broke into the town with their radios bellowing out "Holy War" and "Little Blue Scarf."[23]

Since many theaters, movies, and concert halls closed down, radio became the prime cultural medium. In June 1941 music and literature programing was reduced in order to make room for news, but after

Stalingrad and Kursk the balance was restored. In both front and rear, radio listeners heard the musical and dramatic classics of Russian culture and western civilization in a promotion of Russian nationalism and allied solidarity against barbarism. In time of danger, people are ready to see high culture as national treasure belonging to the masses. Tolstoy's *War and Peace* was adapted for the air in twenty episodes, as was *Terkin*, early sketches for *Young Guard*, and the historical patriotic plays. Contemporary authors were brought closer to public awareness on radio talk shows and readings: Samuil Marshak, Kataev, Surkov, Simonov, and Ehrenburg all regularly appeared. Among the most popular was a trio of women writers who came to prominence during the war. Margarita Aliger (1915–) from Odessa read her poem honoring Kosmodemyanskaya in 1942. Olga Bergholz (Berggolts, 1910–1975) sat by the microphone during the dreadful winter of 1941–1942 at Leningrad radio. Vera Inber (1890–1972), a former avant-garde poet from Odessa also appeared on the air.[24]

An extraordinary public display of emotion on the airwaves was enacted by the reading of letters received by Radio Moscow from and to the frontline soldiers. The reading to the front began a few weeks after the invasion and that to families back home in August 1941. Of the 2 million letters received by the end of the war, 9,000 were broadcast. Although the letters were carefully selected and closely censored, this service linked the two communities separated by war, updated addresses of civilians evacuated or displaced, and continued in the postwar period as a missing persons center.[25]

Wartime radio deepened the bond among Soviet citizens who listened to the open expressions of love, loneliness, despair, fear, and hope that were contained in the letters. Its programing helped to reshape national identity by fusing information, culture, and emotionalism into a picture of a just and martyred people beleaguered by the evil force. Never before had there been such bonding of the Soviet people in the media. This war created a whole generation of popular entertainers and artists as well as a generation of audiences whose memory still rang with the clarion sound of war for decades after 1945.

Hitler as rodent and other images

In July 1941, Alexander Werth saw the first war posters in Moscow: a Russian tank crushing a giant crab with a Hitler moustache; and a Soviet soldier ramming a bayonet down the throat of a rat-like Hitler.

1. Varvara Panina, gypsy songstress (I. Rom-Lebedev, *Ot tsyganskogo khora*, p. 57).

2. The Andreev Balalaika Ensemble, 1898 (*Orkestr imeni V.V. Andreeva*, p. 21).

3. Film poster for *The Abyss*, 1916 (*Testimoni silenziosi*, p. 541).

4. Queen of the linen screen: *Vera Kholodnaya* in *Life for a Life*, film, 1916 (*Testimoni silenziosi*, p. 329).

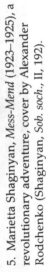

6. Jazz, circus, and the modern poster: the Stenbergs' "Negro Operetta," a circus bill, 1928 (John Bowlt, ed., *Russian Art of the Avant Garde*, New York: Thames and Hudson, 1988, p. 237).

5. Marietta Shaginyan, *Mess-Mend* (1923–1925), a revolutionary adventure, cover by Alexander Rodchenko (Shaginyan, *Sob. soch.*, II, 192).

7. Vladimir Khenkin, standup comedian (Klitin, *Estrada*, p. 96ff.).

8. *Little Red Imps*, 1923, movie blockbuster of the silent era (Yurenev, *Kratkaya istoriya*, p. 232ff.).

9. Facing the town: Isaac Dunaevsky, king of mass song (*Istoriya muzyki narodov SSSR*, II, 352ff.).

10. Facing the country: V. G. Zakharov, voice of folk song (*Istoriya muzyki narodov SSSR*, II, 352ff.).

11. *Chapaev*, 1934, a movie for the millions (*Gody i filmy*, p. 91).

12. Happiness is a Stalinist collective farm: socialist realist painter S. V. Gerasimov's "Kolkhoz Holiday Feast," 1937 (Vanslov, *Chto takoe sotsialisticheskii realizm*, p. 18).

13. Monument to a martyr: M. G. Manizer's "Zoya Kosmodemyanskaya," 1942 (Vanslov, *Chto takoe sotsialisticheskii realizm*, p. 27).

14. Klavdiya Shulzhenko, songbird of World War II (Vasilinina, *Klavdiya Shulzhenko*, p. 176ff.).

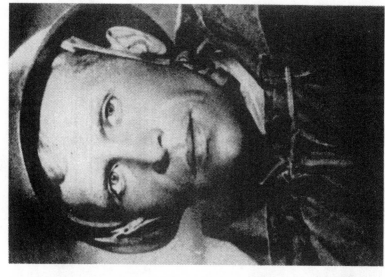

15. Hitler as bride: "I Lost My Ring [at Stalingrad]." Poster by Kukryniksy, 1943 (Kukryniksy, *Po vraҙam mira!*, p. 22).

16. Mark Bernes in the film *Two Warriors* where he sang "Dark is the Night" (*Mark Bernes*, p. 216ff.).

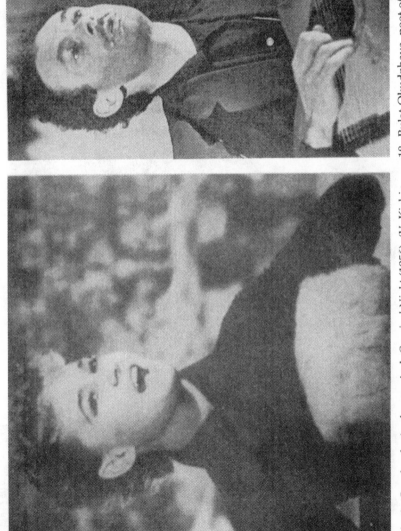

17. Lyudmila Gurchenko in the musical, *Carnival Night* (1956). (V. Kichin, *Lyudmila Gurchenko*).

18. Bulat Okudzhava, poet of the guitar, starting out in the 1960s (*Bulat Okudzhava: 65 pesen*, p. 22).

20. Sergei Bondarchuk as Andryusha in *Fate of a Man*, film, 1959 (*KES*, 368).

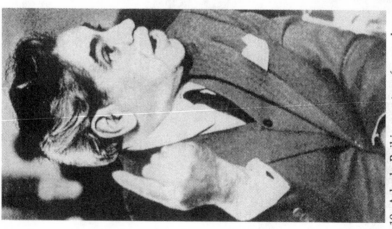

19. Arkady Raikin, master of comedy (*Televizionnaya estrada*, p. 184ff.).

22. Vladimir Vysotsky, national hero (Smith, *Songs to Seven Strings*, p. 146).

21. Alla Pugacheva, queen of pop (*Televizionnaya estrada*, p. 128ff.).

23. The Moiseev Folk Ensemble (*Time*, September 15, 1986, 100).

24. *Moscow Does Not Believe in Tears*, 1980: the hit movie of the Brezhnev era (R. D. English and J. J. Halperin, *The Other Side*. New Brunswick: Transaction, 1987, 116).

25. Yulian Semenov, detective story writer (Semyonov, *Seventeen Moments of Spring*, dust jacket).

26. Cult hero and rock star, the late Viktor Tsoy (Troitsky, *Back in the USSR*, p. 124ff.).

28. Pop Art: "Subscribe to *Soviet Screen* or else!" (SE, December 1990, p.25).

27. Ad for *Little Vera* (Sovexportfilm, 42).

Soon a national system of distribution and display of posters, borrowing from the old ROSTA, came into being: Okno Tass, the Tass Picture Window. The cartoon graphics of World War II strikingly resembled those of the earlier war against the Germans. All the sharp instruments of old Russian *lubok* and revolutionary satire were redeployed in the iconography of World War II – and were soon to be turned against "Yankee imperialists" during the Cold War. Veteran poster artists of the civil war went back into action. The most famous wartime cartooning team was "Kukryniksy," an acronym for Mikhail Kuprianov, Porfiry Krylov, and Nikolai Sokolov – all born at the dawn of the century – who in the 1930s had aimed their pencils against European capitalists and socialists and who would receive the Stalin prize in 1942.[26] Although they cleverly hooked into all the wartime themes, their style was no more than an extension of the anti-fascist cartoons of the 1930s.

Nazis were almost literally too horrible for words; so they had to be insulted graphically, and at this the Soviet cartoonists excelled through the use of rodent-like creatures – a species somehow lower than the ancient dragon – for the German foe. "Parasites on parasites" presented a pack of lice-infested Germans; another showed them as jackals looting corpses. Hitler was represented as a hysteric, a hyena, an indeterminate rodent with sharp claws and ugly features, a leader with brains in his posterior, a bride who has lost her "ring" (see fig. 15), and a misbegotten disciple of Napoleon. German soldiers were "Winter Fritzes," blue-skinned and shivering, unaccustomed to the Russian frosts and addicted to stealing women's garments. Artists also employed the pairing of opposites for comic effect, especially the juxtaposition of a "skinny" (Goebbels) and a "fatso" (Goering), familiar to audiences from clown teams and variety show comedians. The war created an ideal atmosphere for hyperbole and the grotesque of political satire.[27]

But it also projected solemn national imagery. Allegory which had disappeared in the 1930s reemerged in force. Red knights slew fascist vermin that were more disgusting than mythological dragons. Dmitry Moor's "Then and Now, 1812–1941" foregrounded Hitler with a Napoleonic silhouette lurking behind him; Kukryniksy placed the ghosts of Alexander Nevsky and Chapaev marching behind the Soviet troops. Woman as emblem of the motherland began to emerge in 1942. Often it was a defenseless one with child menaced or victimized by a German. There was nothing tendentious about this: women and children were being slaughtered by the thousands in cold blood. But its persistence plus the absence of posters about combat women did mask the fact that women were also fighting at the front and in partisan bands. What came to be one of the most famous posters in history, I. M. Toidze's "The Motherland Calls" (Rodina-mat zovet!) created a startling universal mother clad completely in red with a beautiful Slavic face and a penetrating gaze that was seen all over the Soviet Union from 1941 onward.

Birches, martyrs, and Nazi beasts: wartime cinema

All the fighting countries made film preach – as did the churches – the heroism and justice of their side and the evil of the foe. The Soviets were much more active than other powers in bending the industry to this purpose. Of the 1,313 films produced in Hollywood in 1942–1944, only 374 were about the war. The Nazis also fell far short of total control of film for propaganda purposes. In contrast, the bulk of Soviet wartime films dealt with the war, if sometimes only indirectly. Studios were evacuated to the towns of the Volga, the Urals, Central Asia, and the Causasus. Movie programs supplemented live shows for the troops. Thousands of Soviet cameramen went to the front to capture the war on film. Some striking documentaries were made: the first on June 5 and then every three days. The big success was *Defeat of the German Armies Near Moscow* which drew huge Soviet crowds and was released in the States as *Moscow Strikes Back*, an Oscar winner with narration by Edward G. Robinson and an unforgettable cinema experience.[28]

Fiction filmmakers responded to the emergency as they had during the civil war with *agitki* – fiction shorts released as Fighting Film Albums. Prewar movie character figures were pulled in as narrators: Chirikov as "Maxim" and Orlova as Tanya from *Radiant Road*. Four of these shorts have earned lasting fame. *In the Sentry Box* shows how a German spy who speaks fluent Russian can infiltrate Russian lines – but can never "become" a Russian. His failure to recognize Stalin's baby picture gives him away (a similar device was used in the American film, *Battleground* where baseball was the cultural artifact that tripped up the spy). *Three in a Shell Hole* is another lesson in German perfidy and the need for vigilance: when a Soviet nurse treats a wounded German soldier who shares the crater with her and a wounded Russian, the German tries to kill her but is shot by the Russian soldier. (Here one involuntarily thinks of Alfred Hitchcock's 1944 classic *Lifeboat*.) The pithy *Incident at the Telegraph Office* has one scene: Napoleon sending Hitler a message: "I have tried it. I do not recommend it." The most harrowing of these shorts was *Feast at Zhirmunka* which has an old Russian peasant woman bearing the ancient rustic name Praskovya poisoning herself and a German detachment at a feast she has prepared for them. These shorts did not always match the seriousness of the war and they were superseded by feature films in 1942.

While comedy in the form of anti-Nazi satire was easy to insert into posters and the entertainment stage, it was problematic for fiction film. The very popular *Actress* was criticized because of its light and sentimental treatment of the war. In it, a blinded soldier is enamored of an operetta singer he has never seen. They meet by chance at a hospital bedside (she has become a nurse) and love takes its course. The filmed version of *Schweik*, made in the form of folktale and *lubok* art, had some success: it rejoined the team from *Man with a Gun* (Yutkevich and Tenin) in an anti-fascist caricature of Hitler that resembled Chaplin's *Great Dictator* (1940). The best remembered comedy was Pyrev's *At 6 O'Clock after the War*, a triangle that introduced the one-legged soldier – a common enough sight at the time – who wishes to hide from his beloved but who is taken back by her with great feeling (a theme used most famously in *Ballad of a Soldier*). Moviemakers and their political bosses felt that comedy was not appropriate in this war, although the lighter prewar films such as the Orlova musicals were richly enjoyed in the dark days of combat. Older women – the bulk of the movie audience – still recall a half century after the war began how those films filled them with strength, hope, and optimism.[29]

Of the seventy full-length features produced in 1942–1945, forty-eight were war movies, most of the rest being historical films. One of the earliest was a screening of *The Front*, starring Babochkin, and directed by the Vasiliev brothers who had to reverse their earlier romance of the partisan in *Chapaev*. The two major themes running through serious feature films were the unity and virtue of the Russian people and the hideous bestiality of the German invader. The most famous example of both is *Alexander Nevsky* which was taken off the shelf and reissued after the invasion. Films that people could identify with were those like *The Girl from Leningrad* (1941) and *Two Warriors*. The first deploys a favorite theme: the wartime triangular romance in which misinformation interferes for a time with love. In this case love triumphs at the end under the compassionate portrait of Stalin. In *Two Warriors* (1943), the friends are representatives of two different kinds of Soviet men: Sasha the quiet Russian; and Arkady, the garrulous southern type from Odessa, played by Mark Bernes. Bernes (1911–1969; see fig. 16), who had made a half dozen films before the war, came into his own as a brave, sincere, and good natured – if a bit too extrovert – soldier with a song in his heart. His rendition of "Dark is the Night" in the dugout with the faces of homesick soldiers in the background made that song a classic of the popular repertoire.[30]

The Soviets produced some exceptionally grim and powerful cinematic accounts of the German atrocities. The best of them came after the turning point of Stalingrad when audiences were able to deal with the shock of barbarism without succumbing to despair. *She Defends the Motherland* (1943; released in the States as *No Greater Love*) was directed by the veteran Fridrikh Ermler, with a script by Alexei Kapler, and a superior musical score by Grigory Popov. It opens with an idyllic montage of prewar rural Russia, a troika ride through a birch forest, and a happy family scene of the champion tractor driver, Praslovya (Pasha), brilliantly played by Vera Maretskaya. When the Germans arrive, Pasha loses her husband and then watches in horror as their little son is run over by a tank. Dazed with grief, she wanders in the woods and stops to stroke a birch tree. Pasha then becomes a partisan leader, Comrade P, a ferocious avenging angel garbed in black who wreaks havoc on the occupying forces. *Rainbow* (1944) directed by Mark Donskoy and taken from a novelette by Wanda Wasilewska uses similar material – child murder and torture – with even greater shock effect. A partisan woman's newborn baby is executed in front of her eyes by the German commandant. Equally shocking is the collaboration of a village woman who becomes his mistress, lies around in her underwear, and eats chocolates. The Nazi-ape motif is provided by a stuffed monkey above her bed. Nazi barbarism, augmented by Lev Shvarts' use of "Deutschland, uber Alles" in a Walpurgisnacht arrangement, is contrasted with Russian folk themes and Chaikovskyesque elegies in the score.

Lev Arnshtam's *Zoya* (1944) squeezes as much emotion out of this familiar episode as the screen would bear – and it could bear plenty in those days. But it is also a brilliantly executed Stalinist fairy tale – even Shostakovich's music for the childhood scenes yields nothing to the dreamy lyricism of the score of Walt Disney's *Snow White*. Framed between scenes of her captivity and torment, the film recounts Zoya's childhood and school years and a stern Komsomol career. She learns the meaning of heroism from the exploits of Pavel Korchagin and Valery Chkalov and recites in school the story of the famous martyr, Ivan Susanin, interrogated, tortured, and killed by Polish invaders in

1613. The last scene before the war is an idyllic stroll – almost a travelogue – through new and old Moscow on a bright day in 1941 – the apotheosis of romantic adolescence, Russian nationalism, and Soviet achievement. After the torture scenes, Zoya is led to the gibbet where she reassures the sobbing village women that she is happy to die for Russia. The camera jump cuts from the hanging to footage of the Russian offensive with the smiling, angelic face of Zoya in the foreground.

Women in these three films represent the innocence of the violated and martyred Mother Russia (*rodina*) and they make the perfect foil to the brutalized German occupiers and their ghastly crimes. Women are portrayed in a religious mode as vessels of love in their suffering and sacrifice and in their emotional bonding with each other. But, as in the poster "Mat-Rodina," women are also represented as active figures. Peasant women suffer and die, weep for other victims, and cross themselves constantly; but some take up the rifle and machine gun and – at the conclusion of *Rainbow* – pitchforks and axes, recalling the year 1812. Contrasts and linkages are found everywhere in the *mise-en-scène* and in subtexts. Women are identified with holy and invincible Moscow and with the wintry beauty of the Russian landscape. That landscape is turned into hell by the Germans who force women to march barefoot and almost naked through the snow. In a sequence of *Zoya*, the exasperated German tormentor cannot bear the cold, though he is fully dressed, and he curses his victim with the strange words: "You are a Russian woman!" Rat-like soldiers and officers are filmed in deep shadow. Every possible cinematic device is deployed to establish a vivid contrast between national heroes and evil predators; the use of women to illustrate this theme was a brilliant conception.

The cumulative effect of these and other films was to dehumanize the enemy, which is exactly what all the other belligerents did. More than any other art, the movie stamped the image of the Nazi beast and the Russian martyr deep into the national consciousness. Soviet films during the war also strengthened the image of the friendship of ethnic minorities by teaming them up in combat – just as foxholes and warships in US combat films always had their complement of Italians or Jews from Brooklyn, a Slav, and an Irishman to supplement the WASPy Robert Taylors and John Waynes who commanded them. Nationalism, homeland, Russian history, lore, legend, and classical culture underlay the whole experience – in film and in all the popular arts. The war so deeply popularized and legitimized these that they survived the renewed onslaught of Marxist ideology in the postwar period.[31]

It would be a mistake to read Russian wartime movies as simply elongated *agitki* or moving posters. The plots were harshly simplified and the characters certainly reduced to "types." But it was not all hackwork. Soviet filmmakers, like their Hollywood counterparts, knew how to enhance the emotional impact of a film by means of scenery, set design, and music. Experimental montage would have been out of the question, even had it not been banned before the war. The studios made every effort to evoke the familiar and the "real" for Soviet moviegoers sitting numb in their grief and terror; and they suffused their films with an element of viable hope. Thus the blend of military fantasy, frontline romanticism, rear-area romance, and stark realism that characterized wartime cinema. Working under extremely difficult conditions in their studios and lots in the Uzbek desert or in cities of the Caucasus, the directors wielded lights, cameras, and physical properties in a way that would communicate filmically to mass citizenry. And they underlined the pathos of their stories with some of the best film music ever written.

Coming home

On the great day of victory over the Germans no salutes to spontaneity and authenticity in cultural life were fired. The end of the Holy War ushered in the Cold War and its accompanying flourish of Russian chauvinism and anti-cosmopolitanism, a re-tightening of ideological orthodoxy and control, an austerity program that was covered over with a glistening cultural smile, and the escalation of the Stalin cult to unprecedented heights. Consciousness reasserted itself over the spontaneity born of battle, hardship, heroism, and adventure. Life returned to a tedious round of "prosaic tasks." The Cold War – with America as the principal adversary – deepened the East–West dichotomy, the xenophobia, and the talk of western "decadence" that had dwelt inside the Russian mentality for centuries. The regime sponsored a vaulting sense of national superiority and a smugness about the Soviet victory over the dark and evil forces of fascism. Stalin singled out the Russian people for special commendation on their mammoth wartime heroism. Propaganda managers stressed the great cultural and scientific achievements of the Russian and Soviet people; in the later 1940s Westerners were offended by claims about Russian inventions that consigned Edison and Marconi to an obscure place in history; and Soviet audiences were treated to inflated screen biographies of famous Russian scholars, scientists, and warriors.

A great cultural pogrom, the *zhdanovshchina* was launched in the years 1946–1948. Andrei Zhdanov and his associates railed against foreign influence and formalism and made it crystal clear that Soviet art was superior to all others. He called for a fusion of politics and culture, the hegemony of the party over art, "mass interest" over the whims of artists, and sharp hostility to both elitism in art and to popular culture from below through commercial mechanisms. More dogmatic than most previous figures in the history of cultural control, Zhdanov proclaimed that "incorrect art" was an ideological diversion and he proceeded to punish those who strayed. Shostakovich and Prokofiev fell into the mesh of discord once again along with other major Soviet composers because Zhdanov (and Stalin) saw them drifting back into the sinful zone of formalism, abstraction, atonalism, and excessive complexity – all traceable to foreign sources. Music, said Zhdanov in a major onslaught against musical modernism in 1948, had to be rooted in the people and accessible to them, nationalist in content, tied to classical traditions, and programmatic. This all reflected of course the upsurge of Russian nationalism and the tremendous exaltation of the folk that the war had accomplished. The co-director of the Pyatnitsky Choir V. G. Zakharov was the sharpest and bluntest of those who attacked music not of the people. State promotion of folk music shot upward. In cinema Eisenstein and other prominent film people – many of them Jewish – were punished or made to confess errors and sins against the people, including excessive admiration for Griffiths and Chaplin.[32]

What the guardians of "Soviet" culture disliked most of all was foreign inspiration which produced both frivolity (as in jazz) and excessive difficulty (in classical music). What linked these alien elements was of course novelty. Novelty was the enemy of familiarity and familiarity seemed to guarantee both political and psychological security through comfort and tranquility. Tempos of change in culture always have larger social ramifications and in a state where change can be induced or inhibited by force, the ramifications become enormous. Nostalgia, represented most vividly by "folk" music, became the handmaiden of stability – or even stasis. This is why a lord of the folk establishment, Zakharov, played such a key role in chastising the "difficult" composers and the cosmopolites; and why folksong writing and performance grew so luxuriantly from this time onward. Conservatives feared the far away and the new – both embodied in the young; and the authorities easily took up the old moralistic critique of popular culture as the ally of vice, sex, and alienation from the system.

The revival of anti-Semitism, never admitted as such, was a

byproduct of the war, fueled partly by nationalism and partly by the desire for more upward mobility on the part of Russian officials. It was a toxic revival of the battle between old and new, Slavic and Western, rural and urban, native and foreign. The catch phrase of the cultural pogrom was "rootless cosmopolitan," a person devoid of mystical attachment to the land, "un-Russian" though bearing a Russian name, and inclined to exalt foreign culture. Anti-Semitism cut right through the world of Soviet entertainment and popular culture. As in many other countries, a heavy proportion of entertainment figures were Jews. If many an early Jewish Hollywood producer could trace associations back to New York and even to Central Europe and the Pale, so could a Jew of the Moscow entertainment industry in the thirties and forties find a *landsman* from Odessa or the *shtetls* of Ukraine and Belorussia. Khenkin, Utesov, the song writer Oskar Feltsman, and the film director Mark Donskoy hailed from Odessa, a rich pool of Jewish entertainment life. Donskoy and Utesov would often play a memory game to see who best recalled the old haunts of their home town.[33] These Jews were fully assimilated into Russian and Soviet culture and society. There is no cause to see them as outsiders peering into Soviet reality. Just as Gershwin, Irving Berlin, and Louis B. Mayer created an authentic but hardly "pure" American popular culture, so did their Soviet counterparts mold various themes and styles into Soviet Russian popular culture.

After the war, the Anti-Fascist Jewish Committee was disbanded, its members arrested and some executed. Shlomo Mikhoels, star of movies and the Jewish stage was killed in an arranged accident and his famous lullaby scene was deleted in 1948 from the 1936 film *Circus*. The Yiddish Theater and other Jewish cultural establishments were closed. Alexei Kapler, who wrote the script for that eminently patriotic film, *She Defends the Motherland*, had his name removed from the screen credits. Satire was attacked and since many stage comics were Jewish, *estrada* comedy fell under jeopardy. Alexander Galich and Georgy Munblit, both Jews, were censured for their stage comedy, *Moscow Does Not Believe in Tears*. Arkady Raikin was assaulted by critics in 1946 and the warning he received pushed him into anticapitalist satire. "Positive comedy," Cold War politics, and the doctrine of "non-conflict" gripped all of *estrada*, circus, and operetta. In 1948–1949, all Jews were dismissed from the radio committee. Many of the bandleaders, singers, and figures in the film industry arrested or demoted were Jews.[34]

The deadly purge of American jazz was a byproduct of the cultural pogrom. Beginning in late 1946, the anti-decadent arguments were revived; later bandleaders were arrested, jazz groups dissolved or toned down and renamed, and, in 1949, saxophones confiscated. What Max Lerner once called "the American instrument" was to Soviet high priests the evil emblem of an alien civilization. With renewed vigor, folk ensembles were again promoted by the state and balalaikas were mass-produced. Komsomol teams again raided performances and guards were posted on the dance floor. Dances were even renamed: the foxtrot became the "quick-step," the tango the "slow dance," and the waltz the "ballroom dance." To fill the ears of loyal Soviets, the mass song composers, Blanter, Dunaevsky, and the rest turned out cheerful operettas, musicals, and songs of patriotic optimism. But even the king of the light genre in music, Dunaevsky, came under fire for his operetta, *The Free Wind* (1947) and other works for their alleged "light-minded" or "archaic" elements. A near renewal of the old RAPM campaigns against operetta occurred. A popular singer of the time, Izabella Yureva was attacked for too much emotionalism in her songs.[35]

Anti-cosmopolitanism was also used to divert attention from the harrowing social and economic conditions that afflicted the Soviet people in the immediate postwar period. Much suffering was entailed in the massive shortfall of men as war casualties and the resultant surplus of single women; in devastated housing which augmented the urban overcrowding already well established in the 1930s; in anti-peasant state policies which helped to reduce the rural standard of living; and in the new wave of orphanhood that threatened to replicate the terrible *besprizornik* problem of the 1920s. Yet these years marked the apogee of the Stalin cult that had been partly muted during the "people's war" of 1941–1945. Statues and monuments to him appeared now in many new places in the USSR and also found their way to the public squares of Warsaw, Sofia, and Prague. Painters outdid themselves in portraying him as a wise and mighty ruler of the socialist peoples and as a sainted figure radiating benevolence and love.

The fiction of the late 1940s seems excruciatingly dull to outsiders but it certainly fit into a cultural system which reached a pinnacle in the postwar years. *Bezkonfliknost* (absence of major conflict) was its avowed organizing principle and *lakirovka* (glossing over reality with a bright smile) was its hidden agenda. The role of the party was elevated and the political element served to de-emotionalize the plot and reduce the action. This is evident even in Boris Polevoi's once stupendously popular *Story About a Real Man* (novel, 1946; radio drama and film, 1947). Its pilot-hero is shot down in a snowy forest, locked in struggle with the elements and with a ferocious bear, rescued, loses his feet to the surgeon's saw, and is then – like so many heroes in socialist realism – converted to consciousness by a "real man," an old civil war commissar. The pathos of this fine Jack London-style story is only slightly muted by the ideological content. In spy novels, the American villains were the usual assortment of faceless gorillas, mirror images of those in American anti-communist fiction. Domestic "novels" of collective farm and urban enterprise celebrated solid family values, non-erotic love, and the materialist, even philistine, values of an upwardly mobile class. Semen Babaevsky's *Cavalier of the Golden Star* (novel 1947; operetta and film, 1950) was a *tableau vivant* in a pastoral setting: no conflict except a contrived romantic one, no drama except the forced drama of electrification, and almost no action. In the industrial tales of socialist realism, the hero was now a middle-aged engineer or "organization man" caught in a very mild trauma of obstructionism or corruption, resolved under the guidance of the familiar "conscious" elder.[36]

Prestige films celebrating the national virtues of the composers Modest Musorgsky and Mikhail Glinka enjoyed the kind of success garnered by the American film about Chopin, *A Song to Remember* (1944). Cinematic biographies and even a musical comedy (*Spring*) exalted Russian scientists. The Stalin cult films, such as *Unforgettable 1919* (1951) and *Fall of Berlin* (1949), were monumental and pictorial, like the great edifices built and canvases painted to Stalin's glory at the same time. Film critics have described them as a continuously moving display of museum battle paintings arranged in narrative form. In *Fall of Berlin*, a grotesquely bad movie, Stalin was portrayed by Mikhail Geliani as a tranquil and godlike warlord assisted by dignified leaders contrasting to a hysterical Hitler and his cowardly court. Even in combat films – a genre built for violence – the conflict was subdued and stylized and the stress was on Russian heroics opposing canned evil. As the Cold War unfolded, the United States was depicted as an evil empire, a pendant to the virtuous communists and the sainted Stalin. Talented directors turned out relevant boilerplate such as Alexandrov's *Meeting on the Elbe*, with Orlova as a nasty and seductive American spy. In moral message, casting, and *mise-en-scène*, they were the Soviet equivalents of the American anti-communist pictures, *Red Menace* and *I Married a Communist*.[37]

The thirties musical was revived, sunny and optimistic. Orlova, Alexandrov, and Dunaevsky showed no signs of diminishing enthusiasm for painting a smile across the Soviet land. In *Spring* (1947), Orlova played a double role as solar scientist and dancer in a story that managed to put a humanistic frame around science, celebrate Moscow, and exalt Russian culture – all within the plot of a standard operetta. The ultimate glossy film, released at a time of severe shortages and the ravages of recovery, was *Kuban Cossacks* (1949), said to be one of Stalin's favorites, directed by Ivan Pyrev – master of the rural music comedy. Featuring the clownish Volodin, a veteran of *Circus* who again dished up a spicy diet of corn and ham, it is a horse operetta about cossack collective farmers competing in a "country fair" venue (like Rodgers and Hammerstein's *State Fair*, 1945) and a couple of standard love plots. In addition to Dunaevsky's bright score, this light-hearted frolic is embellished with provincial *estrada* acts – a female folk company, a cossack sword dance, a weight-lifter, and two peasant women delivering saucy *chastushkas*. From the opening chorus amid fields of grain to the fairbooths bulging with melons, bikes, books, and shoes, *Cossacks* mystified the economic life of rural Russia. When young Mikhail Gorbachev saw it in the early 1950s, he said to his companion: 'It's not like that at all." This film, the emblem of an age, is currently the object of a hot debate between critics who see it as an evil mask obscuring reality and defenders who recall the ray of happiness it brought them in dark days.[38] They are, of course, both right.

The insistence on gloss and non-conflict produced a parade of bland and sunny films. When filmmakers ignored the unwritten canon, they were attacked. Leonid Lukov felt the sting of political censorship. His *Grand Life* of 1946, a film about Donetsk miners, displayed drunken workers, miserable housing, and callous bosses. Worse yet, Lukov made a clear reference to the use of popular entertainment to obscure the harsh realities of life: the managers, in response to workers' needs, send them harmonicas and guitars. Producers' fear of making films that could bring trouble was partly the cause of the film famine (*malokartina*) when Soviet production fell to its lowest ebb in Stalin's last years. By 1947, the prewar level in the production of feature films was reached, and then dropped to seventeen in 1948 and to five in 1952. The void was partly filled by trophy films from Europe, confiscated in the wars and occupations of 1939–1945, including innocuous light German movies and captured American films. Ironically, the latter helped shape a subculture totally alien to Stalinist values (see next chapter).

A totally different cultural environment which would also flow over into public life in the 1950s was the gulag. The social phenomenon of the 1940s which offers the richest collection of ironies about the Stalin system is the counterculture of camp life. It replicated some while reversing other aspects of twentieth-century Russian experience. Each camp possessed its own lifeways, but there existed for many years a cultural system which divided the convict population into three major types: the politicals, the "thieves," and the "bitches." The culture of the politicals was a fossilized version of their previous party affiliations – SR, anarchist, Menshevik, Bolshevik, and others. The thieves (*vory*) represented the last remnants of a Pugachev mentality, with their enormous energy and violence imploding on their fellow prisoners. They possessed a communal, ascetic, and male bonding code of behavior with stringent rules: addressing prison officials by the familiar *ty* form of "you"; refusing to work for them; enduring excruciating pain unto death; and prepared to kill over a breach of etiquette. They also affected a "cool" style of speech and spoke often in couplets or *chastushki*. The "bitches" were more complicated. They worked with the authorities but retained a self-image of criminality and toughness, even when they were recruited as prison guards.

A stunning irony of camp life was that "Gulag jazz" flourished there, while almost ceasing to exist in Soviet society. It was performed by arrestees such as Eddie Rosner. And prisoners of an earlier generation continued to sing their own songs all through the years of incarceration. This was possible because the powerful camp administrators had turned them into autonomous fiefs. The most famous camp singer was Vadim Kozin who was arrested in 1943 (for reasons still not clear), and spent most of his subsequent life in Magadan – where as of this writing he still lives. His recordings were rereleased in the 1980s. After the Khrushchev amnesty, these subcultures were brought back to the towns and villages.[39]

5   Springtime for Khrushchev
1953–1964

Coming up for air

The death of the fearsome dictator in February 1953 marked the end of a terrible era and was followed immediately by destalinization of the deed. The heirs of Stalin declared a collective leadership and split the executive between Georgy Malenkov as head of government and Nikita Khrushchev as head of party. They arrested and executed the dread security police chief, Lavrenty Beria and within the next few years released masses of camp prisoners and rehabilitated some of the terror victims. In 1956, Khrushchev, having emerged as the leading figure in government and party, unveiled the shocking destalinization of the word. In his "secret speech" at the XX party congress, he launched a selective but harsh attack upon the crimes of the Stalin era and the gross cult of Stalin himself. Khrushchev survived both the major fallouts from this startling reversal – the unrest in Eastern Europe later in the year and an anti-Khrushchev putsch of 1957. At the XXII congress of the Communist Party in 1961, Khrushchev performed two powerful symbolic acts: he removed Stalin's embalmed cadaver from Lenin's tomb and removed Stalin's name from the legendary city of Stalingrad, which now was renamed Volgograd. This was accompanied by a bloodless purge of old bureaucrats, some important social reforms, a more open cultural atmosphere, and the start of a genuine if turbulent new era of contact with the West.

These momentous changes worked a profound influence on Soviet culture, high and low, and created a climate called "the thaw." In the present era of glasnost it is easy to underestimate the euphoria that gripped the younger generation in the Khrushchev years. The main thrust against the rigid and stupefying cultural system came from the artistic intelligentsia, writers in particular, who usually outstripped other cultural figures in critical boldness, moral conscience, and civic courage. Purveyors of popular culture were, as they tend to be

123

everywhere, more conservative and accommodating. Soon after Stalin's death, voices spoke out. Vladimir Pomerantsev made a stir in the pages of *Novy mir* in December 1953 when he ridiculed the hollowness and falseness of Stalinist literature. Mikhail Sholokhov used the term "gray trash" and Simonov "bakers' confections" to characterize recent fiction. Ehrenburg with his customary pungency saw it as a world of "communal apartments painted in gold, workshops in factories looking like laboratories, *kolkhoz* clubs resembling palatial mansions – a world of stage properties, of tinsel trinkets inhabited by primitives or model children made of wax."[1] Literature came up for air and tried to breathe, to probe long-neglected themes of interior spiritual life, the bleakness of the countryside, the victims of Stalinism, and the glossed over problems of adultery, sexuality, divorce, abortion, illegitimacy, and alcohol abuse. The other arts followed suit.

Tarzan in Moscow

The thaw was not wholly the work of the intelligentsia. Nor did it begin on the day Stalin died. The hunger for Western music and movies in the late 1940s and early 1950s was proof that many people desired something more than *kolkhoz* feasts, wartime exploits, industrial melodramas, and the endless performance of reworked folk songs on radio and in clubs. The long-time cultivation of jazz among many in the intelligentsia and officialdom and the recent exposure to it in the front lines during the war fed this hunger. The most ravenous of all was the new generation, too young to have fought in the war, but victims of it nonetheless: orphans or children with working mothers, casually cared for and lacking male role models at home. The cramped housing of the communal apartments led young boys into the courtyards and sometimes into gangs for the companionship of peers. Informal subcultures arose out of a need for identity and assertion. Serezha Tyulenin, a character played by Sergei Gurzo in the film *Young Guard* (1948), became a culture hero for urban male adolescents precisely because he was coarse and streetwise.[2]

Sexual tension no doubt played a role in shaping values into "macho" systems of toughness and sexual coarseness. The puritanical official values of the regime and its sponsored mass culture acted as a spur to defiance. As in the slums of Harlem and the *barrios* of Los Angeles, where the alienation arose from different causes, Soviet youngsters adapted the outer affects of marginality: short, tight skirts and lots of lipstick for the girls; a modified zoot-suit – broad-shouldered jacket, fat tie adorned with cactus or cowboys, narrow pants, and boxy shoes for the boys. The costuming, a "cool" personal style, terse speech forms, a special argot, and other symbols and codes were statements about differentness, toughness, and a vague foreignness. A 1949 satirical piece in *Crocodile* called them *stilyagi*, rude and ignorant freaks who did weird dances and knew more about Viennese operetta than about Russian culture.[3] This cultural stereotype became one of the big targets of official satire from the late 1940s through the 1950s.

The inflow of foreign films during and after the war fed directly into the newly emerging culture of the *stilyagi*. The German musical *Dream Woman* (Soviet title: *Girl of My Dreams*, 1944), starring the Hungarian singer, Marika Rokk, was many times more popular than any Soviet film. A rash of Deanna Durbin films kept that American singer famous in Russia even down to today, decades after she is all but forgotten in her homeland. Rokk, Durbin, and Jeannette MacDonald were idols to a whole generation of little Russian girls, one of whom, Lyudmila Gurchenko (1935–), became a far more serious and versatile film actress than her models (see fig. 17). For the non-musical trophy films an old form of editing was reintroduced: new titles and ideological lectures to explain their "real" meaning. John Ford's *Stagecoach* (1940), starring John Wayne, was released as *The Journey Will Be Dangerous* and described as an epic about the struggle of Indians against White imperialists on the frontier. Frank Capra's *Mr. Deeds Goes to Town* (1936), an anti-establishment story starring Gary Cooper, was renamed *The Dollar Rules*. *The Roaring Twenties* (1939) – a prohibition era gangster film which made the song "Melancholy Baby" a big hit in Russia – was called *A Soldier's Fate in America*, underlining capitalist heartlessness toward veterans.[4]

Audiences, especially young ones, took little heed of the political gloss attached to these movies. They were entranced by acting styles, adventure, and music. Moscow youths emulated the gestures and memorized lines of American macho actors such as James Cagney and Johnny Weismuller. The latter became a legend through his 1942 movie, *Tarzan's New York Adventure*, which featured the great jungle lord, zoot-suited and running amok in Manhattan in search of his kidnapped son. The word *tarzanets* (Tarzan type) took its place beside *stilyaga*. The fellow students of Mikhail Gorbachev – a contemporary of Aksenov – reminisced about how they enjoyed the Tarzan movies shown in their dorm at Moscow University and filled its corridors at night with ape-man howling. Deep in the "jungles" of postwar

Belorussia, amid the ruins of war and the hunger of the late forties, little boys with no access to the media would devour the Johnny Weismuller Tarzan movies brought to their village on horse carts and shown outdoors. Tarzan, Jane, and Boy were a "holy family" to one of them who recollected decades later how the myth of Tarzan seemed so much more genuine to his generation of youngsters than did the distant myth of Stalin because Tarzan represented a retreat from technological civilization.[5]

The gangster–cowboy genre appealed mainly to boys and the musicals to both sexes. The most influential American film was *Sun Valley Serenade* (1941) which arrived in Russia in 1944. A skiing idyll featuring the ice-skater Sonja Henie and the Glenn Miller orchestra playing "Chattanooga Choo-choo," it gave a boost to the popularity of American big band jazz and swing already fueled by the illegal import and black-market distribution of American recordings. While Aksenov was studying in Moscow in 1952 – the year before Stalin died – he attended a party of gilded youth who owned a "radiola" with stacked records of Bing Crosby, Nat Cole, Peggy Lee, Louis Armstrong, and Woody Herman. He watched astonished as the young guests did the jitterbug, smoked Camels and Pall Malls, addressed each other as "darling" and "baby," and identified themselves as *shtatniki* (Americans). All of this in the midst of one of the greatest cultural freezes of modern times at the very center of a totalitarian state! American jazz sounds were a bonding force for Aksenov and a whole generation that was looking forward and outward to new modes of personal expression.[6]

A time for youth

The *stilyagi*, with their tight suits and short skirts, were as much a part of the 1950s thaw generation as was the cultural intelligentsia. The sharp anti-*stilyagi* media campaign sometimes flowed over into an assault on the younger generation – even though most of that generation were not *stilyagi*. But a cluster of new writers approached "youth" with a different temper. Vasily Aksënov (1932–), one of the most famous of them, was a bridge between the literary conscience and the surging wave of disaffected youth. His childhood had been scarred during the great purges by the long imprisonment of his parents, but he was morally unscathed and shared the yearnings of his Moscow contemporaries for honesty and truth and for real art. Although a man of high culture, Aksenov was a jazz lover and he fed into the popular culture by depicting real people of his alienated generation who scorned ideology, possessed no heroes, and sought something like the jazz, sex, and open road of the American beatniks. In the author's unforgettable metaphor, they gazed out through a nocturnal urban frame at a "starry ticket" into another world and another future. Aksenov's use of off-color urban slang lent authenticity to his work.

Reading Aksenov's ironic contrast between the official and the self images of youth in *Starry Ticket* (1961), one can appreciate the almost permanent mutual alienation. At an "evening party for young people" in the novel, its adult organizers offer an "open talk about personal matters," a documentary film on oral bacteria, and dancing to accordion music. Against this, the young characters denigrate school, imitate Lolita Torres (a popular Argentine singer of the time), and display their preference for loud rock and roll over the folk song "Rowenberry" ("Ryabinushka"). These decent and loyal youngsters are tired of *kvass* patriotism, official bombast, and village-style surveillance by the neighbors of their clothing, their morals, and their leisure habits. As Aksenov explained later, they wanted to head westward to the beaches and not eastward to the construction sites, a brilliantly terse summary of what had transpired between youth and the state since the singing, smiling, and building days of the 1930s. Aksenov was bitterly attacked in the press for the clarity of his revelations which were seen as a corrupting influence. He was only one among several writers who sought the meaning of youth rebellion of the time.[7]

Although socialist realism continued to dominate the literary scene, the great generation of 1960 – Aksenov, the poets Evgeny Evtushenko, Andrei Voznesensky, Bella Akhmadulina, Robert Rozhdestvensky, the poet and singer Bulat Okudzhava, and the sculptor Ernst Neizvestny, born in the mid 1920s to early 1930s – tried to set a new tone not only in high culture but for popular culture to a large degree. Young poets became idols of open-air poetry readings, a genre of mass entertainment from the 1920s revived in 1956 with the founding of poetry days that could fill Moscow stadium with ten to fifteen thousand listeners. Mass declamation of poetry was such a familiar part of the cityscape that film director Vladimir Menshov, in recreating the ambience of youth for his movie *Moscow Does Not Believe in Tears*, filmed Andrei Voznesensky reciting *Antiworlds* on Mayakovsky Square in the late 1950s.

The literature of conscience – Nekrasov, Dudintsev, Pasternak, Solzhenitsyn, and others – rose up to challenge the falsities of socialist realism in the Khrushchev period and conservatives lashed back at them. Their battle is the best-known leitmotif in the literary history of the time. But the popular genres of detective, adventure, and science fiction, revivified in the fifties, took largely a middle ground in which "modernization" was always controlled by a Soviet morality. Two writers from the journal *Youth* illustrate this trend. Arkady Adamov (1920–) inspired by the police novels of Yury German, published in its pages in 1955 *The Case of the Speckled Gang*, a detective and spy tale which offered plenty of entertainment for mass audiences through crime plot and narrative action. Its police hero possessed a high level of civility and morality, Soviet virtues that were set against the primitive or "dark" culture of the underworld and the decadent culture of "westernized" villains. In trying to reach youth through a popular medium and move beyond the canon of non-conflict, Adamov could do no more than trace the source of evil and "low culture" to remnants of NEP and to the influence of speculators and foreign powers. But the very appearance of the genre helped stir a whole new debate about the nature of social problems.[8]

Another member of the *Youth* magazine circle was Yulian Semenov (1931–), destined to become the major writer of Soviet detective novels and thrillers. His first success was *In the Performance of Duty* (1962), an arctic aviation thriller complete with propeller planes, ice flows, and ever lurking danger. Here is the earliest display of Semenov's genius at achieving success and popularity by "having it both ways," by synthesizing old and new – the Soviet and the not so Soviet. The tale is strongly reminiscent of the polar adventures of the 1930s, but the pilot hero is the son of a victim wrongly executed in the Stalinist purges. Alongside "Internationale," Mark Bernes, and "Rowenberry" we hear Lolita Torres and the thump of jazz in a restaurant – almost exactly the same musical components that were at war in Aksenov's *Starry Ticket*. In the conversations about the two (often overlapping) kinds of "westernized" youth, black market dealers (*fartsovshchiki*) are clearly denounced as aliens but the *stilyagi* are treated with sympathy and tolerance. The arctic team contains three Russians, an Armenian, and a Jew – all individualized, all equally sympathetic. The last is even permitted to sing the Shlomo Mikhoels Yiddish lullaby that had just been restored to the footage of *Circus* (Semenov is partly Jewish). Cautious references to sex, the film world, foreign travel, and elite life are mingled with patriotic memories of the war, Soviet official morality, high culture, and a classic mentor–disciple relationship.[9]

The arctic romance no longer beckoned youth as it had in the 1930s and the rickety ski-planes could not vie with the interstellar ships that now began to soar through light fiction. In 1957 Soviet youths were enraptured by the Sputnik launch and the publication of *The Andromeda Nebula* by Academician Ivan Efremov (1907–1972), a landmark in the history of Soviet science fiction. Efremov had been a seaman, a geologist, and a paleontologist, one of the first to reconnoiter the Soviet Far East for construction projects in the 1930s. In the forties he began writing science adventure tales modeled on Jules Verne and in the 1950s added technology. *Andromeda* was the first communist Utopia since the period of revolutionary speculation into the future, a theme not permitted in the Stalin era. The sprawling but well-written story embraces the cosmos, the world of technological fantasy, humane characters, and human dilemmas. Efremov projected a global victory of communism over capitalism and the merger of all races into a beauteous humanity living free of conflict or conquest: "a unified, affluent, humanist, classless, and state-less world." He also offered harsh critiques of Stalin and Stalinism, for which *Andromeda* was attacked by hard liners. But it was published, eventually in dozens of editions and many languages and, while summarizing the destalinized ideology of the Khrushchev period, was extremely popular.[10]

The success of *Andromeda* and the readers' thirst that made it successful – springing in part from the postwar surge in technical education – unleashed a flood of science fiction books with print runs in the hundreds of thousands. Scientists with imaginative minds lent their technical know-how to the genre. Science and engineering students devoured it with a thirst made sharper by the new military technology, freer scientific inquiry in the mid 1950s, and the space sagas of the time, especially Sputnik and the 1961 Gagarin flight. Foreign science fiction made its way rapidly into this burgeoning market and the translated works of Asimov, Heinlein, and Bradbury took their place beside the old favorite classics of Wells and Verne. Science fiction lifted readers out of the everyday into another time and space and provided adventure, suspense, and puzzling situations. It took standard jabs at capitalism. But unlike the detective genre, science fiction sometimes fashioned scenarios that were anti-Western in form but which could be interpreted as critiques of Soviet society and policy. The built-in obsession with the frontiers of science and with rapid technological advances excited its main audience: young urban males, especially those with aspirations for a scientific or technical career.[11]

Singing a new tune

The atmosphere of relative freedom, euphoria, and pluralism was reflected in popular music; for one thing, more songs were written because – as in filmmaking – creators were less afraid of unexpected political consequences. The "mass song" however, with its patina of *kazennaya kultura* or official optimistic gloss, continued to thrive on state subsidy and favoritism: Khrushchev for example commissioned the Pokrass brothers to write a song about Moscow with words by Lebedev-Kumach; and when the leader admitted in public his fondness for a Ukrainian folk song, it was played ten times on the radio that day.[12] Mass song was also promoted by professional song writers who made good money cranking it out. Songs like Evtushenko's "Do the Russians Want War?" (music by Kolmanovsky, 1961), with its folklore, birches, plowed fields, and political rhetoric may seem irrelevant to Westerners. And "Let There Be Sunshine" (Alexander Ostrovsky/Lev Oshanin, 1962) may sound utterly banal:

> Let the sun shine forever,
> Let the sky always be,
> Let there always be mama
> Let there always be me.

The hymn "We, Communists" (Tulikov/Gradov, 1958) is all military bluster, but it hardly differs from the patriotic songs of England or America. "I Love You Life" (Kolmanovsky/Vanshenkin, 1956) is certainly "priggish," but sex was also almost totally absent from Anglo-Saxon popular song for two decades. And "Long Gone from the Donbass" (Bogoslovsky/Dorizo, 1956) – certainly a "grab bag" of clichés as an English critic has shown – performs the same function as the country western song that took hold in the United States at about the same time. Artistry aside, it must be said that such songs were genuinely popular. There is no question that thousands, indeed millions, sang and enjoyed them, partly because the music compensated for the banal words. On the other hand, some Soviets despised mass songs and parodied them. The lyrics "We were born to make fairytales come true" (see ch. 3) were rendered "We were born to make Kafka's nightmare come true" in an underground version.[13] The bard poetry movement (see p. 134) was partly a revolt against mass song.

Side by side with mass song, and often feeding on it, flourished Soviet pop – an inscrutable genre that eludes definition. A sensible way to understand it is to listen to what was for decades the most famous and most popular Russian song: "Evenings Outside Moscow" ("Podmoskovnye vechera"; words by M. L. Matusovsky, 1956) by the prolific and skilful Vasily Solovëv-Sedoi (1907–1979), a veteran of the conservatory, radio, and wartime entertainment brigades, who began writing war songs and mass songs in the 1940s. Known in the West as "Moscow Nights" or "Midnight in Moscow" (wrongly suggesting an urban setting), "Evenings" was the first non-political Soviet song since the 1930s that made its way into Western markets. This was helped by a strikingly energetic dixieland arrangement in the late 1960s by the Englishman Kenny Ball. The banal lyrics describe a chaste and dreamy courtship on a summer night in the wooded suburbs of the capital:

> Now the daybreak comes ever gradually.
> So my darling please be so good,
> As to keep these nights in your memory,
> Summer nights in the Moscow wood.

But the elegiac music is enchanting and eminently singable. The secret of its success probably lies in the ambivalent and pleasant feelings created by words of love and hope to a melancholy minor melody. Such contrastive devices which helped American popular composers like Irving Berlin (as in "Always") to world prominence were readily employed by Russian songwriters. "Evenings" endures in the Soviet consciousness as the hourly musical signal of Radio Moscow (replacing Dunaevsky's "Song of the Motherland" in 1956). This obscure and seemingly trivial change of songs also signaled a shift in national and official mood – from the sunny urban optimism of the 1930s to a more tranquil and nostalgic celebration of rural life; as such it was a landmark in the depoliticization of popular song.[14]

Younger songwriters – Oskar Feltsman (1921–), Venyamin Basner (1925–), Alexandra Pakhmutova (1929–), and others – brought in new styles; and singers such as Muslim Magomaev and Edita Pekha emerged alongside older stars like Mark Bernes to popularize both foreign and Soviet pop songs. In most of the upbeat songs banality ruled supreme, both in melody and words. Kolya Vasin (1945–), a future rock man, recalls the nausea he felt on hearing pop songs like "Misha, Misha, Where's Your Smile?" Yet these songs and big band music were sung and danced to by several generations. The continuing urbanization, the appearance of new restaurants, a relative upgrading in affluence, an upswing in radio listening, and the greater availability of recordings spurred the composition of Soviet pop; and the softening of relations with America and Europe brought in a flood of Western songs. Two of the vocal stars of the late 1950s were the Italian teenager with a falsetto voice, Robertino Loretti, and the Argentinean Lolita Torres.[15]

Although the severe late Stalinist bans were lifted, jazz was still seen by many critics as an alien art and it continued to fight for a place in the galaxy of popular music and public performance – not to mention recording and radio programming. The smooth *estrada* jazz was ever present on bandstands and in restaurants. It was the music of the jitterbugs and *stilyagi* and of hundreds of thousands of youngsters who tuned in to the jazz programs of Willis Conover on Voice of America starting in 1955. Dixieland groups, combos, and jazz clubs proliferated in Soviet towns where couples danced at parties to the strains of Peggy Lee and Duke Ellington. The evening of jazz became, in the words of Frederick Starr, "a community rite of the younger generation." But officials were still ambivalent. In Kiev a "citizens" movement protested the outpouring of "trash" by the Melodia record company. Khrushchev had his own particular notions about jazz: "When I hear jazz," he said at the 1962 Manège exhibition, "it's as if I had gas on the stomach. I used to think it was static when I heard it on the radio ... Or take these new dances which are so fashionable now ... You wiggle a certain section of the anatomy ... it's indecent." In his last years, clubs were closed and the silly Komsomol patrols again began to prowl. The arch-enemy of jazz and rock, Leonid Ilychev, a major party functionary of *agitprop* and ideology, spoke of the "yowling" of foreign bands. Cultural conservatives tended to conflate jazz and rock the way political ones conflate liberalism and radicalism.[16]

Soviet people first began hearing rock and roll in the 1950s over Voice of America. This generated an industry of smuggled records and homemade recordings done on X-ray plates and a large underground market that was linked by the accusing authorities to the underworld of violent crime. At the 1957 World Youth Festival – a great turning point in cultural history – foreign rock was played alongside jazz. Soviet youngsters, like those all over Europe, began bidding each other farewell with the words "See ya later alligator" (from the Bill Haley song). "Love Potion Number 9" and "Tutti Frutti, Well All Rooty" were blasting out in Soviet apartments, recorded or played live by enthusiasts. At some point around 1960, those in the subculture of young urbanites attuned to Western styles divided into *shtatniki* ("Americans" who adhered to the zoot suit and big band) and *bitniki* (proto-hippies in jeans and sweaters who preferred "beat" or rock music). In a few years, "Beatlemania" would drown out the differences. The new musical beat once again transformed dance styles. The durability of the folk dance, foxtrot, waltz, and tango which coexisted freely with the jitterbug or boogie – when not persecuted – made Soviet dance floors into museums of dance history. When the twist arrived in the sixties, the sight of Soviet couples gyrating with fists and knees jutting out in different directions to Chubby Checker tunes dismayed the guardians of culture and morality, including the old-time steppers who shared the dance floor with them.[17]

But what did they do about it? Shostakovich spoke angrily of its "alien primitivism" and ex-foreign minister Shepilov echoed him at a congress of composers in 1957. Jazz groups, aware of rock's attraction, employed the false parody, pretending to make fun of rock as they played it to loving audiences. Moiseev did the same thing in a number called "Back to Monkeys" at Moscow's sober Chaikovsky Concert Hall; again, audiences loved what they were supposed to laugh at. In response to the menace of rock and roll and to the complaints of Soviet composers who were losing royalties, Kiev Komsomol patrols in 1960 were trained to distinguish between acceptable popular music and *bugi-vugi*. They "infiltrated" restaurants and youth hangouts, boogied with the rest, kept lists of the unacceptable songs, and confronted the musicians with their evidence. As a result of this piece of espionage, swing and rock-type bands were replaced by folk ensembles throughout the city.[18]

On a visit to Tashkent in 1956, an American journalist saw *stilyagi* dancing to "Stompin' at the Savoy" played by a loud combo. An indignant MVD (security police) officer spoke out: "All this energy could be invested in building a hydro-electric power station, rather than wasted here on a dance floor." This mood was translated into policy. As an antidote to boogie-woogie and jitterbug, the Komsomol in 1961 endorsed the "Lipsi," a fast waltz invented in East Germany to rival the decadent Western dances. In the spring, a conference on ballroom dancing was convened to discuss what was acceptable on the dance floor. It approved invented dances such as "The Walk," "The Russian Lyrical," and "Friendship" which sought to combine rhythmic energy with respectable deportment. Igor Moiseev, the great impresario of ensemble dancing, tried to eliminate Western vulgarity from Soviet dance floors by designing popular and dynamic dances rooted in tradition. For two years, the press and television promoted Moiseev's new dances – "Moscow Girl," "Russian patterns," "Herringbone," and many others. The steps were imaginative, but young people, in spite of Komsomol efforts at promotion, ignored them and danced the way they wanted. This foolish exercise in socialist choreography for the masses was never really forced on dancers, and was a complete failure. While the Moiseev troupe was selling Russian "folk" to American audiences as part of its country's cultural diplomacy, urban Soviets, old and young, twisted and boogied their way through the 1960s.[19]

A genuinely new music genre that swelled into a mass movement in these years was guitar poetry or "composer's song," words and music written and performed by the artist. Rooted in previous decades and preceded by a wave of camp songs brought back to the cities by victims of Stalin's gulag released by the new regime, it was heard publicly only in the 1950s. Like underground poems, songs, and jokes, guitar poetry was part of the antidote to official culture. Its chief pioneers were Alexander Galich (see ch. 6) and Bulat Okudzhava. Okudzhava (1924–; see fig. 18) was, like his friend Aksënov, a child of the purges, having lost his father in the 1930s. Both a poet and a novelist, Okudzhava imprinted his art on an entire generation with his incomparable guitar songs. He began writing them in 1956 and became a genuine cult figure among students and the urban intelligentsia. His cult reached an even wider audience since much of his work was known from unofficially produced and circulated tapes, particularly of the unpublished songs. This mode of cultural dispersion, called *magnitizdat* or "tape recorder publishing," was the major vehicle for the popularity of Galich, Okudzhava, and later Vysotsky. Okudzhava became a veritable challenge to the official Soviet pop music industry in the early 1960s through recordings, film music, and public performances.

Okudzhava spun the theme of loneliness, loss, despair, and nostalgia, made cryptic references to the terror, and displayed mystical attachment to the old Arbat district in Moscow. His exaltation of the spiritual strength of women ("Your Majesty, Woman") has sources in nineteenth-century Russian literature. His honest songs about World War II, in which he fought, contrast vividly to those of official patriotism. His performance style, a simple and modest demeanor, was a refreshing contrast to the declamatory mode of Soviet popular and mass song artists. His lyrics were poetic and personal, tragic or comic, but always authentic. Places, times, loves, and moods come alive in the realia of his verses about the Arabat, the last trolleybus, an old jacket, or the Smolensk Road. But the lyrics alone, as spoken poetry, could never replicate the response that this artist evoked with his music.

"Georgian Song" (Okudzhava is half-Georgian by birth) and the "Prayer of Francois Villon" are among the most beautiful and singable melodies in all of Russian music.

Okudzhava's art has been called "the folklore of the urban intelligentsia," particularly the generation born between 1930 and 1950. Okudzhava's music still serves as the nostalgic "sound track" for those who were young in the late fifties; one of his songs was used exactly this way in the film *Moscow Does Not Believe in Tears* (1980) and in a documentary on the fate of Soviet art, *Black Square* (1987). Vladimir Frumkin recalls how, as a young communist believer and an enthusiast for the songs of Dunaevsky and Blanter, he and many of his generation were converted to artistic and emotional truth on hearing Okudzhava sing of a noctunal ride of pain and despair through the city on a trolleybus, by the reference to "my religion" in "Old Arbat," and by the simple tale of an "Old Jacket" which gets repaired while the owner's life is still in tatters – all of which evoked feelings that were simply unknown in official culture. "Old Jacket," much to the disgust of Okudzhava's admirers, was set to a banal melody by Blanter and sung by the pop and mass singer, Eduard Khil, in a masterpiece of perverted bombast which lost every trace of the original.[20]

Under the impact of these voices expressing new sensibilities, Soviet youth began forming guitar song groups that congregated out of doors and in people's flats. Their songs and those of the camps – especially among the intelligentsia – offered a new musical mood that differed from what was heard on radio and cut on records. Once banned emigré singers, like Alexander Vertinsky, who had returned to the Soviet Union during the war, were given wide publicity through recordings, appearances, and film.

The crocodile's teeth

In March 1963, Nikita Khrushchev pronounced the following words at a gathering of art and literature figures:

Satire is like the surgeon's scalpel: you find harmful growths inside a human body and like a good surgeon you remove them right away. But to know how to wield the weapon of satire skillfully the way the surgeon uses his knife, to remove the deadly growth without harming the organism – that requires mastery.

This pithy comment sums up almost the entire political history of Soviet satire. The healthy organism is state, party, and Soviet values;

the malignant tumors are what the state says they are. The problem is that tumors so defined are always mechanical rather than organic; mere lapses from a good system. An endless row of Western articles and books on Soviet propaganda have shown us how it works. The major organ of Soviet satire was the magazine, *Crocodile* (founded in 1923), whose circulation rose during the Khrushchev decade from 300,000 in 1953 to 1,700,000 in 1963, reflecting the freer atmosphere in the press. The style of its cartoons and short satirical prose pieces and their targets had changed along with the larger cultural and political configurations of each era since 1923. But the major categories were still in place in the 1950s – and on into the Brezhnev era.[21]

The first was defamation of current foreign enemies. From the 1920s caricature of Lord Curzon to those in the 1950s of NATO warmongers, neo-Nazi revanchists, and Yankee imperialists, there is a remarkable consistency in the imaging of the enemy. He tends to be fat, ugly, brutish, cunning, and arrogant. As a result, an Alabama sheriff, a British colonialist, and a Latin American dictator can even look alike. Some of the cartoons are pungent, a few even brilliant – such as the one of the little black schoolchild standing on the steps of an American school that is guarded by assorted racist thugs. Most of them are uninspired and repetitive. As in type-casting for spy or war movies, the faces remained the same and only the outer garments and emblems were changed. But it was precisely the type-casting that – as in the West – made for effective political cartooning. The second theme was the exaltation of current heroes and campaigns – the cosmonauts, the Virgin Landers, labor stars, soldiers. The third, and largest, was ridicule of accepted domestic abuses and abusers such as laziness, bad work habits, shoddy goods and services, corruption, pilfering, May– December marriages, disrespect for parents, overspending at restaurants, religion, Muslim chauvinism toward women, farm and factory mismanagement, and oversensitivity to criticism. "Decadence" in clothing, dance, and music styles and foreign elements in popular culture came in for special abuse. Jazz and operetta (both admired by the *stilyagi*) were periodically scorned. The methods of *Crocodile* and other satirical publications remained the same; but the number of permissible targets had grown.

Stage whispers

The thaw partially melted the icy monument into which the popular performing arts had been frozen during the last years of Stalin. Circus, standup comedy, variety show – live and on the radio – took on new life. But how far could one go? The uncertainty lent excitement and tension to some of the genres of live entertainment. The tongue of saturn was loosened by the XX party congress and comics became bolder in their sniffing about poor social conditions. Many of their satirical themes were identical to those in *Crocodile*. In Vladimir Polyakov's "Conversation with a Dog" a man brags to a dog about the number of people he has ruined that day and the dog assails him for immoral behavior. Question: is it normal for a dog to talk? Is it normal for a human being to act this way? In their routine, "The Talking Magazine," the comedy duo Vladimir Dykhovichy and Moris Slobodskoi manage to touch on three social realities of the day when one of them says: "I have to live in Moscow because I'm doing a doctorate on roaches." On the other hand, comics were still expected to take jabs at foreign imperialism. A typical Cold War couplet of the early 1960s:

> Once a Greek sailed cross a river
> And in the river saw a crab
> He stuck his hand into the river
> But found instead a Yankee sub.[22]

The brightest spot in the world of comedy *estrada* was Arkady Raikin (see fig. 19). In the last years of Stalinism, Raikin had to turn his satirical face against the Western menace in skits such as "Around the World in Eighty Days" (1951) – a fusion of Jules Verne with the revolutionary fairy tale *Four Brothers* (see ch. 1) – about the bad life under capitalism. During the thaw, he matured into a great comic artist, broadened his range of satire, and achieved the top rank among verbal comedians which he held until his death in 1987. Raikin was a major celebrity in the 1950s and 1960s and the audience in his little theater on Zhelyabov Street in Leningrad was always packed with stars of stage and screen, officials, and ordinary people. What was the attraction? Raikin possessed the gift of the ghetto – that peculiarly Jewish approach to humor that combines Juvenal and Horace – searing satire with gentle sympathy for our flawed humanity. He walked the edge of official censure and delivered sharp social commentary. His routines – lengthy, complex, even learned – were topical and more theatrical than those of American comics, with their chains of one-liners, and certainly less *risqué* than either European cabaret or American nightclub comedy. Raikin used structure and narrative with stunning cumulative effect and embellished it with "a thousand faces" and a repertory of gestures and voice registers that kept Soviet audiences roaring with laughter. Though much of his material was written by others, it was Raikin's delivery, a product of rigorous rehearsal, that raised everyday satire to performance art.

One of Raikin's most famous acts was "Man Alone," a brilliant pantomime about a man who has set a lavish table to impress his bosses and a female co-worker and then finds that he has lost the key and locked his guests out. The one-man conversation with them through the locked door is a masterpiece of timing, visual gags, and social satire. Raikin's repertoire was a virtual catalogue of the permissible themes of social criticism in Soviet life since the death of Stalin: lack of day care, poor restaurant service, shoddy workmanship, careerism, Oblomovite bosses, stupid bureaucrats, philandering, mindless pedagogy, and alcohol abuse. Perpetual shortages led him to invent the name *avoska* for the string bag that everyone carries, "just in case" something is for sale. The dialogue of two drunks in mushy alcoholic voices is so famous that it has entered the language:

> Do you respect me?
> Yes. Do you respect me?
> I respect you.
> Then we're both respectable people.

"The Last Scandal" (1960), using several actors, delved into Russian emotions with bittersweet commentary about communal apartment dwellers, who had been living together and fighting for years, sitting down to say goodbye as they moved off to separate apartments. They recalled the war, they laughed and cried, had a few more fights ("scandals"), and displayed nostalgia for a way of life that for many was passing away.[23]

Circus comedy mingled moralizing with straight clowning. One routine, called "Golden Boy" was directed at parents who spoiled their children – a major subtheme of the anti-*stilyagi* campaign. In this one the boy bites his teacher ("How so?" asks a friend; "I don't know," answers mother, "probably with his teeth"), then marries a rich girl and has "coffee in bed, the paper in bed, everything in bed" – much to the mother's delight. Other subjects of social criticism were resort and restaurant life, poorly run workers' clubs, foreign fashion, and excessive drink – very much like mainstream *estrada* comedy, but softened for youngsters. A rather stern warning against *stilyagi* was issued in a circus skit called "Fashion" (1955), in which a young girl is cruelly expelled from a high school ball by her fellow students for dressing like a *stilyaga*. A rhymed song traced a direct line from the jazz band, movie house, and restaurant to the birth clinic and welfare; and from the beer bar and dance floor to the courtroom and prison.[24] The constant flow of jibes on the Soviet comedy stage reflected not only regime values but also mainstream parental concerns and customs and generational tensions.

Moving pictures

Many accounts tell of how the movie houses in Stalin's last years were showing *Happy-Go-Lucky Guys*, *Volga, Volga* and other films of the thirties instead of new ones. This partly accounts for why many millions of people saw those hits so many times. In the early fifties the nadir of the "film hunger" had been reached: five or ten a year, few of them dealing with contemporary life. But the revival came. By 1954 forty-five were released and by 1955, sixty-six. In the late fifties, the centralized approval of film scripts was abolished – only to be restored under Brezhnev. The character of movies also changed. Almost all of them were "demonumentalized." Life was put up on screen once again, partly defantasized, made intimate, and drawn to a human scale. Viewers could gaze back on the revolution and the war now with calmer eyes; and directors could inject a trace of irony instead of only solemnity. Formerly proscribed films were taken off the shelf and screened. Foreign classics – Shakespeare and Cervantes – were given refined cinematic treatment. All this, together with the debut of the cinematic genius Andrei Tarkovsky with his masterful but never popular *Ivan's Childhood* (1962), clearly pointed away from the stiff conventions of socialist realism but also to renewed tensions between "honest art" and commercial values. In any case, the true side of everyday life began creeping into pictures; and since bolder shooting began to replace the frozen frames of the late Stalin period, films became more "moving" – cinematically as well as emotionally.[25]

One of the popular films of the era was *Pavel Korchagin* (1956), based on Ostrovsky's *How the Steel Was Tempered* (see ch. 3). It is vastly superior to the turgid novel, thanks to the direction of Alov and Naumov who trace the hero from an orphaned childhood, through the revolutionary epic with Budenny's forces in the Ukraine, to his tragic fate. In this film, cinematic art constantly overcomes the banality of the material. No other civil war movie comes close to it in richness of detail, the elegant rhythm of the editing, and sheer visual excitement. A more intimate and moving film was *Serezha* (1960) by G. Daneliya and I. Talankin based on Vera Panova's simple story of a postwar childhood – among the most enduring themes in the last half century of Soviet cinema, reaching right up to recent years with *Orphans* and *Come and Behold*. Behind the central story of a little boy and his new stepfather, played superbly by Sergei Bondarchuk, lurks the theme of a dying countryside and the lure of the city, with its schools, dorms, radios, and social diversions. The cyclical, unchanging nature of the farm life is gently but sadly illuminated in the self-referential scene in which the farmers watch themselves over and over in a documentary production film. The contrast between the bubbling rural idyll depicted in *Kuban Cossacks* and the bleakness of *Serezha* is a striking instance of the new quest for cinematic truth, paralleling the turn to ruralism in fiction.

Grigory Chukhrai deepened the paradox of human beings at war in his remake of *The Forty First* (1956), a simple story of the civil war (see ch. 2) whose theme had enormous hidden appeal in the slowly depoliticizing climate of post-Stalin Russia: the dread conflict between love and politics, between personal feelings and civic obligations. Chukhrai's film displayed on the screen for the first time since the 1920s a subliminally sympathetic portrait of a White officer, a man of the old regime. The very notion of an upright Bolshevik woman falling in love of her own accord with (and not seduced by) an aristocratic male would have been unthinkable and was indeed unfilmable throughout the Stalin period. In spite of the "correct" ending, the director presents the ambivalence, the conflict, and the pathos as something the viewers themselves must resolve. Although this version suffers cinematically in comparison to Protazanov's, it was exciting enough and entirely within the canons of Soviet sexual culture. When the love scene begins, the camera cuts to tropical waters accompanied by the swelling voices of a female chorus. The music of the prolific film composer Nikolai Kryukov was delightfully eclectic and anachronistic: Scriabinesque orchestral textures, atmospheric "desert" music redolent of Havana around 1940, Utesov-like jazz of the 1930s, and some Russian folk tunes. When someone died on screen, the viewer was told twice: once visually and once by slowly descending double-bass notes in the score. Thus, *The Forty First* managed to smuggle into the familiar socialist realist frame forbidden love, illicit sex, and exotic adventure.

In the new cycle of films about the Great Patriotic War, heroes became humans. Chukhrai's spectacularly successful *Ballad of a Soldier* (1959) is visually similar to the standard wartime or postwar Soviet movie: the Russian countryside rolling past the train on which the hero Alesha makes his way home, the endless stands of birch, and the final epiphany of the village and his mother who locks him in a wordless embrace for a few minutes before he returns to die at the front. It is also about young love ruptured by war. But some of the uglier sides of the Russian wartime experience are also shown: the venal guard who sells stowaway space in a boxcar for American Spam; the adulterous wife to whom the hero delivers a bar of soap from her husband at the front – soap that cannot cleanse the ultimate sin of betrayal. Although the cinematography is largely conventional, the opening scene of Alesha pursued by German tanks is riveting in its menace, dizzying in its camera angles, recalling dimly some of the classic film editing of the 1920s. One of the vivid moments in *Ballad* is when Yury Levitan's voice comes over the radio loudspeakers to announce the fall of Rostov in the black summer of 1942.

The Cranes are Flying (1957) by Mikhail Kalatozov (1903–1973), often paired with *Ballad* in terms of huge popularity, is a more serious and honest film based on the play *Eternally Alive* by Viktor Rozov. Here the issue of adultery is central and the perpetrator, Veronika (Tatyana Samoilova), is treated with great sympathy and ambivalence. She is seduced by the cousin of her fiance right after the latter has gone to the front and she has lost her parents. She is lonely and vulnerable and frightened by an air raid over Moscow. But Veronika is redeemed when, in an attempted suicide under the wheels of a train (a literary reference no Russian could miss), she rescues and adopts a lost child whom she names after her fiance; and she is redeemed again in the poignant denouement when, after learning that the fiance has been killed, she gives flowers to her fellow citizens on victory day, affirming life and joining them in the celebration of goodness over evil. Tatyana Samoilova's performance in this film was so affecting that she became a cult figure among young girls who admired her to the point of copying her hairdo.

Soviet clichés surround some of the characters, especially the fiance, Boris, a worker (Alexei Batalov, nephew of Nikolai), and his virtuous intelligentsia family who inhabit a prettified apartment in 1941. But the shady side of homefront life is also revealed in Mark, the seducer, an educated musician, a draft-dodger, a philanderer, and a consorter with decadent old regime types who drink and dance to jazz. There is even a comic sendup of a Komsomol meeting, something unthinkable in a Stalin period film. The familiar and the daring are also blended 'in the *mise-en-scène*. We hear Dunaevsky's "Song of the Motherland" played on the Kremlin bells and the singing of "Katyusha" at the embarkation point. But the low angle shot of a birch clump, the last thing Boris sees, is joined by an imaginative slow montage of the dying man's wedding dream. And poetic montage is employed to underline the moral contrasts in the story when the scene of Mark carrying Veronika to the bedroom with boots crunching splintered glass (shattered virginity and broken vows) dissolves into a shot of Boris' boots slopping through the mud of the battlefront. In the finale, the victory celebration is staged as a popular emotional event without a trace of the official bombast of Red Square parades.

The last in this trio of popular war films – there were many of them – was *The Fate of a Man* (1959) based on a Sholokhov story written for the radio in 1957. Bondarchuk, as leading actor and director, lifted his career to new heights as the orphan boy, Andryusha, who finds happiness in family life, fights the war, is taken prisoner, loses his wife and children, and at the end claims another orphaned boy as his son. The singing of the nasty version of "Katyusha" by Russian war prisoners to their uncomprehending German captors, the hero's embrace of the newly found "son" in the cab of a truck, and his famous vodka drinking victory in the German commandant's office (see fig. 20) – a moment loaded with national symbolism – are unforgettable scenes, filled with emotion but rendered with restraint. The bestiality of the German captors is portrayed with much more clarity than in most previous war films precisely because it is desimplified. No less crucial in the success of this film is the adventure element provided by the final escape sequence which ends, predictably, with the exhausted hero gazing up as he collapses at the symbolic cathedral of sanctuary: the soaring birch trees.

The success of these films and others like them showed that audiences, though still perfectly happy to sit through pure entertainment works of high gloss, music, action, and adventure, also desired emotional catharsis of the kind provided by nostalgic war romances and melodramas. Cinema critics of course could always find flaws in these movies, especially when comparing them to works of high art. But mass audiences – in Russia as elsewhere – have always preferred "simple" emotional subjects and a display of familiar feelings – even to the point of sentimentalism. However, the high quality of many popular movies of the Khrushchëv era also bore testimony that the public was quite capable of absorbing artistic and poetic embellishments in works of entertainment. By boldly but indirectly depoliticizing cinema in some films and putting something resembling real life back on the screen, directors of the era pointed the way to that massive flight from politics that was to characterize the Brezhnev entertainment scene.

The peasant in the machine

Although the fifties was by no means a decade of abundance, the long-suffering Soviet people began to experience some modest material recovery from the war, contact with the West, and an atmosphere of reform. Beneath it all urbanization, educational levels, and media coverage swelled. Although leisure patterns had not changed much since the Stalin times, the reduction of the work day to seven hours in 1959–1960 allowed more time for movies, TV, reading, and sports. Visiting and going out remained predominant and the courtyard culture of the past and the street gangs kept replicating themselves. The perceived and real alienation of youth loomed large. Restless adolescents worried the moralizers. To a generation which had spent its youth in uniform, the costumes and gestures of the *stilyagi* were offensive as was their sin of rejecting the work ethic that the regime had always promoted among the proletariat. To ideological watchdogs, Western music and dance were emblems of treason. This old theme was given a boost by the Soviet discovery of a misconceived article in a NATO military journal in 1958 advocating the spread of Western popular music as a means of winning Soviet bloc youth from communism. The article has been cited for more than thirty years as "proof" of the dangers of alien music. *Krokodil* constantly bared its teeth at the *stilyagi* and even commissioned songs ridiculing them. The Komsomol attacked them as spoiled children, Westernizers, and parasites who wasted time and money in restaurants.[26]

But satire and ridicule alone did not seem to work. After all, most of the youth turned off by official values were not *stilyagi* or dealers in foreign goods. The *stilyagi* were no numerical threat, but their signifiers were a public rejection of official values and the authorities continued to fear "infection" of all by the few. It also seemed harder now to win over youth because they were already tired of hearing about the war. The brazen image of Stalin was cast down and the camps were releasing priests who arrived home with a burning faith and criminals who brought the songs and the toughness and tribal bravado of their subculture. Where were the positive heroes to be emulated? Officials fretted about the use of free time by workers and youth and they "discovered" the drinking problem in the fifties because social inquiry was now legal again. Workers could get drunk and fail to show up for work; youngsters were vulnerable to foreign influences. Although the regime may have been perturbed both by errant workers and by *stilyagi*, these had little in common. An

American journalist in 1956 noted that workers in a beer parlor tended to lump together *stilyagi*, Westerners, "Germans," and other well-fed people.[27]

The social and cultural mobilization campaigns of the Khrushchev years – modeled on those of the thirties – were partly designed to recapture the energies and the faith of the younger generation. The most important by far was the Virgin Lands project from 1954 onward, a pet scheme of Khrushchev to increase agricultural production by cultivating previously non-arable land in Central Asia and nearby areas. Though hatched for practical reasons, it helped siphon off the energies of hundreds of thousands of young people who were mobilized by the Komsomol or who enlisted, as in a crusade or an army. They were culturally represented as pioneers on a frontier with patriotic overtones and references to the great construction adventures of the 1930s and to cult figures such as Pavlik Morozov and Pavel Korchagin. The campaign was suffused with the rhetoric of altruism, duty, and self-sacrifice. Over 640,000 volunteers went out in the first three years, more than half of whom were youth and the rest mostly workers. The Komsomol was the chief recruiter and the whole enterprise was surrounded by official pomp: send-off ceremonies in the Kremlin and receptions and parades in towns along the way. A region the size of Western Europe without France was invaded by travelers on trains, buses, sleds, and all kinds of wheeled conveyances. A delightful popular movie musical of the fifties, *Ivan Brovkin in the Virgin Lands*, captured the lighter side of the campaign by pitting a watered-down epic of construction against an equally attractive village abandoned by the youthful hero in favor of the frontier wilderness.

The *tselinniki*, as the virgin landers were called, developed a kind of frontier subculture and unleashed a flood of poems and songs. Courtship and a high marriage rate among the settlers was a primary feeder of the culture. The romance of the wild, of "tent cities," and sleeping under the stars was another. For women, the romantic element may have faded quickly since many were shunted into "female" roles of housekeeping. Nikolai Pogodin wrote a play in 1956 entitled *We Three Went to the Virgin Lands*. The tractor was the central symbol of the campaign and the real-life tractor driver Ivan Rudskoi became another of those numberless heroes conquering the land in metallic machines. But alongside the officially sponsored spirit, there arose an undercurrent of pure individualism celebrated in such songs as "We Drink to the Malcontents, the Different Ones," expressing what was probably the deepest layer of values among the young who were mostly apolitical – certainly not dissident but bored with the magniloquent words and gestures of the parent state. Related to the virgin landers were mountain climbers, explorers, expeditionary scientists of various kinds, and prospectors (called geologists in Soviet terminology), who wrote and sang their own songs and developed their own subculture of "the road," a road as different from that of the American Beatniks as were the two societies themselves in the 1950s.[28]

The anti-religious movement, muted since the war, was revived in 1959 with a nasty physical assault on churches which then softened into a propaganda campaign with an emphasis on science, space, and technology – the Scientific Technical Revolution – as a surrogate for religion. The popular media were enlisted in this crusade to win over the new generation from god to science. Yury Gagarin, on his return from the 1961 space flight, spoke of the heavens he had seen devoid of any gods. His brother claimed that the cosmonaut received hundreds of letters from believers converted to atheism by his flight. Gagarin became the prototypical cult figure in the 1960s. Fictionalized biographies and popular tales linked cosmonauts to Valery Chkalov and to wartime fighter pilots, exalted their families, and provided them with mentors. Another surrogate for religion were the new Soviet rituals. This was a partial revival of the ritual movement of the 1920s, but much larger, more consciously directed, more subtle in its anthropology, and more readily accepted by the population. Rituals were designed for new calendric holidays and family and life-cycle rituals, keyed variously to themes of the revolution, the labor tradition, and patriotism – the most popular being the new nuptial ceremonies enacted in ornamental Palaces of Weddings, the first of which appeared in Leningrad in 1959. Overarching the whole system was a greatly magnified cult of Lenin, surpassing in scope (and vulgarity) the earlier cult and also designed to enhance a sense of supranational "Soviet" identity among the ethnic minority nations.[29]

One reason for the dual campaign was the perceived (and real) revival of religious activity among believers, itself related to the death of the Stalin cult, to the loss of so many men in the war, and to the work of priests released from the camps. Another was the obvious decline of ideology and gradual erosion of the memory of the revolution. This, together with the loosening of the repression apparatus of fear and terror, led the regime to seek a new social cement, a revival of the myth of October – a secular balance to the memory of the war which was replete with Russian national, religious, and individual overtones as well as a powerful element of Soviet patriotism. Although the new rituals were artificially designed, many of them were sufficiently artful, emotional, and "authentic" to insure some success among Soviet citizens; and the Komsomol gave them its full support – which it had not done in the 1920s. The anti-religious and ritual movements were, with the popularization of space travel and the rebirth of science fiction, part of a "remodernization" movement launched by the regime to counter the effects of wartime religious emotionalism and the fantasy world that Stalin had built.

But Khrushchev and the remodernizers drew the line at "modernism" in high or popular culture. Khrushchev's personal style, his earthy manner, the bawdy peasant sayings that sometimes adorned his speech, and his willingness to engage in mild self-mockery paralleled the looser political atmosphere. On his visit to America in 1959, Khrushchev described capitalism as a dead herring in the moonlight: shining brilliantly as it rotted. But on returning to Russia, he said: "I have seen the slaves of capitalism – and they live very well." He also related the story (drawn from an earlier anti-Goebbels joke) about a Soviet man who ran along the Kremlin wall screaming "Khrushchev – durak!" ("Khrushchev is an imbecile") for which he received six months for disturbing the peace and nineteen and a half years for revealing a state secret. Some Russians with either affection or irony called him *kukuruznik* for his promotion of a corn crop in the USSR. Others disliked his "peasant" manners and were appalled when he banged his shoe on the table at the United Nations; they missed the dignity of Stalin and Lenin. A joke that surfaced at the time called all the great communists by the letters "TK": Marx, the *teoretik kommunizma* (theoretician of communism); Lenin, the *tvorets kommunizma* (creator of communism); Stalin, the *tiran kommunizma* (tyrant of communism); and Khrushchev merely the *trepach kommunizma* (babbler of communism).

Like the Russian spring itself, Khrushchev's was a short one, full of warmth and hope, breezy with new forms of expression, fertile with new life. But it ended on a chilling note a few years before his fall from power. At the Manège art show in 1962, Khrushchev regaled the artists and his companions with homespun criticism. On modernism, he was astringent and offensive: "We aren't going to give a kopeck for pictures painted by jackasses ... on this dog shit." When the movie, *The Gates of Ilych*, was praised by Viktor Nekrasov for the absence in it of the iconic proletarian sage, Khrushchev became publicly angry.[30] That anger was translated into signals for all the arts.

Khrushchev was a transitional figure and his reign was a landmark in the long road back from Stalinism, a road that the Soviet people are still treading. His reading of what the Russian masses and administrators of the land could tolerate, the conservatism of his party comrades, fear of cultural chaos – urban vulgarity, youth, Westernizers – all these were danger signals from the past that were joined to his own personal taste which was fundamentally shaped by peasant values. And those values, fears, and cultural anxieties were to be the hallmarks of cultural policy in the long reign of Brezhnev and his immediate successors.

6 The Brezhnev culture wars 1964–1984

Little land

The Brezhnev period (1964–1982), the second longest in Soviet history, was both stable and for the most part peaceful. To dissidents, reformers, and many other kinds of people this was the peace of the graveyard: a graveyard of ideas, openness, and free expression. Though Khrushchev and Brezhnev came from roughly similar lower-class backgrounds (both were born of peasant families) and were raised up by the revolution, the former had a broader if erratic view of change. Brezhnev – certainly a vigorous wartime commissar and postwar administrator – succumbed to stagnation after he reached the apex of power and allowed a huge cult of personality to arise around him, not as sickly as that of Stalin but constricting none the less. Like many people who rise from humble origins to supreme power, Leonid Ilych was not content with the lordship of command but wanted cultural eminence as well. He had the book *Little Land* ghosted for him. Its title – which provoked many jokes – described a 1943 campaign in which Brezhnev played a role. But it eventually came to symbolize a potentially great nation spiritually throttled and contracted into a "little land."

Brezhnev and his colleagues also delivered impressive results in material growth, full employment (if underemployment), and peace – until the late seventies. Refrigerators, TVs, cars, telephones, and housing space increased in quantity. Only 15–18 percent of the urban population lived in communal or shared apartments at the end of the 1980s compared to about 40 percent in the late 1960s. In a survey of emigres who left the country in the second half of his reign, only 14 percent were very distressed with the standard of living there and fewer still with the housing situation. Many expressed satisfaction with health care, education, police protection, and job security. The population in the Brezhnev years became urban (about two-thirds by

1985) with fairly high educational levels. But the economic, political, and cultural system remained so rigid that counter-systems arose to parallel them: a second economy of black and gray markets, a dissident intellectual and political underground, and various countercultures. Agricultural decay, low efficiency, technological lag, corruption, and a declining birthrate of the Slavic nationalities presented major problems for the regime. Too often, instead of answers and solutions, it offered smug slogans about progress. The era was later called one of "vulgar optimism [which] covered everything with a vigorous phrase and a glistening smile."[1]

Public gloss, monumentalism, desiccated oratory, and the relentless ritualism of the state[2] offered little compensation for the growing malaise. The tension between the pomposity of power and the search for personal authenticity by those outside it ignited culture wars about the airing of such themes as sex and politics and the inflow of Western styles and fashion. The battle was complicated by the fact that large segments of the population continued to prefer traditional Soviet forms of culture. Indeed, many retreated into religion, nationalism, cultural preservation, questing for a lost yesterday, and exaltation of the rural way of life in a continuous and growing divergence between urban dynamic and rural nostalgic mentalities.

The past, the future, and the faraway

In spite of the inroads of television during the Brezhnev era, Soviet people were still reading much more per person than many other nations.[3] Rural prose and historical novels on the one hand and science and detective fiction on the other represent two opposing cultural perspectives on modern Russian life. The first fed that familiar yen to escape from modernity into the past or the pastorale; the second were busy with the here and now, the city, and the future of technology. This did not make for two strictly separate readerships – Russians, like other people, have broad reading tastes – but it did illustrate a deep division in value systems. Before the coming of glasnost, these genres of fiction – along with classics and foreign translations (mostly of older authors) – formed the staple of Russian popular reading. In them one finds almost no explicit sex, organized violence, vaulting ambition, baroque acts of vengeance, or scenes from the world of business, international tourism, or fashion, precisely the themes of Western entertainment fiction which are now appearing in the era of glasnost.

Rural or village prose (*derevenskaya proza*) has received extensive scholarly attention because it lies in the mainstream of Russian and Soviet literature and is thus more highly regarded than historical, detective, or science fiction. Its main practitioners – Vasily Shukshin, Valentin Rasputin, Vasily Belov, Vasil Bykov, and a dozen others – were well-known in the West even before some of them became political icons. The enormous popularity of rural prose in a rapidly urbanizing society is no puzzle. The prospect of the disappearance of the peasant way of life – or what is left of it after collectivization and the anti-religious campaigns – induces many to gaze fondly upon the countryside as the last refuge of real Russian values: honesty, simplicity, harmony, stability, family warmth enshrined in the rich and colorful realms of nature and ritual. This is nothing new: at least since the eighteenth century, readers and writers have identified virtue with rural life. But ruralism was fueled in the last generation by fears of the physical destruction of the environment and the spiritual erosion of the soul. For some readers village prose is a long and loving farewell to village life and not an invitation to go back. It is the sad and nostalgic break with a world that will never return.

In striking contrast to socialist realist novels, rural fiction contains coarse language, rustic speech patterns, religious and folk traditions, camp songs and anecdotes. It deals with environmental wreckage and vanishing rural mentalities. Authentic family and religious values are often personified by an aging peasant woman. For evocative power, it would be hard to surpass the much loved story "Horse with a Pink Mane" by Viktor Astafev, which evokes Siberia and its deeply Russian associations, the war, an orphaned childhood of poverty and simplicity, and the beloved *babushka*. Rural fiction contained neither the optimistic veneer of Soviet slogans nor the facile idealization of the countryside. It offered readers a refreshing picture of serene and dignified sadness and a "radiant past" in contrast to the pseudo-folklore, the *kolkhoz* smiles, and the official vision of a "radiant future." The sheer honesty of the authors helps explain their popularity. An enormous gulf in sensibilities lies between the busy urban technological genres and the often bleak nostalgic world of the village writers; but it is a gulf that cleaves individual persons as much as it divides the Russian population.[4]

War novels, which have never ceased to flow in large numbers from the presses, belong to a special category which in tone and magnitude few nations share. It is hard to say when memory was replaced by "historical" thinking in the construction of these novels which continued to satisfy millions who fought or lived through it. Fiction dealing with tsarist court life, a theme long ignored by Soviet historians and novelists, began attracting wide readership in the Brezhnev era largely due to Valentin Pikul (1928–1990) a name hardly known to literary scholars but the most widely read author in the Soviet Union from the seventies to today. In addition to writing stirring tales of World War II, Pikul vividly recreated the military, diplomatic, aristocratic, and dynastic life of eighteenth- and nineteenth-century Russia and Europe, a realm largely neglected or depersonalized by Soviet professional historians, but one that aroused great curiosity. With garish colors and piquant details, Pikul could depict elegant battlefields or throngs of camels swinging through the desert on their way to Khiva as well as details of court life. He was in some ways a reincarnation of Count Amori, whose meretricious tales of palace boudoirs sold so well in prerevolutionary bookstalls; and like the makers of costume films of the 1920s, he satisfied a thirst. Pikul's works were wildly popular in the book market (in the years 1967–1979 over a million copies were printed), but politically controversial because of his ardent Russian nationalism and xenophobia which was sometimes expressed in thinly veiled anti-Semitism. His 1979 novel about Grigory Rasputin and the Jews as the "evil spirits" behind the 1917 revolution evoked angry criticism and, he claimed, personal assault.[5]

On the urban front, the modern crime novel came into its own with the Vainer brothers, Arkady (1931–) and Grigory (1938–). After studying law, one became a policeman working in the famous station at Petrovka, 38 in Moscow and the other became a journalist. By the late sixties their bestsellers were being made into films and TV shows. *A Cure for Fear* (1974) provided an entertaining plot about gangsters who steal a tranquilizer from a scientist, drug a policeman with it, frame him, and then use his documents to extort money from other criminals. The villain is a perfect embodiment of anti-Soviet behavior. He is a denim-suited speculator and nude model surrounded by Western goods, including recordings of Jimi Hendrix and Janis Joplin. *Era of Mercy* (1975), though glorifying wartime bonding as a salvation mechanism, smudges the old glossy image of the postwar years by revealing the crime and hooliganism of that era. It also evoked the mood through contemporary news clippings interspersed in the text and references to jazz at the Hotel Savoy and the Orlova musicals. *Era* provided the plot of one of Vladimir Vysotsky's police movies, *The Rendezvous Cannot be Changed*. In some ways, the Vainers' novels resemble American police procedurals, for example those of Joseph Wambaugh. Both contain unblinking glimpses of the dregs of society, criminal jargon, a complicated view of the police, and an ultimate optimism about life.[6]

Yulian Semenov is the giant of crime writing in the Soviet Union. A man of the Gorbachev generation, he has traveled widely and experienced life as journalist, linguist, and quasi-policeman. He has for decades maintained openly admitted connections to the KGB. An urbanist like the Vainers, he is more cosmopolitan and "liberal" than they, in spite of his tales about the marriage between capitalism and the CIA (*TASS is Authorized to Announce*) and conspiracies for a separate US–British peace with the Third Reich (*Seventeen Moments of Spring*). Semenov is immensely popular (some 35 million copies of his sixty or so books in print, many of them filmed) and immensely wealthy. Some have estimated that he was the best-selling writer of the Brezhnev period. Like no other Soviet writer, he is able to present the realia of KGB investigative procedures and technologies which he knows intimately; and, like Pikul, he evokes a past that Soviet historians have neglected – in this case Nazi Germany.

Seventeen Moments of Spring (1968) was Semenov's biggest success. Its hero Stirlitz is a Soviet agent posing as a loyal officer of Hitlerite Germany; his situation adds melodrama to the saga of wartime Europe and offers plenty of suspense. For the *cognoscenti*, there are coded references to Weimar culture: the Soviet agents "Erwin" (read Piscator) and "Kathe" (read Kolwitz) live in Kopenick (read *Captain of Kopenick*). For the prurient there is a bit of illicit sex among Hitler's courtiers. And for those with long memories, the title is from the 1945 hit song of the Hungarian movie star Marika Rokk. *TASS* (1979) is an anti-imperialist yarn about an African revolutionary state menaced by counter-revolutionaries who specialize in hideous tortures and are aided by the CIA, the US military industrial complex, and a mole in the Soviet government. The plot is silly and the characters cardboard, but Semenov gives it motivation and action. With a feel for Soviet reading habits, memories, and sensibilities, he cleverly combines the familiar (references to Hemingway and the Spanish Civil War, feminized villains, and learned cops) with titillating elements of the new (exotica, atrocities, light sex, some social criticism). The literary and historical allusions are facile and fun, though not always accurate. Soviet readers can enjoy a feeling of "seriousness" while they are entertained and plugged into their everyday by references to celebrities, in this case Alla Pugacheva singing her first big hit, "Harlequin."[7]

Soviet science fiction, sometimes called the folklore of the Scientific Technical Revolution, continued to flourish in the Brezhnev era. In 1975, an estimated 600 science fiction writers were at work, fifty of them full time, most of them scientists or scholars. About half the readers were in the 15–25 age bracket and included a heavy contingent of technical and science students, mostly male. Their demand for science fiction always exceeded the supply: editions of 2–300,000 sold out at once. The new SF books and stories were more scientifically literate than those of earlier periods, reflecting a higher level of technical education among young people. In the early 1980s, Soviet science fiction moved in a trendy, Western-style direction with the appearance of the "Aelita" annual award for excellence in science fiction (inspired by Alexei Tolstoy's 1923 novel and analogous to the American "Hugo").[8]

What kind of values did science fiction convey? Women – usually treated as icons of tradition in village prose – were portrayed pretty much as they actually operated in urban Soviet society: prominent in the world of science and technology but distinctly subordinate to men. This representation helped perpetuate patriarchal notions but at least it lacked the crude sexism that sometimes occurs in western science fiction. Non-Russian ethnic minorities, however, were integrated naturally into the stories without a trace of prejudice. This masked genuine ethnic tensions in Soviet life; but it also taught tolerance. Like all popular culture of the era, science fiction aimed its critical barbs at flaws in the system – low scientific literacy, bureaucratic conservatism, careerism, and mindless TV watching – not at the system itself. The heroes of Vladimir Savchenko's *Self Discovery* (1967) addressed the chronic shortage of technically-minded people by creating a computer-designed human super-achiever. In "Personality Probe," the professional "reptile" who made his career by informing on others was symbolically assaulted by a retrospective unmasking of a nineteenth-century cultural figure, Faddei Bulgarin, known to all students as a man who denounced writers during the time of Pushkin. Vladimir Savchenko's "Success Algorithm" (1964) was a manual for making it to the top through manipulation, betrayal, venality, and false deference.

Soviet science fiction, like all others, has always been compulsively focused on technology, things that make life easier, solve problems, and carry people to new worlds – airbuses, holograms, videophones, robots, mini-computers, cybernetic systems for arranging everyday life, and machines to ward off emotional distress and sorrow. There is a certain pathos in this longing for a world of efficiency in a land where it is in such short supply. But technology was often also portrayed as life-denying: a device which measures the worth of an artwork by the number of "ahs" uttered by onlookers; green cleansing rain and intrusive "servo-robots" that ruin an artist's attempt to paint the earth's last acre of unspoiled environment; and a computer which threatens to emend old office procedures, eliminate jobs, and dehumanize the workplace. Some of the ostensibly anti-capitalist or anti-fascist plots of science fiction works can be read as attacks on things Soviet. The honesty serum used in Emtsev and Parnov's *World Soul* (1964) to expose the mendacity of capitalists could well be applied to Soviet officialdom. And Sveshnikova's 1984 lament about the sorrow caused by a distant war, an apparent allusion to Vietnam where "Joe" is killed, could not help but remind readers of the then raging Afghanistan war.

Many prominent science fiction authors – the Strugatskys, Emtsev-Parnov, Shefner, Varshavsky, Brandis, and others, most of them Jews – have been linked with the dissident democratic or liberal currents of the time. This accounts for the institutionalized decline in production and translations in the late 1970s. The Strugatsky brothers, Arkady (1925–) and Boris (1933–) were the most popular science fiction writers throughout most of the era and also the most ambivalent about Utopia. Their first major success, *Homecoming* (1962) in the late Khrushchev era was almost a clone of Efremov's *Andromeda*. But in their bestseller, *Hard to Be God* (1964), a totalitarian society set in another time dimension could be read either as a fascist or a communist tyranny. Because of this it was attacked by orthodox critics who argued that stories dealing with the future had to project a beautiful classless society. Things became tense for the Strugatskys after the dissident movement emerged around 1965, and they see-sawed through the sixties and seventies between "safe" and unacceptable fiction. As their vision of progress and technology darkened, their projected terror states became more and more frightening. Their works, when available, were devoured avidly by readers.[9]

By popular demand and state command

Soviet mass song continued to drench the airwaves, the dance floors, and the concert stages. Sometimes it was delivered in the pleasant and sentimental style of the aging icon, Mark Bernes, whose last hit record "Cranes" (music by Yan Frenkel) embodied Rasul Gamzatov's famous legend that fallen soldiers did not die but ascend to the sky as cranes.

More often it was done in the stiff commandeering manner of singers like Eduard Khil, Vladimir Makarov, or Iosif Kobzon who dominated the television *estrada* scene, backed up by Soviet style big bands. Repertory commissions plugged the songs they liked or those written by composers they knew as well as those that evoked patriotic feelings and which still possessed charm to the older generation. A 1967 song that typifies the mass genre in the Brezhnev era is "Where Does the Motherland Begin?" (Basner/Matusovsky):

> Where does the motherland begin?
> With the pictures in your schoolbook
> With comrades good and true
> Living in the next courtyard.
> ... with that song our mother sang us
> ... the old bench at the gate
> That birch tree in the field ...

Nostalgic? Sentimental? Of course. American popular song lyrics of just a generation earlier were replete with similar figures: "the house I live in"; "that old oak tree." Parallels to the elegiac sentimentality of Basner's melody can be found in a hundred American and European pop tunes of the same period.[10]

Solo folksongs still enjoyed a mass hearing in this era, with Lyudmila Zykina and others replacing the now retired or deceased Ruslanova and Shulzhenko. But Zhanna Bichevskaya, who has often been compared to Joan Baez, pioneered a 1960s style, variously called "folk bard" or "country folk" by Soviet critics. Bichevskaya studied medicine, attended the Circus Academy, studied voice and guitar, and worked at the Bolshoi Opera studio. Inspired by Okudzhava to become a guitar songster, she collected folksongs in the far north of Russia and began performing and recording. By 1987, she had sales of 10 million records to her credit. The core of Bichevskaya's repertoire is the Russian folksong in a modern arrangement and without folkloric trappings or costumes. She also recorded old romances and pseudo-folksongs composed by popular and mass song composers such as Solovev-Sedoi. In the sixties and seventies, some of the gypsy songs and urban romances that had been long banned from Soviet airwaves and record grooves, were revived by the Gypsy singer Nikolai Slichenko and others. These ran from classics such as "Dark Eyes," "Two Guitars," and "Dear One" ("Milaya," a waltz) to Sergei Esenin's once famous drunken elegy "My Leafless Maple Tree" and "Brick Factory."[11]

The most popular indigenous music throughout most of the

Brezhnev era was that which foreigners know the least and find the strangest: Soviet pop, usually called *"estrada* music" in Russian. In 1978, the director of Melodia, the country's only record company, founded in 1964 to centralize record production, announced that 75 percent of all records sold (about 200 million pieces a year at that time) contained popular music (including foreign).[12] Even when prices of classical discs were lowered, the masses still preferred popular music. Much of it was a blend of mass song, old time romance and gypsy, and Western pop forms. When Sovpop was bad, it was – to most foreign ears – pretty bad. But at its finest, it was equal to the best of Western love songs. Alexandra Pakhmutova's (1929–) "Tenderness" (1966, words by Grebennikov and Dobronravov) won the hearts of Soviet listeners for years and is still heard on the air. In later years the songs of Raimond Pauls (1936–; recently Latvian Minister of Culture) were regulars on the Soviet hit parade.[13] In 1978, number one in urban Russia was his "Yellow Leaves," an utterly simple tune which matched perfectly the sad-sweet mood of a city in autumn, but whose syncopated 4/4 beat made it eminently danceable just as the lyrics made it very singable:

> Leaves of yellow rustle round the city street,
> Leaves of yellow sadly falling 'neath our feet.
> From these autumn days you can't escape to summer,
> Won't you tell us, yellow leaves, just what your dreams are.

Songs with a sharper edge and a more Western coloration catapulted two singers to stardom: Alla Pugacheva and Valery Leontev. Leontev exudes sexual ambivalence: the long hair and flamboyant costumes, standard items of modern male singers, have an androgynous quality. His postures and the chorus line of athletic young men provide an almost homoerotic atmosphere. Leontev's emotional range is as wide as his voice register, and this accounts for his extraordinary popularity among all kinds of people. A consummate showman with a precise sense of timing, he knows how to manage audiences. Pugacheva (1949–; see fig. 21) was trained as a choral director and then became a pop singer, achieving star status in 1975 with her hit, "Harlequin," after which she became one of the biggest record sellers in history. Since her career coincided with the maturing of television, she became the all-time Soviet media celebrity. Pugacheva offered a roughness in style that contrasted with other female vocalists of her time – such as the sweet-voiced Edita Pekha whose Polish accent was widely imitated by young girls in the 1960s. Pugacheva's luxuriant red hair and passionate temperament matched the furious intensity of her singing; and these were enhanced in the public eye by her propensity for stormy love affairs and scandals. In the Brezhnev era, she was the single female cult figure in a world dominated by males. Scorned by the intelligentsia as a vulgar pop figure, and occasionally branded "wild" by official commentators, Pugacheva was (and is) adored by the millions.[14]

By the mid 1960s guitar poetry was in its heyday. The three major figures, Okudzhava, Galich, and Vysotsky were joined by dozens of lesser-known figures in a kind of alternative culture. Galich and Vysotsky went beyond Okudzhava into the lore of the underworld, the street, and the camps, drawing on materials that were already widely sung in private circles. The seemingly uncontrolled popularity of guitar poetry induced a backlash. The king of popular and mass song, Solovev-Sedoi, compared its music to "dance hall tunes." The lyricist Isakovsky found it excessively Western. Some classical composers did not consider it music at all.[15]

Alexander Galich (real name, Ginzburg, 1918–1977) was a multi-talented Moscow boy, a "Lord Fauntleroy of Crooked Knee Street" as an old friend recalled him in youth. He sang, danced, played the piano, and looked forward to a bright future in a country he believed in. After acting in the theater and in troop entertainment brigades, he became a successful playwright, film scenarist, and song lyricist for Blanter and Solovev-Sedoi. From 1962 to 1974, Galich became a guitar poet. Angered by the regime's persecution of dissidents and hostile attitude toward Jews, he constructed his own song art dealing with the dispossessed elements in Soviet life – workers, prisoners, soldiers, drivers, and alcoholics. Unlike Okudzhava or Vysotsky, he sang his political bitterness; and starting in 1962 he created doleful laments about the great terror. Galich's music swept through the "underground auditorium" of the intelligentsia – *magnitizdat*. A man of high culture, he nevertheless knew the world of bars, barracks, and jails; and the moods of his songs ranged from salon conversation to the coarse idiom of the street. Condemned as anti-Soviet in 1971, Galich was expelled from the Union of Writers and his previous work discredited and obscured in a smear campaign with anti-Semitic overtones. He joined the Orthodox church, emigrated, and died in Paris by a fluke accident in 1977. Rehabilitated, he is currently the subject of numerous stage productions, record releases, and television programs.[16]

In Soviet culture, the 1970s may well be remembered as the age of

Vladimir Vysotsky (1938–1980; see fig. 22), born in Moscow of a Russian mother and a Jewish father who served as a colonel in the war. His colossal popularity – far greater than Galich's – remains undiluted a decade after his death. His work has been called "an encyclopedia of Soviet life" because he poked fun at Semenov's detective novels, morning exercises on television, Soviet heroes, revolutionary traditions, and Russian literature; and aimed his furious guitar at inequality, privilege, official hypocrisy, the harshness of urban life, and both the joys and woes of liquor and sex. The candor of his song was enhanced by the language of the street, the army, the tent city, and the camps; and by the raucous pitch of his voice, so starkly different from the velvety and hollow sounds of mass song crooners. He was attacked in the press for lyrics that allegedly disfigured the Russian language and for singing "in the name of and on behalf of alcoholics, soldiers in disciplinary units and criminals."[17] Known to Muscovites as an actor at the world-famous Taganka Theater from 1964 onward, Vysotsky was visible to an entire nation through movies and numerous personal (though mostly unofficial) appearances; and audible through thousands of underground tapes and a few official recordings. Vysotsky's twenty-six films cast him mostly as a tough guy resembling his own movie idol, the Pennsylvania-born Russo-American, Charles Bronson.

The Vysotsky cult was enlivened by gossip about his life style, romances, marriage to the French actress Marina Vlady, fast cars, and drinking bouts. It was reminiscent of the celebrity legends in the last years of Tsarist Russia, and it revealed as much about Russian character as the officially invented cults of the Soviet period. Vysotsky's early death in 1980, though hardly noted by the official press, unleashed a wave of national mourning. Thousands attended his funeral and thousands more have made the pilgrimage to the Vagankovskoe Cemetery every year since. Masses of "little people" for whom he had undisguised but unsentimental compassion wept at his passing. When a conservative critic lamented the cult of Vysotsky in 1984, he received a storm of abusive letters and calls. A typical one demanded that he not "sully the people's favorites, our heroes, our idols." In the same year the Soviet regime recognized Vysotsky's stature and began showing his films on television. Under Gorbachev, Vysotsky has been accorded full recognition in plays, TV specials, books, record releases, and plans to memorialize him. But old-style cult-making dies hard: some of the sponsored folklore on Vysotsky resembles the hagiography of the Stalin era.[18]

In a paean to Galich after his death, the emigre writer Lev Kopelev touched upon an aspect of the man and of Russian creative culture generally that can be applied to Vysotsky as well and which has often been ignored or avoided in the literature: alcohol. Drunkenness and alcoholism, in Kopelev's opinion, are destructive and evil; but drinking, he maintains, has under certain conditions positive features in that it induces an aura of freedom, equality, and brotherhood, however artificial and temporary.[19] These terse and qualified comments from an insider to Soviet life go far in explaining the attachment that many Soviet people of all stations have to the conviviality of the bottle. It also explains the sense of identity between an errant celebrity who overdrinks and his public. The poet Sergei Esenin had created this bond back in the 1920s and when he committed suicide he became a cult figure among the young. One of Vysotsky's greatest stage successes was his recreation of Esenin.

In addition to the hundreds of imitators of the major bards, amateur and professional, modern "tellers" continued to create underground folklore in hilarious takeoffs, particularly on the gods of Russian literature, Pushkin and Tolstoy, who were targeted not out of hostility but simply because of the pious official aura that surrounded them. Russia's first major military engagement since 1945, the Afghan war, also produced a swelling of spontaneous soldier songs. Unlike those of the last war, their message ran from ambivalence to downright opposition to the war.[20] In the summer of 1981, a red army officer recorded this verse:

> Kabul is far away and is the steppe without life
> I've had enough of this land.
> You will never again see many of your sons. O my country
> cry, sob with sorrow, they have gone, left you.

Even more devastating was the reworking of an old symbol, the dying commissar, celebrated in the famous revolutionary painting by Petrov-Vodkin and in the book and movie, *Story about a Real Man* (see ch. 4):

> The battle waned on the ravaged bridge,
> The enemy dissolved into the darkness.
> The commissar, who doesn't like comfort, is dying on the moistened
> ground.
> A warmth unknown to Russia gathers on his lips.
> The stars of the foreign sky fade in his blue eyes.
> He dies, without believing in tales, gripping his broken gun.

In the realm of imported Western music, almost all Western popular forms – excluding rock but including folk, disco, and jazz – were acceptable to musical and political authorities in the Brezhnev era, though kept under control by record producers and repertory committees. Some foreign singers were welcomed. This was true of the American-born radical singer, Dean Reed, who became an East German citizen and a Soviet bloc star from the late sixties until his mysterious death in 1986. Reed made his first Moscow appearance to wild applause in 1966 and won the Komsomol Lenin Prize in 1979. The Reed repertoire included folk, fifties-style rock and roll, and songs of Third World liberation. Dean Reed was, metaphorically speaking, Pat Boone with a Marxist vision; that is to say he possessed an evangelical, clean-cut manner of singing, gesticulating, and speaking that had gone out of style in his native land, but that was taken by Russians as quintessentially American. Although most Americans had never heard of Reed (and still have not), a 1976 poll showed that he was one of the Americans best known to Soviet citizens; and on a 1989 television retrospective on his life, political pundit Georgy Arbatov and pop–rock musician Stas Namin recalled Reed fondly as the conscience of America. Most Russians admired him at least as much for his song style, his smile, and his engaging manner as for his leftist politics.[21]

Jazz and "disco" music both achieved legitimacy. The former reached its peak of development in the Brezhnev era and became fully accepted. Cool, hot, progressive, and dixie were heard on radio and recordings and at numerous festivals and jazz became the object of books, lectures, and discussions. Jazzmen could even offer upbeat arrangements of Russian folksongs and Dunaevsky and Blanter hits from the forties. Ironically, the triumph of jazz coincided with its decline in popularity among the young. Some of its brightest stars – many of them Jews – emigrated. But more important, jazz had ceased being raucous and bubbly dance music and had become a concert art that required reverence and even study. Young people who wanted to shake no longer found sufficient energy in jazz. In 1976, disco became the rage and the music from the American film *Saturday Night Fever* rushed instantly into the USSR. Soviet cities were captivated by European disco groups, Abba, Baccarat, and Boney-M whose famous "Rah, rah, Rasputin!" was a smash hit in restaurants. British sound equipment was installed all over the country: Moscow alone had 187 discos. The word *disko* became a generic name for almost any contemporary dance venue, with either recorded or live music.[22]

Rock and roll gradually took up residence in the wayward hearts of the young. In the 1960s, Alexander Gradsky formed one of the first rock bands, The Slavs, a clone of the Beatles. By the late sixties there were 263 unofficial bands in Moscow alone. Among them, Hairy Glass, Soft Suede Corners, Young Comanches, Little Red Imps (alluding to the movie classic), and Russo-Turkish War (one of its members was a Bulgarian). Beat clubs came and went, often closed down by authorities fearful of the menace of a new cultural assault. Young people, for their part, resented the style of official performance, "the same buttoned-up suits, the same expressionless faces, brightened only occasionally by a poster-style smile." Soviet "hippies" appeared wearing jeans, bell bottoms, peace medallions, miniskirts, and even bare feet. Gorky Street, once known as "Broadway" by jazzmen, now became simply "Street." A new sense of community – including communes and free love – enveloped rock fans who had regular hangouts in Soviet towns and their own new jargon. Although music and self-expression, not politics, were at the core of their revolt, hippies and rockers were occasionally abused by the police who beat them, jailed them, or cut their hair.[23]

The scope of rock widened in the 1970s with the production of rock operas which helped win friends among some intellectuals; the rapid growth of underground groups; and the pressing of the first rock records by Stas Namin and his group, Flowers. Namin (real name, Anastas Mikoyan), the grandson of the famous Mikoyan, was also the first rocker to be admitted to the Union of Composers. As had happened with jazzmen, the slavish imitation (especially of the Beatles) ended and Russian lyrics took over with the ascendance of Andrei Makarevich's (1953–) unofficial Time Machine, founded in 1968. Makarevich reflected the malaise of young Soviet people and achieved legendary status as the leader of "bard rock," a critique of conformism, hypocrisy, and indifference to society.

> Here is my house, windows shut tight,
> Let the whole world turn upside down,
> My house will preserve me.

In 1979, Makarevich went professional and media fame followed: radio, TV, movies, and foreign travel. By 1982, Time Machine concerts were causing near riots. Some have accused Makarevich of selling out by moving from underground status to accommodation. But the dizzying tempo of popular music taste ought not to obscure the genuine talents of this group in all its stages.[24]

The early eighties exploded in festivals, rock clubs, and new groups: an estimated 1,500 in Moscow Oblast alone and hundreds of thousands of registered and unofficial ones blaring across the land. Soviet youth loved rock for the things the older generation found repugnant: outrageous costumes and gestures, scratchy vocal styling, enormous volume, lyrics that punctured official piety. Alisa, an underground band of the early 1980s, played a song called "Experimentor," an impolite sendup of every tractor song ever written. Strange Games parodied the wartime "Baron von der Pshik." Boris Grebenshchikov's Aquarium, Viktor Tsoy's Kino, and others mercilessly mocked official life and displayed an irreverent attitude to the revolution and the war and to pop stars of the past – to "baldy" Eddie Rosner as one rocker called him and to the reigning pop crooner Iosif Kobzon, lampooned in song and described by a rock critic as a "mainstream singer of patriotic songs who looks like a statue."[25] These were fighting words; and the fight came.

But it was complex. Cultural authorities could not always distinguish rock from pop and they were reluctant to prohibit rock outright because of its immense popularity. So they tried cooptation and selective assault. In the 1960s the term VIA (vocal-instrumental ensemble) was contrived for groups who played a hybrid of rock, jazz, and pop with safe repertoires and who wore mod but moderate costumes, a compromise which got some of them television appearances, recordings, and concert bookings. One of the first, Happy-Go-Lucky Guys, won acceptance and also adopted a name with great nostalgic power. They and groups like them mingled mass songs with soft rock and pop in a bland style with keyboard, guitar, and electronic rhythm box, gradually replacing the big band mode in Soviet restaurants. The Komsomol booked VIAs into their clubs, although local managers still tried to suppress the twist and the shake. Baku officials fell back on the tried and untrue devices of the 1920s: thematic "youth" evenings of speeches and reports followed by ballroom dancing. The organizers had to post guards at the door to prevent people from escaping.[26]

The musical backlash of the Brezhnev period recapitulated many themes of previous times. At its heart was cultural fear and the ideologization of self-interest – a thing hardly unique to the Soviet scene. The bosses of the entertainment world – like those in the United States who were attuned to "the diluted and sweetened values of kitsch" – could not understand the new music and what went with it. A musical jury walked out of a concert in Tbilisi in 1980 when Boris Grebenshchikov played his guitar in the prone position. Old-style songwriters stood armed and defensive behind the walls of the Union of Composers, a vast edifice of privilege, with fat state contracts, juicy royalties, and easy access to TV and radio. The average age of these

3,000 composers in the 1970s was sixty; and many of them were conservatives and Russian nationalists. They resented the drop in their royalty payments due to the tendency of rock musicians to improvise, copy foreign tunes, or simply "self-compose," thus obviating the need to play and pay the professional composers. The neat little deals worked out by song writers, bands, and singers broke down. The seventy-year-old Nikita Bogoslovsky, composer of the iconic wartime song, "Dark is the Night" (see ch. 4) complained bitterly in *Pravda* about "noisy, deafening groups that all sound alike" – precisely the ones that were draining royalties.[27]

But since the thirst for money is not an alluring banner to fight under, some composers masked it behind the façade of culture, morality, and ideological righteousness. They called rockers "illiterate" charlatans and pronounced their music non-musical, indecent, and unpatriotic. Even back in the 1960s, jazz veteran Alexander Tsfasman, on the basis of a Beatles clone concert he saw in Warsaw, dismissed the Beatles as artistic nonentities, a familiar outcry of musicians everywhere whose own style is on the wane. In the 1960s, American groups as different as the Christian Crusade and ASCAP (the songwriters) opposed rock music, but they could not dent its success. In the Soviet Union, however, Broadway, Tin Pan Alley, Motown, Nashville, and Hollywood are all in Moscow and their autocrats could step on the throat of other people's song when generational taste linked up with politics. Their ready allies were Brezhnev, who admired "healthy musical tastes and a sense of melody in our clear-voiced young people" and the folk devotees deeply entrenched in the Ministry of Culture.[28]

A 1982 Time Machine concert in Krasnoyarsk raised a storm of protest from intellectuals (including Viktor Astafev) against the cynical despair of the performers, their falsetto whining, and their disrespectful raiment of fur coats, beach hats, sneakers, and "imported jeans." The conservative journalist, Stanislav Kunyaev (1932–) – currently one of the intellectual leaders of the Russian Right – claimed not to oppose the "sweet tyranny" of mass culture in general, but at the same time assaulted rock music and almost all mass entertainment as trivial, insidious, and alien to the precious memory of wartime suffering and hunger. Kunyaev's cultural disgust is deepest when, at a rock dance in the park, he interprets the greasy hair, pessimistic and fatalistic lyrics, and young people swaying in a trance with half-closed eyes as signs of decadence, "a hypnotically weakened spirit," and a flight from life – virtually the same language used by early Soviet critics of jazz and by the cultural critics of Saninism a decade before the revolution.[29]

The crackdown came during the brief reigns of Andropov and Chernenko. The composers' union, angered at the massive underground distribution of popular music beyond their ken or control, mandated that 80 percent of all songs performed had to be those of Soviet composers – practically a reversal of the natural assortment – and set up review commissions to vet all rock groups – exactly what had happened to popular musicians during the first five year plan. The Komsomol reverted to the dreary habit of sending out music patrols and one of its writers revived the old fear that rock was part of a psychological assault on the USSR by NATO. Groups that later surfaced into celebrity status – Viktor Tsoy, Kostya Kinchev, "Mike" Naumenko, and others went deep into the urban underground.[30]

Kings and queens of entertainment

Estrada – which nowadays means the broad world of entertainment – included most of the popular music and its performers just discussed: they along with the comics, the dancers, and the clowns became its "kings and queens." The nonverbal genres of *estrada* such as circus and folk ensembles remained conservative. In the late Brezhnev period the USSR had seventy permanent and thirty touring circus companies, all coordinated by the government agency Soyuzgostsirk which also maintained a circus academy. About eighty students were accepted annually from some 3,000 applicants to the academy where they learned all the genres of the trade and the rudiments of Marxist ideology which they were expected to incorporate into their acts. In practice this meant a regular dose of patriotism, war songs, and even documentary footage of German atrocities. Respect for authority was conveyed to young and old alike when an elephant dressed as a Soviet policeman "arrested" a stubborn and mischievous donkey in a famous clown act. Pop and circus music was balanced by old tunes of revolutionary or patriotic sacrality. The mythic meaning of a famous aerial act, The Flying Cranes, was instantly recognized from the accompanying "Cranes" sung by Mark Bernes. As in other media, officially approved targets were duly mocked: abstract art, fashion hounds, and fans of cowboy and adventure films.[31]

In the main, circus trod the old paths, amusing and delighting an estimated 100 million Soviets each year in the 1980s by offering familiar acts: acrobatics, high wire, dancing bears, cossack riders, and clowning. Routines with no political message made audiences roar, such as the well-known slapstick performance of a Liszt Rhapsody by Amvrozeva and Shakhnin (partners since 1959), each dressed convincingly as members of the opposite sex. Clowns remained the great stars of the era: Oleg Popov "the sunny clown" became fabulously wealthy; Yury Nikulin's talents led him to a career in motion pictures and then on as president of the Moscow Circus. Behind the scenes, things were not always so jolly. Circus, like other entertainment institutions, was enmeshed in rigid hierarchy and inequality and riddled with favoritism and corruption which exploded into scandals in the 1980s. One was caused by Brezhnev's daughter's close ties with circus. When twenty, Galina Brezhneva married an acrobat twice her age, then married Igor Kio (son of the great illusionist), a much younger man. She traveled with the Moscow Circus and sometimes worked as a make-up artist. Her finale was the affair with the clown Boris Buryatiya ("the Gypsy") which led to criminal activities and his arrest in the Spring of 1982. At the time she was married to a high-ranking KGB official, Yury Churbanov.[32]

The folk ensemble industry grew prodigiously in this era, replicating on a side street the magisterial progress of conservative Russian political and literary nostalgia. The Moiseev, Virsky, and Berezka companies stood at the top of a network of dozens of Russian and republic dance ensembles. Igor Moiseev's company remained the most illustrious example of state-sponsored folk art. But when he toured Europe and America (first visit 1958), he had to face what might be called "market fossilism," that is the demand of foreign audiences for traditional Russian folk numbers and not the kind he and his dancers wanted to do. Moiseev tried to amplify the vocabulary of the dance through experimentation and through playing with other national forms, but he was forced by his own government and by foreign demand to cling largely to the folk repertoires that have made his ensemble world famous (see fig. 23). Pavel Virsky, founder in 1937 of the ninety-nine member Virsky Ukrainian State Dance Company was also a trained ballet dancer who maintained the marriage between the formalism of ballet and the lyrical spontaneity of folk dance for forty years. Since 1980 his successor has preserved the old tradition: "to maintain Virsky's style in every dance, we are duty-bound to do it in Virsky's way."[33] Because of this conservatism, Soviet people and the world at large can still delight in the stylized ethnic variety show with rustic flirtation dances, majestically moving women, boot-slapping and high-kicking peasants, and sword-wielding Caucasians. But it has also caused Soviet young people to become very bored with it.

The Soviet Army Chorus, Band, and Dance Ensemble, under the

direction of Boris Alexandrov (son of its founder), represented the far right of *estrada* culture – if such things can be measured on a political scale. Here "right" means the patriotic culture that military bands usually promote but steeped in folk traditions. A typical performance, filmed for television in the early eighties, opened with swaying ranks of uniformed soldiers singing a march by Solovev-Sedoi to the accompaniment of balalaikas and accordions, with Red Square in the background. The men were then filmed sitting under birches singing "Birch Tree," a traditional Russian folk song. "Volga Boatmen" (Ei ukhnem) was performed in a wedge formation, perhaps signaling the unseen but infinite number of soldiers ready to defend the country. In one of the numbers, the camera lingers on the cupolas of an Orthodox church; another begins as a *tableau vivant* of Ilya Repin's painting of the Zaporozhian Cossacks which then breaks into a cossack dance. A village ring dance and contest, the song of Stenka Razin, and Knipper's "Meadowland" all evoke the rural, the ancient, the eternal Russia – without a single urban motif in sight. The cumulative image was that of an army of strong, healthy, and happy farm boys, full of the spirit of their country and willing to fight for it. It was clear where the army stood in the rural–urban geography of modern Soviet political cosmology. But this show was also an example of what happens to "folk" when it is one further step removed from its own milieu onto the TV screen.[34]

Estrada comedy, though hardly dissident in the political sense, was the opposite of folk entertainment in almost every way; it was urban, topical, irreverent. If a birch tree was ever mentioned there was probably a drunk leaning against it. The Soviet comedian not only had to amuse and entertain, but also display empathy about people's everyday problems: work, in-laws, dating, corruption, bureaucracy, and especially apartment neighbors (who were often across the wall, not the hall). Satirical comedy is partly created by its audience and its environment. The laughter connecting the standup comics to their listeners about the shortcomings of Soviet life in the post-Stalin era may have been more socially significant than the muted exclamations and breathless silences at the Taganka Theater that Western visitors so often noted. In the Brezhnev era, the old jokes about shortages of televisions and refrigerators tended to decline as these products became more readily available. Students may find the social barometer of satire as interesting as official production figures on durable goods. Soviet drunkenness, bribery, and bureaucracy – as well as capitalist politics and lifestyles – remained on the firing range and environmental pollution popped up to join them.[35] Arkady Raikin retained the throne of comedy, moved to Moscow in 1981 and, at the age of seventy, was named Hero of Socialist Labor. In his last years, Raikin turned to long, moralistic monologues. He died in 1988, leaving behind a pleiad of apprentices, including his son Konstantin.[36]

One of Raikin's proteges, Mikhail Zhvanetsky (b. 1933) turned from engineering in the 1950s to comedy writing and then to performance. His "Odessa style" is strictly Jewish in rhythm, tempo, gestural language, and intonation, resembling that of New York borscht-belt comedians of a slightly earlier epoch. The content however was Soviet – not the ghetto, golden or otherwise – and dealt with bureaucrats, pilfering, power relations at the workplace, and materialism. In a brilliant satire, Zhvanetsky tried to persuade the audience how inhumanly boring life would be without bureaucratic obstructionism and theft of state property. Sexual and marital complications, a favorite theme for Soviet audiences, were illustrated in the following conversation between a man and woman:

> Can I come and see you?
> Yes, but there's a hitch.
> What's that.
> My husband.
> Oh, you're married. Good for you. How's married life?
> Fine.
> Good husband?
> Very good, but there's a hitch.
> What's that?
> He has another family.
> I see, so he's with her?
> Yes, but there's a hitch.
> What's that?
> He's always at my place.
> Well, is that o.k.?
> Fine, but there's a hitch.
> What's that?
> I love somebody else.
> Why aren't you with him then?
> He doesn't love me.
> So can I come over?
> Of course.

Zhvanetsky was bolder than Raikin in weaving his monologue into a specifically Soviet cultural text. In the interlocution, "Have you ever been to the Bahamas? No, too busy," everyone knew that the vast majority of Soviet people could never travel anywhere outside the

Soviet bloc; and those who could would never be "too busy" to do so. The allusion to the Bahama Islands simply adds hyperbolic and exotic spice to the sad–funny joke.[37]

Television in the 1960s and 1970s became the dominant mass entertainment medium. By 1968 there were 30 million sets compared to 2.5 million in 1958; the number of transmitters trebled between 1964 and 1974. By the late seventies, television was all but universal. In the Black Sea town of Taganrog, 97 percent of the population had radios and 70 percent television; in Leningrad, the second largest city, 93.3 percent of the homes had a TV and 70 percent watched it every day. There and in smaller towns surveyed, the overwhelming favorites were TV films and pop concerts. Soviet programming was more European than American – no sitcoms or canned laughter, less violence (none in children's programs), and a generally muted level of emotional communication. On the other hand government control was complete. In these years, TV managed the news chiefly on its nightly program *Vremya* (*Time*) in such a way as to influence and reassure the population by highlighting leaders, party functions, and economic achievements and by muting internal problems and natural disasters. Themes of manichean world relations and the unity of the Soviet people were conveyed through heavy use of ceremonial and official texts and symbolized by Vremya's logo of the Spassky Tower in the Kremlin. But it was not until Gorbachev that political leaders learned to use the medium for charismatic communication.[38]

Surveys show that Soviet people at that time were more interested in international news, sports, high culture, and programs dealing with moral behavior than in programs on ideological and economic matters. But entertainment was the most popular, with movie showings at the very top. A variety-game show called *Ready, Girls!* blended celebrity guests, silly but harmless skill contests, and lots of laughter. Family audiences loved it. The TV serialization of Semenov's *Seventeen Moments of Spring* in 1973 and *Tass is Authorized to Announce* in 1984 were blockbuster successes.[39] Live *estrada* artists found it relatively easy to make the transition from the theater boards to the sound stage at Ostankino and other studios. Folk ensembles, circus, variety shows, pop music and jazz, and comedy routines migrated there and enjoyed great success. Raikin, Pugacheva, and Iosif Kobzon became national entertainment icons. The frequency with which Kobzon sang on television gave rise to an underground couplet among rock musicians:

> It's as hard to stop the singing of Kobzon
> As it is to stop the charging of a bison (*bizon*).

Goskino: moviemakers and moviegoers

Goskino (Gosfilm until 1963) – the State Committee on Cinema – was a vast establishment riddled by politics, bossism, patronage, hierarchy, and censorship, beholden ideologically to the film sector of the Central Committee's cultural apparatus and financially to the Council of Ministers. It functioned through four heavily bureaucratic committees dealing with scenarios, production, distribution, and foreign sales and purchases. Beneath these came the studios, of which Mosfilm was the largest, and then production units. At every level watchdogs guarded the interests of the state. The military and the police had the right to censor any film that might affect their image. The Communist Party could even order all members to buy tickets to certain films, as happened with *Liberation* in 1972. The tsar of the cinema empire in the first decade of the Brezhnev period was Alexei Romanov, a party man who became angry at the slightest suggestion of sex in a movie – down to rumpled bedclothes. His successor, Filipp Ermash, who was well-connected in the Kremlin, ruled with an iron hand until his overthrow in 1986. Like Boris Shumyatsky of the 1930s, Ermash admired Hollywood, preferred iron scenarios to directorial freedom, and was sensitive to the market. During his tenure, many films of high artistic quality were shelved until the Gorbachev revolution. The Union of Filmmakers, led by Lev Kulidzhanov – originally a "thaw" director who swam with a tide that floated him upward – provided its members little defence against the machine.[40]

But this was far from being an age of "grey" cinema. Goskino put out about 150 films per year shown in 151,000 movie houses and 138,000 clubs, plus about 100 for television. Although the number of viewers decreased in 1970–1985 from 4.6 billion to 4.1 under the impact of television, the Soviets were very much a movie-going people. About 62 percent of them were urbanites. In 1966 two-thirds of farm workers and intelligentsia and four-fifths of the workers went regularly. The range of subject and genre grew rapidly to create a complicated body of works, many of them masterful. The drift away from politics was massive and the realities of Soviet life and personal destinies loomed ever larger on the screens. A prominent American sociologist of Soviet origin wrote recently that movies "generally documented Soviet life better than social scientists," particularly issues of corruption, materialism, intimate life, and indifference to ideology.[41]

What kind of films did Soviet people like the most? Research conducted in the 1970s showed that the leading genres were melodrama, romance, comedy, crime, science fiction, the epic, and the musical. Twenty-six Soviet and fourteen foreign crime films alone accounted for 250 million tickets in 1980, that is an average of more than 6,000,000 tickets per film as against the overall average of 3 million. Audiences did not flock to heavily socialist realist potboilers or to masterpieces of cinema art. Surveys revealed that audiences were drawn by contemporary themes, fast tempo, spectacle, and simple editing. (The last is why a marvelous film like the present minister of culture Nikolai Gubenko's *Orphans*, 1976, which is full of flashbacks, could never be a box-office hit.) Maya Turovskaya, a noted film scholar, observed that "the melodrama is still the unchallenged box-office hit." Her analysis of the folkloric elements in a Mexican film shown in Moscow in 1975, *Eseniya*, featuring Gypsies, a kidnapped infant, and a handsome officer, is a classic and witty exploration of moviegoers' motivation. The stupendous success of *Eseniya* led some Soviet directors to "rediscover" the melodrama.[42] Folklore, along with plenty of action, adventure, and exotic color, also enlivened Vladimir Motyl's hugely successful and vividly remembered adventure film, *White Sun of the Desert* (1970), a special favorite among Soviet cosmonauts who adored its action sequences.

The Brezhnev cinema revived a genre that had been largely dormant since the late Stalin period: the cold war political thriller. *Unmarked Freight*, a grisly tale of CIA atrocity, and *Can-Can in the English Garden*, a silly and clumsy indictment of the American radio stations in Munich (both 1985), were typical products of the heating up the cold war in the early 1980s which witnessed the Afghan invasion, the KAL airliner incident, the Olympics fiasco, and the tensions over Jewish emigration. Even the talented Sergei Mikaelyan entered the genre with *Flight 222*, a fictionalization of the episode at Kennedy airport when an Aeroflot craft was detained over the desired defection of ballet dancers. The villains were the United States government, not the American "people." This was the era when Ronald Reagan was depicted in the press as a western sheriff with a swastika on his badge. The film series, *Seventeen Moments of Spring* (1973) was a Semenov television blockbuster. The cinematic Stirlitz, played by the well-known actor Vyacheslav Tikhonov, became something of a cult figure and dozens of jokes about him sprung up as they had about Chapaev. The public liked its historical details, clearcut villains, intrigue, chase, and occasional violence. But some neo-Nazi youths in Soviet cities were also inspired by the film to emulate Nazi leaders and assume their names (see ch. 7).[43]

The Soviet screen comedy of this era was low key and socially oriented rather than slapstick. The major exceptions were the hilarious films of Leonid Gaidai, especially his adaptation of Ilf and Petrov's classic farce of the 1920s, *The Twelve Chairs*, which is superior in every way to the two Hollywood versions made by Fred Allen and Mel Brooks. (The story is deathless: Mark Zakharov's TV version recently enjoyed enormous popularity.) Eldar Ryazanov, a master of wry social comedy with a critical bite, could inject crime, corruption, and architectural conformity into love stories and still make people laugh (*Train Station for Two* [1983] and *Irony of Fate* [1975]). In *Garage* (1980), he presented a grotesque tale about a whole collective of employees locked together for the night and revealing their hidden sins and inner thoughts. One of the best and most Russian of the comedy films was Georgy Daneliya's *Autumn Marathon* (1979; 20 million tickets sold), a gentle portrait of a modern Oblomov whose indecision traps him in an impossible situation between wife, mistress, and friends. The Leningrad setting, the university atmosphere, the acting of the principals, and the wonderful performance of Norbert Kukhinke playing a Danish scholar add luster to this engaging work. Musical comedies were promoted again by Goskino in order to balance the "serious genres" and to make money. For this reason celebrities of the music world were featured. Gerasimov's *Don't Get Married, Girls* (1980) put the kinetic talents of pop singer Valery Leontev on the screen; *I'm Here to Talk* (1985) did the same for Pugacheva. *Jazzman* (1983) was a musical romp that quoted heavily from *Happy-Go-Lucky Guys* of the 1930s.

The most famous self-proclaimed melodrama of the 1970s was Nikita Mikhalkov's *Slave of Love* (1976; 11 million tickets sold), a parody of the prerevolutionary genre. Set in a southern town under White control during the civil war, it recaptured the end of the age of Drankov, Bauer, and Kholodnaya. The heroine, played by Elena Solovei, was a silent screen star trying to make a movie, raise children, have a love affair, and survive the murderous forces of the political struggle which kill her lover. The cinematography contains typical trademarks of the director: quaint and archaic characters, theatrical tip-toeing, some poetic moments (the sudden windstorm in the garden), and near perfect costuming and *mise-en-scène*. The affectionate irony and the high artistry of this film did not prevent it from becoming a moderate success with film audiences.

The major epic movie of the period was Sergei Bondarchuk's *War and Peace* (1966–1967) in which he played Pierre Bezukhov. Bondarchuk had been an actor of great power. His directed films however (except for *Fate of a Man*) were ponderous. *War and Peace* is a collection of monuments and battle paintings. Audiences loved it none the less or for just that reason. Konchalovsky's *Siberiade* (1979), a much better film, was seen by masses of Soviet viewers before it was withdrawn for political reasons (he emigrated). It is a multi-generational epic of a Siberian family from the nineteenth century to modern times, loaded with the symbolism of the village prose school. His brother Mikhalkov's *Oblomov* was an adaptation that shattered an old cliché of literature and of Leninism, first drafted by Nikolai Dobrolyubov, that Ilya Oblomov, the phlegmatic and lazy hero of Ivan Goncharov's magnificent sprawling novel of 1860, embodied the worst features of Russian backwardness. In reversing this, Mikhalkov made the sleepy Utopian pastorale of Oblomov's dream the emblem of precious and sacred old Russia; and projected Oblomov as an endearing, poetic, nurturing, generous embodiment of the Russian folk. *Oblomov*, together with *Slave of Love* and a few other films made Nikita Mikhalkov (1945–) a celebrity. He was also very well connected: on his mother's side great grandson of the painter Surikov and grandson of a Soviet painter Konchalovsky; son of Sergei Mikhalkov, conservative writer and author of the Soviet national anthem; one-time husband of Anastasia Vertinskaya; brother of Andron Konchalovsky (Andrei Mikhalkov); and sometime brother-in-law of Yulian Semenov.[44]

Most Soviet movies dealt with everyday life in the present and wholly ignored politics. Shukshin's *Snowballberry Red* (1974; 50 million tickets sold) which he wrote, directed, and played in, won best film award that year in *Soviet Screen*'s poll and generated tens of thousands of letters. Both the story and the symbolism evoked national and rural values. The picture opens with the singing of "Vesper Bells" ("Vechernyi zvon," an ancient Russian song). The main character bears an archaic name, Egor, the setting is the remote village of Yasnoe – perhaps a coy reference to Tolstoy – and birch trees are never far from the camera. Sergei Mikaelyan's *Bonus* (1975) dealt with a confrontation of workers and management in a Soviet enterprise and highlighted the complacency of the latter. The protagonist embodied the simple, slightly awkward folk hero who battles against forces of "sophistication." One of the last, best, and most popular films of the period, Rolan Bykov's *Scarecrow* (1984), shocked audiences by its daring exposure of the tyranny of the collective – in this case over a schoolgirl who was nicknamed "Scarecrow" by her classmates. The ostracism, the denunciation, and finally the burning in effigy of "scarecrow" were shocking reminders of a mentality that had once cost the lives of

millions. The Stalinist motif was driven home in the final scene of a
military band. The fact that the protagonist was played by Kristina
Orbokaite, daughter of the legendary nonconformist Alla Pugacheva,
added piquancy to the film.

The biggest movie hit of the era was *Moscow Does Not Believe in Tears*
(1980; see fig. 24), a fact that caused much upturning of noses among
the intelligentsia, thus illustrating perfectly the enormous gap between
popular taste and elitist aesthetics. The film opens in the late 1950s, as
the heroine sadly walks into her women workers' dorm while Western
pop music and an Okudzhava song are heard through the windows.
The era is also evoked by cameo appearances of the poet Voznesensky
declaiming on a Moscow square and of the then budding actor,
Innokenty Smoktunovsky (1925–); and by recalling the craze for
foreign movie stars and the euphoria of early television when *estrada*
comics Pavel Rudakov and Venyamin Nechaev recited couplets to
accordion music. The simple story, a Cinderella variant, is about three
young women who come to Moscow, take up low-skill jobs (almost the
only way to get there in those days), and hope to make a life. One
marries a rural boy and lives in the country. The second plays at social
mobility by seducing a hockey star who then turns to drink. The
heroine Katya (Vera Alentova) fails her examination and has a child
out of wedlock in the first part of the film. But twenty years later – in
the Brezhnev era – she has become the manager of her factory, lives in
a beautiful flat, and has found a real Russian hero, a simple proletarian
(played by Alexei Batalov) whose character compares favorably with
the "European" lovers of her past. The happy ending suggests marital
bliss and success for at least one of the Cinderellas.

Moscow is full of sexism and populism as well as a good deal of gloss.
In Hollywood it won an Academy Award, a fact sufficient to indict it
for many Soviet critics. But it sold a record 75 million tickets; in two
Moscow cinemas, 1,860,000 people saw it in the two months after its
release. Twenty-five times more people went to see *Moscow Does Not
Believe in Tears* than saw Andrei Tarkovsky's stark masterpiece, *Stalker*
in 1980. Soviet viewers expressed their admiration of the film's
closeness to real life and what they saw as honesty, and they used the
word *dobryi*, kind, to denote what we in the West often call a "feel
good" movie. It was clear that the Cinderella ending made viewers
happy. The director, Vladimir Menshov (b. 1939) explained its success
tersely in an interview: "I made this film, having in view a clear-cut
audience: the mass viewer." He is not alone in believing that this
movie may become the second *Chapaev* of Soviet cinema history. In

many ways, the anxiety-ridden debate about taste and art in cinema circles was set by the spectacular success of this film.[45]

Man and woman after work

Scholars sometimes exaggerate the importance of high culture over low, of one genre over others, of all cultural production over unstructured leisure activity. It has been estimated that as many as 40–50 percent of the population did little reading of books or movie going and almost never went to the theater. Attendance at clubs and other public places of leisure and entertainment declined with the growth of privatization and television. Leisure culture was still dominated by visiting (or entertaining) friends and "going out." For young people this meant being with companions outside the home, workplace, or school – at cafes, bars, restaurants, or "hangouts" such as street corners, parks, and hotel entrances – to talk, tell jokes, flirt, neck, play cards, dance, or generally have fun. Urban Russians visit or hang out not only because of poor housing or the shortage of alternative cultural opportunities. They do so by choice. By the end of the Brezhnev period, the Soviet Union was an urbanized society. Soviet studies of selected towns in the late 1960s showed that men had much more leisure time than women; that young people had more unstructured entertainment than their elders; that male bonding – including drinking – still occupied an important place in self-entertainment.[46]

Television certainly changed the pattern of entertainment for many, as new media technologies often do. Video players entered the scene through the black market in the late seventies and viewers could see foreign films of violence, sex, and mysticism as well as old Soviet movies. By 1985, an estimated 450 titles were on the market. People in the USSR did all kinds of things in their spare time from familiar hobbies (the word khobbi entered discourse in the mid 1960s) such as chess, book hunting, and icon collecting to the lesser-known ones of pet maintenance, motorcycle hockey, UFO watching, yoga, spiritualism, and collecting pins, records, and Beatles' memorabilia. The big boom in foreign labels for jeans, buttons, novelty tee-shirts, and other kitschy artifacts occurred years before perestroika. Fads such as break dance and skateboards came and went.[47]

The restaurant was still the major locus of urban leisure in Soviet towns, especially for those eighteen or over. Bars, clubs, and cafes were small and few in number. Restaurants were hard to get into because waiters and managers dislike crowds and the prospect of overwork and because they want to control the food supplies for their own use. In fact to this day, many "Soviet" restaurants are virtually autonomous economic units in the hands of their employees. But the attractions of restaurants are manifold: the bright, noisy hall (often called a "stable" by their denizens), the conviviality of the table, a talkfest, appetizers and vodka, live music, and – because Russians have retained the European custom of dancing and dining – a room full of dancing partners. Soviet dance floors projected energy, eclecticism, and the generational mix that has all but disappeared in societies where popular culture is strictly stratified by age or style and where the dance has been largely separated from dining. Pluralism of audiences was and is still on display when older people begin singing folk songs during the break in the pop and rock dance music or when folk dance forms mingle freely with jitterbug, disco styles, and the twist.

Sport was and is a major aspect of leisure time, especially for males. At the pinnacle of the sports community is the USSR Committee on Physical Culture and Sport of the Council of Ministers. This state agency manages huge networks of clubs and teams, the largest of which are Spartacus, Dynamo, and the Soviet Army. Some sixty soccer training schools are attended by 20,000 athletes. The stated mission of organized athletics is to promote physical health, local pride through comradely competition, and a culture of efficiency, patriotism, and the "collective spirit." Sports stars ranked with film and entertainment figures in celebrity and were held up as model citizens: the "Golden Goalie," Vladislav Tretyak, often spoke to young audiences about his roles as Komsomol leader and army captain; Anatoly Firsov rose from being a delinquent orphan to world fame in the 1970s. In the 1980s scores of documentary films on sports were issued each year as well as about 900 books and pamphlets with a print run of over 15.5 million. Thirty-four journals and periodicals and some 900 television and 700 radio hours a year are devoted to sports activity. And yet some surveys show that the general population participates very little in an active way – as with everything else, this is blamed on TV watching.[48]

As urbanization proceeded and the moral authority of the Komsomol eroded, the gap widened between official values and the unofficial culture of youth. Subcultures of territorial identity and countercultures arose cutting across geography or class and based on common interests. Detente quickened the influx of Western visitors and goods. For the first time on a major scale, rock, fashion, hedonism, and consumerism captivated Soviet youth. Hippies, Mods, rockers, skinheads, bikers, pacifists, and punks appeared in the big cities and made the *stilyagi* of the 1950s seem altogether tame. In the seventies the hippie culture, known as "the system" by insiders, included a network of cafes, hangouts, and crash pads. In the same years, the gap between the official myth of success and the realities of low-paid manual labor in the rust belt towns led underprivileged youth into courtyard and suburban groupings that hardened into gangs with their own artifacts, rituals, forms of address, and language. One of these subcultures – that of sports fans (*fanaty* or *bolelshchiki*) – organized itself around favorite teams, wore the blue and white tee shirts of Dynamo or the red and white of Spartacus, marked up walls with their graffiti, rooted at games, and beat each other up.[49]

The Brezhnev regime, severely lacking in the social imagination to win over the youthful masses to its programs, reverted to the old device of pioneer construction epic. This was the Baikal-Amur Mainline (BAM), a highway and rail complex designed to link Siberia with the Soviet Far East, bypass the vulnerable Trans-Siberian line, increase the population in a sensitive frontier zone, and augment the flow of goods in and out through the Pacific ports. After some false starts in the 1930s and 1960s, the scheme got up steam in 1974. In mythology and recruitment techniques it resembled the Virgin Lands project. Youth who volunteered explained their motivations as independence, escape, high pay scales, mating, and the romance and adventure of faraway places. But BAM enjoyed fewer successes as an idealistic project than the Virgin Lands of the 1960s – perhaps because workers, engineers, soldiers, and even convicts were targets of recruitment. (In an anecdote of the time, Brezhnev, misreading the striped prison costumes of a BAM work detail, addressed it as "My dear comrade sailors.") Hardship, a shortage of women, and a free flow of alcohol were a way of life out on the Siberian–Asian frontier lands.

The government consciously "culturalized" the project with amateur artistic troupes and an opportunity for the best of them to travel to various sites on BAM: a 1977 contest yielded 10,000 participants. Folk dance numbers and plays about BAM life were the main staple of this cultural scene. Entertainment celebrities and foreign guests, including the ubiquitous Dean Reed, made their way out to the sites. In 1974, the composer Alexander Morozov toured the line and performed his song cycle dedicated to BAM workers. Accounts of these visits resemble those dealing with frontline soldiers and entertainers in World War II. The temporary volunteers experienced something resembling a subculture, the biggest product of which was songs and poems about their work, about exotic places, romance, and love of country. But for all the hullabaloo, cultural life seems to have been rather empty. A 1989 documentary revealed a nest of mismanagement, poor housing, and lack of amenities for those who stayed on. Neither state sponsored adventure nor the tired offerings of the Komsomol could stem the growing tide of disaffected youth, reflected so vividly in the popular culture.[50]

Many jokes surfaced in this period dealing with Jewish emigration, Georgian speculators, everyday life, shortages, the neutron bomb, alcohol, and political repression. The sharpest of them targeted the leader himself. Brezhnev's intellectual pretensions led inevitably to anecdotes about his cultural primitivism. Brezhnev became so senile at the end of his life that rumor and anecdote conspired to render him senseless and uncultured. One of the most famous of these seemed to sum up what many Soviet people felt about his achievements. When the sculptor Ernst Neizvestny made his famous bust of Khrushchev in black and white to denote the two sides of his reign (a historical fact), Brezhnev, in the anecdote, commissioned one of himself from the sculptor. When it was unveiled Brezhnev saw a perfect likeness of his face but noticed that he also had two female breasts: one brown and one yellow. When asked to explain, the sculptor said they represented the nurture and support Brezhnev had given the peoples of Africa (brown) and Asia (yellow). "But can't you show what I have done for the Russian people?" asked Brezhnev. "You asked only for a bust," answered Neizvestny.[51]

7 Perestroika and the people's taste 1985–

Glories of glasnost

The reordering of popular culture since Mikhail Gorbachev's advent to power in 1985 after the brief interludes of Andropov and Chernenko was marked by unprecedented freedom of expression – the cultural side of glasnost – and a legitimation by the authorities of spontaneously generated culture from below. This brought changes in reading habits, show attendance, film and television viewing, musical styles, and non-structured leisure; the quickening of amateur culture; and a decentralization of cultural life through the spread of electronic media. Among the institutional and personnel changes sanctioned by the government were the reorganization of the filmmakers' union in 1986; two new successive ministers of culture, the latest a well-known liberal actor and director, Nikolai Gubenko; and similar changes in various cultural establishments. New alliances, friendships, networks, partnerships, and patronage relations arose, changing the diagram of celebrity interlock that has always linked "stars" of popular culture with the other arts and with influential leaders of Soviet society, journalism, and politics.

The new popular culture – much of it legalized "old" culture – contained strong currents of iconoclasm, demythologizing, and open irreverence. The ridicule of sacred icons that could previously be voiced only in underground anecdotes, paintings, and songs was now publicly heard. For the first time in memory, nude pictures and obscene lyrics appeared in public places as did heretofore unseen levels of shock and violence in movies and TV. This evoked counter currents of envy, resentment, and hostility. The cultural duel continued the critique leveled by a moralizing intelligentsia since the early 1900s against popular forms of entertainment and revealed strikingly that people from all parts of the political spectrum loathed and feared many features of the emerging popular taste. The infighting in repertory committees, censors' offices, ideological headquarters, and all arenas of entertainment came out in the open. At the core of the struggle was the Gorbachev challenge to the spirit not only of the Brezhnev era, but to the whole tradition of culturalism, moral control, and censorship in Russian history. The cultural landscape that opened up challenged beliefs long held in the West that only dissident culture was legitimate, authentic, or popular, that cultural rebels were *ipso facto* politically motivated, or that official, traditional, and old-fashioned tastes were imposed from above and had no following among the people.

In the last full winter of glasnost (1989–1990) before the crackdown, the coup, and the subsequent reorganization of the state, Moscow and Leningrad were living museums of the history of popular culture. One could see a revival of *The Boat* and The Bat, old regime cabaret and variety performances, and Anastasia Vertinskaya singing her father's songs on stage and television. Bichevskaya had added White Army songs of the civil war to her live and recorded repertoire. Illegal songs of NEP were heard publicly in restaurants; old-time singer Alla Boyanova ended a television performance of "Bublichki" whose last words are "I'm just a poor private trader" with a shout to the audience: "cooperatives!" Gypsy songs of every period and big band music from the thirties and forties coexisted with mass showings of Tarzan movies accompanied by historical lectures. From out of the fifties could be heard again mainstream jazz, Bill Haley, Robertino Loretti (who returned to Moscow in 1989 for a nostalgic comeback), and Lolita Torres (interviewed from Buenos Aires on television). But it was not only the past that was being recovered; eyes were turned ever more to Western forms and styles, revealing publicly what any discerning person had long known: when given a chance, most Russians wanted to sample everything from the cultural storehouse of the world; some Russians were afraid of it; still others were happy with the cultures of the past, the present, *and* the faraway. The people's tastes were on full display.

The free Russian word

Soviet commentators long claimed that their people were the world's most voracious readers. In recent years critics questioned this assumption with anguished laments about the alleged decline of reading habits. Their complaint, far from new, argued that the masses were turning from reading to other forms of relaxation or that they were reading the wrong things. The eminent art critic, Maria Chegodaeva, juxtaposed "real" art which is cathartic and cleansing to "comforting art" – books that are light, easy to consume, unburdened with big ideas, and far from the storms and passions of reality. Another critic wrung his hands over a poll which reported that only 45 percent of adult males read books regularly – a figure that would seem impressively high in many other societies but which reflected a decline in the USSR. Alluding to the passion for television and popular music among the young, he concluded wistfully that the USSR has become "the most dancing" instead of the most reading nation. Many observers were upset by amateurism and vulgarity in writing and by the belief that the "lesser" literary genres such as crime, historical novels, and science fiction, were crowding out serious literature in readers' preference. These laments escalated as Soviet writers and booksellers rushed to answer popular tastes in the new uncensored environment.[1]

Pikul and Semenov, the extraordinarily productive bestselling authors, represented opposing political mentalities. Pikul had become an icon in conservative and military circles who cherished his linking of Russian blood and genes to patriotic duty and the officers' honor code – whether on eighteenth-century Balkan battlefields, the steppes of Central Asia, or in the recent Afghan war. Pikul came out publicly in the pages of the conservative nationalist journal *Our Contemporary* as an ardent upholder of military virtues and foe of the Masons, the Bolsheviks, the liberal press, and, by implication, the Jews. He also hated the detective or thriller as exemplified by Semenov whose Stirlitz novels Pikul singled out for criticism. In answer to critics who called him a pulp writer, he produced just before he died a pure "boulevard novel" redolent of the old regime, complete with a wronged woman, a murder, and a trial – bringing us almost full circle to Count Amori. Pikul used familiar code words such as "hairy," "dirty," and "out of control" to describe mass youth culture on television. A staunch individualist who disliked Brezhnev as well as Stalin, he represented that element in Russian society that gloried in the past, opposed both liberal reform and neo-Stalinist conservatism, and sought to locate the source of Russia's suffering in some alien force or "evil spirit" such as Masons or Jews.[2]

Semenov (see fig. 25), on the other hand, produced straight-out fictional apologias for perestroika and its leaders. The protagonist of *The Reporter* (1988), embodies the virtues of the Gorbachev generation. Son of a World War II hero unjustly repressed by Stalin, he is an investigative reporter who discovers a blackmail plot against a reform-minded industrialist and himself becomes the victim of character assassination by high-ranking right-wing bureaucrats (who very much resemble those who launched the *putsch* in 1991). Such things were of course going on as he wrote. To the usual assortment of good cops, references to World War II, and entertaining plot twists, some very bad Stalinist villains were added. Semenov began publishing his own books, a journal, and a newspaper and branching out into various enterprises. Science fiction writers also came out openly for glasnost and perestroika. In 1988, Eremei Parnov lashed out against the "medieval era" of Stalinism; and the Writers' Union's Subcommittee on Adventure and Entertainment fiction resolved to turn their art to the struggle against "reaction" – in other words against the right-wing foes of Gorbachev. Detective and science fiction writers, including the Strugatskys and the Vainers, joined forces in the journal *Detective Story and Political Novel*, edited and published by Semenov, containing crime stories, spy thrillers, documents from the Stalin terror, and pro-Gorbachev commentary, thus closing the ranks of practitioners of urban popular fiction along liberal lines.[3]

Subgenres of fiction proliferated rapidly. There was no Soviet "horror" novel as yet, but East–West love and sex novels created literary scandals. Vladimir Kunin's sensational *Intergirl* (1988), dealing with hard currency prostitutes (see below), popularized the debate, replicating the one that had broken out eighty years earlier over Alexander Kuprin's *Yama*. Yury Nikitin's *Hologram* (1986) – with its scenes of resort romance, hotel sex, a starry-eyed young American woman visiting the Don, foreign bars, drunken tourists, and a total absence of ideas – suggested that writers had crossed a great divide and raised the specter of a revival of old Russian boulevard novels. Conservative writers spoke of the menace of a new *saninshchina* (see ch. 1). Once dull journals and newspapers – *Novyi mir*, *Sovetskaya kultura*, *Znamya*, *Moscow News*, *Znanie*, and *Ogonek* became popular because of their content and the invigorating prose. A fresh reportorial style also emerged. While still far from the "new journalism" of Norman Mailer, Tom Wolfe, or Hunter Thompson, it contained elements of drama, subjective angles, full dialogues, and "status details" borrowed from fiction and cinema. In Artem Borovik's reportage on Afghanistan, for example, one could hear authentic soldiers' slang and a Rod Stewart tape amid the clamor of guns and the clatter of helicopters.[4] Styles of popular culture began influencing the languages of official discourse and this helped new ways of thinking to emerge.

Everyone on stage

Theater at last entered the stream of mass culture in the era of glasnost. Thousands of self-financed companies – private in almost every way – sprang up all over the USSR. In Moscow alone hundreds of them were located in basements and shop fronts, largely run by young people who grew up in a culture of rock and video. The variety of formats, styles, and arrangements with authorities was infinite. The sort of avant-garde performances that in earlier years were put on in suburban train cars and in private flats came out in the open. Nudity, audience shock, dark references to the army and the police became commonplace. The "studio" theater groups who embraced topical themes (rather than the eternal or existential) began garnering large audiences. Their themes included breakdance, disco, organized crime, and the Afghanistan war.[5]

A stunning example of theater that was potentially popular and undeniably artful was Grigory Gurev's 1989 revival of Baliev's pre-revolutionary cabaret, The Bat. It brilliantly merged comedic nostalgia with politics as it commented on Tsar Nicholas and his mistress, the 1917 revolution, Stalinist mass culture, the war, the Robertino Loretti craze of the Khrushchev era, Jewish emigration, and current themes such as AIDS, gays, Boris Eltsin, and the television faith healer, Kashpirovsky (see p. 191). The highlight of the show was a vignette about Intourist guides for the 1957 Youth Festival, at the service of their guests "day and night"; in the denouement, they removed their colorful Russian scarves to reveal to their foreign boyfriends the epaulets of KGB officers as the band broke into "Evenings Outside Moscow." The Bat was a stunning example of the growing thirst among audiences to recapture some of the verve and sophistication of the old regime.

Even the hallowed circus ring was blasted by the gales of change that were howling over the cultural landscape. The press talked openly of circus tyrants, mistreatment of artists, poor safety devices, injuries and deaths, and extreme inequalities of pay. The virtual dictator of Soyuzgostsirk, Leonid Kostyuk, was removed because of his rude behavior toward employees and his archaic and grandiose style which grew out of the Olympic shows of 1980.[6] In the show itself, depoliticization proceeded rapidly. In September 1989 the old circus on Tsvetnoi Boulevard, thoroughly rebuilt, reopened under the direction of the elderly clown and movie actor, Yury Nikulin. Striking was the almost complete absence of standard Soviet elements: classical music, folk culture, World War II, and politics. The closest thing to preaching was a lesson about drunk driving performed by a clown. Rock, pop, reggae, and big band dominated the musical background. Since some circus officials feared a decline in circus attendance, the new face and sound of the arena was obviously designed to pull in the younger generations.

Folk ensemble performance continued to thrive – in large permanent companies, in variety shows, and on television and radio, and in a huge network of folklore clubs.[7] The Andreev centenary was widely celebrated in 1987. A film of Pyatnitsky's life and art was aired on Soviet television in 1989. The Moiseev troupe partially broke the steel vice of "folklorism" clamped upon it by its own success. The opener of a 1989 performance featured men and women in ballet gear with touches of folk costume. Syncretism was present in almost every subsequent number: folkish kicks alternating with pirouettes, the strains of Chaikovsky and Stravinsky giving way to circus and pop songs played by a big band devoid of balalaikas. The combination of elegy and energy raised this performance from mere entertainment to stage art. A 1989 performance of the Osipov ensemble, however, showed not a hint of modernism. Above the dark and whispered chords played pianissimo by a bank of balalaikas rose the plaintive voice of the accordion – over and over again. But the issue of the ideological perversion of folk culture in Soviet history was raised – for the first time – in a jarring film, *Prishvin's Paper Eyes* (1989) which intercut a Russian folk ensemble with clips of Hitler, Stalin, Mussolini, and fascist parades.

Live *estrada* was still next in popularity to television and movies in these years. Hundreds of thousands of concerts were mounted for tens of millions of people each year, placing its attendance figures far ahead of drama, opera, and ballet. A 1989 production at Moscow's famous Theater of Estrada offered a wide assortment: a comedy song on the history of variety shows in Russia ("It all got fouled up in 1917," sang Boris Brunov, director of the theater), several rock vocalists, a short folk number, and the popular teenage group, Tender May. But the customary eclecticism reflected in this show which drew an audience of all ages was rapidly giving way to *estrada* concerts featuring only rock bands. As a result, the word *estrada* became virtually synonymous with popular music.

For stage comedians, Aesopian language no longer worked because the new openness in public discourse cut at the heart of oblique social satire. Comedy became much bolder, sharper, more vulgar and direct.

Mikhail Zhvanetsky (see ch. 6), the master, played to huge audiences live and on television. Not far from him in popularity were Roman Kartsev and Viktor Ilchenko, fellow Odessans, and Gennady Khazanov, all of whom combined high comic art and civic message. But they were now much freer. Once aiming solely at middle- and lower-level social ailments, comics went for high politics, real issues, and prominent personalities. A 1990 television comedy hour presented a comedian's impression of Anatoly Kashpirovsky, the star of television faith-healing, promising his viewers – if they would only have faith – food in the shops, new apartments, and Fords and Cadillacs for all. Mikhail Zadornov publicly performed a hilarious impersonation of Gorbachev which not only replicated the leader's peculiar speech patterns and grammatical errors, but actually made fun of him. Gorbachev heard the tape and had a good laugh at it. Khazanov did the same thing at the Moscow White House during the August 1991 *putsch*. This was unprecedented in modern Russian history. Sendups of public and media figures, though angering some people, broke the ice of solemnity for others and seemed to say that the ambivalence toward authority which most people felt could be publicly aired without any real damage to anyone.[8]

New model cinema

The revolt of directors at the V Congress of the Filmmakers Union in May 1986, with tacit backing by political leaders, marked the onset of a new era in Soviet cinema. Elem Klimov replaced Kulidzhanov as head of the union and a largely new slate of officers was elected. In addition, Ermash of Goskino was replaced by a less rigid official.[9] The movie world – comprising as it did the power holders (Goskino), the filmmakers (the union), the critical establishment (institutes and journals), and the public – was thrown into a whirlpool of change rotating around two main issues: freedom and survival. In this sense, its quandary resembled that of the Soviet reforms in general: freedom of expression had been much easier to attain than economic security. On the freedom front came the release of many previously shelved and censored films and a good deal of artistic liberty. State censorship was greatly reduced and even for a while eliminated. Once taboo political, social, and sexual themes – including homosexuality – were vividly treated on screen. Pressure still emanated from party and cultural leaders; and the military and police establishments still tried to dissuade filmmakers from showing them in a bad light.

Films shelved for political or other reasons in the Brezhnev era included Klimov's own *Agony* (*Rasputin*, 1975, 1985) which was shelved because of its sympathetic portrait of the last tsar. Alexei German's *My Friend Ivan Lapshin* (1982, 1985) candidly displayed gloomy dorms, criminals, prostitutes, and beleaguered policemen in a small town on the eve of the great purges. Alexander Askoldov's stunning wide-screen black and white film *Commissar* harnessed the talents of the long deceased Vasily Grossman for its story, Alfred Shnitke, the USSR's foremost composer, Nona Mordyukova in the title role, Vasily Shukshin, and Rolan Bykov who delivered a virtuoso performance as the Jewish tinker. Askoldov broke two taboos when he made this film in 1967: putting on screen a female Bolshevik commissar who is pregnant out of wedlock and presenting a sympathetic and unsentimental treatment of ghetto life in Berdichev and a flash forward to the Holocaust. It was shelved until 1987. The most famous of the "unshelved" films, Tengiz Abuladze's *Repentance* (1984, 1986) was a landmark in political filmmaking, a beautifully wrought allegorical indictment of terror and dictatorship and of those who maintain silence in the face of evil. In Moscow cinemas more people saw this film (over 4 million) in two months than saw the popular hit *Pirates of the Twentieth Century*, and it sold 14 million tickets in a year – a record for an innovative film. But audiences comprised mostly educated people and *Repentance* did not enjoy success among the general public, particularly the young.[10]

Of the films made under perestroika, one that drew large audiences and critical acclaim was Klimov's *Come and Behold* (1985), a horrifying account of German troops gone amok in a Belorussian village whose inhabitants they burn alive. This event, based on a historical episode, is seen through the eyes of the young partisan boy, Florya, played brilliantly by Alexei Kravchenko who was hypnotized during the shooting of some scenes to give him a manic look. The soundtrack captures some of the spirit of the moment in partisan songs and the radio singing of Lyubov Orlova and Vadim Kozin. The finale of this color film is an enthralling backward roll of black and white footage on the rise of Hitler set to the music of the Mozart *Requiem*.

Documentary filmmakers were and still are at the forefront of social criticism and openness – indeed they were far out in front of professional historians. *More Light* (1988, narrated by Mikhail Ulyanov, a well-known actor and a staunch Gorbachevite) and *Defence Counselor Sedov* (1990) partially restored the historical truth about the Russian Revolution, early Bolshevism, and Stalinism. Documentaries dealt with the rehabilitation of artists, architects, and writers silenced or destroyed in the 1930s or harassed and persecuted in the 1960s and 1970s (Iosif Pasternak's *Black Square* and *Krivoarbatsky, 12*) and with current problems long glossed over or ignored by the media: environmental disaster, crime, drugs, prostitution, the Afghan war, bureaucracy, youth alienation, and rock culture. Herz Frank's *Highest Court* was a camera study of a condemned murderer awaiting execution. Georgy Gavrilov's *Confession: Chronicle of Alienation* did the same thing with a drug addict. They afforded raw and riveting glimpses into the underside of Soviet life, unthinkable in the previous era. Major facets of the youth scene were captured on film. *Is It Easy to be Young?* (1987) by Latvian director Juris Podnieks, chalked up record attendance figures for a documentary for its skillful unobtrusive interviews with young people involved in a destructive rampage at a rock concert. He extended his inquiry in the series *Soviets* (shown on American TV), whose Latvian cameraman was shot and killed by Russian troops in the Riga events of early 1991. *Homecoming* demythologized the Afghan war which was formerly hailed as a comradely internationalist struggle on behalf of a neighboring people. Among the pathbreaking documentaries, this was perhaps the most unnerving for many in that it was probably the first ambivalent screen treatment of a Soviet war in its cinema history.[11]

But the public did not rush to see all the masterpieces and documentaries. Soviet movie audiences, like those the world over, had not changed much since the birth of the cinema – they still preferred professionally made films of action, adventure, and pure entertainment over allegorical, symbolic, experimental, or political films. Movie audiences diminished in the face of the competition from upgraded television shows and televised films, foreign hits, and video. But since the new order in filmmaking wanted independence, this also meant a diminution in subsidy. The industry responded with the widely touted scheme for a "new model cinema" by independent or semi-independent studios and with joint venture and cooperative productions. The entire industry was streamlined, decentralized, and relatively democratized over the course of five years. Self-financing accelerated the process of diversification.[12]

All this fueled a big debate – a new version of a recurrent one – about taste and art. Many critics continued to scorn commercially successful films and wished to sustain the distance between filmmaker and mass audience. Others openly recognized the people's taste and discussed its implications; researchers used audience questionnaires to assess the age, gender, and occupation of the viewers. The ferment was mostly about how to make films with high moral and artistic value that were also box-office attractions (usually defined at 30–40 million tickets sold as opposed to the average of 3 million). This replicated the dilemma of the 1920s. The problem was partially solved back then by financing artistically worthy but poorly attended films with the receipts from popular ones. Another strategy was to make better popular movies. Critics knew in the 1980s that audiences did not flock to see "great" films. Survey research revealed that three-quarters of the movie-going public were young people who wanted action, compelling (*ostrosyuz-hetnye*) themes, and exciting plots. Detective movies, wrote a well-known film historian, were "the locomotive of the box office," and since, he claimed, most Soviet crime movies were trashy, the industry should import more well-made foreign ones. Conservative critics denounced "cinematic trash" (*kinoshka*) but they could not keep the masses from rushing to see it.[13]

The most important response was to make new kinds of popular movies, films which addressed problems of alienated youth, sexual tension, and hooliganism. Rock musicians began regularly appearing in them. In *The Burglar* and *Messenger Boy* (which includes break-dance scenes) – both 1987 – it was a backdrop. But in *Assa* (1988), rock culture was the symbol of a coming era just as the mafia-like boss was emblematic of the corrupt age about to fade away. At the end, rock star Viktor Tsoy (see fig. 26) sang: "We are expecting change." *Little Vera* (1988) was a wrenching, unvarnished closeup of working-class life in Maryupol (then called Zhdanov), a provincial smokestack and harbor town that drains the industrial Ukraine. In addition to dance-halls and disorderly youth (including a wall-to-wall gang fight), it showed sexual intimacy between a boy and a girl unprecedented on the Soviet screen. The female lead, Natalia Negoda (see fig. 27) was later the subject of a *Playboy* magazine picture story (May 1989). Director Vasily Pichul and screenwriter Maria Khmelik (his wife) were attacked and defended in the press. As for the public, 50 million tickets were sold in the first three months. The "first Soviet horror film" (so advertised) was *Mister Designer* (1988), an entertaining piece of gothic art, but far too tame to slake the thirst for shock that was growing fast. Ernst Yasan's *Evil Spirit* (1989) went further by depicting witches, labor camps, and homosexual gang rape; and *Guard* (1989) featured army brutality, multiple murder, male nudity, and lesbian sex.

Hollywood has only sporadically influenced Soviet cinema in the past, but two slick movies seemed to symbolize the time of frenetic glasnost. *Intergirl*, based on the Kunin novel, was the first film to deal openly with the long-established practice of prostitution at Intourist hotels. In spite of critical disdain – although one defended it as the new *Yama*[14] – it drew huge box-office receipts. The film delivered shock effect with brutal dialogue when a prostitute says to her colleague after a grueling session with a client: "he fucked and banged you the way Pol-Pot did it to Cambodia." It also presented, along with the nasty sides of Soviet life, the mystique of Russia – rendered musically by a stunning choral singing of the folksong "Baikal" as the heroine flies over Leningrad to join her Swedish husband. Most important, the film offered a balanced and sympathetic portrait of the "inter-girl" – a woman torn between two worlds – decked out in western clothes but clearly endowed with a Russian "soul"; and the contrasting picture of the Swedish businessman who is kind and decent but who adds up his dinner check with a calculator, an act all but unthinkable to a Russian. The heroine and her mother perish because of the daughter's sins – part of the moral message. But director Petr Todorovsky clearly wanted to get that message to the masses by infusing his picture with action, street life, and exotica.

A direct instance of *amerikanizm* in movies was *Déjà vu* (1989) a riotous Odessa Studio production set in 1925 and advertised as having "American style action." The plot of this manic parody of the gangster film – which recalls the cinematic gifts of Billy Wilder – revolves around a Chicago prohibition war and a Polish–American hit man sent to Odessa to wipe out an informer. It offers shameless quotations from Cagney films, *The Godfather*, and *Potemkin* (whose staircase scene is woven into the chase) and hilarious reactions of foreigners to Soviet life in the twenties. The large audience in Leningrad never stopped laughing and almost exploded at the shot of a mafioso with a civil war machine-gun pointed through a loft window – a direct quotation from *Chapaev*. The lavish depiction of the Odessa criminal underworld of bootlegging, American jazz, and sex during NEP was an affectionate reminder of another age, a sharp commentary on the kingdoms of illegality that flourished in the USSR in the late twentieth century, and a sidesplitting mockery of everything Soviet and communist in the early days of the revolution.

The film industry was beset by flux, tension, and debate in the Gorbachev years. Officials feared the total loss of ideological control and a descent into cinematic anarchy; artists and critics feared that bowing to mass taste would simply destroy film art. And there was unrest among actors and directors, a shortage of basic technical equipment to make marketable films, and a dearth of efficient managers and broadly educated, sensitive critics. But in spite of these problems and many others, the Soviet film world had not seen such euphoria and creative excitement since the 1920s, a time when both popular taste and great art had their days and nights in the dark salons.

Blue screen

Glasnost reestablished the nexus between real and even sensationalized news and popular culture that characterized the early years of this century. The main vehicle for this revival was television. In 1986, it was accessible to 93 percent of the population, 150 million people watched TV news daily (80 percent of all adults), and some 63 percent of blue and white collar workers named it as the chief source of information and moral values. The power of real news, politics, social candor, and the new popular entertainment relentlessly reduced the public's consumption of reading matter, theater, shows, concerts, and cinema-viewed movies – or so it was claimed. In May 1986 the news program *Time* replaced its logo of the old Kremlin tower with a global symbol; other changes came in quick order, including a new director, Eduard Sagalaev, in 1989. The new regime at *Time* sharply increased the function of timeliness (*operativnost*), giving viewers fast-breaking, authentic, and concrete news. This was a response to Gorbachev's remarks at the XXVII Party Congress in 1986 on the dullness of the media and the need to infuse them with life and appeal to audiences. On *Time* – increased to three times a day – news about the United States prevailed over that about the Third World or the socialist bloc – even during the revolutions of 1989. Reporters could meticulously demonstrate American voting machines and fast-food retailing procedures on Soviet TV. Disasters, violent crimes, and civil disorders, once hidden from sight, were reported. Although crackdowns and personnel changes of 1990–1991 jeopardized the new freedom, it was fully restored after the *putsch*.[15]

Straight news was surrounded by even more dramatically formated reportorial, interview, and call-in shows. *Twelfth Floor* was launched in 1986 by Sagalaev, at that time director of youth programing. Spinoffs included *Glance* (canceled and restored in 1991), *Before and After Midnight*, *Talk Show (Tok shou)*, *World and Youth*, *120 Minutes*, *Information TV*, the exposure program *Fact*, *Fifth Wheel*, and the meaty and kinetic *600 Seconds*. Some of these were lively, hard-hitting programs in which the visual medium clearly out-dramatized the press in treating rock culture, drug abuse, prostitution, youth disaffection, violence, and corruption with unprecedented candor and energy. On screen one could see young Soviet neo-Nazis expounding racism, body builders explaining why they beat up punks, and rockers and veterans talking about alienation. Cameras and microphones picked up the anger and the sharp clashes of opinion; and announcers responded to it with sympathy and a desire to defuse tensions and solve problems. *600 Seconds* was extremely popular because in it the personal opinion of the commentator – Alexander Nevzorov (b. 1958), an ex-circus performer and a confessed Russian nationalist – offered a voice that did not (at least before 1991) reverberate with the authority of the state. He asserted that the refined educated type of commentator (an *intelligent*) was unsuitable for the new TV journalism because it was soldier's work, dirty and rude, done by people who stick their noses everywhere and ask impolite questions.[16]

The entertainment sector of television got larger, though still proportionately smaller than in the US. Sports coverage was wider than in the states and women appeared more often both as athletes and as announcers. The biggest audience favorites were adventure films, popular music, comedy reviews, and games and youth shows that test the wit and skill of participants but without lavish prizes for winners. Half of all weekday viewing time was taken by movies, culture, and sports. TV films accounted for half of that time. They tended to be less sharply critical or challenging than those shown solely in theaters.

Musical programming on weekdays was about one-third classical; but on the weekend, 78 percent of cultural programs were rock, pop and mass song, and folk; only 6 percent of it was classical. The old morning exercise show became an aerobic ballet of chic females gyrating to rock or disco in the background. Rock was the thematic music for some news and commentary shows. Music video arrived on Soviet television and included outrageous costumes, lots of flesh, and vulgar foreign words such as "shit" uttered and written. In one, a pop female singer was driven in a limousine to a Soviet ministry to show the starchy men how to run the country. With the growth of cooperatives, joint ventures, and more active foreign firms, "sponsors" and commercials appeared, many in the format of the music video. In 1988, Michael Jackson, clad in leather and studs, sang for the first Pepsi commercial on Soviet TV.[17] In November 1989, the first commercial channel was opened and in 1991 cable TV appeared.

Although religious leaders regularly began to appear on television and freely voice their ideas – unheard of in the media throughout

Soviet history – it was the phenomenon of pseudo-medical faith healing that won millions of viewers. Anatoly Kashpirovsky, a physician and hypnotist, was for a time the second most famous person in the Soviet Union after Gorbachev. He combined religious and psychic imagery to promote mental, spiritual, and physical health. His style of delivery, riveting eyes, soothing voice, and velvet musical accompaniment, cured – he claimed – hundreds of thousands in the USSR and abroad. Although he and other TV healers were attacked by the academic and medical establishments, they throve as no other single kind of television personality.

The massive expansion of television popularity – now including commercial and cable channels – evoked criticism. The Soviet intelligentsia was more alienated from the general offerings on television than the American educated elite. The eminent scholar and standard-bearer of culturally conservative values, Dmitry Likhachev, saw television as a "great force" but one that was littered with bad programs – a wholly familiar complaint in "media" societies. Irina Tokmakova, one of the best-known children's writers, called it simply "a terrorist and aggressor who tries to oust literature."[18] Soviet television was becoming more like that in the west – though it still lacked sitcoms, gossip shows, canned laughter, formulaic silliness, violence on children's shows, and massive consumerism. Polling techniques were used to determine viewers' wants. Television news and entertainment mutually framed and defined one another. Frankness and timeliness in news coverage and analysis was paralleled by the sharpening of the themes of popular culture as a whole which were accessible on television to almost everybody simultaneously – historical revisionism, strident social commentary, iconoclastic styles of dress and speech, and audacious criticism of authority.

A word about radio and video. The former fell well behind TV among the mass media, though the radio speaker continued to hang in the workplace. Independent radio stations sprang up in 1991. Video – called Third Screen – grew rapidly. Video players cost about 1,200 rubles (before the currency reforms) and only 4,000 a year were produced; the great bulk of those in use were imported. They could also be rented. Owners of underground players and tapes viewed, bought, sold, and rented porno films and Western products such as Bruce Lee, *Rambo*, *The Last Tango in Paris*, and *One Flew Over the Cuckoo's Nest*. Public video sprung up everywhere after 1987 – at railroad stations, parks, and other public places, in private salons run by cooperatives who pirated foreign films, and by a state network of video bars, cafes, and salons, showing overwhelmingly foreign films of sex and violence. The House of Culture, once a stronghold of Soviet folk and "mass" entertainment became a house of rock and video.

Rock, shock, and schlock

The driving force behind urban youth culture in large Soviet cities was rock music. The burgeoning musical pogrom under Brezhnev and his successors died with them. Under Gorbachev, formerly proscribed rock bands were recognized and all styles of rock blossomed – hard, soft, punk, art, folk, fusion, retro, and heavy metal. The number of registered rock groups ran into the hundreds of thousands and it grew with great speed. Professional rockers belonged to one of about 200 concert agencies. They performed in clubs, restaurants, concert halls, radio shows, television programs, recording studios, and films; and they were paid on the basis of skill, training, and content of lyrics. Amateurs got no state bookings or pay but were free to drift from gig to gig, to shape their own programs, and to make informal wage deals. Beyond the pros and paid amateurs lay a whole world of garage bands, barracks groups, and workplace ensembles who played for themselves and friends. Thus a great deal of rock performance was unmonitored. Visiting rock stars did much to augment the music's popularity and Soviet groups found it much easier to travel to the West.[19]

What kind of people performed rock music? Overwhelmingly they were, as elsewhere in the world, young males. Ethnic peoples produced their own rock at home; but many rockers in the Russian Republic were also of non-Russian background – Korean, Jewish, Armenian, and all the rest. Some entered the scene through love of poetry and music; others saw it as an exit from intolerable surroundings – a moral outlet and a mode of free expression. Some are or were poor (Igor Sukachev of S-Brigade is an ex-worker; the late Viktor Tsoy worked as a stoker; Grebenshchikov lived in a seventh floor communal walk-up). Others came from famous families – of an architect (Andrei Makarevich), an aviation designer (Vsevolod Gakkel of Aquarium), even a politburo member (Stas Namin). Guitarist Sasha Skylar of Va Bank continued to play rock while serving as a junior diplomat in North Korea. Vyacheslav Bukusov of Nautilus Pompilius was trained as an architect. The level of musical background varied immensely from the self-taught to conservatory graduates. They were often portrayed in the media as hooligans. The film *Burglar* (1987) had rockers stealing a synthesizer and furiously smashing old trolley cars. But in the documentary, *Rock*, Boris Grebenshchikov, Viktor Tsoy, and Yury Shevchuk – often objects of strident press abuse – came across in low-key interviews as ordinary decent people, family men, lost and alienated from Soviet values, but not intent on violence of any kind.[20]

Boris Grebenshchikov (b. 1953) of Aquarium was for a time a cult figure for Soviet urban youth. The fifteen years of Aquariums' underground recordings (*kassetnaya kultura*) which reached millions, ended in 1987 when Melodia released his first legal album – 200,000 of which were bought within hours of release although unadvertised. Since then it has sold millions. Grebenshchikov left Aquarium and in 1989 went to live for a while in New York's Greenwich Village and made his first American release (in English). There was a very strongly perceived spiritual element in Grebenshchikov that distinguished him sharply from his Western counterparts – though this was not the only reason for his popularity. The tall, thin, sandy-haired, pony-tailed singer, resembled an aging hippie at first glance. But as Andrei Voznesensky pointed out, he was also truly poetic and possessed of a deep knowledge of Russian culture. This explains the breadth of his popularity at that time – like that of the bards earlier – to thousands of students, soldiers, officers, taiga dwellers, and ordinary people – though probably not to nosy grandmothers as one of his verses indicates:

> Farewell, babushkas, your aim was always dead-on target.
> Farewell, babushkas, your looks quenched all the flames.
> Farewell, babushkas, although you are always near the doors.
> But whoever told you that you have the right to rule us?[21]

Soviet rock, like jazz before it, had many well-placed friends and allies. The popularity of such groups as AVIA, Black Coffee, Aquarium, Time Machine, Stas Namin, Bravo, Pop Mekhanika, Kino, Arsenal, Nautilus Pompilius, and Avtograf brought them celebrity and contacts with other figures in the art and entertainment worlds. Raimond Pauls explained that he preferred the intimate sound of jazz to rock, but added: "Why should fifty-year-olds dictate the tastes of the young?" Alla Pugachëva actively supported rock musicians. Voznesensky, a leading Soviet poet, was an enthusiastic promoter of Grebenshchikov. Critic Oleg Panov called rock music the folklore of the Scientific Technical Revolution and urged the public to take it seriously, admit its vast popularity, and criticize it intelligently. The political bosses were not quite so clear cut, yet in 1987, Raisa Gorbachëva greeted John

Lennon's widow Yoko Ono by saying that she and her husband were Beatles' fans.[22]

While some Soviet rock music resembled that of the West right down to instrumentation and electronic gear, it varied greatly. The 1987 festival Rock Panorama featured fifty bands, half of them hard rock. Autograph's debut album of progressive hard rock sold over 6 million copies. It was fronted by Alexander Sitkovetsky, son of a concert violinist. Zvuki Mu, led by Petya Mamonov, took its name from the American film *Sound of Music* (*Zvuki muzyki*). Groups like Bravo specialized in retro; its ex-vocalist, Zhanna Aguzarova, catapulted it and her to fame with fifties style rock and roll (thus dubbed "Neo-Stilyagi" by a rock critic). Rock Hotel (Rokotel) did blue grass and gospel and even renditions of 1930s Estonian pop. The themes of apathy, falseness, indifference, hypocrisy, and conformism were heard more often than amorous or erotic ones and were joined by the glasnost themes of drugs, war, alcoholism, prostitution, corruption, and speculation – but their bite was much sharper than any of the glasnost media. Nautilus Pompilius sang of kindness and reason, Russian woes and Russian dreams. After touring, they always returned to Sverdlovsk in the Urals to maintain, as they say, their Russianness.[23]

But rock continued to make enemies because of its style and its social overflow. The loudness and the harsh vocal phrasing assaulted the ears of older people who for decades had tuned in to smother pop music. Rock lyrics such as "get out of control" or "my father is a fascist" were offensive to Leninists and to those who recalled the war against "fascism" in 1941. A rock lament on the lack of places for couples to make love ended like this:

> In summer we can go together to the woods
> But it takes an hour to get there
> And if the local fuckers get you
> You risk being beaten into a pile of shit.

Or the boast of a corrupt bureaucrat as rendered by the group DK:

> I am a man of the people
> The people chose me
> And raised me over the years.
> That's how it is, boom, boom, fuck you;
> That's how it is.

Rockers presented the satire of sound, sight, and gesture. Song titles like "Atheist Twist" or names of groups such as Crematorium, Female Disease, Pig, Chapaev Detachment, or Mister Twister (from a beloved children's verse), were offensive to an older generation – especially when the last named group played the sacred revolutionary hymn "Varshavianka" to a rock 'n' roll beat. Rock players licked shoes, stripped, threw meat at the audience, fainted into it, and shepherded livestock onto the stage. S-Brigade (Brigada-S), dressed in zoot suits, performed in front of a huge portrait of Brezhnev with the word "proletjazz" on his forehead and a missile in his mouth. Hairstyles and costumes ranged from the hippie look of the 1960s to mocking replicas of Russian civil war uniforms. Like the popular music of other eras and places, rock produced a subculture that was carried onto the streets: a lexicon, facial expressions, gestures, clothes – a code and ethos shared by its members. Heavy metal fans called themselves *metallisty*, a term associated by older people with the steelworkers of the October Revolution.[24]

In the minds of some conservatives, rock was equivalent to vice or disloyalty. In 1987 a Red Army officer identified heavy metal with Zionism and the once powerful writer Sergei Mikhalkov linked rock bands to AIDS, prostitution, drugs, crime, and treason. The right-wing group Pamyat put the matter simply: "Rock groups are satanism." When he was prime minister, the conservative Egor Ligachev opposed the "spread of primitive music" and urged a return to folk and classical. Influential ruralist writers called rock "mentally and morally damaging." Alexander Yakovlev, though a major Gorbachev reformer, on viewing an American rock group and its "frantic" audience on television, said that "such things we shall never accept." Dmitry Likhachev viewed popular music as all "wild rhythms and stupid words." A writer for *Young Guard* managed in its first two pages to sew together carnal lust and nudity with Esperanto, Israel, NATO, Bill Haley, and Elvis Presley. To some observers, the rise of rock and roll was a political danger. Nina Andreeva, author of the notorious pro-Stalin letter of 1988, launched in 1989 a diatribe to a foreign journalist against the suggestive performance of Yury Shevchuk. "His male dignity was protruding!" she said:

In any state there must be order ... This is not a state, it is like some anarchistic gathering. And when there is such a gathering there is no state no order, no nothing. A state, above all, means order, order, order.[25]

But discomfort with the rock revolution arose not only from ideological concerns. Traditional crooners like Iosif Kobzon and Muslim Magomaev lost young listeners to rock singers and were also mocked by them. Kobzon in particular was a constant butt of jokes – open and underground. Zhanna Bichevskaya complained in 1986 that teenagers listen to heavy metal and other "non-descript music." Big band figures who fought for years in order to gain recognition were distressed. Konstantin Orbelyan, a smoothly attired leader of the Armenian State Estrada Orchestra, was a child of the Stalinist purges who fought against all odds to make it to the top of popular music only to find that in the late 1980s his kind of music was ignored by "nearsighted managers" and television producers. He made the mournful and undoubtedly correct observation that if Utesov, Shulzhenko, or Ruslanova should reappear, they would not have a chance.[26]

What happened to mass song, folk music, jazz, and pop in the years of glasnost? Radio and TV programing, records, and lingering affection kept them very much alive. One could often hear Kobzon – who was a People's Deputy in parliament – and others doing mass songs on TV and an occasional retrospective of Blanter or Dunaevsky on the radio. Memory of the war was partly responsible for their enduring popularity. Russian people – not only officials – loved the songs they heard when growing up, falling in love, or fighting in a war. The folk industry was deeply entrenched and widespread. The most debased forms of folk kitsch were performed in tourist restaurants. But real folk songs could be heard daily on the radio. Balalaika lessons were still offered in workers' clubs and amateur folk groups were too numerous to count. Bands in restaurants played a few folk numbers for wedding parties and older guests. But adolescents and young adults were tired of it. At concerts, young people sometimes left when a folk ensemble followed a pop group.

Jazz still had a large following among the intelligentsia, not only those who grew up on it in the 1940s, but some young people as well. The Leningrad Jazz Club, directed by the multi-talented David Goloshchekin, had full houses five nights a week in the winter of 1989–1990 (it was the only such club in the huge city); there people of all ages could eat, drink, and sometimes dance to Soviet and foreign jazz music, although a certain amount of reserve was expected of the public. In Moscow the Igor Bril Quartet (piano, guitar, saxophone, and string bass) continued to play with brilliant technical virtuosity the classical idiom of the 1950s. Mainstream jazzmen filled huge Moscow *estrada* theaters with their concerts. Apostles of New Jazz or Free Jazz, like Vyacheslav Ganelin, Vladimir Chekasin, Vladimir Tarasov, Sergei Kurekhin, and other avant-gardists abandoned the decorum of the "cool" era for an explosive emotionalism, experimental individualism, and political iconoclasm: at concerts they matched the rockers in parodying revolutionary songs or desecrating Stalin's portrait. A promoter of Free Jazz has called it "the most democratic music on this planet" but it has not captured a mass audience.[27]

What about pop? When rock and roll in the States outstripped jazz and "popular" song, the latter genres continued on in narrower outlets – radio, nightclubs, and recordings with greatly diminished sales. In Russia, entrenched mechanisms and institutions and the absence of a market slowed the pace of change. Although big band held out on larger stages, the old "combo" – sax, piano, percussion, and brass – was almost wholly replaced in Soviet restaurants by the VIA with its electronically amplified guitars, keyboard, and drums. Displaced musicians retired into teaching or work in Houses of Culture. Soviet pop song took on some of the trappings of disco and rock. A typical Moscow hit in 1989 was "Music Brought us Together" (Muzyka nas svyazala) sung by Tanya Ovseenko of the group Mirage, a strident song in a minor key backed by a pounding disco rhythm. But most of the other hits were squarely in the Soviet pop melodic tradition. Aside from the world hit, "Lambada," the big favorites bore titles such as "White Roses," "Old Cafe," and "Don't Put Salt on My Wounds."

Two song hits of that year contained social commentary couched in the form of a ballad or "cruel song." Nautilus Pompilius' "Goodbye, America" was the sad if ironic recognition by the singer that he would never see the States. The other, upbeat in melody, was the balladeer's story of a childhood sweetheart who had become a prostitute or "Putana." Its verses recalled the innocent school years and then separation – he to a camp, she to a foreign currency bar from which he cannot retrieve her:

> Putana, Putana, Putana,
> Nocturnal butterfly; well then, who's to blame?
> Putana, Putana, Putana,
> Enchanting night lights always draw you to their flame.[28]

Alla Pugacheva's popularity did not diminish even among the young. In 1987 a school teacher complained that her pupils put "Alla" first on a list of most admired heroes. Her persona continued to add to her lustre: aggressively individualistic and clinging to youth, she concertized in miniskirt and boots and refused to be a "grand old lady of Soviet estrada."[29] In performance, Pugacheva created an alluring combination of moods: the clothes, the backup sound, and the beat were continental European; but the words of her songs were Russian and the music alternated a contemporary disco sound with a melancholy minor and snatches of folk dance and waltz. At a 1989 concert, characteristically called "Christmas Greetings," the mood was accented by a choir singing Orthodox music, a backdrop of a Russian church, and a memorial screening of portraits of deceased heroes of the intelligentsia – Pasternak, Vysotsky, Sakharov (who had died a few days before).

Youth: subculture and social barometer

The Soviet Union has never possessed a monolithic leisure culture. But an unprecedented pluralism flourished openly during the heyday of Gorbachev, resulting from dramatically increased exposure to the West, glasnost, and the attendant sense of self-discovery. Old forms of amusement endured, particularly visiting, going out, restaurant dining, and hobbies. But the diversity in form and the daring of the content in all of these arenas were redolent not of NEP – when it was dangerous to flaunt unacceptable social as well as political values – but to the old regime. Urban Soviet youth retained its habit of hanging out in groups or gangs that shared the same taste – groups of constantly changing shape and composition. A new street culture arose that was popular both as the chosen leisure form of those in it and as an object of entertainment for the general public. On Moscow's pedestrianized Arbat Street and in Izmailovo Park of Culture, one saw not only daring outdoor art, but a whole marketplace of cultural forms – rock bands, singers, poets, youngsters in bizarre costumes, and sellers of kitschy junk bearing bold and topical slogans. In Leningrad subway tunnels, guitarists sang songs of NEP and the prison camps. It was the same array of visual and theatrical elements which twenty years earlier linked the hippie hangouts of a score of American and European cities into a single culture.

Informal youth groups based on interests or "issues" became more diverse and more publicized. One student estimated their number at about 30,000 in the late 1980s. Their interests ranged over nudism, music, the environment, religion, and all kinds of political programs. One of the oldest was the hippies, whose movement slumbered for two decades and resurged around 1985. Some hippies combined social nonconformity with religious sensibility; their main goal was to withdraw from "Soviet" society and shape their own lives. They created their own jargon, hangouts, and values – including a level of sexual activity high even for Russians. On the other hand women were definitely second-class citizens. Hippies were non-Soviet in that they loved the leisure life, supplemented the vodka sometimes with drugs, abhorred military service, and systematically ridiculed Soviet icons and traditions – the medals, the war movies, the flag, and the cult heroes they were told to revere as schoolchildren, such as Lenin, Zoya Kosmodemyanskaya, and Gagarin. This withdrawal from official Soviet life had political implications but was not overtly dissident.[30]

The potentially explosive phenomenon of war veterans in the twentieth century has been little studied in a comparative manner. Yet the experience of veterans' circles in Germany, France, and Eastern Europe between the wars, as well as the very different "Vietnam syndrome" in the United States offers much for historical reflection. Many of the 700,000 Soviet veterans of the war in Afghanistan (1979–1986) – including about 20 percent who saw combat – joined groups that reflected their views – not only about the war, but about society as a whole. The groups included military-patriotic societies and benefit associations. The paramount mood of the veterans (*afgantsy*) was one of puzzlement and disillusionment about their military experience. They spoke publicly about atrocities committed on both sides, about glossy training films showing soldiers milking cows and helping the Afghan people, and about the lack of real coverage of the war back home. Their often-voiced opinion that "they don't understand us" betrayed a sense of alienation from civilian society and a yearning for a bond with their fellow veterans. Though far from unanimous in their opinions (some were proud to kill, others abhorred it), the majority seemed to have had difficulty adjusting to peacetime life and doubts about whom to believe. This led some into taking over Komsomol chapters and street gangs and marching in protest. Those of the patriotic persuasion targeted corrupt bureaucrats and teenage punks and rockers.[31]

The gang phenomenon took on new shape in the era of perestroika. Some gangs simply melted into the criminal syndicates which flourished. Crime, vice, and the gang culture were publicized by the media and popular culture more than at any time in Soviet history – not only in news reportage, but in movies and songs dealing with prostitution rings, the "mafia," and gang wars. Juvenile violence quickened among working-class and vocational school youth in provincial smokestack and rust belt towns and ports and in the new housing developments and proletarian suburbs of big cities that were beset by material and cultural deprivations. City gangs which in the past had little connection with other elements of society except as a force of hooliganism now became vigilantes. In Novosibirsk, a gang assaulted speculators and destroyed their goods in the name of morality and reform. In Kazan gangs performed ring dance rituals, wore short hair, did bodybuilding, subjected their recruits to a fist fighting test, and forbade members to leave the organization once enrolled. Such gangs hated metalheads and wearers of earrings and trinkets whom they deemed weak and morally sick. The Kazan group Cascade, founded by an Afghan veteran, and the Petrozavodsk Union of Struggle for Justice declared an alliance against corruption and rock music. Other gangs surfaced in Pskov, Rostov, Volgograd, Taganrog, Sverdlovsk, Chelyabinsk, Gorky, Vologda, Kurgan, and Alma Ata.[32]

In Moscow, violence was fueled by resentment of speculators and privileged youth (called *goldeny* by a television interviewee). One Moscow group forced speculators to help Afghan war widows; another, The Repairmen, helped mend the minds of "disloyal" rockers and punks. The best-known gang was The Office (Kontora), known to outsiders as the Lyubery, named from the Moscow suburb of Lyubertsy which contains 360,000 residents, mostly working class. Martial arts and bodybuilding – very popular in the media – was their main hobby, and they adopted special clothing, names, rituals, and a way of walking. Moved by a kind of angry redneck patriotism, the Lyubery identified rock music, its cultural style, and its devotees with the West and with disloyalty. They traveled downtown to raid discos, beat up rockers and hippies ("a disgrace to the Soviet way of life"), cut their hair, and smash their artifacts. "We hate punks," one of them said, "and everybody else does too." They also attacked dealers and well-dressed youths, thus revealing an element of social envy beneath the cultural slogans. Although the activities of the Lyubery diminished in the late 1980s, the tone of their limericks was menacing:

> We were born and raised in Lyubertsy
> The center of physical force.
> The center of Russia will be Lyubertsy
> And we believe our dream will come true.[33]

Neo-Nazi youth had been around since the 1960s, a product of boredom and alienation. But in the late eighties it surfaced in urban gangs. One, called Bad Boys (*Bed boiz*) vowed to kill all communists and Komsomols. In 1987, some youth audiences cheered Hitler in a screening of the 1941 newsreel film *Defeat of the German Armies Near Moscow*. Since 1982, these youngsters, short haired, with black shirts, jackboots, dark glasses, and swastikas sporadically celebrated Hitler's birthday on April 20 in Moscow by shouting "Sieg Heil!" in public. Opponents and victims of gang violence organized marches in Moscow and Leningrad in 1987 to protest police inactivity. Some commentators perceived a natural (and perhaps active) alliance between the culturally conservative intelligentsia and the street gangs since both displayed bitter hostility to the dominant mode of youth culture. Their impulses of course were quite different. The former felt a threat to their status and its symbols. The latter were fueled by the socio-geographical resentment of people who lived in a more rigidly controlled environment (working-class suburbs) toward the youth of the inner city who not only had more things but also more freedom. Rock, clothing, and badges were the offensive symbols of this freedom. The polarities created by the cultural element in street politics were part of the painful process of pluralism, free expression, and democracy.

Civil society and civilized life

Since Stalin's death, a continuous tension between popular demand and official offering has been in place – resulting in the painful but relatively quiet cultural wars of the Khrushchev and Brezhnev eras. Beneath the surface, urbanization has continued and all but triumphed; contact with the west – punctuated by occasional setbacks – has grown relentlessly as has technological growth. All of this flowed together in the Gorbachev revolution to strengthen and make possible the glasnost and the explosion of new public forms of expression. Long-felt needs and desires of the population were put on full display. Upon coming to power, Gorbachev sent two strong signals about how glasnost related to popular culture: his appeal for more responsive media and his 1987 appeal to "give young boys and girls scope for their own activities, and spare them petty interference and surveillance."[34] The media echoed this all through the glasnost period: newspapers urged that rock music be given a hearing; television interviewers encouraged disaffected youngsters to speak for themselves. There existed for a time a tacit alliance among reform leaders, media managers, a segment of the intelligentsia, and the huge rock community. At the same time, the authorities, the Komsomol, and entertainment industry leaders tried to tame and coopt rock music culture, to deflect it from nihilistic directions without eliminating its vigor – a difficult task.

Many of the changes in popular culture noted here had beginnings in the pre-Gorbachev era. But one of its functions in the new era was to disseminate in popular and digestible forms the muckraking and revisionism of journalism. Under the old order, fun and social criticism (tightly constrained) were subjected to a certain distancing. Under the new, the two were often combined and they opened to the masses past realities and present problems. This disturbed some as much as it delighted others. But even some of the most eccentric popular culture was defused and legitimized by its very appearance on television in a respectable setting. The openness in the media helped close that enormous and oft-noted gap in Soviet life between the public and the private, the personal and the official as expressed in words, voice, gesture, and behavior patterns. Narrowing this gap was essential in removing the surreal and fantasy-like qualities that imbued so much of the daily round. The whole process was marked by backlash, gaps, and contradictions. But the new popular culture gave those who favored reform a greater sense of participation in national renewal by seeing problems dramatized or fictionalized in song, story, television drama, or comedy routine. The audience thrill of identification supplemented what people got from news and political language. The diverse content of the emerging popular culture reinforced pluralism – existing or in embryo. Religious freedom, greater privacy, personal security and autonomy, preservation of past culture, and conservation of nature were not only promised in speeches but also celebrated in the popular arts. The burning question was: could all this lead to greater civic consciousness among the Soviet people, a prerequisite for any passage to the long-awaited civil society? Or could it be the accompanying song of polarization and chaos?

No one can predict the near or far future of Russian popular culture – or of any major aspect of life. Shortly after his first press conference as minister of culture in 1989, the noted actor and director, Nikolai Gubenko, met with the Supreme Soviet's Commission on Culture, headed by the writer Chingiz Aitmatov, and attended by luminaries of high culture, including the universally revered Dmitry Likhachev. They lamented the still-lingering ideologization of culture and also noted the low level of mass culture. In their effort to raise the overall cultural level of the population, an admirable goal, will they try to control the mechanisms (foreign import and the market) that actually process the people's taste? Gubenko's work at the Taganka and in films did not portend any particular sympathy for mass culture; on the other hand he was the most liberal and democratic culture minister since Lunacharsky. And his colleague Raimond Pauls, briefly the minister of culture in Latvia, had a whole lifetime of popular culture behind him. The election to parliament as People's Deputies of such cultural figures as Evtushenko, Voznesensky, Kobzon, Ales Adamovich (head of the Film Research Institute), Alexander Gelman (film writer and playwright), Mikhail Ulyanov and Kirill Lavrov (actors), and Yury Shchekochikhin (a leading writer on youth subculture) and many others had more significance than, say, the election of Dunaevsky to the Supreme Soviet in Stalin's time – but in which direction?[35]

Nor can glasnost or the freeing up of the cultural scene provide answers to the future of the Gorbachev revolution. After a speech in the Soviet Far East a few years ago, Gorbachev was asked by a listener about glasnost: "What do you eat with it?" Hundreds of kindred remarks were voiced by citizens about the new popular culture. But they said this also about high culture, political and economic reform, and the new detente – and this did not necessarily indicate the unimportance of these things. Popular culture at the peak of glasnost reflected above all the uneven development between top and bottom and the splintering and pluralism of values in Soviet society: new and old, urban and rural, cosmopolitan and chauvinistic, religious and anti-religious, rational and mystical – and many more polarities and conflicting emotional values. But it also indicated spontaneity, freedom, competition, individualism – a market place of ideas and feelings. And this is the absolute prerequisite for the expansion and legitimation of all kinds of popular culture – including that which was long forbidden – and for the satisfaction of the entire gamut of the people's tastes.

Greetings and farewell

Soviet history has come to an end. How can we assess the history of its popular culture and entertainment? Its fate was conditioned by the degree of freedom of communication across frontiers; the presence and power of the market; the extent and quality of competition by non-market forces – especially the state. In the last years of tsarism, both the importing and the marketing mechanisms were relatively free and the state was correspondingly inactive in the realm of entertainment. People in towns had a good deal of access to pulp literature, serialized stories, recordings of popular songs, movies, and stage shows – if they could afford them. Cultural elites tried to compete with these offerings but possessed little power to interdict them. Thus urban popular culture was surrounded by high culture, folk culture, and a modicum of radical culture, but harbored more than enough energy and space in which to grow. World War I, though foreshadowing what was to come, did little to alter the balance.

The changes wrought in the early years of Soviet power altered the balance, though not definitively. Foreign importation and a commercial market were permitted but controlled. The market was feeble and politics constantly intervened and competed on an unequal basis with commercial culture. And the moral sermons uttered by the intelligentsia and culturalists of the old regime were replaced by the thunder of the commissars and Komsomol activists. In this war between alleged proletarian values and commercial ones, the state often lost. At the end of the 1920s, militants of the cultural revolution destroyed the mechanisms of commercial popular culture and tried to replace it with a dry, cramped, and Utopian culture that was anti-intellectual in rhetoric but largely cerebral in inspiration – the product of narrow-minded and puritanical ideologues. Its temporary victory caused the greatest gap between cultural production and demand in Soviet history. And it was repudiated precisely because of its unrealistic and unproductive dogmatism.

The Stalinist order went furthest in trying to control culture and taste – at every level. But, paradoxically, in doing so it created a culture that was far more to the taste of the masses than that of the cultural revolution of the preceding years. Because so much of the cultural production was politically or ideologically mandated, some have argued that popular culture ceased to exist in the Stalin period; that no original culture at all emerged in those years; that, since foreign imports all but ceased in the 1930s and commerce was killed, this left only state-produced sacralizing propaganda possessing neither art nor mass appeal; and that thus the people had no choice. But this is not what happened. Choice did exist within mass culture which was developed to answer public taste as well as state goals. That the culture was monopolistic and that other products could have had even better reception does not change the fact that the masses consumed it and enjoyed it.

This does not mean that Stalinist culture was not mystification. Anyone living or growing up in the USSR in the 1930s with ears and eyes and a minimum of understanding was saturated with certain themes about national life beamed out in news stories and educational materials, themes that served the designs of despotic leaders and were reinforced in the popular media. Indeed it is more than likely that the latter was the most influential conveyor of official values. Missing from the public record so far is the inner story of those who created the mass culture of the time. We have only an inkling of behind-the-scenes plots and fights, tyrannical bosses, casting couches, careerism, treachery, and purges.[1] When the details surface, as they are bound to, some of it will resemble what we know from Hollywood history; but the resemblance is superficial. Can one imagine in the 1940s the execution by federal authorities of Louis B. Mayer and the imprisonment of Bing Crosby, the Andrews sisters, and Harry James? This after all would have been the equivalent of the actual shooting of Boris Shumyatsky and the arrest of Vadim Kozin, Lydia Ruslanova, and Eddie Rosner. Thirty years ago the American comedian Bob Hope, on his return from Russia, joked that "over here [in the US] the losers get to go home." He was comparing Russian political losers to the losers at the Academy Awards. But in fact, there were losers – in a total sense – in the Soviet entertainment world. We do not yet know what, if any, moral losses were felt by those who survived and served the system all the way through.

The changes that occurred after Stalin's death seem pallid when compared with those in the US which saw the dismantling of the

Hollywood studio system, the near total eclipse of big band jazz in favor of rock and roll, the ascendance of television as the principal means of mass entertainment, the growth of drive-in movies and fast food shops, and the flourishing of subcultures and countercultures. Nevertheless throughout the Khrushchev and Brezhnev years, the cultural scene widened. The controlled reentry of foreign culture triggered desires for more and launched the long march of youth for complete cultural autonomy. The commercial market remained closed, but the dominance of officially sponsored culture – through unions, repertory commissions, cultural fiefdoms, and Komsomol crusades – gradually weakened until at the very end of the pre-Gorbachev era, it was on the verge of collapse. Now, the doors to the outer world have been flung wide open, the market is emerging, and the control mechanism almost a shambles. Soviet society – what is left of it – is about to be deluged by the world cultural system, called in some quarters "Americanization."

The intense telescoping of processes of this period, the volcanic effect of spewing out long-pent-up feelings, grievances, and modes of expression invites comparison with the Russian Revolutions of 1905 and 1917 both of which were followed by repression and stifling of the recently vented impulses – the first by tsarist authorities, the second by the Bolsheviks. It also resembles, in its frenetic enthusiasm and critical edge, the May 4th Movement of China which erupted in 1919 and the radical free speech movements in the United States and Western Europe in the 1960s. Eldar Ryazanov's elegiac comedy, *Forgotten Melody for Flute* (1987) presents a scorching satire on state control of taste via a Directorate of Leisure Time whose officials mindlessly bungle the management of amateur theater, modern art, and provincial folk ensembles. But the film also points to the death of censorship and – in the metaphor of its finale – to censorship itself as death. Muckraking, social criticism, and even the ridicule of political leaders has replaced Stalinist panegyric Utopia. The media, in a way unknown in Soviet history, has become the voice of fundamental change.

The history of the Soviet state has ended. But what will become of its popular culture? One of the great misreadings of the Soviet people by foreigners has been to take the part for the whole, to mistake the values and habits of the Moscow and Leningrad intelligentsia for those of all Russian and other Soviet people. Leaving out the non-Russian nationalities whose own inner cultural history is begging to be told, it is clear that the vast majority of Russians were not really represented by the elite that resides at the top and in the center – any more than

New York culture is American culture in miniature. In Soviet times, tourists often arrived in the Soviet Union half expecting to see citizens walking around with *Das Kapital* under one arm and *War and Peace* under the other; to see in other words an entire nation steeped in ideological politics and high culture. Anyone who stayed there for more than a day would, if attentive, have seen that most people cared nothing – or less than nothing – about Marx; and that their cultural pursuits were much more in the directions described in this book than in those of high culture. To learn this, of course, one had to mingle with ordinary people who did not know foreign languages and to haunt places that most scholars were not inclined to visit. But although a number of journalists and exchange students did describe this world, the message never seems to have gotten through. Why?

Part of it is because tourism did not and still does not lend itself to critical observation – the fault of both the tourist and Intourist. The latter organization showed visitors what it thought was the best (or indeed only) side of Russian culture: the ballet, the theater, the galleries. Elite bias on both sides of the border shaped the cultural exchanges: for a long time this was Leonard Bernstein for David Oistrakh or jazz for folk dancing. Ordinary people with common tastes from abroad seldom met their Russian counterparts – the millions of them. When journalists encountered *stilyagi* or rock fans, they often saw them only as signs of political disaffection. Only now, with much openness in the former USSR and sharper observation of what is happening on streets and on stages is this changing. Perhaps in time, while the elites of Russia and the outer world continue to enjoy political and high cultural intercourse – which indeed they should – the people of that country and the rest of the world can find something to share in the kinds of popular culture and entertainment they enjoy.

It is true that many Russians were more steeped in the classics than are, for example, Americans – partly because they had more to be steeped in (a group of Soviet hippies, after the non-appearance of the rock group Santana in Leningrad in 1987, made their way to the family estate of Tolstoy at Yasnaya Polyana).[2] But high culture was not the main occupation of the broad masses in their leisure time. The majority of Soviet Russians enjoyed what some people would call simple, common, or vulgar entertainments. Although many Soviet intellectuals still lament this, it is probably wiser to recognize its truth, avoid the unflattering terminology, and refrain from using this truth as a judgment either on the masses or on culture. But does this mean that there is nothing specific about Russian varieties of popular culture?

That it is simply a local sector of a world culture? Yes and no. Yes, to the extent that it is fast coming under the influence of outside forces – disco, clothing, video, celebrity crazes (Madonna or Lambada), commercial television. No, to the extent that old forms persist, as they have done so stubbornly through the decades both through official aid and through natural patterns of taste (gypsy songs, war ballads, old movies, even folk ensembles).

There was no single popular culture that meshed with a single set of mass values because values varied between generations, locales, genders, and social strata; and they changed over time. Popular arts can never fully and precisely reflect mass values. But if popular culture is but a murky mirror image of certain values and feelings held by a large body of people in a given time, it is a mirror none the less. And it has reflected over time the feelings and aspirations of people, their attitudes to the regime, and their vision of self. Some long-range shifts in popular values are discernable. One is a slow and gradual decline of interest by the masses in ideology and in abstract goals of the state, goals that, in the years 1917–1941, captured hundreds of thousands for the revolution, the cultural revolution, and the great age of construction. During the war, all energy was turned to saving the country from a murderous foreign invader – a far more concrete phenomenon than building communism. The upsurge of patriotism induced a related deepening of personal values and a search for identity apart from the state. In time, the defensive patriotism of the war gave way in many people to nostalgic love for the countryside, for national identity, and for the religion that was associated with them. Russian nationalism was promoted and reinforced by the growth of folk music performance, especially at the local level. The postwar leaders not only allowed this feeling to germinate but themselves shared its nostalgic glow.

Urban elements not bound to the regime, especially each new generation of youth, sought their identity not in birch trees and village choirs but in the exotic appeals of the outside world. There were the jazz musicians who rejected the balalaika for the saxophone; the courtyard teenagers of Aksenov who preferred pop music to folk songs; the rockers who ridiculed the archaic habits of the Russian grandmothers. If one group turned its face to the village and the other to the city, both did an about-face away from the politics of the regime. Needless to say, there never was a simple division of the population into urbanites and ruralists, politicized and depoliticized. People continue to mingle things according to circumstances and desire. But one need only to compare the heroic structures of the most popular songs

and movies of the 1930s to those of the 1970s to see how far a
population, including those who still vaguely believed in the goals of
communism, had banished the rhetoric of revolutionary transformation from the languages of popular culture.

Youth and generational rebellion have always been linked up with
popular culture. The "gilded youth" – or children of the leaders (a
group about which we have yet much to learn) often felt a particular
grievance against state culture which they lived so near. In the 1920s
counter culture grew up in the wake of NEP as a counterweight to the
moralizing revolutionary rhetoric of the new regime. Under Stalin it
took the form of very narrowly constricted jokes and some songs and
lyrics. In the 1940s it was nourished by jazz and imported movies. After
the amnesties of the 1950s, prison camp culture enriched the urban
underground and traces of it found their way into cultural icons like
Vysotsky. The flow became much larger: search for authenticity, thaws
and frosts, the massive apoliticism of the people, and the crude cultural policies of the regime all fed into it. In the Gorbachev period,
undergrounds surfaced to the street and counter cultures almost
merged with the free culture of glasnost and became part of it.

There is reason to celebrate the liberation of youth culture. Honest
and intelligent people in Russia and abroad are greeting it with open
arms. But it is to be hoped that the celebration will be marked by
tolerance. Many Russians understandably wish to obliterate the Soviet
past – including all its culture – to leap back into a mythic, romanticized realm of the tsars. But it was precisely the purloining of the past
that the now detested former leaders were so good at. Young people
have a right to stretch out and embrace the artifacts of global culture,
to feel themselves and to be a part of a modern world, to voice their
own demands and concerns, and to shout an angry and ironic farewell
to the mass culture that their parents and grandparents once enjoyed,
a culture that now seems on the verge of extinction. But those parents
who built dams, fought a war, and carved out a life in the tumultuous
and tragic decades of Soviet history had an inner life as well, a life that
was sometimes lightened or made tolerable by a haunting love song, a
tale of heroism and adventure, the biting satire of a clown, or the
dusky black and white shadows flitting across a screen.

Notes

Introduction

1 Gans, *Popular Culture and High Culture.*
2 For a beginning see the works of Friedberg, Mehnert, and Shlapentokh in the bibliography. I have also omitted any systematic discussion of the important realms of sports and children's culture. For the former, see Riordan, *Sport in Soviet Society*; for the latter Obraztsov, *My Profession*; O'Dell, *Socialisation through Children's Literature*; Hellman, *Barnboken i Sovjetryssland*; Sivokon, *Uroki detskikh klassikov*; Victor Victorov, *The Natalia Sats Children's Musical Theatre* (Moscow, 1986); Klimontovich, *Na ekrane skazka.*
3 Bowers, *Entertainment in Russia*, 215.

1 In old Russia 1900–1917

1 For the link between social moods, hooliganism, and artistic revolt, see Neuberger, *Hooliganism.* On the press, see McReynolds, *News under Russia's Old Regime.*
2 Mikhnevich, *Yazvy Peterberga*, 445; Bushnell, "Urban Leisure Culture in Post-Stalin Russia"; Johnson, *Peasant and Proletarian*; Bradley, *Muzhik and Muscovite*, 78–9, 315–16.
3 *SM*, 12 (1955) 8. All abbreviations are at the beginning of the bibliography. Zelnik, *A Radical Worker in Tsarist Russia.*
4 Mikhnevich, *Yazvy Peterburga*, 445.
5 Rom-Lebedev, *Ot tsyganskogo khora* for the gypsy tavern milieu; Soboleva, *Russkii sovetskii romans*; *Starinnye russkie romansy*, 1–15. Godoshnikov, "Gorodskoi romans kak sotsialnoe i khudozhestvennoe yavlenie." Rothstein, "Death of the Folk Song?" On *volya*, see Stites, *Revolutionary Dreams*, ch. 1.
6 Nestev, *Zvëzdy russkoi estrady*; *Rampa i zhizn*, 3 (1910) 46 and *ibid.*, 23 (1911) 10–11; Kugel, *Teatralnye portrety*, 284–93; recordings of Panina, Vyaltseva, and Plevitskaya in the Hubertus Jahn collection (see discography).
7 Smith, *Songs to Seven Strings*, 60–4; Rothstein, "Popular Song in the NEP Era."
8 Kuznetsov, *Iz proshlogo russkoi estrady*, 350–2; Gendlin, *Iz pesen A. Vertinskogo*; Vertinskii, *Zapiski russkogo pero* and *Pesni i stikhi 1916–1937*; Konstantin Rudnitskii, record jacket notes to *Aleksandr Vertinskii* which was

210

made shortly before his death and contains "Endless Road" and "On a Pink-Tinted Sea" among others. A more complete and recent collection is *Pechalnyya pesenki A. N. Vertinskago: k stoletiya so dnya rozhdeniya, 1889–1989*. See discography for all data on recordings.

9 Starr, *Red and Hot*, 20–36; compare Erenberg, *Steppin' Out*, 1–109.

10 Nestev, *Zvëzdy*, 16; *IIK*, 3 (1960) 154–61.

11 Recordings of the more famous songs on *History of the Soviet Union: I, Revolution and Civil War* (recording). Analysis in Dreiden, *Muzyka-revolyutsii*; Shiryaeva, "Poetic Features and Genre Characteristics of the Songs of Russian Workers" which shows the rich variety of workers' songs; Ament, "Russian Revolutionary Songs"; Frumkin, "Tekhnologiya ubezhdeniya." *Obozrenie*, 5 (July 1983) 17–20.

12 Nekrylova, *Russkie narodnye gorodskie prazdniki*; Von Geldern, *Festivals of the Revolution*; Kuznetsov, *Iz proshlogo*.

13 Astakhova, "Improvisation," in Oinas, *The Study of Folklore*.

14 Savushkina, *Russkii narodnyi teatr*; Warner, *The Russian Folk Theater*.

15 Khaichenko, *Russkii narodnyi teatr*; Thurston, "Theater and Acculturation in Russia" and "The Impact of Russian Popular Theater, 1886–1915."

16 Data supplied by officials at the Ligovsky Nardom in Leningrad, officially the Railroad Workers' House of Culture but now in the process of being renamed in honor of the once repugnant Countess Panina. See also *TE*, III, 1053–4 and *Statisticheskii ezhegodnik Rossii, 1913* (SP, 1914) 14.

17 Dmitriev, *Russkii tsirk* and *Tsirk v Rossii*; Shneer and Slavskii, eds., *Tsirk*; Bouissac, *Circus and Culture*.

18 *A. Durov v zhizni i na arene*; Dvinsky, *Durov and his Performing Animals*, 14–15. Durov's Corner and the Animal (now Mouse) Railway are still in operation in Moscow.

19 For cultural populism see Hilton, *Russian Folk Culture*; for sponsored culture, Brooks, *When Russia Learned to Read*, 295–352.

20 *Orkestr imeni V. V. Andreeva*; *Tvorcheskoe nasledie V. V. Andreeva*; Kuznetsov, *Iz proshlogo*, 315–20.

21 Martynov, *Gosudarstvennyi russkii narodnyi khor imeni Pyatnitskogo*; Kuznetsov, *Iz proshlogo*, 309–15; *Russian Folk Song and Dance* (video), with a recording of Pyatnitsky's voice, stills of the early ensemble, and filmed performances of its later incarnations. See videography.

22 Kuznetsov, *Iz proshlogo*, 241–92; *TE*, V, 1023–6; *NS*, xii/1565 (March, 1908) 2; Yaron, *O lyubimom zhanre*, 48–50.

23 *Rampa i zhizn*, 1909–1917 is rich in material on variety shows and restaurant entertainment.

24 Terikov, *Kuplet na estrade*, 1–76.

25 Seigel, *Bohemian Paris*; Segel, *Turn-of-the-Century Cabaret*, 255–320.

26 Vladimir Propp, "The 'Function' of the Fairy Tale," in Oinas, *Study*, 163–8; Meletinsky, "The 'Low' Hero of the Fairy Tale," in *ibid.*, 236–57; Perrie, "Folklore as Evidence of Peasant Mentalite;" Robin, "Popular Literature of the 1920s."

27 Brooks, *When Russia Learned to Read*; Zorkaya, *Na rubezhe stoletii*, relates this fiction to cinema and other popular arts.

28 Russell, "Red Pinkertonism," 392. For an example of extreme anti-Chinese racism, see the 1915 Nat Pinkerton story, *Krovavyi talisman* (The Bloody Talisman). Foreign adventure was also popular in Russia: at least four multi-volume collections of the works of Jack London, one of them in twenty-one volumes, appeared in Russian prior to 1917, as well as many individual editions.

29 Zorkaya, *Na rubezhe stoletii*, 93–182; Artsybashev, *Sanin*; Verbitskaya, *Klyuchi schastya*; see also her *Prestuplenie Mari Ivanovny i drugie razskazy i ocherki iz zhizni odinokikh*, 2nd edn (Moscow, n.d.).

30 McReynolds: *News under Russia's Old Regime*; "Autocratic Journalism"; and "Imperial Russia's Newspaper Reporters." An attempt to film *Yama* was foiled by the government censors; it was finally put on screen for the first time in 1991.

31 *Four Brothers*: "Gde luchshe? Skazka o chetyrekh bratyakh i ob ikh priklyu-cheniyakh," *Agitatsionnaya literatura*, 267–95. A fine analysis of this genre is in Pearl, "Educating Workers for Revolution." Bogdanov, *Red Star*, texts and commentary on science fiction of the era.

32 Postcard collection in the Slavonic Library, Helsinki; Goulzadian, *L'empire du dernier tsar*; Lofgren, "Wish You Were Here"; Belitskii, *Rasskazy ob otkrytkakh*, 105–36; Baburina, *Russkii plakat*; Count Amori, *Tainy Nevskogo Prospekta*, 177.

33 King and Porter, *Blood and Laughter*; *Testimoni silenziosi*, illustrations, 535–41.

34 Perestiani, *75 let*, 265. Basic works on the subject are Ginsburg, *Kinematogra-fiya dorevolyutsionnoi Rossii*; Sobolev, *Lyudi i filmy russkogo dorevolyutsionnogo kino*; Zorkaya, *Na rubezhe stoletii*; Likhachev, *Kino v Rossii*, I, and "Mater-ialy"; Vishnevskii, "Filmografiya"; *Testimoni silenziosi*; and Leyda, *Kino*, ch. 1. I have also drawn on Taylor, "Kiss of Mary Pickford" and Kepley, "Mr. Kuleshov" which deal mainly with the 1920s. Films I have seen are marked with an asterisk in the filmography.

35 Khanzhonkov, *Pervye gody russkoi kinematografii*; Lemberg, "Iz vospomi-naniya starogo operatora," 119; Zorkaya, *Illustrated History of the Soviet Cinema*, 21.

36 Voznesenskii, "Kinodetstvo" on the process of "star-building" through mass publicity; Zorkaya, *Na rubezhe stoletii*, 275–96.

37 *Ibid.* (qu. p. 94); Chaikovskii, *Mladencheskie gody*; Yaron, *O lyubimom zhanre*, 68; Khanzhonkov, *Pervye gody*; Kenez, *The Birth of the Propaganda State*, 104–5.

38 *SE*, 21 (November 1982) 13 (an assortment of movie ads from early in the century).

39 Ginzburg, *Kino*, 51, 64, 109. Shooting script for *Stenka Razin* in N. Lebedev, *Ocherk*, I, 16–17.

40 Zorkaya, *Na rubezhe stoletii*, 183–246.

41 Catalog libretto for *Do You Remember* in *IIK*, 3 (1960) 91–3.

42 According to Richard Taylor, the epitome of the genre was Bauer's film *Silent Witnesses* (1914) which I have not seen.

43 Jahn, "Patriotic Culture in Russia During World War I"; Brooks, *When Russia Learned to Read*, 161–2, 314; Lapshin, *Khudozhestvennaya zhizn Moskvy i*

Petrograda; Raek: Nemetskaya voina; postcard collection; *Bich,* 4 (September 14, 1916) 5; Kaempfer, *"Der rote Keil": das politische Plakat.* Pamphlets, stories, and songs on Kryuchkov run into the dozens.

44 Kuznetsov, *Iz proshlogo,* 342–5; Halle, *Women in Soviet Russia,* 296; Loewe, "Political Symbols and Rituals of the Russian Radical Right, 1900–1917."

45 Von Geldern, *Festivals of the Revolution;* Dmitriev, *Sovetskii tsirk,* 240; Radunskii, *Zapiski,* 98.

46 Likhachev, "Materialy," 45–57; Zorkaya, *Na rubezhe stoletii,* 231–2. Both parts of the antagonist's name became icons for Germanic villainy in Soviet popular culture: "fritz" was the generic name for German soldiers in World War II; Commandant Muller is the tormentor of Andryusha in the story and film *Fate of a Man* (see ch. 5); "Gestapo" Muller was the villain of Yulian Semenov's bestselling thriller and TV series (see ch. 6).

2 Revolutionary reassortment 1917–1927

1 For two fine introductions to Bolshevik views of culture, see Kenez, *The Birth of the Propaganda State,* and Starr, *Red and Hot,* ch. 1.

2 Maksakova, *Agitpoezd;* Von Geldern, *Festivals of the Revolution;* Stites, *Revolutionary Dreams,* ch. 4.

3 As in Fedor Lopukhov's *Red Whirlwind* (1924) which closed after two performances.

4 Mally, *Culture of the Future.*

5 Brooks, "The Breakdown in Production and Distribution of Printed Material."

6 These and other radical fables may be found in Bednyi, *Izbrannye proizvedeniya,* I.

7 Robin, "Popular Literature of the 1920s"; Kenez, *Birth of the Propaganda State,* 230–2; Brooks, "Competing Modes of Popular Discourse" and "Public and Private Values in the Soviet Press."

8 Kenez, *Birth of the Propaganda State,* 239; Robin, "Popular Literature of the 1920s" citing Halina Stephan, *Lef and the Left Front of the Arts* (Munich, 1981), 160; Andrei Sobol, "V plenu u obezyan," in *Pisateli,* 97–101; Brooks, *When Russia Learned to Read,* 160; Clark, *The Soviet Novel,* 104. See the publication figures on Tarzan books in R. Leblanc, "A Russian Tarzan or 'Aping' Jocko?" *SR,* 46/1 (Spring 1987) 86n.

9 Russell, "Red Pinkertonism."

10 Shaginyan, *Mess-Mend.* The meaningless title was created by the author by combining two English words. She also wrote a sequel, *Laurie Lane, Metal Worker.* See Avins, *Border Crossings.* The wonderful comedy film *Miss-Mend* [sic] loosely based on this story featured the well-known actors Boris Barnet, Vladimir Fogel, and Igor Ilinsky as well as the talented wife of Lunacharsky, Natalia Rozenel.

11 Stites, *Revolutionary Dreams,* 167–89; Belyaev, *The Amphibian.*

12 Gutkin, "Anticipating the Past and Retrospecting the Future."

13 Robin, "Popular Literature of the 1920s"; Clark, *Soviet Novel,* 36–44; Brooks, "Public and Private Values."

14 Furmanov, *Chapaev*. For the cowboy as mythic hero, see the classic account by Henry Nash Smith, *Virgin Land: the American West as Symbol and Myth* (1950; New York, 1957).

15 *Muzykalnaya zhizn Moskvy*, 63–4; Ilina, *Kulturnoe stroitelstvo v Petrograde*, 124–40; for machine music, see Stites, *Revolutionary Dreams*, 159–60.

16 Trotsky in Hosking, *A History of the Soviet Union*, 84; *RSE*, 1, 204–39; Nestev, "Massovaya pesnya."

17 Frumkin, "Tekhnologiya ubezhdeniya" (qu. p. 24).

18 *ME*, I, 687; Schwartz, *Music and Musical Life in Soviet Russia*, 21; *Orkestr imeni V. V. Andreeva*, 50–6; *Tvorcheskoe nasledie V. V. Andreeva*, 1–58; Mally, *Culture of the Future*, 113–14.

19 Frumkin, "Tekhnologiya ubezhdeniya," 24. The next few paragraphs are heavily indebted to Rothstein, "Popular Song in the NEP Era" and "The Quiet Rehabilitation of The Brick Factory."

20 Starr, *Red and Hot*, 39–78; early recordings and data on 1920s bands in *Pervye shagi* (record).

21 *RSE*, 1, 240–80; Stites, *Revolutionary Dreams*, 118; Tirado, *Young Guard* (qu. p. 136).

22 *RSE*, 1; Von Geldern, *Festivals of the Revolution*.

23 *RSE*, 1; Von Geldern, *Festivals of the Revolution*; Yershov, *Comedy in the Soviet Theater*.

24 I have drawn this from my paper, "Trial as Theater in the Russian Revolution," for the Gauss Seminar, Princeton, 1989. Vishnevsky's recollection in *Sovetskie dramaturgi o svoem tvorchestve* (Moscow, 1967). 149–50; Ratchford, "Stalinist Myth on the Soviet Screen."

25 Uvarova, *Estradnyi teatr*, 92–111; Terikov, *Kuplet na estrade*, 87; *RSE*, 1, 302–72; Von Geldern, *Festivals of the Revolution*; Halle, *Women in Soviet Russia*, 297.

26 Gurevich, *O zhanrakh sovetskogo tsirka*, 5; for the attack on circus, see *VT*, 36 (October 7–12, 1919) 9.

27 Uvarova, *Estradnyi teatr*, 70–8, 85; Filippov, *Actors without Makeup*, 206–13; *RSE*, 1, 116–36; Skorokhodov, *Zvezdy*; *Muzykalnaya zhizn Moskvy*, 76. The source for the invention of "Nepman" is N. Lunacharskaya-Rozenel, *Pamyat serdtsa* (Moscow, 1962), 341.

28 Yaron, *O lyubimom zhanre*, 100–69; Yankovskii, *Operetta*, 377–400.

29 Kenez, *The Birth of the Propaganda State*, 113–18; Williams, *Artists*, 71–6; White, *The Bolshevik Political Poster*; Von Geldern, *Festivals of the Revolution*; Robin, "Popular Literature of the 1920s"; Hellberg, "The Hero in Popular Pictures."

30 Leyda, *Kino*, 92–120; Betz, "As The Tycoons Die." Count Amori turned out scripts for six Rasputin films which were shot in two days on the same set with only the furniture moved around: Lemberg, "Iz vospominaniya starogo operatora."

31 Kenez, *The Birth of the Propaganda State*, 109–11, 204; Turovskaya's archive on moviegoing; Taylor, *The Politics of Soviet Cinema* and "Kiss of Mary Pickford"; Youngblood, *Soviet Cinema in the Silent Era* and *Movies for the Masses*. In the latter Youngblood relates that Pudovkin's *Mother*, an exception,

managed to edge out *Mark of Zorro* for ninth place in a popularity poll. She also shows that costume dramas and historical films about the old regime were popular because, unlike history books of the time, these films enlivened the past with strong heroes and narratives.

32 Leyda, *Kino*, 163; Petric, "Cinematic Abstraction"; Kenez, *The Birth of the Propaganda State*, 136.

33 Taylor, "Soviet Cinema as Popular Culture." Between 1922 and 1933, 965 American, 535 German, and 202 French films were shown in the USSR: Petric, "Cinematic Abstraction." The climax of *Great Citizen*, made in the midst of the terror, is held in the cinema of a 1920s workers' club where *Thief of Baghdad* is playing.

34 Perestiani tells how the film was made in *IK*, 3 (1960) 16–24 and *75 let*; Leyda, *Kino*, 168. The Makhno story is now being revised by historians: *Istoriya SSSR*, II (1990) 75–90.

35 Kepley, "Mr Kuleshov in the Land of the Modernists"; Leyda, *Kino*, 172.

36 Youngblood, *Movies for the Masses*, discusses a whole range of popular films by Ermler, Barnet, Protazanov, and others. A famous "social film" of the age, Avram Room's classic *Third Meshchanskaya Street* or *Bed and Sofa* (1928) was a popular success but a critical failure. It is so well known and accessible that I have not discussed it here.

37 Winter, *Red Virtue*, 277–8; *Pioner*, 20 (October, 1929) 1; Zorkaya, *Illustrated History of Soviet Cinema*, 104–6; Kenez, *Cinema and Soviet Society*. There was a rather tame movie magazine, *Sovetskii ekran* and a plethora of film star biographies: Youngblood, *Movies for the Masses*.

38 *Ibid.*, Kenez, *The Birth of the Propaganda State*, 197–8; Youngblood, *Movies for the Masses*; Starr, *Red and Hot*, 64; Lebedev, "Boevye dvadtsatye gody," 90; Khrenov, "K probleme sotsiologii i psikhologii kino 20-kh godov," 163–83.

39 For concepts of taste: Gans, *Popular Culture and High Culture*.

40 For the ambience, see Ball, *Street Children in Soviet Russia* and the films, *Aelita, Katka,* and Boris Barnet's *Girl with a Hatbox* (1927). The desperation sharpened during the cultural revolution: see the novels: Kataev, *The Embezzlers*; Ilf and Petrov, *The Twelve Chairs* and *The Golden Calf*. This kind of literary satire was of course choked off completely in the 1930s.

41 Ball, *Street Children*. The best visual treatment of the *besprizorniki*, though highly romanticized, is the film *Start in Life* (see ch. 3).

42 Kenez, *The Birth of the Propaganda State*, 169–80; Winter, *Red Virtue*, 287; Stites, *Revolutionary Dreams*. For the tension between education and entertainment in workers' clubs of the 1920s, see Hatch, "The Politics of Mass Culture."

3 Stalin by starlight 1928–1941

1 For the larger context see Fitzpatrick, *Cultural Revolution*.

2 Fitzpatrick, "Middle Class Values"; Timasheff, *The Great Retreat*. See Rybakov, *Children of the Arbat* for status details; Groys, *Stalin's Gesamtkunstwerk* and Gunther, *The Culture of the Stalin Period* for the larger framework.

3 On the personality cult, see Nina Tumarkin, *Lenin Lives: the Cult of Lenin*

in the Soviet Union (Cambridge, MA, 1983); Robert Tucker, *Stalin as Revolutionary, 1879–1929* (New York, 1973) 462–87; Stites, "Stalin: Utopian or Anti-utopian?" For organization, see London, *The Seven Soviet Arts*, 39–57.

4 Robin, *Le Réalisme socialiste*, 198, "Stalinism and Popular Culture," and *Soviet Literature of the Thirties*, 7–46; Clark, *The Soviet Novel*.

5 Ostrovsky, *How the Steel Was Tempered*; Robin, "Stalinism and Popular Culture," 26; Gunther offers a fascinating comparison of Ostrovsky's novel with a Nazi favorite, Karl Aloys Schenzinger's *Der Hitlerjunge Quex* (1932) in *The Culture of the Stalin Period*, 193–209; Tolstoy, *Peter the First*; Gutnik, "Anticipating the Past"; Clark, *The Soviet Novel*.

6 German, *Lapshin*; Pogacar, "The Theme of Culture in the Soviet Detective Novel."

7 For a complete revision of the case and the impact of the legend, see Druzhnikov, *Voznesenie Pavlika Morozova*.

8 Garri, *Ldy i lyudi*. The arctic genre was reinforced by Russians' fondness for Jack London.

9 Filippov, *Actors without Makeup*, 81–100; Clark, *The Soviet Novel*; Bailes, *Technology and Society under Lenin and Stalin*, 381–406.

10 Zhukov and Izmailova, *Nachalo goroda*; Ilin, *New Russia's Primer*, tr. of *Rasskaz o velikom plane* (1930). On Ilin, see Sivokon, *Uroki detskikh klassikov*, 159–75.

11 Siegelbaum, *Stakhanovism*, 210–46; Tretyakov, "Nine Girls."

12 *Belomorsko-Baltiiskii Kanal*; Robin, "Stalinism and Popular Culture," 34; Ken Strauss, "Workers' Lives in the 1930s."

13 Miller, *Folklore for Stalin*; Clark, *The Soviet Novel*, 7–50; Oinas, *Study*, 7–8, 91–110, "Folklore and Politics in the Soviet Union." See the magical, folkloric Chapaev tales translated in *IL*, 12 (1937), 10–11 (1938), and 2 (1939).

14 *Dovesti do kontsa borbu s nepmanskoi muzykoi*, 19; Winter, *Red Virtue*, 282–5; Jelagin, *Taming of the Arts*; Sherel, *Rampa u mikrofona*, 63; Skorokhodov, *Zvezdy*, 14; *Umnozhai urozhai*, a typical songbook by a composers' shock brigade.

15 Rothstein, "Popular Song in the NEP Era"; Starr, *Red and Hot*, 83–94; Frumkin, "Tekhnologiya."

16 Starr, *Red and Hot*, 94–111; Rybakov, *Children of the Arbat*; Jelagin, *Taming of the Arts*, 178, 208; Nestev, "Massovaya pesnya." The song "Little Lemons" (1929 or earlier) can be heard on the record *Leonid Utesov, I, Muzykalnyi magazin*.

17 Vasilinina, *Klavdiya Shulzhenko*. Recordings: *Poet Lidiya Ruslanova*; *Izabella Yureva: esli pomnish, esli lyubish*; *Vadim Kozin: pesni i romansy* (2 records); *Vadim Kozin: starinnye romansy*. See also *Ogonek*, March 10, 1987, 15. The 1940 listing of phonograph records produced in the USSR shows Kozin and Lyubov Orlova as the leading recording artists of popular music followed by Ruslanova, Utesov, Tsereteli, Tsfasman, and Yureva: *Katalog gramplastinok*, 327–409.

18 Starr, *Red and Hot*, 107–56; Skorokhodov, *Zvezdy*.

19 Recordings: *Pamyati Leonida Utesova* (2 records); *Leonid Utesov: Recordings of the Forties and Fifties*; *Noch i den*. For the contrast with Tsfasman, see *Pervye shagi*.

20 Siegelbaum, *Stakhanovism*, 230; Timbres, *We Didn't Ask Utopia*, 8.

21 Starr, *Red and Hot*, 157–80; Kater, "Forbidden Fruit? Jazz in the Third Reich." The smoothing out and nativization of Utesov's style from the late 1920s through the 1940s may be traced in the recordings: *Pervye shagi; Leonid Utesov, I, Muzykalnyi magazin; Leonid Utesov, II, Ot vsego serdtsa; Noch i den*; and *Leonid Utesov: zapisi 40-kh-50-kh godov.*

22 Frumkin, "Tekhnologiya" (September 1983) 24; Lebedev, *Pesni rozhdennye v ogne*; Smith, *Songs to Seven Strings*, 10–15; Starr, *Red and Hot*, 172–5; Jelagin, *Taming of the Arts*, 178.

23 Miller, *Jews in Soviet Culture*, 65–106.

24 Dunaevskii, *Vystupleniya*; Jelagin, *Taming of the Arts*, 278–80. For a personal assessment of Dunaevsky see Shafer, "Paradoks."

25 Nestev, "Massovaya pesnya"; Jelagin, *Taming of the Arts*, 68; 241; *RSE*, 1, 238–9.

26 Filippov, *Actors*; *NYT*, January 15, 1989, H1 (Moiseev interview); Kazmin, *S pesnei*, 58–285.

27 Kipriyanov, *Orkestr russkikh narodnykh instrumentov.*

28 Hellberg, "Folklore, Might, and Glory"; Lerman, "Folk Arts in Russia and the Soviet Union."

29 Makarov, *Sovetskaya klounada*, 62–76; *Soviet Circus*; Dmitriev, *Sovetskii tsirk*, 232–41, 254–5; TsiE, all issues for December, 1929; *Makhnovshchina*; performance photos in the Leningrad Circus Museum archive.

30 *RSE*, 2, 16–67; Uvarova, *Estradnyi teatr*, 128–279; Uvarova, *Arkadii Raikin.*

31 Yaron, *O lyubimom zhanre*, 160–226. For the *Ball at the Savoy* episode, see Bowers, *Entertainment in Russia*, 173–4.

32 Gurevich and Ruzhnikov, *Sovetskoe radioveshchanie*, 1–173; Starr, "New Communications Technologies."

33 Mikryukov, "Radioteatr – iskusstvo"; Sherel, *Rampa u mikrofona*; Marchenko, *Radioteatr.*

34 *Radio Gazeta*, 4 (January 18, 1934); *Radiofront* (March, April, and June 1937); Radio Moscow Archives; exhibits at the Museum of Radio Leningrad. For Levitan, see next chapter.

35 Panofsky in Burke, *Popular Culture in Early Modern Europe*, 79; Sartorti, *Pressephotographie und Industrialisierung*; Bonnell, "The Representation of Politics and the Politics of Representation"; Stites, "Adorning the Russian Revolution." For the imaging of Moscow and the labor and aviation heroes see Belitskii, *Rasskazy ob otkrytkakh.*

36 Papernyi, *Kultura "dva"* and "Moscow in the 1930s"; Stites, *Revolutionary Dreams*, 223–53; Jelagin, *Taming of the Arts*; Groys, *Stalin's Gesamtkunstwerk.*

37 London, *The Seven Soviet Arts*, 261; Bliznakov, "Architecture as Decorative Art."

38 Kenez, "Cinema and the 'Cultural Revolution'"; Youngblood, *Soviet Cinema in the Silent Era*, 189–232; Taylor, "Boris Shumyatsky and the Soviet Cinema in the 1930s"; Turovskaya archive.

39 On the search for a deathless Chapaev, see Varshavskii, *Esli film talantliv*, 132. For a brilliant analysis of the film's ideological content, see Farro, "The Fiction Film and Historical Analysis."

40 I am grateful to Maya Turovskaya who not only gave me data on the popularity of *Karo*, but watched it with me in Moscow.

41 Pendo, *Aviation in the Cinema*, useful but full of errors.

42 Leyda, *Kino*, 324.

43 Shumyatskii, *Kinematografiya millionov*, 24–30; Nestev, "Massovaya pesnya," 258.

44 Klimontovich, "The American Theme in Soviet Cinema"; Jelagin, *Taming of the Arts*, 264; Blakeley, *Russia and the Negro*, 160–1.

45 Yaron, *O lyubimom zhanre*, 216; Aleksandrov, *Gody poiskov i truda*, 69; Dunaevskii, *Vystupleniya*, 288. Quotations: Robert Tucker and Stephen Cohen, eds., *The Great Purge Trial* (New York, 1965), 564–5; Mark Kuchment in *SO*, January 26, 1989, 4.

46 Enzensberger, "'We Were Born to Turn a Fairy Tale into Reality.'"

47 Aleksandrov, *Gody poiskov i truda*; Romanov, *Lyubov Orlova v iskusstve i v zhizni*. Recordings of the voice of Orlova in the films discussed and the reminiscences of Alexandrov on the record *Lyubov Orlova*.

48 Turovskaya, "I. A. Pyrev i ego muzykalnye komedii."

49 "Kino totalitarnoi epokhi," *IK*, 1 (1990) 111–21; *Kino totalitarnoi epokhi*.

50 For comparison, see Victoria De Grazia, *The Culture of Consent: Mass Organization of Leisure in Fascist Italy* (Cambridge, 1981) and Detlev Peukert, *Inside Nazi Germany: Conformity, Opposition, and Racism in Everyday Life* (London, 1987).

51 Quoted in Williams, *Keywords*, 145.

52 Turovskaya, "I. A. Pyrev," 115; Ginzburg quoted in Graffy, "Unshelving Stalin," 19.

53 Sartorti, "Stalinism and Carnival" (qu. pp. 65, 71); Stites, *Revolutionary Dreams*, 228–9; *Radiofront*, 13 (1939) 12–13.

54 Bushnell, "Urban Leisure," 61; Fitzpatrick, "Middle Class Values," 25; Scott, *Behind the Urals*, 210; Barber, "Working-class Culture and Political Culture in the 1930s."

4 Holy war and cold war 1941–1953

1 Dunham, "Troublemakers in Uniform" (qu.); Hosking, *A History of the Soviet Union*, 262; Tumarkin, "Russia Remembers the War."

2 Aliger, *Zoya*; Kosmodemyanskaya, *Moya Zoya*; Lidov, *Tanya*; Filippov, *Actors*, 237; Werth, *Russia*, 394, 781.

3 Werth, *Russia at War*, 743; Surkov, *Sochineniya*, II (especially the poems of 1941–1943); Simonov, *Sobranie sochinenii*, I, 105–7.

4 *Ibid.*; Pasternak quoted in Hosking, *History*, 276; Tvardovskii, *Vasilii Terkin*; *LN*, lxxviii/1, 563–601 (letters to Terkin and its author).

5 Simonov, *Sobranie sochinenii*, I, 158–9.

6 *Ibid.*, 88–9; Simonov, *Days and Nights*; Fadeev, *Molodaya gvardiya*; Clark, *The Soviet Novel*, 160–6.

7 Ehrenburg and Simonov, *In One Newspaper*; Werth, *Russia at War*, 414; Goldberg, *Ilya Ehrenburg*; Lucas, *War on the Eastern Front*; Krasilshchik, *World War II Dispatches from the Soviet Front*.

8 Data on wartime radio from Aleksandr Sherel.
9 Danilevich, *Muzyka na frontakh Velikoi Otechestvennoi Voiny*, 43.
10 Lebedev, *Pesni rozhdennye v ogne*, 3–15; Schwartz, *Music and Musical Life*, 181; Werth, *Russia at War*.
11 Sokhor, "*Katyusha*"; Ament, "Soviet Songs of World War II"; Romanov, *Lyubov Orlova*, 192; Lebedev, *Pesni*, 6; Danilevich, *Muzyka na frontakh*, 22.
12 Utesov: *Leonid Utesov: Recordings of the Forties and Fifties*. Rosner: Starr, *Red and Hot*, 183–94.
13 Dementev, *Pesni*; Vasilinina, *Klavdiya Shulzhenko*, 60–79.
14 Gurevich, *Sovetskoe radioveshchanie*, 203–4; Werth, *Russia at War*, 512; Ament, "Soviet Songs of World War II"; *LN*, lxxviii/1, 433–43. Information on songs from Robert Rothstein.
15 Werth, *Russia at War*, 677; *WP*, December 10, 1943. Trans. by Annemarie Ewing, courtesy Am-Russ Music Corporation.
16 Werth, *Russia at War*, 586, 678, 762; Smith, *Songs to Seven Strings*, 66–7.
17 Werth, *Russia at War*, 411–12, 423–5. Three of the most popular wartime Broadway stage hits were *Life with Father*, *Arsenic and Old Lace*, and *Oklahoma*.
18 Werth, *Russia at War*, 411, 480; Makarov, *Sovetskaya klounada*, 93–119; *RSE*, 2, 371–97.
19 Obraztsov, *My Profession*; *TE*, V, 1024–6; *Iskusstvo v boevom stroyu*, 7–29; Romanov, *Lyubov Orlova*, 118–40; Danilevich, *Muzyka na frontakh*. On Ruslanova: Starr, *Red and Hot*, 215; Leningrad radio documentary on her life, January 19, 1990; *MZh* (May, 1975) 18–19; and *Poet Lidiya Ruslanova*, record sleeve notes.
20 *Soviet Circus*; Shneer and Slavskii, *Tsirk*, 158–9; Terikov, *Kuplet na estrade*, 123–34.
21 Ament, "Soviet Songs of World War II"; Schwartz, *Music and Musical Life*, 104; *Playbill of Kennedy Center*, Washington DC, program of the Osipov Ensemble, January 1989. See also Starr, *Red and Hot*, 186.
22 Werth, *Russia at War*, 162; *Radio v dni voiny* (see 177–85 for Levitan); Radio Moscow archives – Levitan reading the surrender document, 1945; Radio Leningrad Museum sound archives.
23 Hopkins, *Mass Media in the Soviet Union*, 101; Werth, *Russia at War*, 684–5, 692; *LN*, lxxviii/1, pp. 407–32; Gurevich and Ruzhnikov, *Sovetskoe radioveshchanie*, 174–211.
24 *Ibid.*; Radio Leningrad Museum sound archives (the voices of Bergholz, Vishnevsky, and others).
25 Gurevich and Ruzhnikov, *Sovetskoe radioveshchanie*, 184–5.
26 Werth, *Russia at War*, 62; Kukryniksy, *Vtroem*, 118–79; Sokolova, *Kukryniksy*, 162–230; *LN*, lxxviii/1, pp. 446–62 (wartime *lubok* and verses).
27 In addition to works cited above, see *Plakaty Velikoi Otechestvennoi*.
28 Kenez, *Cinema and Soviet Society*; Yurenev, *Kratkaya istoriya sovetskogo kino*, 123–30 and his "Na ekrane – natsionalnyi kharakter"; Taylor, *Film Propaganda*.
29 Ratchford, "Soviet Musical Comedies"; Yurenev, *Kratkaya istoriya*, 129.
30 Kenez, *Cinema and Soviet Society*; Bernes, *Stati; vospominaniya o M. N. Bernese*, 59–61.

31 Kenez, *Cinema and Soviet Society*; Short, *Film, and Radio Propaganda in World War II*; Basinger, *World War II Combat Film*.

32 For official statements, see Thomas Riha, *Russian Civilization*, 3 vols. (Chicago IL, 1964) III, 684, 687, 690, 692, 706, 707; and Werth, *Musical Uproar*. The best account of anti-cosmopolitanism in film is Kenez, *Cinema and Soviet Society*.

33 Filippov, *Actors*, 273.

34 Leyda, *Kino*, 398 (Kapler's "crime" had been to have a brief love affair with Stalin's daughter in 1943); Starr, *Red and Hot*, 213; Yershov, *Comedy in the Soviet Theater*; Uvarova, *Raikin*, 123–4; Terikov, *Kuplet na estrade*, 135–49; *Izabella Yureva* (record sleeve notes). Radio purge: personal information.

35 Starr, *Red and Hot*, 205–29; Gleb Skorokhodov in *GiPM*, 50 (December 1989) 6; Yaron, *O lyubimom zhanre*, 227–35; Yankovskii, *Iskusstvo operetty*, 180; see Dunaevsky's spirited reply to critics (including Blanter) in his *Vystupleniya*, 69–77.

36 Polevoi, *A Story about a Real Man*; Clark, *The Soviet Novel*, 102–4, 183–94; Dunham, *In Stalin's Time*.

37 Leyda, *Kino*, 398; Romanov, *Lyubov Orlova*, 61; Liehm and Liehm, *The Most Important Art*, 49–63.

38 Turovskaya, "I. A. Pyrev i ego muzykalnye komedii," a masterful analysis; *SE*, 18 (September, 1988), an issue devoted to 1940s–1950s retro; Morrison, *Gorbachev*, 67–8. Raizman's filming of Babaevsky's *Cavalier*, though finely acted and shot in beautiful color in the same rich Kuban country and offering the same vista of rural affluence, could not equal its magic.

39 Glazov, "'Thieves' in the USSR." For the Gulag and other islands of jazz in the late Stalin years, see Starr, *Red and Hot*, 224–32. I wish to thank the Moscow director Savva Kulish for his reminiscences of Kozin in Magadan.

5 Springtime for Khrushchev 1953–1964

1 Slonim, *Soviet Russian Literature*. For the mood of the time, see the remarks of Akhmadulina, Evtushenko, Okudzhava, Rozhdestvensky, and Voznesensky in *Ogonek*, 9 (1987) 27–31.

2 Yurenev, *Kratkaya istoriya*, 147.

3 Starr, *Red and Hot*, 237–43; D. Belyaev, "Stilyaga" (1949), reprinted in *Krokodilu – 60 let*, 170–3. A recent Moscow play, *Grownup Daughter of a Young Man*, makes *stilyaga* culture its main theme.

4 Turovskaya archive (Marika Rokk); Jelagin, *Taming of the Arts*, 218; Alexander Werth, *Russia at War*, 524; Kichin, *Lyudmila Gurchenko*, 57–9; Aksenov, *In Search of Melancholy Baby*, 17–18. The old trick of framing "tainted" motion pictures with propaganda in order to raise revenue probably backfired again: mature Leningrad audiences to whom I showed and lectured on these films in 1990 recalled the fact but not the messages of the propaganda lessons that preceded them; but they retained a vivid memory of the plots, actors, and songs of the movies.

5 Starr, *Red and Hot*, 237–8; Morrison, *Gorbachev*, 62. Among Gorbachev's fellow students were the Czech dissident Zdenek Mlynar, the mystery

writer Fridrikh Neznansky, and my former colleague Lev Yudovich. V. Mikhalkovich's memories of Tarzan in *SE*, 18 (September 1988). On costume, see Aksenov, *In Search of Melancholy Baby*, 13.

6 *Ibid.*, 12–13.

7 Aksenov, *A Ticket to the Stars*; *In Search of Melancholy Baby*; *WP* (March 24, 1985), C3.

8 Adamov, *Delo "pestrykh"*; Pogacar, "The Theme of Culture in the Soviet Detective Novel."

9 Semenov, *In the Performance of Duty*.

10 Efremov, *Andromeda*; Grebens, *Ivan Efremov's Theory of Science Fiction*; Suvin, "The Utopian Tradition of Soviet Science Fiction," 154 (qu.).

11 McGuire, *Red Stars*, 1–94. See also Glad, *Extrapolations from Dystopia* and Stites, "World Outlook and Inner Fears."

12 *MNE*, 41 (October 15–22, 1989) 16.

13 For the negative side of these songs, see the intelligent analysis in Smith, *Songs to Seven Strings*, 16–30; Frumkin, "Tekhnologiya."

14 *Vasilii Pavlovich Solovev-Sedoi*. Recordings: *Vasilii Solovev-Sedoi: izbrannye pesni*; Kenny Ball: *Midnight in Moscow*; see also Alec Wilder, *American Popular Song*. Dunaevsky died in 1955 in the midst of a family tragedy; some have suggested suicide (Starr, *Red and Hot*, 238). Many who knew Dunaevsky deny this.

15 Troitsky, *Back in the USSR*, 13, on Vasin; Anna Lawton, recollections on Loretti in the 1960s.

16 Starr, *Red and Hot*, 241–75 (qu. p. 251); Khrushchev quotation: Johnson, *Khrushchev and the Arts*, 102–3; Ramet and Zamascikov, "The Soviet Rock Scene," 3.

17 Troitsky, *Back in the USSR*, 6–15; Ryback, *Rock Around the Bloc*, 19–49. For the festival, see Starr, *Red and Hot*, 248–51.

18 Ryback, *Rock Around the Bloc*, 30–4.

19 Kalb, *Eastern Exposure*, 141–2. A popular movie of 1989, *Zero City*, presents a loving portrait of the advent of rock and roll music and dance in a 1950s provincial town and the scandals and life-changing events that it caused. On the dance: Ryback, *Rock Around the Bloc*, 29–30, 53–5. For folk ensembles abroad, see Barghoorn, *The Soviet Cultural Offensive*, 145, 315–18.

20 Smith, *Songs to Seven Strings*, 120–41; Marran, "Bulat Okudzhava"; Okudzhava, *65 Songs* and *Songs*. Recordings: *Bulat Okudzhava: novye pesni ispolnyaet avtor*; see others in discography. Talk and performance by Frumkin, Georgetown University, January 1989.

21 *Krokodil*, 1945–64; Khrushchev quoted in Stykalin and Kremenskaya, *Sovetskaya satiricheskaya pechat*, 5. Circulation figures, 212. See also *Krokodilu – 60 let*.

22 *Satira i yumor: repertuarnyi sbornik*, 85, 114–16; Terikov, *Kuplet na estrade*, 186.

23 Uvarova, *Arkadii Raikin*, 98–299; Samoilov, *Arkadii Raikin* 1–37. Recordings: *Ot 2-kh do 50-ti*; *Mastera sovetskoi estrady: Arkadii Isaakovich Raikin*; *Ego velichestvo teatr*. *Teatr Arkadiya Isaakovicha Raikina* (video) contains "Man Alone." Two samples of his art in the 1930s are contained on the 78-record issued by Trest "Mostor" in the Helen Price collection. The decline of

communal living is discussed in Shlapentokh, *Public and Private Life*, 179. For foreign impressions of Raikin, see Kalb, *Eastern Exposure*, 90–3 and Bowers, *Entertainment in Russia*, 173–6.

24 "Repertuar dlya estrady." Manuscript collection in the library of the Circus Academy, Moscow.

25 There is no adequate work on the cinema of the Khrushchev period; some facts may be gleaned from Liehm and Liehm, *The Most Important Art*, but it is filled with errors and is better for Eastern Europe than for the USSR. Much more interesting is Vronskaya, *Young Soviet Filmmakers*.

26 Bushnell, "Urban Leisure Culture"; Troitsky, *Back in the USSR*, 2–5; Ryback, *Rock Around the Bloc*, 26 (the NATO story). Americans did not invent cultural imperialism. At a Moscow composers' meeting in 1948, a Soviet scholar said that "the success of a good [musical] work with a progressive foreign audience must be regarded as a success for our ideology, as a means of persuasion exercised on ordinary people in the West." Werth, *Musical Uproar*, 84.

27 Kalb, *Eastern Exposure*, 236; for the youth "problem," see Kassof, *The Soviet Youth Program*, 144–71.

28 Heineman, "The Youth Experience on the Virgin Lands and Baikal-Amur Mainline Projects"; Smith, *Songs to Seven Strings*, 25, 40–4; Kopelev in *Kontinent*, 16 (1978) 340.

29 Lane, *Rites of Rulers*; Long, "Antireligious and Ritual Campaigns under Khrushchev"; *Kommunist*, 8 (May 1961) 65–72; *Partiinaya zhizn*, 6 (March, 1963) 49–54; Lewis, "The Image of Cosmonauts in Popular Culture."

30 Johnson, *Khrushchev and the Arts*; *MN*, 41 (October 15–22, 1989) 16.

6 The Brezhnev culture wars 1964–1984

1 Feshbach, report in *At the Harriman Institute* (February 16, 1989); Millar, *Politics, Work, and Daily Life in the USSR*; Moshe Lewin, *The Gorbachev Phenomenon* (Berkeley CA, 1989); Evgeny Sidorov quoted in Olcott, "Glasnost and Soviet Culture," 118.

2 Lewis, "Memorialization of the War."

3 Mehnert, *Russians and their Favorite Books*.

4 Hosking, *Beyond Socialist Realism*; Parthe, "Time Backward." For a sampling, see Rasputin, *Live and Remember* and *Farewell to Matera* or Vasily Shukshin, *Snowballberry Red*.

5 Pikul's bibliography is large; see a convenient collection of short stories, *Miniatury*, and his most scandalous novel: *U poslednei cherty*, originally entitled *Nechistaya sila* or *Evil Spirit*: interview with Pikul: *NS*, 2 (1989) 184–92. Guzanov, *Pravda o zhizni i smerti Valentin Pikulya*; Mehnert, *Russians*, 32, 50–1, 85, 156–60, 268 and Laqueur, *The Long Road to Freedom*, 117–21.

6 Vainer, *Lekarstvo protiv strakha* and *Era miloserdiya. Gorod prinyal!* is excellent for details of police operations.

7 Both novels available in English translation: *Tass* (New York, 1988) and *Seventeen* (New York, 1989). See Laqueur, "Julian Semyonov and the Soviet Political Novel."

8 For a more detailed analysis of these and other stories, see Stites, "World Outlook and Inner Fears." For other perspectives: Glad, "Brave New Worlds" and *Extrapolations from Dystopia*; McGuire, *Red Stars*.

9 Kaganskaya, "Mif dvadtsat pervogo veka"; Hellman, "Paradise Lost"; Suvin, "Criticism" (1972). Most of the Strugatskys' major works have been translated into English. *Roadside Picnic* (1972) was the basis for Andrei Tarkovsky's film, *Stalker*. See also *Ugly Swans*.

10 "Cranes" and "Motherland" in *Ya lyublyu tebya, zhizn!* words and music; see also *Populyarnyi spravochnik-pesennik*, 22–3. Poet Vladimir Makarov (recording) provides a sampling of mass and pop songs of the 70s. Smith, *Songs to Seven Strings*, 18–28.

11 CSM (September 3, 1981) 19; *Zhanna Bichevskaya* (recording); *Nikolai Slichenko* (recording) contains gypsy and urban songs performed by him with the V. Knushevitsky Cinema Orchestra and Chorus of the Romen Gypsy Theater. See also Rothstein, "Quiet Rehabilitation"; and *Pevtsy sovetskoi estrady*, 33–43 (Slichenko) and 201–9 (Bichevskaya).

12 Bushnell, "Urban Leisure Culture," 85; Fisher and Volkov, "The Audience for Classical Music in the USSR"; *ME*, III, 530.

13 Pakhmutova, *Izbrannye pesni*, 155–6; interview with Pauls in *SK* (November 15, 1986) 3.

14 On Leontev, *Estrada* (1988) 312–20. On Pugacheva: *MZh*, 5 (1978) 8–9; lyrics to "Harlequin" (by Bulgarian composer, Emil Dmitrov) in *Populyarnyi spravochnik-pesennik*, 185–6; Pekha, *MZh*, 16 (1968) 10. Recordings: Leontev on *Dialog*, *Komarovo*, and *Parad solistov estrady*; Pugacheva on *Alla Pugacheva v Stokgolme* and *Alla Pugatjova*.

15 Smith, *Songs to Seven Strings*, 45–53.

16 *Ibid.*, 181–228; Kopelev, "Pamyati Aleksandra Galicha"; Betaki, "Galich i russkie bardy"; Galich, *Kogda ya vernus*; *Pesni russkikh bardov*; *Kogda ya vernus*, television documentary, Moscow, February 5, 1990.

17 *Sovetskaya Rossiya* (June 9, 1968) quoted in Ryback, *Rock Around the Bloc*, 46.

18 Lazarski, "Cult of Vysotsky"; *NS* (July, 1984) 179. The literature and discography on Vysotsky is growing by the month. See: Smith, *Songs to Seven Strings*, 146–99; Leonidov, *Vysotskii i drugie*. The fullest collection of his songs is *Sobranie stikhov i pesen* 3 vol. edn Arkadii Lvov and Aleksandr Sumerkin (New York, 1988). One of the best Vysotsky cassettes is *Vladimir Vysotsky*, Toronto, 1987, with spoken and written translations. Funeral of Vladimir Vysotsky (video). The first Soviet TV program about Vysotsky (1987) is reproduced in *Televidenie*, 188–222. A good discussion of all the bards is Sosin, "Magnitizdat."

19 Kopelev, "Pamyati." For a well-informed, though essentially negative discussion of "drinking culture," see Walter Connor, "Alcohol and Soviet Society," *SR*, 30/3 (September, 1971) 570–88.

20 *Harpers'* (November, 1984) 14.

21 Ryback, *Rock Around the Bloc*, 131–4; *New York Times*, November 28, 1966; *MZh*, 2 (1979) 22–3; *Izvestiya*, January 17, 1982, 3; Hayes, "The Dean Reed Story"; Soviet television documentary on Reed, September 24, 1989.

22 Starr, *Red and Hot*, 261–315. For a sampling of recordings: *Jazz 67: the IV*

Moscow Festival of Jazz Ensembles; Leningradskii Diksilend; Leonid Chizhik; and *Igor Bril*. On disco: Ryback, *Rock Around the Bloc*, 159–61.

23 Starr, *Red and Hot*, 289–321; Troitsky, *Back in the USSR*, 15–25, 36 (qu.); conversation with rock drummer, Andrei Grigorev, April 1989; *Vokrug sveta*, 1968 article by Genrikh Borovik cited in Ryback, *Rock Around the Bloc*, 112–14.

24 Ryback, *Rock Around the Bloc*, 152–7; Troitsky, *Back in the USSR*, 28–36 (qu. p. 34).

25 Ramet and Zamascikov, "The Soviet Rock Scene" (KIARS); Troitsky, *Back in the USSR*, 99 (qu.).

26 Ryback, *Rock Around the Bloc*, 106–7, 150–2; Easton, "The Rock Music Community," 49.

27 Troitsky, *Back in the USSR*, 51. Quotations: Belz, *The Story of Rock*, 29; *Pravda* (October 1, 1984) 3. To add to a little more sting to the rivalry, one rock group of the 1980s called itself Union of Composers.

28 Tsfasman interview in *SK* (February 19, 1966) 4; Ryback, *Rock Around the Bloc*, 62–3; Troitsky, *Back in the USSR*, 89–90; Ramet and Zamascikov, "Soviet Rock Scene" (KIARS).

29 *KP* (April 11, 1982), 2; *NS*, 7 (July 1984) 171–82 (qu. p. 177).

30 Troitsky, *Back in the USSR*, 91–104; Ramet and Zamascikov, "Soviet Rock Scene" (KIARS). For the buildup of hostility, see *KP* (September 23, 1984) 4 and (October 11, 1984). For the NATO story, see ch. 5. A vivid picture of the Leningrad underground rock scene in 1986 is given in Rashid Nugmanov's film, *Ya-Ha*.

31 Makarov, *Sovetskaya klounada*, 181–263; Hammarstrom, *Circus Rings Around Russia*; *RSE*, 3, 451–83; *Inside the Soviet Circus* (video).

32 *BDSU*, 53; Dusko Doder, *Shadows and Whispers Power Politics Inside the Kremlin from Brezhnev to Gorbachev* (New York, 1986) 57–9. These sources diverge on the spelling of Boris the Gypsy's last name.

33 *NYT*, January 15, 1989 and January 10, 1988; Playbill, Constitution Hall, Washington, DC, February 9, 1988.

34 *Soviet Army Chorus, Band, and Dance Ensemble* (video). On televising folk ensembles, see *Folklor i viktorina*, especially 32–46. Amateur folk playing remained more "authentic" than the national ensembles which had to fit their work to public and media performance. See *Folkor i khudozhestvennaya samodeyatelnost*.

35 Terikov, *Kuplet na estrade*, 187–214.

36 *Ego velichestvo teatr: Arkadii Raikin* (recording); Uvarova, *Arkadii Raikin*, 143–299. A sample of his late work can be viewed on *Teatr Arkadiya Isaakovicha Raikina* (video). For his influence on other comedians, see Gennadii Khazanov in *Ogonek*, 43 (October 1986) 10–11; *TZh*, 24 (December 1987) 9–10.

37 Zhvanetskii, *Vstrechi*, 125–6; Briker and Vishevskii, "Yumor v populyarnoi kulture." For recent routines: *Diskoteka smekha* (recording), with the three Odessans, Zhvanetsky, Kartsev, and Ilchenko.

38 *Televidenie* (1985) 146–60; Gerner, "Sobornost Secularized"; I. Fomichev, "Ekran obshchestvennogo mneniya," *Televidenie, '89*, 124–34.

39 Mickiewicz, *Split Signals*; White, *Political Culture*, 137–8. Game shows: *Folklor i viktorina*, 47–68.

40 Golovskoy, *Behind the Soviet Screen*, an insider's account. For a sample of Ermash's ideological hash, see *Kommunist*, 12 (August 1982) 83–91.

41 Figures in *SK*, November 25, 1986, 4 and in Shlapentokh, *Public and Private Life* (data on movie houses and clubs, 182; qu. p. 178).

42 Lawton, "Towards a New Openness in Soviet Cinema" and "'Lumiere' and Darkness," discussing Turovskaya; Dymshits, *Sovetskaya kinomelodrama*, 33. Vilchek, *Pod znakom TV*, 105, discusses the obvious folkloric quality of *Eseniya* by comparing it to the Russian folk tale, "Tsarevna-lyagushka." Indian, Arab, and Latin American films have been popular in Russia over the past four decades.

43 Lawton, *Kinoglasnost*, ch. 1.

44 For more detail on Russian nationalism in film, see Dunlop, "Russian Nationalist Themes."

45 *Ibid.*; conversation with Menshov, March 1988. For the importance of nostalgic atmospherics in film, see Klimontovich, "Teatr i kono segodnya," 38.

46 Bushnell, "Urban Leisure Culture"; Gordon and Klopov, *Man after Work*, 104–21, 131–2. Their sample was tens of thousands of workers in Dnepropetrovsk, Zaporozhe, Odessa, and Kostroma.

47 *Ibid.*; Starr, "New Communications Technologies"; *KP* (January 1, 1982) 4 and (February 27, 1983) 2; *Izvestiya* (August 19, 1984) 5.

48 Bennett, "The Politics and Culture of Soviet Sports"; Anatoly Firsov, interview on Moscow television, September 29, 1989.

49 Tanya Frisby, "Soviet Youth Culture,", in Riordan, *Soviet Youth Culture*, 4–6; Bushnell, *Moscow Graffiti* and "Soviet Hippies."

50 Heineman, "The Youth Experience on the Virgin Lands and Baikal-Amur"; *BAM – doroga druzhby*; *BAM: the Permanent Settlers* (documentary film).

51 For numerous Brezhnev jokes, see the index in Telesin, *1001*.

7 Perestroika and the people's taste 1985–

1 *SK* (July 30, 1988) 4; Olcott, "Glasnost and Soviet Culture," 107. For a brief overview as of 1989, see Stites, "Soviet Popular Culture in the Gorbachev Era."

2 Pikul interviews in *Literaturnyi Kirgizstan*, 7 (1988) 121–33 and *NS*, 2 (1989) 184–92. I thank Walter Laqueur for these references. See also afterword to Pikul, *Malchiki*. The latest novel, *Go Forth Without Sin* is in *MG*, 2 and 3, (1990). Pikul died in 1990; see Guzanov, *Pravda o zhizni i smerti Valentina Pikulya*.

3 Semenov, *Reporter*; *People* (1987) 81–97; *Economist* (January 21, 1989) 21; conversations with Semenov and with Anthony Olcott, 1987 and with Abraham Brumberg, 1989. *NF: sbornik nauchnoi fantastiki*, vyp. 32, Moscow, 1988, 184–207; Parnov in *SK* (July 26, 1988) 6; Stites, "World Outlook and Inner Fears": Semenov, ed. *Detektiv i politika* and *Sovershenno sekretno*.

4 Olcott, "Glasnost," 106–9; *LG* (September 17, 1986) 3; Nikitin, *Gologramma*;

Kunin, *Interdevochka*; *DK* (October, 1989) 11; Borovik in *Ogonek*, 28–30 (1987), published in English as *Hidden War*; and war stories in *Znamya*, 3 (1989) 93–119.

5 *SL* (September 1986) 52–3; *CDSP*, 39/11 (1987) 17; *Ogonek*, 2 (January, 1987) 32–3; *SO* (September 29, 1988) 1, 5; Law, "Revolution in the Soviet Theater."

6 *SK* (November 13, 1986) 5.

7 *Klub* (December, 1989).

8 I. Rakhlin, "Estrada – Zolushka?" *LG* (March 11, 1987) 8; *Ogonek*, 43 (October, 1986) 10–11; Briker and Vishevskii, "Yumor v populyarnoi kulture"; interviews with Zhvanetsky and Khazanov in *Estrada* (1988) 276–83, 301–11; conversation with Khazanov, December, 1989; Zadornov, Parodii yumoristicheskie o Gorbacheve i o nashikh lozungakh (tape).

9 Dunlop, "Soviet Cultural Politics"; Ratchford, "Perestroika and the Soviet Cinema." In 1990, the Tadzhik director Dovlat Khudonazarov became the new head of the Union. The best treatment of the subject as a whole is Lawton, *Kinoglasnost*.

10 Askoldov's remarks at the screening of the film in Washington DC, 1988; it had been shown earlier in Moscow but with cuts. *CSM* (August 7, 1987) 19–20; Mikhail Zhabsky, remarks at the Soviet–American Film Conference, Moscow, 1989.

11 Documentaries shown at the Soviet Culture Festival, Imatra, Finland, 1988; the Glasnost Film Festival, Washington DC, April, 1989; Moscow and Leningrad TV, 1989–1990; Soviet Glasnost Symposium, Washington DC, 1991. See also Lawton, "Rewriting History."

12 *SK* (November 25, 1986) 4; *People* (April 6, 1987) 18–19, 28; *SO* (September 29, 1988) 5; Lawton, *Kinoglasnost*.

13 Sobolev, "Grustnye priklyucheniya priklyuchencheskogo filma," *LG* (March 11, 1987) 8; Lawton, "Towards a New Openness" and "'Lumiere' and Darkness." Sharply conflicting opinions on "popularity" and "commercialism" in cinema were voiced openly at the Soviet–American Film Conferences in Moscow (1989) and Washington DC (1990).

14 *DK* (October, 1989) 11.

15 Mickiewicz, *Split Signals*, qu. p. 204; Sanders, "A Very Mass Media"; Hayes, "Glasnost and the Politics of Soviet Media." Egor Yakovlev, former editor of *Moscow News*, was put in charge of Gosteleradio in August 1991.

16 The lively show *Glance* was taken off the air in late 1990 when hard liner Leonid Kravchenko became the new head of Gosteleradio and stymied a story about Shevarnadze's resignation (conversation with Alexander Politkovsky, anchorman of *Glance*, Washington, January 1991). Nevzorov interview in *Elektromash* (July 19, 1989) 4. See also *WP* (February 3, 1991) A16. He was taken off the air after the *putsch*.

17 Pepsi: Ryback, *Rock Around the Bloc*, 7.

18 *Ogonek*, 36 (August, 1985) 22–4; *SK* (July 18, 1988) 8; Gerner, "Soviet Television Viewing in Sweden," quoting Tokmakova.

19 Troitsky, *Back in the USSR*, 18, 67; Ryback, *Rock Around the Bloc*, 222–32; conversation with Nikolai Mikhailov, president of the Leningrad Rock Club.

20 *SK* (October 1, 1988); *People* (1987) 47; *Guitar Player* (December, 1988) 87–103; Fedorov, *Rok v neskolkikh litsakh*.

21 Troitsky, *Back in the USSR*, 129; *Ogonek*, 46 (November, 1986) 14–15. When Grebenshchikov's star declined, Tsoy replaced him as the major idol: after the latter's death by accident in August 1990, several female teenagers committed suicide. There has also been a renewed interest in old-style bard song, its most prominent practitioner now being Alexander Rozenbaum.

22 *SK* (November 15, 1986) 3 and (January 10, 1987) 4; Ryback, *Rock Around the Bloc*, 3.

23 *WP* (April 28, 1989) D8; *SK* (September 6, 1986) 5; Troitsky, *Back in the USSR*, 17; *KiZh* (September, 1989) 44.

24 Troitsky, *Back in the USSR*, 119–20, 127; Easton, "The Rock Music Community" (lyrics pp. 67, 64); *SO* (November 15, 1988) 1, 3.

25 Troitsky, *Back in the USSR*, 125, 131; Ramet and Zamascikov, "The Soviet Rock Scene" (KIARS), 8–11; *WP* (November 27, 1987), section A41, (April 20, 1988) section A24, and (July 28, 1989) section B2 (Andreeva qu.). *MG*, 2 (1990) 217–18; *Ogonek*, 36 (August 1985) 23.

26 Troitsky, *Back in the USSR*, 99; *SK* (July 28, 1988) 5; *Ogonek*, 49 (December, 1986) 17; *People* (1987) 76–8.

27 *SK* (November 15, 1986). Conversations with Roman Kopp, manager of the Leningrad Jazz Club, 1990; *Igraem amerikanskii dzhaz*, program May 28–29, 1988. The program notes by the jazz historian, Alexei Batashev, link the spirit of jazz with the euphoria of perestroika. Concert review: *IHT* (June 10, 1988). Feigin, in *Russian Jazz*, makes the "democratic" claim but is contradicted by the contributors to his book, including Starr.

28 Performed by Eskadron (Squadron); Salnykova tapes.

29 *RLR* (September 10, 1987); *Ogonek*, 11 (March 1987) 17–18.

30 Mark Pomar, conference paper on informal groups in the USSR, AAASS, 1988; Bushnell, "Soviet Hippies"; Troitsky, *Back in the USSR*, 121; Easton, "The Rock Music Community."

31 Pomar; Riordan, "Teenage Gangs"; *Homecoming* (documentary film); interviews on Moscow television, 1989–1990.

32 Bushnell, *Moscow Graffiti*; Riordan, "Teenage Gangs"; Dobson, "Problems Among Soviet Youth"; *What's Happening in Your Courtyard?* (documentary film).

33 *LG* (March 4, 1987) 1, (March 11, 1987) 1; *Ogonek*, 5 (January, 1987) 20–1. For a sociological interpretation, see: "Rok: Muzyka? Subkultura? Stil zhizni?"

34 A. S. Zapekotskii, "Traditsii i novatsii v kulture molodezhi," *Stil i traditsiya v razvitii kultury* (Leningrad, 1989), 86.

35 *MN*, 51 (December 17, 1989) 5.

Greetings and farewell

1 William Campbell, a Scottish-born entertainer who worked in Moscow in the 1930s, played small roles in the Alexandrov films and in stage shows and operetta, offers snippets about these things: *Villi the Clown*, 63–167.

2 Bushnell, "Soviet Hippies," 4.

Bibliography

Abbreviations

AHR	*American Historical Review*
BDSU	*Biographical Dictionary of the Soviet Union.* Ed. Jeanne Vronskaya. London, 1989
CDSP	*Current Digest of the Soviet Press*
CSM	*Christian Science Monitor*
DK	*Dom Kino*
DvM	*Dosug v Moskve*
GiPM	*Govorit i pokazyvaet Moskva*
HJFRT	*Historical Journal of Film, Radio, and Television*
IHT	*International Herald Tribune*
IIK	*Iz istorii kino*
IK	*Iskusstvo kino*
IL	*International Literature*
JPC	*Journal of Popular Culture*
KES	*Kino: enstsiklopedicheskii slovar.* Moscow, 1986
KIARS	Kennan Institute for Advanced Russian Studies
KiZh	*Kultura i zhizn*
KLE	*Kratkaya literaturnaya entskilopediya.* 9 vols. Moscow, 1962–1978
KP	*Komsomolskaya pravda*
KS	*Kinoslovar.* 2 vol. Moscow, 1966–1970
KZ	*Kinovedcheskie zapiski*
LG	*Literaturnaya gazeta*
LN	*Literaturnoe nasledstvo*
ME	*Muzykalnaya entsiklopediya.* 6 vol. Moscow, 1973–1982
MG	*Molodaya gvardiya*
MN	*Moskovskie novosti*
MNE	*Moscow News*
MoE	*Molodezhnaya estrada*
MZh	*Muzykalnaya zhizn*
NJSS	*Nordic Journal of Soviet and East European Studies*
NoS	*Novyi Satirikon*
NS	*Nash sovremennik*
NT	*Narodnoe tvorchestvo*
NYT	*New York Times*

NZ   *Novosti sezona*
PG   *Petrogradskaya gazeta*
POC   *Problems of Communism*
RF   *Radiofront*
RG   *Radio Gazeta*
RH   *Russian History*
RiZh   *Rampa i zhizn*
RLR   *Radio Liberty Report*
RR   *Russian Review*
RSE   *Russkaya sovetskaya estrada*
SE   *Sovetskii ekran*
SEiTs   *Sovetskaya estrada i tsirk*
SF   *Sovetskii film*
SI   *Sotsiologicheskie issledovaniya*
SiU   *Stolitsa i usadba*
SK   *Sovetskaya kultura*
SL   *Soviet Life*
SM   *Sovetskaya muzyka*
SO   *Soviet Observer*
SR   *Slavic Review*
TE   *Teatralnaya entsiklopediya.* 5 vols. Moscow, 1961–1967
TG   *Teatralnaya gazeta*
TiI   *Teatr i iskusstvo*
TKM   *Teatralno-kontsertnaya Moskva*
TsiE   *Tsirk i estrada*
TZh   *Teatralnaya zhizn*
VK   *Voprosy kinoiskusstva*
VT   *Vestnik teatra*
WP   *Washington Post*

Other serials

Bich
Fantastika
Harpers'
Iskry
Izvestiya
Kadr
Kino
Klub
Kommunist
Kontinent
Le monde
Mir detektiva
NF: sbornik nauchnoi fantastiki
Niva
Obozrenie

Ogonek
Partiinaya zhizn
People
Pioner
Sovershenno sekretno
Variety
Znamya

Archival sources

Moscow

Gosteleradio, Teleradio Center: old television programs
Gosteleradio, Radio Moscow Archives: taped recordings of radio programs, 1930s–1940s; texts of Soviet broadcasting, 1930s–1940s
Maya Turovskaya archive: statistical data on Soviet moviegoing
State Circus Academy Library (Gosudarstvennoe Uchilishche Tsirka i Estradnogo Iskusstva imeni M. N. Rumyantseva [Karandash]): photo collection; repertoires and routines of the Soviet circus

Leningrad

Leningrad Radio Museum: graphic and audial materials
Leningrad State Circus Museum Archives: graphic and written materials
Private Collections: manuscripts of song lyrics and jokes

Helsinki

Slavonic Library: postcard and poster collections

Note: For other nonprinted sources, see discography, filmography, and videography. In addition, I have consulted programs and in-house materials of various organizations too numerous to list.

Published sources and scholarly papers

Adamov, Arkadii, *Delo "pestrykh": povest*. Moscow, 1956
A. Durov v zhizni i na arene. Moscow, 1984
Aksenov, Vasily, *In Search of Melancholy Baby*. New York, 1987
  A Ticket to the Stars (1960). New York, 1963
Aleksandrov, Grigorii, *Gody poiskov i truda*. Moscow, 1975
Alekseev, M., *Ekran – eto zhizn*. Moscow, 1985
Aliger, Margarita, *Zoya*. Moscow, 1942
Ament, Suzanne, "Russian Revolutionary Songs of 1905 and 1917: Symbols and Messengers of Protest and Change." MA Thesis, Georgetown University, 1984
  "Soviet Songs of World War II." Ms

Amori, Count [Ippolit Rapgof], *Tainy Nevskogo Prospekta*. Petrograd, 1915

Anisimov, A. I., *Rabota s samodeyatelnym khorom*, 2nd edn Leningrad, 1938

Anisimov, A. V., *Dosug v Moskve*. 3rd edn Moscow, 1989

Artsybashev, Mikhail, *Sanin* (1908). Berlin, 1911

A. V. Aleksandrov: komplekt iz 12 fotootkrytok. Moscow, 1983

Avins, Carol, *Border Crossings: the West and Russian Identity in Soviet Literature, 1917–1934*. Berkeley CA, 1983

Babaevskii, Semen, *Kavaler zolotoi zvezdy*. Moscow, 1947

Baburina, N. I., *Russkii plakat: vtoraya polovina XIX–nachalo XX veka*. Leningrad, 1988

Bagaev, B., *Boris Shumyatskii*. Krasnoyarsk, 1974

Bailes, Kendall, *Technology and Society under Lenin and Stalin*. Princeton NJ, 1978

Bakhtin, Vladimir, and Dmitry Moldavskii, *Russkii lubok, XVII–XIX vv.* Moscow, 1962

Ball, Alan, *Russia's Last Capitalists*. Berkeley CA, 1987

   Street Children in Soviet Russia: the Besprizornye, 1918–1930. Forthcoming

BAM – doroga druzhby. Irkutsk, 1984

Barber, John, "Working-class Culture and Political Culture in the 1930s," in Gunther, *Culture of the Stalin Period*, 3–14

Barghoorn, Frederick, *The Soviet Cultural Offensive: the Role of Cultural diplomacy in Soviet Foreign Policy*. Princeton NJ, 1960

Basinger, J., *World War II Combat Film*. New York, 1956

Bednyi, Demyan, *Izbrannye proizvedeniya*. 2 vols., Moscow, 1959

Beilin, A., *Arkadii Raikin*. Leningrad, 1969

Belitskii, Ya. M., and G. N. Glezer, *Rasskazy ob otkrytkakh*. Moscow, 1986

Belomorsko-Baltiiskii Kanal imeni Stalina: istoriya stroitelstva. ed., M. Gorkii, L. Averbakh, and S. Firin. Moscow, 1934

Belyaev, Alexander, *The Amphibian* (1928). Moscow, 1986

Belz, Carl, *The Story of Rock*. New York, 1972

Bennett, John, "The Politics and Culture of Soviet Sports." Ms. Georgetown University, 1989

Bernes, Mark, *Stati; vospominaniya o M. N. Bernese*. Moscow, 1980

Betaki, V., "Galich i russkie bardy," *Kontinent*, 16 (1978) 349–53

Betz, Kate, "As the Tycoons Die: Class-struggle and Censorship in the Russian Cinema, 1917–1921," in N. A. Nielsson, ed., *Art, Society, Revolution: Russia, 1917–1921*. Stockholm, 1979, 198–236

Bilenkin, Dmitry, *The Uncertainty Principle*, tr., A. Bouis. New York, 1978

Blakeley, Alison, *Russia and the Negro*. Washington DC, 1986

Bliznakov, Milka, "Architecture as Decorative Art: Soviet Architecture During Stalin's Regime." Ms

Bogdanov, Alexander, *Red Star: the First Bolshevik Utopia*. Ed. L. Graham and R. Stites, tr., C. Rougle. Bloomington IN, 1984

Bonnell, Victoria, "The Representation of Politics and the Politics of Representation," RR, xlvii/3 (1988)

Borovik, Artyom, *The Hidden War: a Russian Journalist's Account of the Soviet War in Afghanistan*. New York, 1991

Bouissac, Paul, *Circus and Culture: a Semiotic Approach*. Bloomington IN, 1975

Bowers, Faubion, *Entertainment in Russia*. Edinburgh, 1959

Bradley, Joseph, *Muzhik and Muscovite*. Berkeley CA, 1985

Bratolyubov, S. K., *Na zare sovetskoi kinematografii*. Leningrad, 1976

Brezhnev, L. I., *Little Land* (1978). Moscow, 1990

Bright, Terry, "Soviet Crusade against Pop," in R. Middleton and D. Horn, eds., *Popular Music 5: Continuity and Change*. Cambridge, 1985

Briker, Boris, and Anatoly Vishevskii, "Yumor v populyarnoi kulture sovetskogo intelligenta," *Wiener slawistischer Almanach*, 24 (1989) 148–69

Brooks, Jeffrey, "The Breakdown in Production and Distribution of Printed Material, 1917–1927," in Gleason, *Bolshevik Culture*, 151–74

"Competing Modes of Popular Discourse: Individualism and Class Consciousness in the Russian Print Media." Ms

"Public and Private Values in the Soviet Press, 1921–1928," SR, xlviii/1 (Spring, 1989) 16–35

"Studies of the Reader in the 1920s," RH, 2–3 (1982) 187–202

When Russia Learned to Read. Princeton NJ, 1984

Brower, Daniel, *Russian Urbanism between Tradition and Modernity, 1850–1900*. Berkeley CA, 1990

Budyak, L. M., and V. P. Mikhailov, *Adresa moskovskogo kino*. Moscow, 1987

Bulychev, Kirill [Kir], *Half a Life and other Stories*, tr., H. S. Jacobson. New York, 1977

Burke, Peter, *Popular Culture in Early Modern Europe*. London, 1978

Bushnell, John, *Moscow Graffiti: Language and Subculture*. Boston MA, 1990

"Soviet Hippies," *Harriman Institute Forum*, iii/5 (April, 1990)

"Urban Leisure Culture in Post-Stalin Russia," in Thompson and Sheldon, *Soviet Society and Culture*, 58–86

Campbell, William, *Villi, the Clown*. London, 1981

Chagadaev, A., *V. V. Andreev*. Moscow, 1948

Chaikovskii, Vsevelod, *Mladencheskie gody russkogo kino*. Moscow, 1928

Chapple, Richard, *Soviet Satire of the Twenties*. Gainesville FL, 1980

Chernov, A., and M. Byalik, *O legkoi muzyke, o dzhaze, o khoroshem vkuse*. Leningrad, 1965

Chernyshev, A. A., *Russkaya dooktyabrskaya kinozhurnalistika*. Moscow, 1987

Chesnokov, P., *Khor i upravlenie im*. Moscow, 1940

Clark, Katerina, *The Soviet Novel: History as Ritual*. Chicago IL, 1985

Condee, Nancy, and Vladimir Padunov, "The Frontiers of Soviet Culture: Reaching its Limits?" *Harriman Institute Forum*, i/5 (May, 1988)

Connor, Walter, "Alcohol and Soviet Society," SR, xxx/3 (September, 1971) 570–88

Danilevich, L., *Muzyka na frontakh Velikoi Otechestvennoi Voiny*. Moscow, 1948

Dementev, V. V., *Pesni i sudby soldatskie*. Tashkent, 1982

Desyat let Krasnoznamennogo ansamblya Krasnoarmeiskoi pesni i plyaski Soyuza SSR. Moscow, 1939

Dmitriev, Yurii, *Estrada i tsirk glazami vlyublennogo*. Moscow, 1971

Russkii tsirk. Moscow, 1953

Sovetskii tsirk: ocherki istorii, 1917–1941. Moscow, 1963

Tsirk v Rossii ot istokov do 1917 goda. Moscow, 1977

Dobryi, Roman [I. D. Putilin], *Genii russkogo syska I. D. Putilin: rasskazy o ego pokhozhdennyakh*. (Reprint; Moscow, 1990)

Dobrynin, Vladimir, *V. Dobrynin: pesni dlya golosa v soprovozhdenii fortepiano (bayan, gitary)*. Moscow, 1989

Dobson, Richard, "Problems Among Soviet Youth," KIARS Meeting Report, April, 1988

Dolinskii, I., *Chapaev: dramaturgiya*. Moscow, 1945

Dovesti do kontsa borbu s nepmanskoi muzykoi. Moscow, 1931

Dramaturgiya kino. Moscow, 1935

Dreiden, S. D., *Muzyka-revolyutsii*. 2nd edn, Moscow, 1970

Druzhnikov, Yurii, *Voznesenie Pavlika Morozova*. London, 1988

Dunaevskii, I. O., *Vystupleniya, stati, pisma, vospominaniya*. Moscow, 1961

Dunham, "Troublemakers in Uniform." Ms. n.d.

Dunham, Vera, *In Stalin's Time*. Cambridge, 1976

Dunlop, John, "Russian Nationalist Themes in Soviet Films of the 1970s and 1980s," in Lawton, *Red Screen*

"Soviet Cultural Politics," POC, xxxvi (November–December, 1987) 34–56

Dvinsky, Emmanuel, *Durov and his Performing Animals*. Moscow, nd

Dymshits, N. A., *Sovetskaya kinomelodrama vchera i segodnya*. Moscow, 1987

Easton, Paul, "The Rock Music Community," in Riordan, *Soviet Youth Culture*, 45–82

Efremov, Ivan, *Andromeda: a Space-Age Tale* (1957). Moscow, 1980

Ehrenburg, Ilya, and Konstantin Simonov, *In One Newspaper*. New York, 1985

Ekran, 89: tvorcheskaya tribuna. Moscow, 1989

Emtsev, Mikhail, and Eremei Parnov, *World Soul* (1964), tr., A. Bouis. New York, 1978

Enzensberger, Maria, "'We Were Born to Turn a Fairy Tale into Reality': Grigory Alexandrov's *Bright Path*." Ms, 1990

Erenberg, Lewis, *Steppin' Out: New York Nightlife and the Transformation of American Culture*. Chicago IL, 1981

Ershov (see Yershov)

Estrada: chto? gde? zachem?: stati, intervyu, publikatsiya. Moscow, 1988

Everything But Love: Science Fiction Stories, tr. A. Shkarovsky. Moscow, 1973

Fadeev, Aleksandr, *Molodaya gvardiya*. Moscow, 1946

Fedorov, Evgenii, *Rok v neskolkikh litsakh*. Moscow, 1989

Feigelson, Kristian, *L'U.R.S.S. et sa television*. Paris, 1990

Feigin, Leo, ed., *Russian Jazz: New Identity*. London, 1985

Ferro, Marc, "The Fiction Film and Historical Analysis," in Paul Smith, ed., *The Historian and Film*. Cambridge, 1976, 80–94

Filippov, Boris, *Actors without Makeup*. Moscow, 1977

Filippov, V. I., *Puti samodeyatelnogo teatra*. Moscow, 1927

"Filmografiya," IIK, 4 (1961) 137–43

Fisher, Wesley, and Solomon Volkov, "The Audience for Classical Music in the USSR," SR, xxxviii/3 (September, 1979) 481–3

Fitzpatrick, Sheila, ed., *Cultural Revolution in Russia, 1928–1931*. Bloomington IN, 1978

"'Middle Class Values' and Soviet Life in the 1930s," in Thompson and Sheldon, eds., *Soviet Society and Culture*, 20–38

A. Rabinowitch, and R. Stites, eds., *Russia in the Era of NEP: Explorations in Soviet Society and Culture*. Bloomington IN, 1991

Folklor i khudozhestvennaya samodeyatelnost. Leningrad, 1968

Folklor i viktorina: narodnoe tvorchestvo v vek televideniya. Moscow, 1988

Friedberg, Maurice, *A Decade of Euphoria: Western Literature in Post-Stalin Russia, 1954–64*. Bloomington IN, 1977

Russian Classics in Soviet Jackets. New York, 1962

Frumkin, Vladimir, "Tekhnologiya ubezhdeniya," *Obozrenie*, 5 (July, 1983) 17–20 and 6 (September, 1983) 23–6

Furmanov, Dmitry, *Chapaev* (1923). Moscow, 1974

Gakov, Vladimir, *World Spring*, tr. R. de Garis. New York, 1981

Galich, Aleksandr, *Kogda ya vernus*. Frankfurt, 1977

Gans, Herbert, *Popular Culture and High Culture*. New York, 1975

Garri, Aleksei, *Ldy i lyudi*. Moscow, 1928

Garteveld, V. N., *Kontsertnoe turne po Rossii i Sibiri*. Moscow, 1909

Gendlin, L., *Iz pesen A. Vertinskogo*. Stockholm, 1980

German, Yurii, *Lapshin*. Moscow, 1937

Gerner, Kristian, "Sobornost Secularized," in Claes Arvidsson and Lars Eric Blomqvist, eds., *Symbols of Power*. Stockholm, 1987, 113–40

"Soviet Television Viewing in Sweden." Ms

Ginsburg, S., *Kinematografiya dorevolyutsionnoi Rossii*. Moscow, 1963

Glad, John, "Brave New Worlds," *Wilson Quarterly*, vii/4 (Autumn, 1983) 68–78

Extrapolations from Dystopia: a Critical Study of Soviet Science Fiction. Princeton NJ, 1982

Glazov, Yury, "'Thieves' in the USSR as a Social Phenomenon," *Survey*, xxii/1 (Winter, 1976) 141–56

Gleason, Abbott, *et al.*, eds., *Bolshevik Culture: Experiment and Order in the Russian Revolution*. Bloomington IN, 1985

Goldberg, Anatol, *Ilya Ehrenburg*. New York, 1984

Golovskoy, Val, with John Rimberg, *Behind the Soviet Screen*. Ann Arbor MI, 1986

Gordon Leonid, and E. Klopov, *Man after Work*, tr., J. Bushnell. Moscow, 1975

Goryaeva, Tatyana, and Aleksandr Sherel, eds., *Istoriya sovetskoi radiozhurnalistiki, 1917–1945: dokumenty, teksty, vospominaniya*. Moscow, 1990

Goulzadian, Anne, *L'empire du dernier tsar; 410 cartes postales 1896–1917*. Paris, 1982

Graffy, Julian, "Unshelving Stalin: After the Period of Stagnation" Ms. 1990

Graffy, Julian, and Geoffrey Hosking, eds., *Culture and Media in the USSR Today*. London, 1989

Grebens, G. V., *Ivan Efremov's Theory of Science Fiction*. New York, 1978

Groys, Boris, *Stalin's Gesamtkunstwerk*, tr., Charles Rougle. Forthcoming

Gruppa "Akvarium": fakty biografii. Tallin Estonia, 1989

Gudoshnikov, Ya.I., "Gorodskoi romans kak sotsialnoe i khudozhestvennoe yavlenie," in *Folklor narodov RSFSR*. Ufa, Russia, 1979, 98–104

Gunther, Hans, ed., *The Culture of the Stalin Period*. London, 1990

Gurevich, E., *O zhanrakh sovetskogo tsirka*. Moscow, 1984
Gurevich, P., and V. Ruzhnikov, *Sovetskoe radioveshchanie*. Moscow, 1976
Gutkin, Irina, "Anticipating the Past and Retrospecting the Future: the Soviet Historical Novel in the 1920s and Early 1930s." Ms., 1989
Hammarstrom, David, *Circus Rings Around Russia*. Hamden CT, 1983
Hatch, John, "The Politics of Mass Culture: Workers, Communists, and Prolet-kul't in the Development of Workers' Clubs," RH, xii/2–3 (Summer–Fall 1986) 119–48
Hayes, Nick, "Glasnost and the Politics of Soviet Media." Ms
"The Dean Reed Story," in Ramet, *Rock and Roll*
Heineman, Paul, "The Youth Experience on the Virgin Lands and Baikal-Amur Mainline Projects." Ms., Georgetown University, 1989
Hellberg, Elena, "Folklore, Might, and Glory," NJSS, iii/2 (1986) 9–20
"The Hero in Popular Pictures: Russian Lubok and Soviet Poster," in R. Brednich and A. Hartmann, eds., *Populare Bildmedien*. Reinhausen, 1986, 171–91
Hellman, Ben, *Barnboken i Sovjetryssland*. Helsinki, 1990
"Paradise Lost: the Literary Development of Arkadii and Boris Strugatskii," in L. Kleberg and R. Stites, eds., *Utopia in Russian History, Culture, and Thought*. Special number of RH, xi/2–3 (Summer-Fall, 1984) 311–19
Hilton, Alison, *Russian Folk Culture*. Forthcoming
Hopkins, Mark, *Mass Media in the Soviet Union*. New York, 1970
Hosking, Geoffrey, *Beyond Socialist Realism*. London, 1980
A History of the Soviet Union. London, 1985
Ilin, M., *New Russia's Primer: the Story of the Five Year Plan*, tr., G. Counts and N. Lodge. Boston MA, 1931
Ilina, G. I., *Kulturnoe stroitelstvo v Petrograde*. Leningrad, 1982
Iskusstvo v boevom stroyu: vospominaniya, dnevniki, ocherki. Moscow, 1985
Istoriya muzyki narodov SSSR. 2 vols., Moscow, 1970
Jahn, Hubertus, "Patriotic Culture in Russia During World War I." PhD Dissertation, Georgetown University, 1991
Jalkanen, Pekka, *Alaska, Bombay, ja Billy Boy: Jazzkultuurin murros Helsingissa 1920–luvilla*. Helsinki, 1989
Jelagin, Jury, *Taming of the Arts*, tr., N. Wreden. New York, 1951
Johnson, Priscilla, *Khrushchev and the Arts*. Cambridge MA, 1967
Johnson, Robert, *Peasant and Proletarian*. New Brunswick NJ, 1979
Kaempfer, Frank, *"Der rote Keil": das politische Plakat*. Berlin, 1985
Kaganskaya, Maiya, "Mif dvadtsat pervogo veka, ili Rossiya vo mgle," *Strana i mir*, 11 (1986) 78–85
Kalb, Marvin, *Eastern Exposure*. New York, 1958
Kartseva, Elena, *Sdelano v Gollivude*. Moscow, 1964
Kassof, Allen, *The Soviet Youth Program*. Cambridge MA, 1965
Katalog gramplastinok. Moscow, 1940
Kater, Michael, "Forbidden Fruit? Jazz in the Third Reich," AHR, xciv/1 (February, 1989) 11–43
Kazmin, P. M., *S pesnei: stranitsy iz dnevnika*. Moscow, 1970
Kenez, Peter, *The Birth of the Propaganda State*. Cambridge, 1985

Cinema and Soviet Society, 1917–1953. Forthcoming

"Cinema and the 'Cultural Revolution'," SR, xlvii/3 (Fall, 1988) 414–33

Kepley, Vance, "Mr Kuleshov in the Land of the Modernists," in Lawton, *Red Screen*

Khaichenko, G. A., *Russkii narodnyi teatr kontsa XIX-nachala XX veka*. Moscow, 1975

Khanzhonkov, A. A., *Pervye gody russkoi kinematografii*. Moscow, 1937

Khrenov, N. A., "K probleme sotsiologii i psikhologii kino 20-kh godov," VK, 17 (1976) 163–83

Sotsialno-psikhologicheskie aspekty vzaimodeistsviya iskusstva i publiki. Moscow, 1981

Kichin, V. S., *Lyudmila Gurchenko*. Moscow, 1987

King, David, and Cathy Porter, *Blood and Laughter*. London, 1985

Kino: prokat, reklama, metodika, praktika. Moscow, 1987

Kino totalitarnoi epokhi, 1933–1945. Moscow, 1989

"Kino totalitarnoi epokhi," IK, 1 (1990) 111–20

Kipriyanov, V. P., *Orkestr russkikh narodnykh instrumentov im. V. V. Andreeva: istoricheskii ocherk*. Leningrad, 1940

Klimontovich, Nikolai, "The American Theme in Soviet Cinema." Ms

Na ekrane skazka. Moscow, 1984

"Teatr i kino segodnya," in *Kino i zritel*. Moscow, 1987, II, 34–42

Klitin, S. S., *Estrada: problemy teorii, istorii i metodiki*. Moscow, 1987

Kopelev, Lev, "Pamyati Aleksandra Galicha," *Kontinent*, 16 (1978) 334–43

Kosmodemyanskaya, Lyubov, *Moya Zoya*. Moscow, 1942

Krasilshchik, S., *World War II Dispatches from the Soviet Front*. New York, 1985

Krokodilu – 60 let: yubileinaya letopis. Moscow, 1983

Kugel, A., *Teatralnye portrety* (1923). Leningrad, 1967

Kukryniksy, *Po vragam mira!* Moscow, 1982

Vtroem. Moscow, 1975

Kulturnaya zhizn v SSSR. Moscow, 1975 (multivolume)

Kunin, Vladimir, *Interdevochka*. Moscow, 1988

Kurkela, Vesa, *Musiikkifolklorismi ja Jaryestokulttuuri*. Helsinki, 1989. English summary, 394–414

Kuznetsov, E. M., *Iz proshlogo russkoi estrady*. Moscow, 1958

Tsirk: proiskhozhdenie, razvitie, perspektivy. Moscow, 1971

Lane, Christel, *Rites of Rulers*. Cambridge, 1981

Lapshin, V. P., *Khudozhestvennaya zhizn Moskvy i Petrograda v 1917 godu*. Moscow, 1983

Laqueur, Walter, "Julian Semyonov and the Soviet Political Novel," *Society*, xxiii/5 (July–August, 1986)

The Long Road to Freedom: Russia and Glasnost. Boston MA, 1989

Law, Alma, "Revolution in the Soviet theater," *Harriman Institute Forum*, II/7 (July, 1989)

Lawton, Anna, "Happy Glasnost," *The World and I* (December, 1989) 30–43

Kinoglasnost: Soviet Cinema in Our Time. Cambridge, 1992

"'Lumiere' and Darkness: the Moral Question in the Russian and Soviet Cinema," JGO, 38 (1990) 244–54

"Rewriting History: a New Trend in Documentary Film," SO (September 29, 1988)

ed., *The Red Screen: Politics, Society, and Art in Soviet Cinema*. London, 1992

"Towards a New Openness in Soviet Cinema," in Daniel Gould, ed., *Post New Wave Cinema in the Soviet Union and Eastern Europe*. Bloomington IN, 1989, 1–50

Lazarski, Christopher, "The Cult of Vladimir Vysotsky." Ms., Georgetown University, 1989

Lebedev, N. A., *Ocherk istorii kino SSSR*, vol. I. Moscow, 1974

"Boevye dvadtsatye gody," IK, 12 (1968) 85–99

Lebedev, P. F., ed., *Pesni rozhdennye v ogne*. Volograd, 1983

Lebedev-Kumach, Vasilii, *Pesni*. Moscow, 1947

Lemberg, A. G., "Iz vospominaniya starogo operatora," IIK, 2 (1959) 117–31

Leonidov, Pavel, *Vladimir Vysotskii i drugie*. New York, 1983

Lerman, Seth, "Folk Arts in Russia and the Soviet Union: a Case Study of the Andreev Folk Orchestra, Piatnitskii Folk Choir, and Moiseev Dance Company." Ms. Georgetown University, 1991

Lewis, Cathleen, "The Image of Cosmonauts in Popular Culture." Ms., Georgetown University, 1989

"Memorialization of the War." Ms., Georgetown University, 1988

Leyda, Jay, *Kino: a History of the Russian and Soviet Film* (1960) 3rd edn, Princeton NJ, 1983

Lidov, P., *Tanya*. Moscow, 1944

Liehm, Mira and Antonin, *The Most Important Art: Soviet and Eastern European Film after 1945*. Berkeley CA, 1977

Lif, A. et al., *Forbidden Laughter (Soviet Underground Jokes)*. Los Angeles CA, nd

Likhachev, B. S., *Kino v Rossii, 1896–1927*. 3 vols., London, 1927

"Materialy k istorii kino v Rossii (1914–1916)," IIK, 3 (1960) 33–102

Loewe, Heinz-Dieter, "Political Symbols and Rituals of the Russian Radical Right, 1900–1917." Ms

Lofgren, Orvar, "Wish you Were Here: Holiday Images and Picture Postcards," in Nils-Arvid Bringeus, ed., *Man and Picture*. Stockholm, 1986, 90–107

Lokshin, D., *Zamechatelnye russkie khory i ikh direzhery*. 2nd edn, Moscow, 1963

London, Kurt, *The Seven Soviet Arts*. London, 1937

Long, Jennifer, "Antireligious and Ritual Campaigns under Khrushchev." Ms., Georgetown University, 1989

Lucas, James, *War on the Eastern Front*. New York, 1979

Lyons, Eugene, *Moscow Carousel*. New York, 1935

Makarov, S. M., *Sovetskaya klounada*. Moscow, 1986

Makhnovshchina ("Gulyai-Pole"). Leningrad, 1930

Maksakova, A. V., *Agitpoezd "Oktyabrskaya Revolyutsiya" (1919–1920)*. Moscow, 1956

Mally, Lynn, *Culture of the Future: the Proletkult Movement in Revolutionary Russia*. Berkeley CA, 1990

Marchenko, T., *Radioteatr*. Moscow, 1970

Maro (M. I. Levitin), *Besprizornye*. Moscow, 1925

Marran, "Bulat Okudzhava i ego vremya," *Kontinent*, xxxvi (1983) 329–54

Martynov, I., *Gosudarstvennyi russkii narodnyi khor imeni Pyatnitskogo*. 2nd edn, Moscow, 1953

Materialy po istorii pesni velikoi otechestvennoi voiny. Eds V. Yu. Krupyanskaya and S. I. Mints. Moscow, 1953

McGuire, Patrick, *Red Stars: Political Aspects of Soviet Science Fiction*. Ann Arbor MI, 1985

McReynolds, Louise, "Autocratic Journalism: the Case of the St. Petersburg Telegraph Agency," *SR*, xlix/1 (Spring 1990) 48–57

    "Imperial Russia's Newspaper Reporters: Profile of a Society in Transition, 1865–1914," *SEER*, lxvii/2 (April, 1990) 277–93

    "News and Society: *Russkoe Slovo* and the Development of a Mass Circulation Press in Late Imperial Russia." PhD Dissertation, University of Chicago, 1984

    News Under Russia's Old Regime. Princeton NJ, 1991

Medvedev, M. *Leningradskii tsirk*. Leningrad, 1975

Mehnert, Klaus, *Russians and their Favorite Books*. Stanford CA, 1983

Mickiewicz, Ellen, *Split Signals: Television and Politics in the Soviet Union*. New York, 1988

Mikhailov, Dzh., "SSSR-SShA: imidzhi muzykalnoi kultury," in O. E. Tuganova, ed., *Vzaimodeistvie kultur SSSR i SShA, XVIII–XX vv*. Moscow, 1987, 219–29

Mikhnevich, Vladimir, *Yazvy Peterburga: opyt istoriko-statisticheskago izsledovaniya nravstvennosti stolichnago naseleniya*. SP, 1886

Mikryukov, Mstislav, "Radioteatr – iskusstvo," *Teatr*, 12 (December, 1964) 42–56

Millar, James, ed., *Politics, Work, and Daily Life in the USSR*. Cambridge, 1987

Miller, Frank, *Folklore for Stalin: Russian Folklore and Pseudo folklore of the Stalin Era*. Armonk NY, 1990

Miller, Jack, *Jews in Soviet Culture*. New Brunswick NJ, 1984

Morrison, Donald, ed., *Mikhail S. Gorbachev: an Intimate Biography*. New York, 1988

Mozejko, Edward, *et al.*, eds., *Vasily Pavlovich Aksenov*. Columbus OH, 1986

Muzykalnaya zhizn Moskvy. Moscow, 1972

Nekrylova, A. F., *Russkie narodnye gorodskie prazdniki, uveseleniya i zrelishcha konets XVIII-nachalo XX veka*. Leningrad, 1988

Nestev, I. V., "Massovaya pesnya," in *Ocherki sovetskogo muzykalnogo tvorchestva*, I (1947) 235–76

    Zvëzdy russkoi estrady (Panina, Vyaltseva, Plevitskaya). 2nd edn, Moscow, 1974

Neuberger, Joan, *Hooliganism: Crime, Culture, and Power in St. Petersburg, 1900–1914*. Forthcoming

New Soviet Science Fiction, tr. H. Jacobson. New York, 1979

NF: Sbornik nauchnoi fantastiki, vyp. 32. Moscow, 1988

Niemczyk, Barbara, "Vladimir Vysotsky in the Age of *Glasnost*." Ms. 1987

Nikitin, Yurii, *Gologramma*. Moscow, 1986

Nikulin, L., *Karandash*. Moscow, 1951

Novyi polnyi pesennik s notami. Berlin, 1920

Obolenskaya, Yuliya, and K. V. Kandaurov, *Voina korolei*. Petrograd, 1918

Obraztsov, Sergei, *My Profession*. Moscow, 1981

O'Dell, Felicity, *Socialisation through Children's Literature: the Soviet Example*. Cambridge, 1978

Oinas, Felix, "Folklore and Politics in the Soviet Union," SR, xxxi/1 (March 1973) 45–56

   "The Political Uses and Themes of Folklore in the Soviet Union," in Oinas, ed., *Folklore, Nationalism, and Politics*. Columbus OH, 1978

   ed., *The Study of Folklore*. The Hague, 1975

Okudzhava, Bulat, *65 Songs*, ed., Vladimir Frumkin. Ann Arbor MI, 1980

   Songs, ed., Vladimir Frumkin. Ann Arbor MI, 1986

Olcott, Anthony, "Glasnost and Soviet Culture," in M. Friedberg and H. Isham, eds., *Soviet Society Under Gorbachev*. Armonk NY, 1987, 101–30

Orkestr imeni V. V. Andreeva. Moscow, 1987

Ostrovsky, Nikolai, *The Making of a Hero*. New York, 1937 tr., *How the Steel Was Tempered* (1932–4)

Ot lipetskogo gorkoma VLKSM. Lipetsk, 1958

Ozhegov, M. I., *Moya zhizn i pesni dlya naroda*. 2 vols., Moscow, 1901

Pakhmutova, Aleksandra, *Izbrannye pesni*. Moscow, 1989

Papernyi, Vladimir, *Kultura "dva"*. Ann Arbor MI, 1985

   "Moscow in the 1930s and the Emergence of a New City," in Gunther, *Culture of the Stalin Period*, 229–39

Parthe, Kathleen, "Time Backward: Memory and the Past in Soviet Russian Village Prose," KIARS Occasional paper, 1987

Pearl, Deborah, "Educating Workers for Revolution: Populist Propaganda in St. Petersburg, 1879–1882," RH, xv/2–4 (1988) 255–84

Pendo, Stephen, *Aviation in the Cinema*. Metuchen NJ, 1985

Perestiani, Ivan, *75 let zhizni v iskusstve*. Moscow, 1962

Perrie, Maureen, "Folklore as Evidence of Peasant Mentalite," RR 48/2 (1989) 119–43

Pesni radio, kino i televideniya, 81. Moscow, 1988

Pesni radio, kino i televideniya, 84. Moscow, 1989

Pesni russkikh bardov. Paris, 1977

Pesni voennykh let, 1941–1945. Moscow, 1989

Petric, Vlada, "Cinematic Abstraction as a Means of Conveying Ideological Messages in *The Man with the Movie Camera*," in Lawton, *Red Screen*

Pevtsy sovetskoi estrady: vypusk vtoroi. Moscow, 1985

Pikul, Valentin, *Malchiki s bantikami: povest* (1971). Moscow, 1989

   Miniatury. Moscow, 1983

   U poslednei cherty. Moscow, 1981

Pinegina, L. A., *Sovetskii rabochii klass i khudozhestvennaya kultura, 1917–1932*. Moscow, 1984

["Pinkerton, Nat"], *Krovavyi talisman*. SP, 1915

Pisateli ob iskusstve i o sebe. Moscow, 1924

Plakaty Velikoi Otechestvennoi, 1941–1945. Moscow, 1985

Pogacar, Timothy, "The Theme of Culture in the Soviet Detective Novel," in *Studies in Modern and Classical Languages and Literatures*. Madrid, 1988

Polevoi, Boris, *A Story about a Real Man* (1946). Moscow, 1986
Populyarnyi spravochnik pesennik. Moscow, 1989
Postavnichev, K., *Massovoe penie.* Moscow, 1925
Prazdnik yunosti. Kiev, 1987
Propp, V. Ya., *Down Along the Mother Volga,* tr. Roberta Reeder. Philadelphia
    PA, 1975
    Morphology of the Folk Tale. Austin TX, 1968
Radio v dni voiny. 2nd edn. Moscow, 1982
Radunskii, I. S., *Zapiski starogo klouna.* Moscow, 1954
Raek: Nemetskaya voina. Moscow, [1915]
Ramet, Pedro, and Sergei Zamascikov, "The Soviet Rock Scene," JPC, 24/1
    (Summer 1990) 149–74
    "The Soviet Rock Scene," KIARS Occasional Paper, 223 (1987)
Ramet, Sabrina (formerly Pedro), ed., *Rock and Roll in Eastern Europe and the
    Soviet Union.* Forthcoming
Rasputin, Valentin, *Live and Remember* (1974). New York, 1978
    Farewell to Matera. New York, 1979
Ratchford, Moira, "Perestroika and the Soviet Cinema." Ms. Georgetown
    University, 1988
    "Soviet Musical Comedies of the 1930s: Laughter amidst Terror." Ms. George-
    town University, 1988
    "Stalinist Myth on the Soviet Screen, 1936–1940." MA Thesis, Georgetown
    University, 1989
Reeder, Roberta, "Puppets: Moving Sculpture," *Journal of Decorative and Propa-
    ganda Arts,* 11 (Winter, 1989) 106–25
Riordan, Jim, ed., *Soviet Youth Culture.* Bloomington IN, 1989
    Sport in Soviet Society. Cambridge, 1977
    "Teenage Gangs, 'Afgantsy', and Neofascists," in Riordan, *Soviet Youth
    Culture,* 122–42
Robin, Regine, *Le realisme socialiste, une esthetique impossible.* Paris, 1986
    "Popular Literature of the 1920s: Russian Peasants as Readers," in Fitzpa-
    trick, *Russia in the Era of NEP,* 249–62
    ed, *Soviet Literature of the Thirties: a Reappraisal.* Montreal, 1986
    "Stalinism and Popular Culture," in Gunther, *Culture of the Stalin Period,*
    15–40
"Rok: Muzyka? Subkultura? Stil zhizni?," SI, 6 (1987) 29–51
Romanov, Aleksei, *Lyubov Orlova v iskusstve i v zhizni.* Moscow, 1987
Rom-Lebedev, I. I. *Ot tsyganskogo khora – k teatru 'Romen': zapiski moskovskogo
    tsygana.* Moscow, 1990
Rothstein, Robert, "Death of the Folksong?" in Stephen Frank and Mark
    Steinberg, eds., *Popular Culture in Imperial Russia.* Forthcoming
    "Popular Song in the NEP Era," in Fitzpatrick, *Russia in the Era of NEP,*
    263–83
    "The Quiet Rehabilitation of The Brick Factory: Early Soviet Popular Music
    and its Critics," SR, xxxix/3 (September, 1980) 373–88
Russell, Robert, "Red Pinkertonism: an Aspect of Soviet Literature of the
    1920s," SEER lx/3 (July, 1982) 390–412

Russian Science Fiction, 1969: an Anthology. New York, 1969

Russkaya sovetskaya estrada. Ed. E. Uvarova. 3 vols., Moscow, 1976–81

Russkie sovetskie pesni, 1917–1977. Moscow, 1977

Russkii folklor Velikoi Otechestvennoi Voiny. Moscow, 1964

Ryback, Timothy, *Rock Around the Bloc: a History of Rock Music in Eastern Europe and the Soviet Union*. New York, 1990

Rybakov, Anatoly, *Children of the Arbat*. tr., H. Shukman. Boston MA, 1988

Samoilov, Yakov, *Arkadii Raikin i ego teatr*. Detroit MI, 1984

Sanders, Jonathan, "A Very Mass Media: Soviet Television," *Television Quarterly*, xxii/3 (1986) 7–27

Sartorti, Rosalinda, *Pressephotographie und Industrialisierung in der Sowjetunion*. Berlin, 1981

"Stalinism and Carnival: Organisation and Aesthetics of Political Holidays," in Gunther, *Culture of the Stalin Period*, 41–77

Satira i yumor; repertuarnyi sbornik, ed., N. Igateva. Moscow, 1956

Savchenko, Vladimir, *Self-Discovery* (1967), tr., A. Bouis. New York, 1979

Savenkov, A., and Ya. Shvedov, *Moskva moya*. Moscow, 1964. Song book

Savushkina, N. I., *Russkii narodnyi teatr*. Moscow, 1976

Sbornik pesen i chastushek dlya kolkhoznogo obedinennogo khora. Np, 1936

Schwartz, Boris, *Music and Musical Life in Soviet Russia: 1917–1981*. Rev. edn Bloomington IN, 1983

Scott, John, *Behind the Urals: an American Worker in Russia's City of Steel* (1942), ed., Stephen Kotkin. Bloomington IN, 1989

Segel, Harold, *Turn-of-the-Century Cabaret: Paris, Barcelona, Berlin, Munich, Vienna, Cracow, Moscow, St. Petersburg, Zurich*. New York, 1987

Twentieth Century Russian Drama. New York, 1979

Seigel, Jerold, *Bohemian Paris*. New York, 1986

Semenov, Yulian, ed., *Detektiv i politika*. 3 vols., Moscow, 1988–9

In the Performance of Duty. Moscow, 1962

Reporter. Moscow , 1989

Seventeen Moments of Spring. New York, 1988

TASS is Authorized to Announce. New York, 1987

Shafer, N., "Paradoks Dunaevskogo," *Ogonek*, 30 (July, 1988) 22–3

Shaginyan, Marietta, *Mess-Mend, ili Yanki v Petrograde* (1923–5) Moscow, 1952

Mess-Mend. English edn, Ann Arbor MI, 1991

Sherel, A. A., *Rampa u mikrofona: teatr i radio*. Moscow, 1985

Shilova, I. M., "Film i ego muzyka," in *Kino i zritel*. Moscow, 1987, 11–20

Shiryaeva, P. G., "Poetic Features and Genre Characteristics of the Songs of Russian Workers (Prerevolutionary Period)," *Soviet Anthropology and Archeology* (Summer-Fall, 1975) 71–95

Shlapentokh, Vladimir, *Public and Private Life of the Soviet People*. New York, 1989

Shneer, A. Ya., and R. E. Slavskii, eds., *Tsirk: Malenkaya entsiklopediya*. 2nd edn Moscow, 1979

Short, K., *Film and Radio Propaganda in World War II*. Knoxville TN, 1983

Shukshin, Vasily, *Snowballberry Red and Other Stories*. Ann Arbor MI, 1979

Shumyatskii, Boris, *Kinematografiya millionov*. Moscow, 1935

Siegelbaum, Lewis, *Stakhanovism and the Politics of Productivity in the USSR, 1935–1941*. Cambridge, 1988

Simonov, Konstantin, *Sobranie sochinenii*. 12 vols., Moscow, 1979–87

Sivokon, Sergei, *Uroki detskikh klassikov*. Moscow, 1990

Skorokhodov, G., *Zvezdy sovetskoi estrady*. Moscow, 1982

Slavnym zavoevatelyam Arktiki: sbornik. Moscow, 1934

Slonim, Marc, *Soviet Russian Literature*. New York, 1967

Smirnova, N. I., *Sovetskii teatr kukol, 1918–1922*. Moscow, 1963

Smirnov-Sokolskii, N., *Sorok pyat let na estrade*. Moscow, 1976

Smith, Gerald Stanton, *Songs to Seven Strings: Russian Guitar Poetry and Soviet "Mass Song."* Bloomington, IN, 1984

Smushkova, M. A., *Pervye itogi izucheniya chitatelya*. Moscow, 1926

Sobolev, Romil, *Lyudi i film russkogo dorevolyutsionnogo kino*. Moscow, 1961

Soboleva, G., *Russkii sovetskii romans*. Moscow, 1985

Sokhor, Arnold, *"Katyusha" M. I. Blantera*. Moscow, 1960

  Russkaya sovetskaya pesnya. Leningrad, 1959

Sokolova, Nataliya, *Kukryniksy*. Moscow, 1975

Soldatskaya pesnya, ed., A. Surkov. Moscow, 1945

Sosin, Gene, "Magnitizdat: Uncensored Songs of Dissent," in R. Tokes, ed., *Dissent in the USSR: Politics, Ideology, and People*. Baltimore MD, 1975, 276–309

Sovetskie khudozhestvennye filmy: annotirovannyi katalog. 4 vols., Moscow, 1961–8, with supplements

Sovetskie pisateli na frontakh velikoi otechestvennoi voiny. 2 vols., Moscow, 1966 (LN, lxxviii, 1–2)

Sovetskii dzhaz: problemy, sobytiya, mastera. Ed. A. Medvedev and O. Medvedeva. Moscow, 1987

Sovetskii reklamnyi plakat i reklamnaya grafika, 1933–1973. Moscow, 1977

Soviet Circus: a Collection of Articles. Moscow, 1967

Sredstva massovoi kommunikatsii i sovremennaya khudozhestvennaya kultura. Moscow, 1983

Starinnye russkie romansy. Kiev, 1988

Starr, S. Frederick, "New Communications Technologies in the USSR," in L. Graham, ed., *Science and the Soviet Social Order*. Cambridge, MA, 1990, 19–50

  Red and Hot: the Fate of Jazz in the Soviet Union. New York, 1983

Statisticheskii ezhegodnik Rossii 1913 g. SP, 1914

Stirius, M., *Bolsheviki zavoevyvayut efir*. Leningrad, 1931

Stites, Richard, "Adorning the Russian Revolution: the Primary Symbols of Bolshevism, 1917–1918," *Sbornik*, 10 (1984), 39–42

  "Doing Film History in the Soviet Union: a Research Note," *Russian Review*, 1/4 (October, 1991), 65–7

  "Movies for the Masses and for Historians," HJFRT, xi/2, 1991, 185–94

  Revolutionary Dreams: Utopian Vision and Experimental Life in the Russian Revolution. New York, 1989

  "Soviet Popular Culture in the Gorbachev Era," *Harriman Institute Forum*, ii/3 (March, 1989)

"Stalin: Utopian or Antiutopian?" in J. Held, ed., *The Cult of Power: Dictators in the Twentieth Century*. Boulder CO, 1983, 77–93

"World Outlook and Inner Fears in Soviet Science Fiction," in L. Graham, ed., *Science and the Soviet Social Order*. Cambridge, MA, 1990, 299–324

Strauss, Ken, "Workers' Lives in the 1930s." Ms

Strugatsky, Arkadii and Boris, *Escape Attempt*. New York, 1982

Hard to be a God. New York, 1973

Noon 22nd Century (1962; 1967 as *Homecoming*). New York, 1978

Roadside Picnic (1972). New York, 1977

Ugly Swans (1972). New York, 1979

Stykalin, S., and I. Kremenskaya, *Sovetskaya satiricheskaya pechat, 1917–1963*. Moscow, 1963

Surkov, Aleksei, *Sochineniya*. 2 vols. Moscow, 1954

Suvin, Darko, "Criticism of the Strugatskii Brothers' Work," CASS, v/1–2 (Summer, 1972) 286–307

"The Utopian Tradition of Soviet Science Fiction," *Modern Language Review*, 66 (1979) 139–59

Tarakanov, Mikhail, *Muzykalnaya kultura RSFSR*. Moscow, 1987

Taylor, Richard, "Boris Shumyatsky and the Soviet Cinema in the 1930s: Ideology as Mass Entertainment," HJFRT, vi/i (April, 1986) 43–64

and Ian Christie, eds., *The Film Factory*. Cambridge, MA 1988

Film Propaganda: Soviet Russia and Nazi Germany. New York, 1979

"The Kiss of Mary Pickford: Ideology and Popular Culture in Soviet Cinema," in Lawton, *Red Screen*.

The Politics of Soviet Cinema, 1917–1929. Cambridge, 1979

"Red Star: the Personality Cult and the Positive Hero," Ms.

"Soviet Cinema as Popular Culture, or the Extraordinary Adventures of Mr. Nepman in the Land of the Silver Screen," *Revolutionary Russia*, i/1 (December, 1988) 36–56

Teatry Moskvy (spravochnik). Moscow, 1960

Telesin, Yulius, *1001 [Tysyacha i odin] anekdot*. Tenafly NJ, 1986

Televidenie: vchera, segodnya, zavtra. Moscow, 1985

Televidenie '89: vchera, segodnya, zavtra. Moscow, 1989

Televizionnaya estrada. Moscow, 1981

Teplits, Ezhi (Jerzy Teplic), *Istoriya kinoiskusstva*, tr. V. S. Golovskoi. 3 vols., Moscow, 1968–71

Terikov, G., *Kuplet na estrade*. Moscow, 1987

Terras, Victor, ed., *Handbook of Russian Literature*. New Haven CT, 1985

Testimoni silenziosi: film russi, 1908–1919/Silent Witnesses: Russian Films, 1908–1919 (in English and Italian), ed., Yury Tsvian, *et al*. Pordenone, 1989

Thompson, Terry, and Richard Sheldon, eds., *Soviet Society and Culture: Essays in Honor of Vera S. Dunham*. Boulder CO, 1988

Thurston, Gary, "The Impact of Russian Popular Theater, 1886–1915," *Journal of Modern History*, 1v/2 (January, 1983) 236–67

"Theater and Acculturation in Russia from Peasant Emancipation to the First World War," *Journal of Popular Culture*, xviii/2 (Fall, 1984) 3–16

Timasheff, Nicholas, *The Great Retreat: the Growth and Decline of Communism in Russia*. New York, 1946

Timbres, *We Didn't Ask Utopia* (1939) New York, 1970

Tirado, Isabel, *Young Guard: the Communist Youth League, Petrograd, 1917–1920*. New York, 1988

Tishchenko, Aleksandr, *Dusha soldata: pesennik*. Moscow, 1983. With music

Tkachenko, Tamara, *Narodnyi tanets*. Moscow, 1954

Tolstoy, Alexei, *Peter the First*. New York, 1959

Peter the Great. London, 1932

Tretyakov, Sergei, "Nine Girls," (1935), tr. J. Von Geldern. Forthcoming in Von Geldern and Stites, *Mass Culture in Soviet Society*

Troitsky, Artemy, *Back in the USSR: the True Story of Rock in the Soviet Union*. London, 1987

Tsirk pod vodoi (Chernyi pirat). Leningrad, 1929

Tumarkin, Nina, *Lenin Lives! The Cult of Lenin in the Soviet Union*. Cambridge MA, 1983

"Russia Remembers the War." Ms

Turovskaya, Maiya, "I. A. Pyrev i ego muzykalnye komedii," KZ, 1 (1988) 111–46

Tvardovskii, Aleksandr, *Vasilii Terkin: kniga pro boitsa*. Moscow, 1944

Tvorcheskoe nasledie V. V. Andreeva i praktika samodeyatelnogo instrumentalnogo ispolnitelstva. Leningrad, 1988

Tvorchestvo narodov SSSR, ed., A. M. Gorkii, L. Z. Mekhlis, A. I. Stetskii. Moscow, 1938

Ultimate Threshold: a Collection of the Finest in Soviet Science Fiction, ed., Mirra Ginsburg. Harmondsworth, Middlesex, 1970

Umnozhai urozhai: kolkhoznye pesni i chastushki. Moscow, 1930

Uvarova, Elizaveta, *Arkadii Raikin*. Moscow 1986

Estradnyi teatr: miniatyury, obozreniya, myuzik-kholly (1917–1945). Moscow, 1983

Vainer, A. A. and G. A., *Era miloserdiya* (1975). Minsk, 1988

Gorod prinyal! Moscow, 1980

Lekarstvo protiv strakha (1974). Moscow, 1986, 1–346

Vanslov, V. V. *Chto takoe sotsialisticheskii realizm*. Moscow, 1988

Varshavskii, Ya., *Esli film talantliv*. Moscow, 1984

Vasilii Pavlovich Solovev-Sedoi: vospominaniya, stati, materialy, ed., S. M. Khentova. Leningrad, 1987

Vasilinina, I. A., *Klavdiya Shulzhenko*. Moscow, 1979

Verbitskaya, Anastasiya, *Klyuchi schastya*. 6 vols., 1909–13

Vertinskii, Aleksandr, *Izbrannoe: gody emigratsii*. Moscow, 1990

Pesni i stikhi 1916–1937. Np, nd

Zapiski russkogo pero. New York, 1982

Vilchek, V. M., *Pod znakom TV*. Moscow, 1987

Vishnevskii, Venyamin, *Khudozhestvennye filmy dorevolyutsionnoi Rossii: filmograficheskoe opisanie*. Moscow, 1945

"Filmografiya," IIK, 4 (1961) 137–43

V mire fantastiki. Moscow, 1989

Von Geldern, James, "The Center and the Periphery: Cultural and Social Geography in Mass Culture of the 1930s." Ms
Festivals of the Revolution, 1917–1920. Forthcoming
and R. Stites, eds., *Mass Culture in Soviet Society.* Forthcoming
Voznesenskii, Aleksandr, "Kinodetstvo," IK, 11 (1985) 75–93
Vronskaya, Jeanne. *Young Soviet Filmmakers.* London, 1972
Vysotskii, Vladimir, *Pesni i stikhi.* 2 vols., New York, 1981–3
Walter, Scott, "The Silent Muse: Soviet Theater in World War II." Ms., Georgetown University, 1989
Warner, Elizabeth, *The Russian Folk Theater.* The Hague, 1977
Werth, Alexander, *Musical Uproar in Moscow.* London, 1949
    Russia at War, 1941–1945 (1964). New York, 1984
White, Stephen, *The Bolshevik Political Poster.* New Haven CT, 1988
    Political Culture and Soviet Politics. 1979
Wilder, Alec, *The American Popular Song.* New York, 1972
Williams, Raymond, *Keywords.* New York, 1983
Williams, Robert C., *Artists in Revolution.* Bloomington IN, 1977
Winter, Ella, *Red Virtue: Human Relationships in the New Russia.* New York, 1933
Ya lyublyu tebya, zhizn!; pesni iz repertuara Marka Bernesa. Moscow, 1971
Yankovskii, Mark, *Iskusstvo operetty.* Moscow, 1982
    Operetta. Leningrad, 1937
Yaron, G., *O lyubimom zhanre.* Moscow, 1960
Yershov, Peter, *Comedy in the Soviet Theater.* New York, 1956
Youngblood, Denise, "Entertainment or Enlightenment? Popular Cinema in Soviet Society." Ms
    "The Fate of Soviet Popular Cinema during the Stalin Revolution," RR, 1/2 (April, 1991) 148–62
    Movies for the Masses: Soviet Popular Cinema in the Twenties. Forthcoming
    Soviet Cinema in the Silent Era, 1917–1935. Ann Arbor MI, 1985. Paperback, Austin TX, 1991
    "Soviet Society in Cinema: the Early Films of Fridrikh Ermler," in Lawton, *Red Screen*
Yurenev, Rostislav, *Kratkaya istoriya sovetskogo kino.* Moscow, 1979
    "Na ekrane – natsionalnyi kharakter: o russkom geroe v sovetskom kino," IK, 1 (1985) 102–21
Zakharov-Menskii, N., ed., *Chastushki.* 2nd edn. Moscow, 1927
Zelnik, Reginald, ed., *A Radical Worker in Tsarist Russia.* Stanford CA, 1986
Zhukov, Yurii, and Roza Izmailova, *Nachalo goroda: stranitsy iz khroniki 30-kh godov* (1937). Khabarovsk, 1977
Zhvanetskii, Mikhail, *Vstrechi na ulitsakh.* Moscow, 1980
Zorkaya, Neya, *Illustrated History of the Soviet Cinema.* New York, 1989
    Na rubezhe stoletii: u istokov massovogo iskusstva v Rossii, 1900–1910 godov. Moscow, 1976
Zvezdy na nebe: starinnye russkie romansy. Moscow, 1990. Words and music

Discography
Including tape cassettes

Archival collections

Radio Moscow Archives. Tapes from the 1930s and wartime: Levitan, Stalin, Berggolts, Simonov, Ehrenburg, Khenkin, Utesov, Bernes, Shulzhenko.
Radio Leningrad Archives. Tapes from the blockade: Berggolts, Vishnevsky, singer Efrem Flaks.

Private collections

Suzanne Ament: Private recording. Folk and popular
John Bowlt: tapes of the 1930s
Hubertus Jahn: tapes of Panina, Vyaltseva, Plevitskaya
Vladimir Padunov: Vadim Kozin; Black Coffee
Helen Price: 78 RPMs made in the USSR in the early 1930s and released on Keynote
Anya Salnykova: tapes of popular music
Alexander Sherel: 78 RPMs from the 1930s
Valery Shinder: Mikhail Zadornov performing *Parodii yumoristicheskie o Gorbacheve i o nashikh lozungakh*
James Von Geldern: tapes of the 1920s–1940s from the Stanford University Music Library. Blanter, Dunaevsky, the Pokrasses, Tsfasman, the Pyatnitsky Ensemble, the Red Army Chorus and others – film and mass song

Commercial recordings

All phonograph records with Russian titles are 12-inch long-playing Melodia label unless otherwise noted. S and M in the serial number indicate stereo and mono respectively. (C) indicates tape cassette. A rich discography of jazz records released since 1960 but including recordings of the earliest periods can be found in *Sovetskii dzhaz*, 533–77. There is a rock discography in Troitsky, *Back in the USSR*, 139–57.

Akvarium. S60 25129 005 (1987)
Aleksandr Vertinskii. D026773–026774
Alexei Kuznetsov: Blue Coral. East Wind MC–20648
Alla Pugacheva v Stokgolme. S60 23481 002

Alla Pugatjova: Soviet Superstar. 2 records. Track. Hits of 1984
Antologiya sovetskogo dzhaza. 14 records. Recordings, 1920s–1940s. See *Noch i den*
    and *Pervye shagi* below
Antologiya sovetskoi pesni dlya shkolnikov. Vol. 5, comp. by Yu. Aliev. M50 46765
    004 (1985). Songs by Blanter, Dunaevsky, and others sung by Bernes,
    Kobzon, and others
Arsenal: With Our own Hands. East Wind MC–20649
B. Okudzhava. M40–38867–68
Boulat Okoudjava: poete, compositeur sovietique. Harmonia Mundi, LDX 74358
Bravo. BIEM LJMK 1071a and b (C)
Bulat Okudzhava. S60–13331–2
Bulat Okudzhava: novye pesni ispolnyaet avtor. S60 25001 009 (1984)
Chants revolutionnaires. Musidisc CV 949
Dialog Raimond Pauls; poet Valerii Leontev. S60 21271 006
Diskoteka smekha. S60 25215 005. Zhvanetsky, Kartsev, and Ilchenko (1986)
Ego velichestvo teatr: Arkadii Raikin. 2 records, S–60–21145–000 (1984; recorded
    1983)
Exercises. Leo, LR 113. Chekasin, Grebenshchikov, Kurekhin
Galina Kareva: starinnye romansy. SM04519–20. Old romances
Ganelin, Tarasov, Chekasov: Poi Segue. East Wind MC–20647
Gde zhe vy teper moi odnopolchane? Pesni o Velikoi Otechestvennoi Voine. S60
    2195–004. War songs. Bernes, Shulzhenko, Kobzon, and others
Gosudarstvennyi estradnyi orkestr Armenii. S60 20321 005. The Orbelyan band
*Gosudarstvennyi gimn Soyuza Sovetskikh Sotsialisticheskikh Respublik; Internatsio-
    nal.* 10-inch, S01–13057–58 (1980). Two versions of each played by sympho-
    nic orchestra and military band
Gosudarstvennyi Russkii Narodnyi Orkestr imeni N. Osipova. S01689–90
*History of the Soviet Union in Ballad and Song, v. I: Songs of the Revolution and Civil
    War.* Folkways FH 5420
Igor Bril: Before the Sun Sets. East Wind MC–20646
Instrumental Rock-Group "Zodiac." SM01158. (C)
Izabella Yureva: Esli pomnish, esli lyubish. M60 48357 001 (1988)
Jazz 67: the IV Moscow Festival of Jazz Ensembles. S01889–90(a)
Kollazh: dzhaz-ansambli Leningrada. S60 20671 003
Komarovo: pesni na stikhi Mikhaila Tanicha. S60 24063 007 (1986). Songs by Pauls,
    Tukhmanov, and others performed by Leontev, Pugacheva, and others
Krasnoznamennyi imeni A. V. Aleksandrova ansambl pesni i plyaski Sovetskoi Armii.
    D019973–019974
Leningradskii Diksilend. SM 02787–02788
Leningradskii rok-klub. (1988). Auction, Jungle, Zoo, Alisa, AVIA, and others
Leonid Chizhik: reministsentsii. 2 records. S60–16155–8
Leonid Utesov: Recordings of the Forties and Fifties. M60 36931–32(a)
Lyubov Orlova: tvorcheskii portret. M40–44665–66. Film songs with commentary
    by Igor Ilinsky and Grigory Alexandrov
Mashina vremeni: reki i mosty. 2 records. S60 25617 001 and S60 25619 006 (1987)
Mastera sovetskoi estrady: Arkadii Raikin. 33d–6285–86(a). 10-inch
Muslim Magomaev. S 04719–20

New Wine. Leo, LR 112. Ganelin, Chekasin, Tarasov
Nikolai Slichenko. Gost 5289–68/D–626697 (1968)
Noch i den. Vol. 14 of *Antologiya sovetskogo dzhaza.* M60 48285 000 (1988). Utesov recordings, 1930s–1940s
Olympic Fanfares Resound in Moscow. FULP 4
Osipov Russian Folk Orchestra. S 01689–90
Ot 2-kh do 50-ti. 4 records. 33d, 12517–24. Arkady Raikin
Pamyati Leonida Utesova. Vol. I: *Muzykalnyi magazin.* M60 4997–001. Early 1930s
Pamyati Leonida Utesova. Vol. II: *Ot vsego serdtsa.* M60 4999006. The 1930s
Panorama-86: Festival molodezhnoi populyarnoi muzyki. S60 25131 003 (1987). Cruise, EVM, Bravo, The Architects, and others
Parad ansamblei. S60 20703 009 (1984). Earthmen, Happy-Go-Lucky Guys, Stas Namin, Time Machine, Autograph, and others
Parad solistov estrady. S60–18809–10 (1983). Pugacheva, Leontev, Kobzon, and others
Pechalnyya pesenki A. N. Vertinskago: k stoletiyu so dnya rozhdeniya, 1889–1989. 2 records. M60 48689 001 and 48691 001 (1989)
Pervye shagi. Vol. I of *Antologiya sovetskogo dzhaza.* M60 45827 006. Tsfasman, Utesov, and others, 1920s–1930s
Pesni sovetskikh kompozitorov. S60–08863–4. Soviet Army Song and Dance Ensemble, Boris Alexandrov, director
Poet Boris Shtokolov. S 01277–01278. Romances
Poet Lidiya Ruslanova: Russkie narodnye pesni. D 035125–26
Poet Vladimir Makarov. 33d 029993–35006(a). Folk songs
Red Wave. (1986). Recordings of 1982–5 by Joanna Stingray of four Soviet rock groups
Rok-otel. S60 24421 009 (1986)
Russkaya Troika. S20–17831–2. The Osipov Russian Folk Orchestra and V. Gorodovskaya
Russkie narodnye pesni: Gosudarstvennyi Akademicheskii Russkii Khor SSSR. S 0599–0600. A. Sveshnikov, director
Russkie narodnye pesni: Lyudmila Zykina. S 01807–01808
Russkie narodnye pesni: Yurii Gulyaev. SM 01811–01812
Schastya tebe, zemlya moya: pesni sovetskikh kompozitorov. 2 records. S60 2629 006 (1988). Mass and pop songs
Selskii prazdnik: muzykalnye kartinki XIX veka; Rural Holiday: Musical Pictures, XIXth Century. S20 20313 006 (1984). Folk ensembles, 1979–83
6 pesen Bulata Okudzhavy. Samizdat "Narzan" (C)
Songs and Poems by Vladimir Vysotsky (1938–1980). Septima S–101. Toronto performance with readings in English
Starinnye russkie valsy. A20 00145 001. Academic Orchestra of Russian Folk Instruments of Central Television and Radio, Nikolai Nekrasov, director
Starye romansy: Galina Kareva. S 01277–01278
Teatr Arkadiya Isaakovicha Raikina. (C)
Trio "Romen." S201052. Ethnic Gypsy songs by artists of the Romen Gypsy Theater in Moscow. (C)
Vadim Kozin: pesni i romansy. M60 48575 000 (1988). 1930s and 1940s

Vadim Kozin: pesni i romansy. M60 47725 005 (1989). 1940s

Vadim Kozin: starinnye romansy i pesni. M60–46669–007 (1985). 1937–40

Vasilii Solovev-Sedoi: izbrannye pesni. Gost 5289–61 33d–19557. 10-inch

Vechernyi zvon: Russkie pesni. C10 25889 002. A collection of old songs by the Leningrad Television and Radio Chorus

Viimeinen tango (The Last Tango). KK–35, with Finnish language notes. Oskar Strok

Vladimir Vysotskii poet svoi pesni. S90 10769 002

Vladimir Vysotskii: Synovya ukhodyat v boi. M60 47431 006

Vstrecha druzei. S60 26191 006. Okudzhava, Novella Matveeva, Yuly Kim, Yury Vizbor, and other guitar poets

Vyacheslav Dobrynin: Sinii tuman. S60 27865 009

Ways of Freedom. Leo, LR 107, 1981. Sergei Kurekhin

"Yunona" i "Avos": opera. 2 records. S60 18627 008 (1982). Rock opera by Alexei Rybnikov and Andrei Voznesensky

Yurii Levitan: stranitsy zhizni. M40 46257 007

Zhanna Bichevskaya. S60 14015 006

Zhanna Bichevskaya poet pesni Bulata Okudzhavy. S21103–000

Filmography

Films mentioned in the text in English alphabetical order followed by original Russian titles, director, and date of release when known in parentheses. The sign (*) indicates a film I have seen; the sign (-) means partly seen; m = when made; r = when released. Also listed are some films which have shaped my thinking but which are not mentioned in the text.

Feature films

   Actress (Aktrisa; Erdman and Trauberg, 1943)
* Aelita (Protazanov, 1924)
* Alexander Nevsky (Aleksandr Nevskii; Eisenstein, 1938)
   Amid the Thunder of Cannon, the Prussian Rapists (Pod grokhot pushek: Prusskie nasilniki; 1914)
   Amorous Adventures of Mme. V. (Lyubovnye pokhozhdeniya gospozhi V.; Chardynin, 1915)
   Amphibious Man (Chelovek-amfibiya; Kazansky and Chebotarev, 1962)
   Anna on the Neck (Anna na shee; Annensky, 1954)
   Antosha Rybkin (Yudin, 1941)
* Arsenal (Dovzhenko, 1929)
- Assa (Soloviev, 1988)
   At 6 O'Clock after the War (V shest chasov vechera posle voiny; Pyrev, 1944)
* Autumn Marathon (Osennii marafon; Daneliya, 1979)
* Ballad of a Soldier (Ballada o soldate; Chukhrai, 1959)
* Battleship Potemkin (Bronenosets Potemkin; Eisenstein, 1926)
* Bear's Wedding (Medvezhya svadba; Eggert, 1926)
   Beauty and the Bolshevik (see Brigade Commander Ivanov)
* Bed and Sofa (see Third Meshchanskaya Street)
* Be Still My Grief (Molchi, grust, molchi; Chardynin, 1918)
- Bezhin Meadow (Bezhin lug; Eisenstein, 1933–5, unfinished)
* Bonus (Premiya; Mikaelyan, 1975)
* Borderlands (Okraina; Barnet, 1933)
   Border Troops (see On the Frontier)

Brigade Commander Ivanov (Kombrig Ivanov; 1923)
Bright Path (see Radiant Road)
Burglar (Vzlomshchik; Ogorodnikov, 1987)
* By the Law (Po zakonu; Kuleshov, 1926)
Can-can in the English Garden (Kankan v angliiskom parke; Pidpaly, 1984)
* Carnival Night (Karnivalnaya noch; Ryazanov, 1956)
Case of the Three Million (see Trial of the Three Million)
* Cavalier of the Golden Star (Kavaler zolotoi zvezdy; Raizman, 1950)
* Chapaev (The Vasilev "brothers," 1934)
* Chess Fever (Shakhmatnaya goryachka; Pudovkin and Shpikovsky, 1925)
* Children of the Age (Deti veka; Bauer, 1915)
* Cigarette Girl from Mosselprom (Papirosnitsa ot Mosselprom; Zhelyabuzhsky, 1924)
* Circus (Tsirk; Alexandrov, 1936)
* Come and Behold (Id i smotri; Klimov, 1986)
* Commissar (Komissar; Askoldov, m 1967, r 1988)
- Counterplan (Vstrechnyi; Ermler and Yutkevich, 1932)
* Country Teacher (Selskaya uchitelnitsa; Donskoy, 1947)
Courier (see Messenger Boy)
* Cranes are Flying (Letyat zhuravli; Kalatozov, 1957)
Crew (Ekipazh; Mitta, 1979)
* Criminal Quartet (Kriminalnyi kvartet; Muratov, 1989)
* Dark Eyes (Ochi chernye; co-production Italy-USSR; Mikhalkov, 1988)
* Defence Counsel Sedov (Zashchitnik Sedov; Tsimbal, 1990)
* Defence of Sevastopol (Oborona Sevastopolya; Goncharov and Khanzhonkov, 1911)
* Deja vu (Dezha vyu; Machulski, 1989)
* Deserter (Dezertir; Pudovkin, 1933)
Devil's Wheel (Chertovo koleso; Kozintsev and Trauberg, 1926)
Don Diego and Pelagea (Don Diego i Pelageya; Protazanov, 1927)
Don't Get Married, Girls (Ne khodite devki zamuzh; E. Gerasimov, 1985)
Do You Remember? (Ty pomnish li?; Chardynin, 1916)
Dream of a Cossack (see Cavalier of the Golden Star)
* Earth (Zemlya; Dovzhenko, 1930)
* End of St. Petersburg (Konets Sankt-Peterburga; Pudovkin, 1927)
* Enthusiasm (Entuziazm; Vertov, 1930)
* Evil Spirit (Nechistaya sila; Yasan, 1989)
* Extraordinary Adventures of Mr West in the Land of the Bolsheviks (Neobychainye priklyucheniya mistera Vesta v strane bolshevikov; Kuleshov, 1924)
* Fall of Berlin (Padenie Berlina; Chiaureli, 1949)
* Fate of a Man (Sudba cheloveka; Bondarchuk, 1959)
* Father Sergius (Otets Sergii; Protazanov, m 1917; r 1918)
Feast at Zhirmunka (Pir v Zhirmunke; Pudovkin, 1941) Fighting Film Album, 1941)

* Flight (Beg; Alov and Naumov, 1971)
* Flyers (Letchiki; Raizman, 1935)
* Forgotten Melody for Flute (Zabytaya melodiya dlya fleita; Ryazanov, 1987)
* For the Sake of Happiness (Za schastem; Bauer, 1917)
* Forty-First (Sorok pervyi; Protazanov, 1926)
* Forty-First (Sorok pervyi; Chukhrai, 1956)
* Fragment of an Empire (Oblomok imperii; Ermler, 1929)
* Garage (Garazh; Ryazanov, 1979)
  General Line (see Old and New)
  Girlfriends at the Front (Frontovye podrugi; Eisymont, 1941)
  Girls from Leningrad (see Girlfriends at the Front)
* Girl with a Hatbox (Devushka s korobkoi; Barnet, 1927)
  Glinka (Kompozitor Glinka; Pavlenko, 1952)
* Glory to Us – Death to the Foe (Slava nam, smert vragam; Bauer, 1914)
* Great Citizen (Velikii grazhdanin; Ermler, 1938–9)
* Grunya Kornakova (Ekk, 1936)
* Guard (Karaul; Rogoshkin, 1989)
* Happiness (Schaste; Medvedkin, 1935)
* Happy-Go-Lucky Guys (Veselye rebyata; Alexandrov, 1934)
* Heir of Chinggis Khan (Potomok Chingis-khana; Pudovkin, 1929)
  I'm Here to Talk (Prishla i govoryu; Ardoshnikov, 1985)
  Incident at a Telegraph Office (Sluchai na telegrafe; Arnshtam, 1941).
  Fighting Film Album
* Intergirl (Interdevochka; Todorovsky, 1989)
  In the Sentry Box (1941). Fighting Film Album
* Irony of Fate (Ironiya sudby, ili s legkim parom; Ryazanov, 1975)
* It (Ono; Ovcharov, 1989)
* Ivan Brovkin in the Virgin Lands (Ivan Brovkin na tseline; 1959)
* Ivan's Childhood (Ivanovo detstvo; Tarkovsky, 1962)
* Jazzmen (My iz dzhaza; Shakhnazarov, 1983)
* Jobs and People (Dela i lyudi; Macheret, 1932)
* Journalist (Zhurnalist; Gerasimov, 1967)
* Jubilee (Yubilei; Petrov, 1944)
* Karo (Ai-Artyan and Taits, 1937)
* Katka, the Reinette Apple Seller (Katka – bumazhnyi ranet; Ermler and Ioganson, 1926)
  Keys to Happiness (Klyuchi schastya; Protazanov and Gardin, 1913)
* King of Paris (Korol Parizha; Bauer, 1917)
  Kings of Crime (Vory v zakone; Kara, 1988)
* Kiss of Mary Pickford (Potselui Meri Pikford; Komarov, 1927)
* Komsomolsk (Gerasimov, 1938)
- Kreutzer Sonata (Kreitserova sonata; Chardynin, 1911)
- Kreutzer Sonata (Gardin, 1914)
* Kuban Cossacks (Kubanskie kazaki; Pyrev, 1949)
* Lady and the Hooligan (Baryshnya i khuligan; Slavinsky, 1918)
* Last Tango (Poslednee tango; Viskovsky, 1918)
* Life for a Life (Zhizn za zhizn; Bauer, 1916)

* Light-Fingered Sonka (Sonka zolotaya ruchka; Yurevsky, 1914–5)
* Little House in Kolomna (Domik v Kolomne; Chardynin, 1913)
* Little Red Imps (Krasnye dyavolyata; Perestiani, 1923)
* Little Vera (Malenkaya Vera; Pichul, 1988)
  Man from Boulevard des Capucines (Chelovek s Bulvara Kaputsinov; Surikova, 1987)
  Man from the Restaurant (Chelovek iz restorana; Protazanov, 1927)
* Man with a Gun (Chelovek s ruzhem; Yutkevich, 1938)
* Man with a Movie Camera (Chelovek s kinoapparatom; Dziga Vertov, 1929)
* Marionettes (Marionetki; Protazanov, 1934)
- Maxim's Return (Vozvrashchenie Maksima; Kozintsev and Trauberg, 1937) Part Two of the Maxim Trilogy
* Maxim's Youth (Yunost Maksima; Kozintsev and Trauberg, 1935) Part One of the Maxim Trilogy
* Member of the Government (Chlen pravitelstva; Zarkhi and Kheifits, 1940)
  Men and Jobs (see Jobs and People)
* Messenger Boy (Kurer; Shakhnazarov, 1987)
  Miracle Worker (Chudotvorets; Pantaleev, 1922)
* Mirages (Mirazhi; Chardynin, 1915)
* Miss-Mend (Otsep and Barnet, 1926)
* Mister Designer (Gospodin Oformitel; Teptsov, 1988)
* Moscow Does Not Believe in Tears (Moskva slezam ne verit; Menshov, 1980)
  Moscow Laughs (see Happy-Go-Lucky Guys)
* Mother (Mat; Pudovkin, 1926)
* My Friend Ivan Lapshin (Moi drug Ivan Lapshin; German, m 1984, r 1986)
* Name Day (Den angela; Selyanov, 1989)
* Neptune Festival (Prazdnik neptuna; Mamin, 1987)
  New Adventures of Schweik (Novye pokhozhdeniya Shveika; Yutkevich, 1941)
* New Babylon (Novyi Vavilon; Kozintsev and Trauberg, 1929)
* Night is Short (Noch korotka; Belikov, 1986)
* Nights are Dark in Sochi (V gorode Sochi temnye nochi; Pichul, 1989)
  No Greater Love (see She Defends the Motherland)
* Oblomov (Neskolko dnei iz zhizni Oblomova; Mikhalkov, 1980)
* October (Oktyabr; Eisenstein, 1927)
  Oktyabrina (Pokhozhdeniya Oktyabriny; Kozintsev and Trauberg, 1924)
* Old and New (Staroe i novoe; Eisenstein, 1929)
  On the Frontier (Na granitse; Ivanov, 1938)
* Orphans (Podranki; Gubenko, 1977)
  Our Circus (Nash tsirk; Simkov, 1939)
* Overcoat (Shinel; Kozintsev and Trauberg, 1926)
* Parisian Cobbler (Parizhskii sapozhnik; Ermler, 1927)
  Patriots (see Outskirts)
* Pavel Korchagin (Alov and Naumov, 1957)
* Peasants (Krestyane; Ermler, 1935)
* Peasant Women of Ryazan (Baby ryazanskie; Preobrazhenskaya, 1927)

* Perfect Crime (Idealnoe prestuplenie; 1989)
* Peter I (Petr pervyi; Petrov, 1937–9)
  Peter the Great (see Peter I)
  Pirates of the Twentieth Century (Piraty XX veka; Durov, 1979)
  Postal Sleigh (Vot mchitsya troika pochtovaya; Sabinsky, 1915)
  Praise of Madness (Khvala bezumiyu; Uralsky, 1915)
* Prishvin's Paper Eyes (Bumazhnye glaza Prishvina; Ogorodnikov, 1989)
* Radiant Road (Svetlyi put; Alexandrov, 1940)
* Rainbow (Raduga; Donskoy, 1944)
  Reach for the Sky (see Story about a Real Man)
* Repentance (Pokayanie; Abuladze, m. 1984, r. 1987)
* Return of Nathan Becker (Vozvrashchenie Neitana Bekkera; Shpis and Milman, 1932)
  Road to Life (see Start in Life)
* Satan Exultant (Satana likuyushchii; Protazanov, 1917)
* Scarecrow (Chuchelo; Bykov, 1984)
* Serezha (Daneliya and Talankin, 1960)
  Seventeen Moments of Spring (Semnadtsat mgnovenii vesny; Leznova, 1973), a television film
  Several Days from the Life of Oblomov (see Oblomov)
* She Defends the Motherland (Ona zashchishchaet rodinu; Ermler, 1943)
* Siberiade (Sibiriada; Konchalovsky, 1979)
* Sideburns (Bakinbardy; Mamin, 1990)
* Silent Witnesses (Nemye svideteli; Bauer, 1914)
* Slave of Love (Raba lyubvi; Mikhalkov, 1975)
  Snatchers (see Happiness)
* Snowballberry Red (Kalina krasnaya; Shukshin, 1974)
  Solo Voyage (Odinochnoe plavanie; Tumanishvili, 1986)
* Spring (Vesna; Alexandrov, 1947)
* Springtime (Vesnoi; Kaufman, 1929)
* Start in Life (Putevka v zhizn; Ekk, 1931)
* Stenka Razin (Stenka Razin: ponizovaya volnitsa; Romashkov, 1908)
* Stern Youth (Strogii yunosha; Room, m. 1935, r. 1974)
  Storm Over Asia (see Heir of Chinggis Khan)
* Story about a Real Man (Povest o nastoyashchem cheloveke; Stolper, 1948)
* Strike (Stachka; Eisenstein, 1925)
  Summer to Remember (see Serezha)
  Swineherd and the Shepherd (Svinarka i pastukh; Pyrev, 1941)
  Symphony of the Donbass (see Enthusiasm)
  Tanya (see Radiant Road)
* Taxi Blues (Taksi blyuz; Longin, 1990)
  Ten Days that Shook the World (see October)
* Third Meshchanskaya Street (Tretya Meshchanskaya; Room, 1928)
  Three in a Shell Hole (Troe v voronke; Mutanov, 1941). Fighting Film Album
  Three Russian Girls (see Girlfriends at the Front)
* Three Songs of Lenin (Tri pesni o Lenine; Vertov, 1934)

* Train Station for Two (Vokzal dlya dvoikh; Ryazanov, 1983)
* Trial of the Three Million (Protsess trekh millionov; Protazanov, 1926)
* Twelve Chairs (Dvenadtsat stulev; Gaidai, 1971)
* Twenty Days without War (Dvadtsat dnei bez voiny; German, m. 1977, r. 1986)
  Two Arrows (Dve strely; Surikova, 1989)
* Two Buldis (Dva-Buldi-dva; Kuleshov, 1930)
* Two Warriors (Dva boitsa; Lukov, 1943)
* Unfinished Lesson (Neokonchennyi urok; Tyutyunikov, 1980)
  Unmarked Freight (Gruz bez markirovki; Popkov, 1985)
  Unsent Letter (Neotpravlennoe pismo; Kalatozov, 1959)
* Valery Chkalov (Valerii Chkalov; Kalatozov, 1941)
* Valiant Seven (Semero smelykh; Gerasimov, 1936)
* Vassa (Panfilov, 1983)
* Volga, Volga (Alexandrov, 1938)
  Vyborg Side (Vyborgskaya Storona; Kozintsev and Trauberg, 1938) Part three of the Maxim Trilogy
- War and Peace (Voina i mir; Bondarchuk, 1966–7)
- War and Peace (Gardin and Protazanov, 1915)
  War and Peace (Kamensky, 1915)
* We Are From Kronstadt (My iz Kronshtadta; Dzigan, 1936)
* Wedding (Svadba; Annensky, 1944)
* Wedding in Malinovka (Svadba na Malinovke; 1967)
* White Sun of the Desert (Beloe solntse pustyni; Motyl, 1970)
  Wings of Victory (see Valery Chkalov)
* Winter Evening in Gagry (Zimnyi vecher v Gagrakh; Shakhnazarov, 1986)
  Wrestler and the Clown (Borets i kloun; Barnet and Yudin, 1957)
- Year 1812 (1812 god; Goncharov et al., 1912)
  Young Guard (Molodaya gvardiya; Gerasimov, 1948)
* Your Contemporary (Tvoi sovremennik; Raizman, 1968)
* Zero City (Gorod Zero; Shakhnazarov, 1989)
* Zoya (Arnshtam, 1944)
* Zvenigora (Dovzhenko, 1928)

Documentary films and newsreels

* Against the Current (Delov, 1988). The "greenies"
  All That Jazz, BBC. Interview with and music of Sergei Kurekhin
* Alto Sonata (Altovaya sonata; Sokurov and Aranovich; 1989). On the life of D. D. Shostakovich
* And the Past is But a Dream (A proshloe kazhetsya snom; Mirosh-nichenko; narrated by Viktor Astafev, 1987). Returning camp inmates
* Are You Going to the Ball? (Khvorova, 1987). The rigors of dance training for children
* Arkadii Raikin (1989). A retrospective
* BAM Zone: Permanent Residents (Zona Bama: postoyannye zhiteli; Pavlov, 1987). Realism vs. fanfare in the BAM epic

* Bell of Chernobyl (Kolokol Chernobylya; Sergienko, 1987)
* Black Square (Chernyi kvadrat; Pasternak, 1988). Persecution of Soviet artists
* Chernobyl: Chronicles of Difficult Weeks (Shevchenko, 1986)
* Dam (Plotina; Kuznetsov, 1987). Environmental issues
* Defeat of the German Armies Near Moscow (Varlamov and Kopalin, 1941)
* Dialogues (Dialogi; Obukhovich, 1987). Jazz and rock
* Evening Sacrifice (Zhertva vechernyaya; Sokurov, m. 1984, r. 1987)
* Funeral of Vera Kholodnaya, 1919. Newsreel
* Homecoming (Vozvrashchenie; Chubakova, 1987). Afghan War veterans.
* I Served in Stalin's Guard (Ya sluzhil v okhrane Stalina; Aranovich, 1989)
* Is it Easy to be Young? (Legko li byt molodym?; Podnieks, 1987). Rock culture and youth alienation in Latvia
* Lost Monuments (Utrachennye pamyatniki, 1989). The destruction of churches and art treasures
  Moscow Strikes Back (see Defeat of the German Armies Near Moscow)
* Risk Group (Gruppa riska; Nikishin, 1988). AIDS, prostitutes, gays
  Risk-II (Barshchevsky and Violina, 1988). Destalinized history
  Rock (Rok; Uchitel, 1987)
  Solovki Power (Vlast solovetskaya; Goldovskaya, 1989)
* Soviets (Podnieks, 5 parts, 1991)
* Stalin is with Us (Stalin s nami; Shakhverdiev, 1989)
* Supreme Judgement (Vysshii sud; Frank, 1987). Murderer on death row
* Temple (Khram; Dyakonov, 1987). Religious revival
* To the Soldiers in the Trenches (Soldatam v okopakh, 1915?). Newsreel of World War I charity bazaar
* What's Happening in Your Courtyard? (A u vas vo dvore?, 1988). Kazan street gang culture
* Ya-Ha (Ia-Khkha [sic]; Nugmanov, 1986). Underground Leningrad rock

Videography

I do not include here Soviet TV programs that I viewed except as they have been made into available videos. Reviews of videos, including films, can now be followed in the journals *Russian Review* and *Soviet Union*.

All the Best of Russia (Kultur, no date)
BBC Documentary Video: Interviews with directors Soloviev, Askoldov, Klimov, Nikita Mikhalkov, Nana Dzhordzhadze, Abuladze, and others
Birth of Soviet Cinema. Films for the Humanities
Dialogues. Video Project. Documentary Rock and Jazz Concert by Sergei Kurekhin, Boris Grebenshchikov, Vladimir Chekasin, and others, 1989
Durov's Dynasty; Beriozka Dance Company. SUNY/Soviet TV Project
Funeral of Vladimir Vysotsky. Samuel Rachlin, Danish Radio
Inside Russia. International Historic Films, 1985. Scenes of Soviet life in the 1930s produced in 1941 by Charles Stuart, American engineer
Inside the Soviet Circus. Narrated by Theodore Bikel, National Geographic, 1988
Life and Times of Josef Stalin. Films for the Humanities. Includes footage from popular movies and performances of the 1930s and 1940s
Rock Around the Kremlin. Billon and others. Filmmakers Library, 1986
Rock at the Crossroads. SUNY/Soviet TV Project. Written by Artemy Troitsky
Russian Folk Song and Dance. Kultur, V1107
Soviet Army Chorus, Band, and Dance Ensemble. Kultur, V1106
Teatr Arkadiya Isaakovicha Raikina (no production data)
This is How We Live. Video Project. Youth interviews
Voice of Russia. Samuel Rachlin, Danish Radio. On Vysotsky
Yiddish to Rock: Soviet Culture Today. PBS Adult Learning

I wish to thank Nick Hayes of Minneapolis television and radio and Sergei Zamascikov for their Soviet video presentations on youth culture and media.

Index

Note: Moscow and Leningrad (and its variants) are not indexed in that they appear on virtually every page. Most movies are listed under director and alphabetized in English by title in the Filmography.

258

CPSIA information can be obtained
at www.ICGtesting.com
Printed in the USA
LVHW091929120321
681373LV00005B/74